AUGUSTINE AND THE CURE OF SOULS

CHRISTIANITY AND JUDAISM IN ANTIQUITY SERIES

Gregory E. Sterling, Series Editor

Volume 17

The University of Notre Dame Press gratefully acknowledges the generous support of Jack and Joan Conroy of Naples, Florida, in the publication of titles in this series.

AUGUSTINE
AND THE
CURE OF SOULS

Revising a Classical Ideal

PAUL R. KOLBET

University of Notre Dame Press

Notre Dame, Indiana

Library of Congress Cataloging-in-Publication Data

Kolbet, Paul R.
Augustine and the cure of souls : revising a classical ideal / Paul R. Kolbet
p. cm. — (Christianity and Judaism in antiquity)
Includes bibliographical references and index.
ISBN-13: 978-0-268-03321-7 (pbk. : alk. paper)
ISBN-10: 0-268-03321-8 (pbk. : alk. paper)
1. Augustine, Saint, Bishop of Hippo.   I. Title.
BR65. A9K59 2010
253.0937— dc22

                                           2009042050

For Amy Egloff

with love and gratitude

Christianity and Judaism in Antiquity Series (CJAS)

The Christianity and Judaism in Antiquity Program at the University of Notre Dame came into existence during the afterglow of the Second Vatican Council. The doctoral program combines the distinct academic disciplines of the Hebrew Bible, Judaism, the New Testament, and the Early Church in an effort to explore the religion of the ancient Hebrews, the diverse forms of Second Temple Judaism, and its offspring into religions of Rabbinic Judaism and the multiple incarnations of early Christianity. While the scope of the program thus extends from the late Bronze and Early Iron Ages to the late antique world, the fulcrum lies in the Second Temple and Early Christian periods. Each religion is explored in its own right, although the program cultivates a History-of-Religions approach that examines their reciprocally illuminating interrelationships and their place in the larger context of the ancient world. During the 1970s a monograph series was launched to reflect and promote the orientation of the program. Initially known as Studies in Judaism and Christianity in Antiquity, the series was published under the auspices of the Center of the Study of Judaism and Christianity in Antiquity. Six volumes appeared from 1975 to 1986. In 1988 the series name became Christianity and Judaism in Antiquity as the editorship passed to Charles Kannengiesser, who oversaw the release of nine volumes. Professor Kannengiesser's departure from Notre Dame necessitated the appointment of a new editor. At the same time, the historic connection between the series and the CJA doctoral program was strengthened by the appointment of all CJA faculty to the editorial board. Throughout these institutional permutations, the purpose of the series has continued to be the promotion of research into the origins of Judaism and Christianity with the hope that a better grasp of the common ancestry and relationship of the two world's religions will illuminate not only the ancient world but the modern world as well.

Gregory E. Sterling, Series Editor

Contents

Acknowledgments

A project of this scope is only possible because many people have been exceedingly generous with their time, energy, and expertise. Its best insights have their source in more conversations and readings than I can acknowledge adequately either here or in notes. It was the late Jaroslav Pelikan who first brought to my attention the intriguingly complex relationship between Christianity and the classical world. The personal and scholarly influence of John Cavadini is evident throughout the work. He encouraged me at each point never to lose sight of either Augustine's rhetoric or his theology. Others whose help has been indispensable at critical stages of the work include Brian Daley, S.J., Allan Fitzgerald, Stephen Gersh, Rowan Greer, Carol Harrison, Marina McCoy, Gretchen Reydams-Schils, Gregory Sterling, James Wetzel, and Randall Zachman. Thanks are also due to my colleagues both in the Department of Theology at Boston College—especially Stephen Brown, Boyd Taylor Coolman, Robert Daly, S.J., Charles Hefling, Pheme Perkins, and Stephen Pope—and those in the Boston Area Patristics Group for their collegiality and support. John Slotemaker kindly helped me compile the index. The research and writing were partially funded by a fellowship provided by the J. M. Ormond Center of Duke University and subsequently by a postdoctoral fellowship at the University of Notre Dame.

Witnessing the failure of his best efforts, Augustine ultimately concluded that divine love was the only true source of resiliency for the human spirit in difficult times. When he was most disheartened by the limitations of his own strength, he admonished himself to be more receptive to the love that penetrated every dark corner of the human heart and was capable of turning even the worst into something with a beauty all its own. In this regard, I am especially grateful for the sustaining love of my wife, Amy Egloff, the wonder of our daughter, Chloe, and for my parents, Robert and Diana Kolbet.

Abbreviations

Series

ANRW   *Aufstieg und Niedergang der römischen Welt* (Berlin: Walter de Gruyter, 1972–)

CCL   Corpus Christianorum, Series Latina (Turnhout: Brepols, 1953–)

CSEL   Corpus Scriptorum Ecclesiasticorum Latinorum (Vienna: Tempsky, 1865–)

LCL   Loeb Classical Library (Cambridge, MA: Harvard University Press)

MA   *Miscellanea Agostiniana* (Rome: Tipografia Poliglotta Vaticana, 1930–1931)

NPNF   Nicene and Post-Nicene Fathers, Series 1–2 (Edinburgh, 1886–)

PG   Patrologia Graeca, ed. J.-P. Migne (Paris: 1857–1866)

PL   Patrologia Latina, Cursus Completus, ed. by J.-P. Migne (Paris: 1844–1864)

PLS   Supplement to the Patrologiae Cursus Completus, Series Latina, ed. A. Hamman (Paris: 1958–1963)

SBLTT   Society of Biblical Literature Texts and Translations

SC   Sources chrétiennes (Paris: Cerf, 1942–)

WSA   *The Works of St. Augustine: A Translation for the 21st Century,* ed. John E. Rotelle (Hyde Park, NY: New City Press, 1990–)

Ancient Authors and Editions

Alcidamas
   Soph.   *Peri sophiston* (ed. Muir)
Ambrose of Milan
   Abr.   *De Abraham* (CSEL 32.1: 501–638)
   bon. mort.   *De bono mortis* (CSEL 32.1: 703–53)
   Cain   *De Cain et Abel* (CSEL 32.1: 339–409)
   ep.   *Epistulae* (CSEL 82.1–4)
   ex.   *Exaemeron* (CSEL 32.1: 3–261)
   expl. symb.   *Explanatio symboli ad initiandos* (CSEL 73: 1–12)
   expos. Ps. cxviii *Expositio Psalmi cxviii* (CSEL 62: 53–510)
   fid.   *De fide ad Gratianum* (CSEL 78: 3–307)
   fuga   *De fuga saeculi* (CSEL 32.2: 163–207)
   Ios.   *De Ioseph* (CSEL 32.1: 73–122)
   Luc.   *Expositio euangelii secundum Lucam* (CCL 14: 1–400)
   myst.   *De mysteriis* (SC 25bis)
   Nab.   *De Nabuthae historiae* (CSEL 32.2: 469–516)
   off.   *De officiis ministrorum* (CCL 15)
   parad.   *De paradiso* (CSEL 32.1: 263–336)
   sacr.   *De sacramentis* (SC 25bis)
Apuleius
   Apol.   *Apologia* (Teubner, ed. R. Helm)
   Flor.   *Florida* (Teubner, ed. R. Helm)
   Soc.   *De Deo Socratis* (Teubner, ed. C. Moreschini)
Aristophanes
   Au.   *Aues* (LCL 179)
Aristotle
   En.   *Ethica Nicomachea* (LCL 73)
   Metaph.   *Metaphysica* (LCL 271, 287)
   Pol.   *Politica* (LCL 264)
   Rh.   *Rhetorica* (LCL 193)
Augustine
   Acad.   *De Academicis libri tres* (CCL 29: 3–61)
   agon.   *De agone christiano liber unus* (CSEL 41: 99–138)
   an. quant.   *De animae quantitate liber unus* (CSEL 89: 129–231)
   bapt.   *De baptismo libri septem* (CSEL 51: 143–375)
   beata u.   *De beata uita liber unus* (CCL 29: 65–85)
   cat. rud.   *De catechizandis rudibus liber unus* (CCL 46: 115–78)

ciu.	*De ciuitate dei libri uiginti duo* (CCL 47–48)
conf.	*Confessionum libri tredecim* (CCL 27)
cons. eu.	*De consensu euangelistarum libri quattuor* (CSEL 43)
corrept.	*De correptione et gratia liber unus* (PL 44: 915–46)
doctr. chr.	*De doctrina christiana libri quattuor* (CCL 32: 1–167)
en. Ps.	*Enarrationes in Psalmos* (CCL 38–40)
ep.	*Epistulae* (CSEL 34.1–2, 44, 57, 58, 88)
ep. Io. tr.	*In epistulam Iohannis ad Parthos tractatus decem* (SC 75)
c. ep. Man.	*Contra epistulam Manichaei quam uocant fundamenti liber unas* (CSEL 25.1: 191–248)
c. Faust.	*Contra Faustum Manicheum libri triginta tres* (CSEL 25.1: 249–797)
f. et symb.	*De fide et symbolo liber unus* (CSEL 41: 1–32)
gest. Pel.	*De gestis Pelagii liber unus* (CSEL 42)
Gn. adu. Man.	*De Genesi aduersus Manicheos libri duo* (CSEL 91)
gr. et pecc. or.	*De gratia Christi et de peccato originali libri duo* (CSEL 42)
haer.	*De haeresibus ad Quoduultdeum liber unus* (CCL 46: 286–345)
Io. eu. tr.	*In Iohannis euangelium tractatus CXXIV* (CCL 36)
lib. arb.	*De libero arbitrio libri tres* (CCL 29: 211–321)
c. litt. Pet.	*Contra litteras Petiliani libri tres* (CSEL 52: 3–227)
mag.	*De magistro liber unus* (CCL 29: 157–203)
mor.	*De moribus ecclesiae catholicae et de moribus Manicheorum libri duo* (CSEL 90)
mus.	*De musica libri sex* (PL 32: 1081–1194)
op. mon.	*De opere monachorum liber unus* (PL 40: 547–82; CSEL 41)
ord.	*De ordine libri duo* (CCL 29: 89–137)
perseu.	*De dono perseuerantiae liber ad Prosperum et Hilarium secundus* (PL 45: 993–1034)
retr.	*Retractationum libri duo* (CCL 57: 5–143)
s.	*Sermones* (CCL 41; PL 38: 332–1484, 39: 1493–1718, 46; PLS 2: 417–743, 1348–56; MA)
s. dom. m.	*De sermone domini in monte libri duo* (CCL 35)
Simpl.	*Ad Simplicianum libri duo* (CCL 44)
sol.	*Soliloquiorum liber duo* (CSEL 89: 3–98)
symb. cat.	*De symbolo ad catechumenos* (CCL 46: 179–99)
trin.	*De trinitate libri quindecim* (CCL 50–50A)
uera rel.	*De uera religione liber unus* (CCL 32: 187–260)
util. cred.	*De utilitate credendi liber unus* (CSEL 25.1: 3–48)

Cicero
    Acad.   *Academica* (LCL 268)
    Inu.   *De inuentione* (LCL 386)
    Lig.   *Pro Ligario* (LCL 252)
    N.D.   *De natura Deorum* (LCL 268)
    Off.   *De officiis* (LCL 30)
    Orat.   *Orator* (LCL 342)
    De orat.   *De oratore* (LCL 348, 349)
    Part.   *De partitiones oratoriae* (LCL 349)
    Tusc. Disp. *Tusculanae disputationes* (LCL 141)
Claudian
    Cons. Mall. *De Consulatu Fl. Mallii Theodori* (LCL 135)
       Theod.
Dio Cassius
    Hist. Rom. *Historia Romana* (LCL 32, 37, 53, 66, 82, 83, 175, 176, 177)
Dio Chrysostom
    Or.   *Orationes* (LCL 257, 339, 358, 376, 385)
Diogenes Laertius
    Vit. phil.   *Vitae philosophorum* (LCL 184, 185)
Epictetus
    Diss.   *Dissertationes* (LCL 131, 218)
    Ench.   *Enchiridion* (LCL 218)
Epicurus
    Fr.   *Fragmenta* (Teubner, ed. H. Usener)
    VS   *Vaticanae Sententiae* (Teubner, ed. Mühll)
Gorgias
    Hel.   *Helena* (ed. H. Diels, vol. 2.288–94)
Homer
    Il.   *Iliad* (LCL 170, 171)
    Od.   *Odyssey* (LCL 104, 105)
Horace
    Sat.   *Satirae* (LCL 194)
Jerome
    Apol.   *Apologia aduersus libros Rufini* (SC 303)
    Ep.   *Epistulae* (LCL 262)
Julian
    Gal.   *Contra Galilaeos* (LCL 157)
Lucian
    Dial. Mort. *Dialogi Mortuorum* (LCL 431)
    Musc. Enc. *Muscae Encomium* (LCL 14)

Nigr.	*Nigrinus* (LCL 14)
Peregr.	*De morte Peregrini* (LCL 302)
Pisc.	*Piscator* (LCL 130)

Maximus of Tyre
Diss.	*Dissertationes* (Teubner, ed. M. Trapp)

Musonius Rufus
Fr.	*Reliquiae* (ed. C. Lutz)

Optatus of Milevis
De Schism.	*De Schismate Donatistarum Libri Septem* (SC 412, 413)
Donatist.	

Paulinus of Milan
Vit. Ambr.	*Vita Ambrosii* (PL 14: 27–46)

Paulinus of Nola
Ep.	*Epistulae* (CSEL 29)

Pelagius
Dem.	*Epistula ad Demetriadem* (PL 30: 15–45, 33: 1099–1120)
Vit. chr.	*Liber de uita christiana* (PL 40: 1031–46, 50: 383–402)

Philodemus
Lib.	*De libertate dicendi* (SBLTT 43, ed. David Konstan et al.)

Philostratus
Vit. Soph.	*Vitae sophistarum* (LCL 134)

Pindar
Nem.	*Nemean* (LCL 485)
Pyth.	*Pythian* (LCL 56)

Plato
Apol.	*Apology* (LCL 36)
Chrm.	*Charmides* (LCL 201)
Ep.	*Epistles* (LCL 234)
Grg.	*Gorgias* (LCL 166)
Hipp. Min.	*Hippias Minor* (LCL 167)
La.	*Laches* (LCL 165)
Lg.	*Laws* (LCL 187, 192)
Mx.	*Menexenus* (LCL 234)
Men.	*Meno* (LCL 165)
Phdr.	*Phaedrus* (LCL 36)
Plt.	*Politicus* (LCL 164)
Prt.	*Protagoras* (LCL 165)
Rep.	*Republic* (LCL 237, 276)
Sph.	*Sophist* (LCL 123)
Smp.	*Symposium* (LCL 166)

Tht.	*Theaetetus* (LCL 123)
Ti.	*Timaeus* (LCL 234)

Plotinus
En.	*Enneads* (LCL 440–68)

Plutarch
Adol. poet. aud.	*Quomodo adolescens poetas audire debeat* (LCL 197)
Adul. amic.	*Quomodo adulator ab amico internoscatur* (LCL 197)
Cic.	*Cicero* (LCL 99)
Cohib. ira	*De cohibenda ira* (LCL 337)
Rect. rat. aud.	*De recta ratione audiendi* (LCL 197)

Porphyry
Marc.	*Ad Marcellam* (SBLTT 28, ed. Kathleen O'Brien Wicker)
Plot.	*Vita Plotini* (LCL 440)

Possidius
Vit. Aug.	*Vita Augustini* (PL 32: 33–66)

Rufinus
Apol. adu. Hier.	*Apologia contra Hieronymum* (CCL 20: 29–123)

Seneca
Const.	*De Constantia Sapientis* (LCL 214: 48–104)
Ep.	*Epistulae Morales ad Lucilium* (LCL 75–77)
Ira	*De ira* (LCL 214: 106–354)
Otio	*De otio* 4.1 (LCL 254)
Vit. beat.	*De uita beata* (LCL 254: 98–179)

Sextus Empiricus
Math.	*Aduersus mathematicos* (LCL 291, 311, 382)

Suetonius
Dom.	*Domitian* (LCL 38)

Symmachus
Ep.	*Epistulae* (ed. O. Seeck)
Rel.	*relatio* (CSEL 82.3: 21–33)

Tacitus
Ann.	*Annales* (LCL 312, 322)

Tertullian
Apol.	*Apologeticum* (CCL 1: 85–171)
Praescr.	*De praescriptione haereticorum* (CCL 1: 187–224)

Xenophon
Smp.	*Symposium* (LCL 168)

Introduction

Who, then, will be this doctor of souls?
What will his drugs be like, and what form will
the regimen he prescribes take?
                    —Maximus of Tyre, *Diss.* 28.1

Rhetoric and Christian Identity in the Roman Empire

The sudden, extraordinary influence of Christian bishops in the fourth and fifth centuries was due in no small part to their ability to make the publicly recognized practices and strategies of the Greco-Roman orators and philosophers their own—even as they adapted them to conform to Christian principles.[1] Christian bishops who were versed in classical rhetorical and philosophical literature became a public presence as Christianity emerged as the dominant religion of the Roman Empire.[2] Research on their public affairs has revealed their involvement in a wide range of remarkable activities as they exercised their office under the pervasive patronage systems of the Empire.[3] Aside from their responsibilities regarding the Church's teaching and worship, they created programs concerned with the welfare of the poor,[4] founded hospitals,[5] held their own courts to arbitrate disputes,[6] and ransomed those taken prisoner.[7]

As Christianity asserted itself in the Roman Empire and embraced its newly acquired status as a legal religion, it struggled with the challenge of redefinition that came with its new, more public presence. It is no co-incidence that an unprecedented number of theoretical texts on Christian ministry come from this time period.[8] Indeed, the very instability of these changing times forced upon the minds of serious Christians the question of what form Christian leadership ought to take in a culture that already had well-established and vigorous political, religious, and philosophical traditions of its own. The relationship between Christianity and the other religious and philosophical traditions that surrounded it in this pluralistic environment remained unclear. This situation was further aggravated by Emperor Julian's prohibition of Christians from teaching the classic texts of the Empire, separating them from a literary inheritance they had, by and large, taken for granted.[9] Confronted by the increasing prominence of Christians, pagans found themselves struggling with their own identity as their founding traditions appeared to be receding into a "classical" past.[10]

Among Christians and their leaders was a wide diversity of opinion concerning their relationship both to Roman culture and to the classical traditions undergirding it. Questions abounded regarding how to relate the Church of the martyrs to the newly born Church of the Empire. Christians still remembered how in former times Tertullian famously exclaimed that truth was found in Jerusalem rather than Athens and that the seed of the Church was the blood of Christian martyrs.[11] The uneasy relationship between Christianity and Roman culture is evident in the debate between two of the leading Christian scholars of the fourth century, Rufinus and Jerome. Rufinus chastised Jerome for teaching pagan texts in his monastic community in Bethlehem to "young boys who had been entrusted to him that he might teach them the fear of the Lord."[12] Rufinus recounts that when the well-respected Christian scholar visited him in Jerusalem, Jerome brought with him "a book which contained a single dialogue of Cicero and also one of Plato's in Greek."[13] For Rufinus, Jerome's fondness for classical learning marked him as a Ciceronian rather than a Christian. Jerome responded by inquiring from where Rufinus had "obtained that flow of words, that lucidity of thought, that variety of translation" he used to write his attacks. Jerome continued, "I must be very much mistaken if you do not study Cicero in secret?"[14]

As a bishop in Tertullian's North Africa—where a rigorous Christianity had existed for centuries—Augustine of Hippo found these questions to be particularly acute during his episcopacy.[15] The North African Christians whom Augustine referred to as "Donatists" criticized the Empire as well as the apparently compromised position of Catholic Christians in relation to it. As a bishop, Augustine adopted the strategy modeled for him by his mentor, Ambrose of Milan, of wide-ranging engagement in the Empire's philosophical and political life, but brought to it North African concerns regarding the purity of Christian identity.[16] The "social implications of Christianity itself" were at stake.[17] One finds in Augustine's leadership a sophisticated struggle to form in his hearers a vital Christian identity as they remained actively engaged in the imperial culture which was spread across the whole Roman world. The bishop sought to further a Christianity that could sustain intermingling with the wider culture without so diminishing its critical edge that it became merely "cultural."

Although Augustine was never a professional philosopher, he was— prior to his conversion—a professional orator paid to deliver public speeches that were both persuasive and entertaining. His skill at this craft was such that by it alone he rose to the proximate edges of imperial power in the Roman capital. This professional experience and the intellectual formation that made it possible undoubtedly "left a permanent mark on his later years as a Christian priest and bishop."[18] After he abandoned his imperial careerism, Augustine never ceased giving persuasive speeches. He drew upon the expertise of his former profession as he sought to influence and shape the Roman world. Indeed, the most abundant and direct evidence of the appropriation of the practices and strategies of classical rhetoric by late antique bishops is provided by their own sermons. Preaching was one of the principle means by which Christian bishops engaged their surrounding culture and extended the influence of Christianity throughout the Roman world.[19] The immense quantity of homiletical material produced (and preserved) during this period testifies both to the great value ascribed to public oratory in late antiquity and to the extensive time and effort Christians devoted to preaching.

A scant few years after Augustine's death, Possidius, Augustine's fifth-century biographer, drew the attention of his readers, above all, to the bishop's preaching and to the harmony between his words and deeds. Possidius noted that during his nearly forty years as priest or bishop Augustine "preached God's word in the church right up to his last illness unceasingly, vigorously and powerfully, with sound mind and sound judgment." Possidius continued: "No one can read what he wrote about divinity without profit. But I think that those were able to profit still more who could hear him speak in church and see him with their own eyes. . . . Truly, he was indeed one of those of whom it is written, 'speak this way and act the same way'" (Jas. 2:12).[20] As a result of the very talent and dedication described by Possidius, "the largest body of oratory surviving from any ancient speaker" is the Christian preaching of Augustine of Hippo, some 1,000 surviving sermons.[21] Although these preserved sermons are only a small number of those he preached over the course of his thirty-nine-year ministry, they still amount to "more than a third of A[ugustine]'s own surviving *œuvre*."[22]

Despite this large quantity of material and the importance ascribed to it at the time of its composition, when compared with the amount of secondary literature concerned with other sources, late antique sermons are relatively little studied. Augustine's sermons amount to, in the words of J. J. O'Donnell, "long known but under-studied masses of texts."[23] In the epilogue to the recent second edition of his influential biography of the bishop of Hippo, Peter Brown states that if he were to write it over again, he would take more account of the sermons.[24] It is not at all surprising that he did not make much use of these materials in the 1960s. In fact, to this day, scholarly attention given to homilies continues to lag behind that given to other early Christian literature such as the apologetic, doctrinal, polemical, or political works.

This neglect has occurred and continues to occur for understandable reasons. For one, although collections of homilies circulated through the centuries, it has been a daunting task to sift through such collections, determine which sermons are authentic, and establish reliable texts for them. Second, once one has reliable texts of authentic sermons, the sermons themselves are often impossible to date precisely because they nearly always lack internal references that can be securely connected to external, verifiable facts or events.[25] Third, the sermons almost universally have an exegetical quality to them whose logic continues to remain obscure. For example, in his biography of Augustine, Peter Brown has likened such scriptural exegesis to Freudian analysis of dreams (far from an exact science).[26] Fourth, the sermons have a "popular" feel to them. While this makes them more accessible to a general audience, they can lack the precision necessary for them to be that useful to historians, philosophers, or theologians. Finally, since they were oral performances, only the notes made by those who originally heard them survive.[27] Contemporary readers are consequently in a position not unlike that of paleontologists examining the bones of some ancient creature and attempting to imagine what it actually looked like.

The studies of Augustine's homilies tend to fall within two categories: those concerned with philology, authenticity, and dating or those that employ the sermons in service of some other project whether doctrinal, thematic, or sociological. Most prominent among the former is Dom Pierre-Patrick Verbraken's fine work.[28] Studies of the latter category have found the sermons to be a rich source of information about the liturgy of Augustine's time[29] as well as providing further discussions of topics present in the written treatises.[30] The investigation of late antique homilies by social historians that has only just begun promises to expand knowledge of late antique life all across the Empire.[31]

What remains elusive is how one would study the homily itself, on its own terms. While assessing the state of research on late antique Christian bishops, Pauline Allen and Wendy Mayer conclude that a comprehensive pastoral theory uniting their diverse activities remains a desideratum.[32] They attribute this in part to the manner in which scholars experienced in the practice of pastoral care tend to bring with them little understanding of the world of late antiquity and instead are concerned primarily with modern questions and presuppositions about effective pastoral counseling. While specialists in late antiquity have avoided imposing on the period such contemporary concerns, they "have made no attempt to examine pastoral care in this setting in its own right," preferring to explore particular practices "without in any way attempting to pull these fragments together or to formulate a theory which might make coherent sense of them."[33]

Historians know all too well how perilous it is to assume that current practices correspond with those of antiquity. If it has become obvious that the meaning has shifted of such common societal conditions and practices as gender and meals, it would be foolhardy to assume that the delivery and hearing of late antique sermons in any way mirrors our present-day experience. To preserve this historical distance, it is appealing to resort to the methods and insights of the social sciences. From this perspective, late antique sermons are examples of ideological legitimation, buttressing and defining the identity of Christian communities.[34] To be sure, sermons are such examples and may be used in this general sociological category to explain a great deal about the late Empire. To use homilies only as supporting texts, however, neglects the study of the internal structure and distinctive genius of the late antique Christian sermon.

Thus, what is needed is a clarification of the theory informing the original composition of the sermons themselves, one that situates them within the philosophical and social constraints of the time.[35] Throughout his works, Pierre Hadot has warned that overlooking the centrality of certain cultural assumptions of late Roman antiquity easily obscures important features of the literary evidence. He contends that "in order to understand the works of the philosophers of antiquity we must take account of all the concrete conditions in which they wrote, all the constraints that weighed upon them: the framework of the school, the very nature of *philosophia,* literary genres, rhetorical rules, dogmatic imperatives, and traditional modes of reasoning."[36]

> Understanding a work of antiquity requires placing it in the group from which it emanates, in the tradition of its dogmas, its literary genre, and requires understanding its goals. . . . For the ancient author's art consists in his skillfully using, in order to arrive at his goals, all of the constraints that weigh upon him as well as the models furnished by the tradition. Most of the time, furthermore, he uses not only ideas, images, and patterns of argument in this way but also texts or at least pre-existing formulae.[37]

Taking Hadot's admonition seriously requires the interpreter of Augustine's sermons to be attentive to the skillful way the bishop employed the formal assumptions and methods of the classical traditions that he and other Christians inherited.

For centuries discussions of philosophical therapy in Greek and Roman philosophical schools addressed how the philosopher could most effectively employ speech to guide students in the philosophic life. In a well-regarded study, A. D. Nock points to the continuity between later Christian homiletic and its philosophic predecessor, remarking: "A man who heard Musonius Rufus or Epictetus at Rome was doing the thing most nearly equivalent to hearing a Christian sermon later: the technique was in fact inherited."[38] George Kennedy characterizes an oration of Dio Chrysostom at the Olympic games as "in fact, a pagan sermon, preaching the faith of Hellenism, its gods, its poetry, its art, and its culture as a whole."[39]

In his cultural history of the second sophistic, Graham Anderson demonstrates how prevalent sophistic oratory and presuppositions were in the first four centuries of the Christian Church. Hellenistic rhetoric was a resource so flexible that it was used to a greater or lesser extent by each of the Hellenistic philosophical schools, Platonic, Stoic, Epicurean, Cynic, and Peripatetic. Likewise, Hellenistic rhetoric was no less amenable to being employed by "educated and eloquent Jewish and Christian performers."[40] Anderson describes sophists as such "familiar figures" that it was "inevitable that any educated Christian should find himself either using or reacting to the tools of the sophists' trade. Where there was Christian rhetoric, one would expect an element of 'Christian Sophistic,' of cultural or ornamental display in the service of Christ." This led to an "unexpected cultural convergence" where the founder of Christianity could be perceived by educated pagans to be "a crucified sophist" who was "during his lifetime a popular public speaker with an inner circle of disciples."[41] In such times, "anyone with serious educational aspirations" could "import these into their Christianity, and in the event this was clearly done."[42] Christians internalized not only sophistic reflexes and habits of thought but fundamental presuppositions regarding the nature of speech itself and its effects upon the soul (for better or worse).

Classical traditions of philosophical therapy have been referred to as "psychagogy" in recent scholarship. Abraham Malherbe states, "The constant attention philosophers devoted to their followers' intellectual, spiritual, and moral growth resulted in a well developed system of care known as psychagogy."[43] In fact, these psychagogic traditions were so widespread and influential that they are present in the Christian New Testament itself.[44] Indeed, the ideal of an orator who cures the souls of hearers in the same way that a physician cures the body both preceded Christianity and influenced its earliest expressions. Malherbe continues, "The psychagogic tradition became increasingly important to Christians in later centuries [after the New Testament] as more structure was given to the spiritual life by developing devotional and spiritual exercises."[45] Ilsetraut Hadot describes a process whereby the "highly developed practice of spiritual guidance was completely adopted by Christians, albeit with different premises." In succeeding centuries, "the figure of the philosopher as spiritual guide with the philosophical schools as the center of his activity" was eventually "replaced by the person of the clerical spiritual guide."[46]

To use the term "psychagogy" in this manner to refer to a "well developed system of care" is to give the term a precise range of meaning that it did not have in antiquity. In its earliest usage, it was "a term from magic; it is the raising of spirits of the deceased."[47] Psychagogy later came to be used in rhetoric and poetics to refer to the influencing of the souls of the living: "bringing into ecstasy (the mind of) the audience by the magic of speech, carrying it away to the fictitious world that one (as a poet) has created, or to the emotional state that will make it take the decision one (as an orator) hopes for."[48] This kind of ψυχαγωγία, this seductive enchantment, often carried with it negative connotations of manipulation, flattery, or beguilement as well.[49]

The term seems never to have shed entirely its unfavorable associations in antiquity. Accordingly, when someone sought to cure souls through the use of psychagogy, it meant engaging in more ambiguous practices than what is implied by the alternatives of pedagogy, education, or even dialectic. Only one who believed that the human condition was such that appeals to reason alone were therapeutically ineffective would resort to such measures. Rational arguments were thus thought to need supplementation by various techniques consciously designed to enlist the non-rational faculties of the human person into the therapeutic process and assimilate them to its therapeutic aims. Unlike the straightforward value of rational argumentation, psychagogy involved one in a complicated, indirect, time-consuming process. Christian and non-Christian alike were suspicious of the conscious use of non-rational means of persuasion due to the considerable potential for abuse. For this reason, the extent that philosophers and Christian leaders believed that human flourishing necessitated psychagogic methods is all the more striking.

Psychagogy is, therefore, a useful term for identifying specific practices and strategies employed by classical and late antique philosophers, poets, and rhetoricians. A working definition would be that psychagogy refers to those philosophically articulated traditions of therapy—common in Hellenistic literature—pertaining to how a mature person leads the less mature to perceive and internalize wisdom for themselves. These traditions, moreover, stress that for therapeutic speech to be effective, it must be based on knowledge and persuade by adapting itself in specific ways both to the psychic state of the recipient and to the particular occasion. Thus, as a contemporary investigative category, psychagogy is a distinctive use of rhetoric for philosophic or religious ends. It can be difficult to identify since powerful movements in recent centuries set up a binary opposition between rhetoric and reality separating the art of persuasion from disinterested logic and observation. As John Locke declared, "[I]f we would speak of Things as they are, we must allow, that all the Art of Rhetorick, besides Order and Clearness, all the artificial and figurative application of Words Eloquence hath invented, are for nothing else but to insinuate wrong *Ideas,* move the Passions, and thereby mislead the Judgment; and so indeed are perfect cheat."[50] To understand ancient psychagogy requires one to set aside such polarities and imagine the possibility of a kind of speech whose persuasiveness does not diminish its truthfulness. In this case words would lead to, or even mediate, the apprehension of "things as they are."

The primary venue of ancient rhetoric was the day-to-day business of civic life, whether in legal proceedings, deliberative bodies, or any number of public occasions. As will become clear in the opening chapter, the line between psychagogy and rhetoric (much as that between philosophy and sophistry) is difficult to draw. Those practicing psychagogy — Socrates and Augustine included — were usually quite ambivalent about rhetoric itself and keenly sensitive to the many ways it could be used in the service of any unjust cause. In practice, psychagogic speech deployed many of the same strategies and even commonplace examples as other forms of rhetoric. What distinguishes psychagogy from rhetoric is its fairly narrowly defined end, namely, the inculcation of the philosophic life. It should, therefore, be kept in mind that the use of words for psychagogic purposes was a real but minority tradition within ancient rhetoric that, as argued here, was especially influential upon early Christians.

The early chapters of this study pay substantial attention to Augustine's predecessors on their own terms. This is necessary not only to prove how classical psychagogic traditions were transmitted to Augustine, but also to add to our understanding of him. The difficulty of obtaining an accurate image of Augustine should not be underestimated. Much like gaining perspective on a mountain, it is always tempting to marvel at the peak rather than doing the work of tracing the whole figure rising from the plain. Despite the astonishing manner in which Augustine towers over history and casts an unusually immense shadow, he truly had a local context and *all* of his thoughts and feelings grew organically out of the actual life he lived. The more at home one can become with the antique, florid rhetoric of Cicero, the arcane, strangely insightful philosophy of the Platonists, and the urbane, sophisticated Christianity of Ambrose of Milan, the more likely one will be able to see Augustine as he was. The wide-angle lens employed here, therefore, is not meant to take the focus away from its subject, but to accurately take him in. Through examining classical psychagogic traditions in their own right and delving into those with which Augustine was familiar, the true shape of his own initial revision of the methods and aims of philosophical therapy becomes apparent. Of special note is Augustine's retreat from public life at Cassiciacum where he gathered his friends and students around him and made his first steps not as a teacher of rhetorical techniques alone, but as one who used rhetorical techniques in the service of the philosophically informed Christian life. In the first five years after his conversion, Augustine gradually formulated a brilliantly Christian appropriation of the psychagogic tradition in which both the methods and aims of the Hellenistic philosophical schools, especially those of the Platonists, are visible in his description of the fleshly expressions of the divine rhetoric.

Augustine's life and thought, however, underwent a profound shift in the 390s primarily due to his ordination to the priesthood and then to the episcopate. His reflections on spiritual guidance came to maturity in the context of his duties as a Christian bishop. Like other bishops of his day, Augustine engaged in a wide range of activities caring for the souls and bodies of those for whom he was responsible, including assorted forms of charity and social welfare, hearing legal cases, preaching, leading liturgical rites, ransoming captives, and offering personal guidance to individuals. Augustine made these often-burdensome duties the subject of inquiry and developed a sophisticated pastoral theory in which these ministries of *care* could be understood as various expressions of more fundamental convictions regarding the soul's *cure*. Indeed, in Augustine's Latin, the word *cura* had two distinct but overlapping meanings. On the one hand, it meant "to be charged with administration." On the other hand, medically, it meant "healing treatment."[51] In time, the *cura animarum* became synonymous with Christian ministry itself.[52] For this reason, one seeking Augustine's advice could readily appeal to him as a "physician of the soul" (*medicum spiritalem*).[53]

Augustine's fame is attributable less to his ministries of care than to his written works whose insights into psychology, politics, philosophy, and theology continue to interest readers. For centuries Augustine has been approached theologically beginning not with his rhetorical practice, but with his most characteristic doctrine: his teaching on grace and the further corollaries, predestination and perseverance, harnessed by him to protect this insight from critics.[54] Of course, subsequent Christian writers found these topics so rich in meaning that for more than a thousand years after Augustine's death there was a continuous series of treatises interpreting his teaching on how creatures are moved to know and love God. As this topic in Augustine's writings generated such interest and controversy, it tended to become so central to perceptions of him that it obscured the very context in which his convictions originally developed.

Stephen Duffy has lamented how aspects of Augustine's doctrine of grace have over time "been disengaged from his total vision and have become influential in a one-sided way in later presentations"—especially when "deployed as weaponry in polemics."[55] This disengagement continues to present the danger of imbuing his teaching on grace and its corollaries with a freestanding quality. This risks detaching them from their original context within the bishop's ministry and his more basic conviction in the incarnation of the divine Word: a Word spoken rhetorically, adapted to the human condition, and meant to persuade us. It is this Word who sought to "entice" us and "enkindle" love in us by flirting with us through the window of our own flesh.[56] The very eloquence of this divine Word is what both reveals the world as the contingent sign Augustine perceived it to be and heals by becoming the ultimate object of creaturely desire.[57] In this way, rhetorical theory is so internalized by Augustine that it not only expresses his theological vision, but also informs it. Moreover, even as it is employed, rhetoric itself is revised and infused with theological content. The deep philosophical link between language, vulnerability, and desire is one of Augustine's chief insights. For Augustine the Christian, these underlying existential particulars cohere in the manner in which the divine Word becomes present to our all-too-fleshly desires by becoming vulnerable.

The following pages seek to retrieve the living context of Augustine's theological conclusions by, among other things, showing the cure of souls to be an enduring commitment of his—from his earliest pre-baptismal writings to his final acts as bishop. This retrieval entails investigating how this fundamental concern was borne out in the variety of contexts in which

Augustine functioned, whether as the brilliant young rhetorician, the teacher of Christian philosophy at Cassiciacum, the newly ordained priest, or the formidable Catholic bishop. This study demonstrates that, rather than rejecting his earlier ideals, Augustine adapted them to inform his mature pastoral theory and his homiletical practice. Formal features of classical philosophical therapy persist in Augustine's homilies, but they have been materially altered and recontextualized as an exegetical exercise in the Christian liturgy. Augustine's acceptance of the tasks posed to him by this classical tradition accounts for certain structural features of his homilies even as he undertook these tasks in new ways. The full integration of Christian exegetical and sacramental traditions into his classically informed psychagogy is the hallmark of his homilies.

Sources and Method

Although many leaders of late antique Christianity were capable, philosophically informed orators, Augustine is particularly suited for this study due to the preservation of homilies in which his own practice can be observed as well as a number of theoretical works where he addresses the task of preaching. The abstract discussion of psychagogic tasks and methods that follows should not obscure the personal setting in which such theory was realized. Graham Anderson describes the second sophistic as producing "a literature of performance which requires almost as much of a *skene,* a stage-set, and a sense of audience and occasion as the dramatic genres." He laments, "It is a pity that our appreciation of sophistic literature should so seldom take this living context into account."[58] This sentiment is no less applicable to Christian materials.

Augustine himself warns his readers against drawing hasty conclusions from his theoretical writings without first consulting his sermons—"if anything in us has so pleased you that you want to hear from us some plan to be observed by you in preaching, you would learn better by watching us and listening to us when actually engaged in the work itself than by reading what we dictate."[59] This study takes up the bishop's suggestion by observing him at work and discerning the structural features of his actual homilies. The bishop, nevertheless, could have added that his theoretical works supply a conceptual clarity and a wider perspective that are unavailable in the homilies themselves.

This study seeks a balance between two modes of inquiry: one devoted to Augustine's reception of classical traditions of the cure of souls and another to his transformation of these classical traditions in his Christian rhetoric. It is quite possible, on the one hand, to overemphasize the first and be content merely to document a genetic connection without doing the hard work of establishing what has changed in the process. In such a study, Augustine and his sermons would be a footnote to the philosophical tradition. On the other hand, overemphasizing the uniquely Christian aspects of Augustine's homilies risks obscuring those features derived from Roman culture that made them intelligible to their original audiences. In short, my inquiry strives to respect the integrity of the homily itself, in its original context, as its own discrete task, measured by its own criteria of effectiveness.

Rather than using contemporary models to understand late antique preaching, I appeal to theories derived from the culture itself that were well known at the time. This research is possible only because of the current revival of interest in post-classical philosophy and its practices.[60] The following chapters especially clarify the manner in which Augustine shared the concern of the Hellenistic philosophical schools to pass on spiritual practices that foster a way of life in harmony with doctrinal principles drawn from a distant past. Situating Augustine's sermons in their native philosophical and liturgical context allows us to understand them through the criteria that informed their original composition. Viewing them in this manner not only illumines their formal and material features, but also makes more intelligible the logic informing the scriptural exegesis that pervades them. Moreover, the following chapters show the extent that powerful classical ideals informed both Augustine's theoretical speculation and his public activities at each stage of his development. His engagement with classical traditions of philosophical therapy influenced both his early rhetorical career and his philosophical leisure at Cassiciacum. Rather than receding into the background, in his Christian preaching such traditions became more manifest, even as he transformed them in the process. Even as Augustine openly accepted inherited philosophical categories, he often simultaneously pointed out their limitations and relativity, and nearly always made them his own to such a degree that they become nearly unrecognizable.[61]

The available sources themselves present the researcher with at least the following formidable obstacles. First, in determining the extent to which classical traditions of philosophical therapy inform Augustine's works, it is necessary to discern clearly how they were transmitted to him. Fortunately, the literary sources directly available to him have been the subject of much study.[62] The classical sources employed from the third chapter forward will be limited to sources that can be shown to be ones of which Augustine was directly aware, primarily Cicero, Seneca, and Ambrose supplemented by portions of Plotinus. All of these contain sufficient material for Augustine to have assimilated psychagogic traditions. In the very sources that Augustine himself read, therefore, it is possible to trace philologically the use of the characteristic vocabulary of the psychagogic traditions he inherited such as the stock metaphors used to describe the process of reforming the soul drawn from medicine and athletic training and the particular use of terms to refer to sources of belief such as rumor, opinion, truth, rhetoric, and philosophy as well as the vocabulary related both to the function of beliefs and to methods that aim to bring about a harmony between beliefs and deeds.

Sources to which Augustine did not have firsthand access, such as Plato's *Phaedrus* and the *Orations* of Dio Chrysostom, will be used in the first chapters because they clarify and inform the materials that he did have. In treating such materials, the Platonic (and secondarily Cynic-Stoic) trajectory of the psychagogic tradition is privileged because the psychagogy Augustine learned was one principally shaped by this tradition. While there are overlaps with other philosophical traditions (such as use of frank speech and adaptation), there are some distinctive features as well (primarily its cognitive ascent and understanding of the telos of human life). Consequently, I omit much that could be said regarding classical psychagogy, especially in reference to the different ways of life arising from the diverse doctrines of the Hellenistic schools.[63]

After determining that Augustine knew the relevant classical traditions, in turning to Augustine's sermons, one discovers that they are notoriously difficult to date, and no study at this time would be credible whose conclusions relied on asserting precise dates for many of the homilies. This problem becomes acute when combined with perhaps the most perplexing question in Augustine scholarship—how to understand the development of Augustine's thought. Near the end of his life, Augustine himself suggested that if his future readers read his works "in the order in which they were written," they will discover how he "progressed while writing."[64]

It has been customary to locate the critical juncture of Augustine's development in the 390s, the decade between Augustine's first written works at Cassiciacum and his writing of the *Confessions*. Thus, Peter Brown, in a poignant chapter entitled "The Lost Future," described how "Augustine moved imperceptibly into a new world," surrendered "the bright future he thought he had gained," and abandoned the "long-established classical ideal of perfection."[65] Echoing Brown, Robert Markus has emphasized the same decade: "His re-reading of Saint Paul in the mid-390's is one of the great divides of Augustine's intellectual development. It marks the end of his belief in human self-determination and the beginnings of the theology of grace he would deploy against Pelagius. . . . Augustine came to abandon his previous confidence in man's intellectual and moral capabilities."[66] Accepting this particular understanding of the development of Augustine's thought means that anyone examining a specific topic within it must, in one way or another, write a "history of the way Augustine coped with the intellectual landslide brought about in his mind by the collapse of this vision."[67]

While for the most part following Augustine's advice to read his books in order, this study does not find the kind of radical discontinuity in Augustine's thought that has become traditionally accepted. In fact, Augustine's use of psychagogic traditions reveals a profound continuity in his fundamental concerns. The most conspicuous changes in his Christian thought are largely adaptations to the different contexts in which he lived. The structural features of Augustine's psychagogy were already in place by the time he preached his first homilies. Certainly, Augustine grew and developed as he wrote, and the writings he composed in the first years following his ordination to the priesthood are especially important in showing how he adapted his earlier insights to his ecclesial role, but this growth is best understood as a deepening or enriching of his pre-ordination practice. Accordingly, this study takes its place in a series of studies that have underscored the continuity in Augustine's thought and rhetorical methods.[68] Rather than tracing how the early "philosopher" was superseded by the strident "theologian," the following pages reveal an early Augustine that was more Christian than is often assumed and a later Augustine that remained highly philosophical to the end.

Finally, one needs to keep in mind that although most of the homilies retain the shape of a spoken address, others have been more or less heavily redacted to take on a more literary form (primarily *In Iohannis euangelium tractatus* 55–124, portions of the *Enarrationes in Psalmos,* and his *De sermone domini in monte*).[69] Such redaction did not always erase their original oral quality.[70] It did, nevertheless, make these materials less helpful in capturing Augustine's manner of oral performance, yet they remain valuable in determining Augustine's homiletical concerns and the sort of things he regularly preached. Difficulties like these require the researcher to be circumspect.

Part One

A Classical Ideal

Chapter One

Classical Therapy:
Its Origins, Tasks, and Methods

The soul is cured by means of certain charms,
and these charms consist of beautiful words.
　　　　　　　—Plato, *Chrm.* 157a

Psychagogy as a Cultural Ideal

On the 18th of September, 96 CE, the Roman emperor, Domitian, was stabbed to death. Since Domitian had no heir, the conspiracy resulted in the end of the Flavian dynasty and raised the perilous problem of succession. Indeed, as he executed senators and banished philosophers to undermine any opposition to his power, Domitian feared that such a thing would happen. He was known to say that "the lot of rulers was most unhappy since when they discovered a conspiracy, no one believed them unless they had been killed."[1] Although the Roman senators greeted the news of his death with relief, the armies remained loyal to Domitian. He had cultivated this relationship by giving them a 25 percent pay increase — the first in nearly a century.[2] Due to recent conflicts in Dacia, many soldiers were stationed on the northern border across the Danube River. Domitian had personally led troops into that region ten years earlier.[3] When the news arrived in an army camp, it sent the troops into turmoil. If the murder was to be avenged, it would be by someone from the ranks of the army.[4] Amid the discord, a man in rags walked through them, ascended the high altar, stripped off his tattered clothing, and shouted, "Then the resourceful Odysseus stripped away his rags"—an echo of Homer's account of Odysseus' return from his long absence and expulsion of the suitors who had unjustly occupied his home.[5]

At this outburst, those present realized that the man was not actually a beggar, but the sophist Dio in the garb of a cynic philosopher announcing his own return. Exiled by Domitian, he had been banished both from Rome and from his homeland of Bythinia.[6] He was known as a man who in exile combined the philosophy of Plato with the eloquence of Demosthenes.[7] Dio, the enemy of the soldiers' fallen leader, faced the army armed with nothing but words. He proceeded to deliver an oration against Domitian's tyranny by invoking Roman traditions of governance and order. The early third-century historian Philostratus remarks that Dio's "persuasiveness was indeed able to cast a spell (καταθέλξαι) over even those not deeply versed in Greek letters."[8] Ultimately, Dio persuaded the soldiers to aspire to these higher traditions and quelled the mutiny as his speech (λογοῦ) overcame the disorder (ἀταξίαν).[9]

This narration by Philostratus, far from being an isolated tale, exemplifies a widespread Hellenic cultural ideal that only gained force as it traveled through time into the Roman Hellenistic world. Amphitheaters across the Empire were commonly filled with spectators gathered to hear the discourse of rhetors. It was a culture that admired speech and made mastery of it central to its educational aspirations.[10] Speeches were even a featured part of the Olympic games.[11] Orators were greatly admired who could visit a city and in an extemporaneous speech turn even the city's greatest faults into attributes deserving of lavish praise. If the city had been destroyed three times, the orator argued that this fact actually enhanced the city on account of the greater availability of farmland. If the city was not located directly on the ocean, the orator extolled its insulation from threatening weather and the immorality of sailors. If the city had no claim to a single deity or native race as founders, the rhetor argued that immigration had, in fact, attracted the finest of everything to a single place.[12]

Audiences were entertained by the beguiling quality of such a speech as common perceptions were easily overturned before their very eyes.

What they had previously thought to be of little value was rhetorically turned into that which they could not live without. Plutarch remarks that there were those who "not without a certain plausibility" could extol the virtues of such things as vomiting, fever, or a kitchen pot.[13] Dio's oration in praise of hair was so well regarded that Synesius, some three hundred years later, used the same techniques to speak in tribute of the virtues of baldness.[14] Persuasive words could discredit a historical fact that had never been previously doubted. Dio famously traveled to Illium (the city descended from Troy) and before the citizens of that city argued that their ancestors had, in fact, triumphed over their famed attackers—a victory obscured only by an elaborate Homeric deception.[15]

To a sophist's audience, such oratorical display appeared spontaneous and effortless—the ad lib creation of the moment coming into existence in their very presence—but that spontaneity was, in fact, an illusion made possible through intense preparation and skillful use of known rhetorical methods. Philostratus says the sophist Scopelian "no doubt gave an impression of indolence and negligence, since during the period before a declamation he was generally in the company of the magistrates of Smyrna transacting public business . . . in fact during the daytime he did not work much, but he was the most sleepless of men. . . . Indeed, it is said that he used to work continuously from evening until dawn."[16] Students flocked to learn the art by studying with its most famous practitioners.[17]

A trained speaker could employ such skills to any desired end. If, under the sway of oratory, a fly or a fever could be made to appear attractive, how much more so could it affect the outcome of legal cases or civic decisions? Indeed, such matters are the paramount concern of the rhetorical handbooks of the period.[18] Rhetorical training could also be put in the service of philosophy. Dio describes himself as doing exactly this, especially during his exile.[19] He presented himself as a physician who brought with him medicine truly curative of the soul and productive of the moral good. In doing so, he embodied an ideal that had been developing for centuries.[20] While traveling he admonished crowds and told them that they were foolish in the sense that they neither did any of the things that they should do—such as liberating their souls by living more virtuous and better lives—nor did they rid themselves of such evils as ignorance and confusion of mind. Instead, things such as money, reputation, and certain pleasures of the body were sweeping them about. This was so much the case that they found themselves caught in a kind of whirlpool from which they were unable to free themselves.[21]

Dio regularly set himself up as the instructor of whole cities, coming "by divine guidance to address and counsel" them.[22] He often contrasted himself with rhetors who were mere "sophists"—those who commonly used oratorical techniques irresponsibly for personal gain. He likened such sophists to physicians who were more interested in being admired for showing off their knowledge than in curing their patients, or else, who "disregard their [patients'] treatment and restoration of health," preferring to "bring them flowers and courtesans and perfume."[23] He warned his hearers that there were many in the schools of the sophists "growing old in ignorance" because the speeches that they heard there were like sexual encounters with a eunuch: no matter how constant they prove to be, they will never produce offspring.[24] Instead of providing mere entertainment, Dio claimed that discourses like his own "make people happier (εὐδαιμονοῦσι) and better and more self-controlled and more able to administer effectively the cities in which they dwell."[25]

Crowds of thousands filled amphitheaters to attend Dio's performances and considered his oratory as pleasurable as any other entertainment.[26] On these occasions, he remarked, "I will explain to you more clearly . . . the nature of yourselves. In fact such an explanation is a useful thing, and it will do you more good than if I were to speak about heaven and earth."[27] He nevertheless cautioned those listening that the truth about themselves was not something that they would want to hear. They would likely resist the stinging words of philosophy by claiming instead that they had suffered "abuse and mischief."[28] "I believe most people feel toward the words of philosophy exactly as they do toward the medicines which physicians administer; that is, no one resorts to them at first, nor buys them until he contracts some unmistakable illness and has pain in some part of his body. And in the same way people are, as a general rule, not willing to listen to the words of the philosopher until some affliction visits them, something which they consider grievous."[29] Dio explained that whenever people find "falsehood to be sweet and pleasurable," the "truth is bitter and unpleasant." Like those "with sore eyes—they find the light painful, while the darkness, which permits them to see nothing, is restful and agreeable." Having grown accustomed to listening to falsehood generation after generation, "it is no easy matter to disabuse these of their opinion, no matter how clearly you prove it (ἐξελέγχῃ) to be wrong."[30]

In such a situation, where whole cities have grown accustomed to false-hood, entertaining rhetoric that flatters those listening only perpetuates the problem. Of much more help is a speaker who can "expose human sins by words" in a manner that overcomes the audience members' resistance so that they actually become receptive to hearing the truth about themselves.[31] Dio, accordingly, extols those orators "who have the ability through persuasion and reason to calm and soothe the soul."[32] Observing in his day "a great shortage of experts" in this kind of healing, Dio describes them as "the saviors and guardians of all who can be saved, confining and controlling vice before it reaches its final stage."[33]

Dio sought to guide those hearing him in the city of Tarsus to see the truth about themselves. He assured them that his therapeutic speech would not be "overly frank" and "not touch upon all the ailments that afflict" them, but would rather limit itself "to just one item or maybe two."[34] Consequently, he explained to the people of Tarsus, "it is a very mild medicine you are getting in this speech of mine, much less severe than your case calls for."[35] He told them that even though they walked and talked, most of them were in fact asleep. This may not be apparent to one untrained at perceiving the signs (σημεῖα).[36] To the trained eye it is evident that "practically all their actions bear a resemblance to the dream state." Although "they experience joy and sorrow, and courage and timidity," they do so "for no reason at all." Although "they are enthusiastic, they desire the impossible, and what is unreal they regard as real, while what is real they fail to perceive."[37]

He cautioned them, more specifically, that they considered themselves happy (εὐδαίμονας) and blessed (μακαρίους) because of such things that orators regularly praised: Tarsus was the capital city of Cilicia; it occupied a fertile land where the necessities of life were found in abundance and had a river running through the heart of the city.[38] He, nevertheless, sought to persuade them saying that these things "do not make you happy (οὐκ ἐστὲ εὐδαίμονες), not even if the mighty Nile itself should flow through your city with waters clearer than Castalia."[39] Indeed, when Dio visited Alexandria, Egypt, he praised their river and soil and harbors, and then asked the crowd why they were pleased since he had praised everything but them—things independent of their own personal attributes.[40] According to Dio, the populations of both cities suffered the emotional and physical effects of their mistaken judgments of value.

He exhorted the Alexandrians, "perhaps it is high time for you to cease your Bacchic revels and instead attend (προσέχειν) to yourselves."[41] Rather than wait until some catastrophe upset their way of life, or to continue to lose themselves in distractions like the theater, Dio challenged them to begin to care for themselves and reorder their lives so that they would live according to a better set of values that places a premium on more stable and permanent goods. In doing so perhaps they will, in words drawn from one of his speeches at Tarsus, see that "the greatest things, yes the only things worthy of serious pursuit, were present then [in the classical age], are present now, and always will be. Over these no one, surely, has authority, whether to confer them on another or to take them away from the one who has them, but, on the contrary, they are always at one's disposal, whether it be a private citizen or the body politic."[42]

Internalizing this mental conversion to such a degree that it actually reshapes daily activities is like an extended recuperation from an illness or injury. Dio states,

[T]he process of healing and knitting together requires time and serious attention, so it is also in the case of cities. . . . For not among you alone, I dare say, but also among all other peoples, such a result requires a great deal of therapy (θεραπείας)—or, shall I say, prayer? For [it will] only [occur] by getting rid of the vices that excite and disturb people, the vices of envy, greed, contentiousness, the striving in each case to promote one's own welfare at the expense of both one's native land and the common weal.[43]

Dio commends both education (παιδείαν) and reason (λόγον) as the essential ingredients of the curative process, stating that the one "who throughout life employs that remedy with consistency finally comes to a healthy, happy end" (τέλος ὑγιὲς καὶ εὔδαιμον).[44] By contrast, those who avoid the cure of their souls by never "giving ear to chastening reason" have no protection from their own passions and survive adrift on "a sea of senseless opinion and misery."[45]

Psychagogy in Its Classical Form

Dio was but one celebrated instance of a larger cultural phenomenon.[46] Philostratus states that the flourishing of eloquence that is the subject of his history was nothing new in his time. It was instead a renewal of something old, a "second sophistic."[47] Indeed, every practitioner would trace the origins of the art back to an earlier time.[48] Consequently, to understand a figure like Dio, it is necessary to look back to the Greek classical age. There one finds the conditions that make possible the cultural category of the philosophical orator who acts as a physician that cures souls with words.

Homer's *Odyssey* begins not with the epic heroism of Odysseus, but with the young Telemachos grieving over the absence of his father who had not been heard from in the years following the war with Troy. Telemachos sits passively among his mother's shameless suitors as they unjustly consume the household goods while eating, drinking, singing, and dancing. The situation changes only because of the intervention of the goddess Athena who, disguised as the elderly family friend Mentes, provides guidance to the young man. Mentes asks Telemachos, "Are you, grown as you are, the very child of Odysseus?" He answers, "My mother says indeed I am his. I, for my part, do not know."[49] Although Telemachos bears an outward resemblance to his father, he has no certainty of his own identity.[50] Without this conviction, he sits idly among his mother's suitors—remarkably indistinguishable from them, or from any other citizen of Ithaca for that matter.

Telemachos lacks not only self-knowledge, but also a sense of his own agency. After remarking that Odysseus, Telemachos' father, certainly would drive out the suitors, Mentes laments, "How great your need is now of the absent Odysseus!"[51] Rather than remain passive and continue to wait as a spectator for his father's return or the eventual triumph of the suitors, Mentes admonishes the young man to consider how he could force the suitors out of his household.[52] This charge requires Telemachos to mature into the image of his father and realize that identity in resolute action. The divine Athena asserts through Mentes, "You should not go on clinging to your childhood! You are no longer of an age for that." She, then, instructs him to make a journey to determine what happened to his father and then to settle matters himself on his return. Telemachos responds by telling the old man that he has spoken to him like a father would speak to his son.[53] The narrator reports that Athena's guidance "left in his spirit determination and courage, and he remembered his father even more than he had before."[54]

Throughout the rest of the epic, another "old man" (γέροντι) named Mentor accompanies Telemachos and aids his maturation and formation.[55]

By "likening herself to Mentor in voice and appearance," Athena also continues to counsel the young man.[56] She is his companion on his journey and instructs him by introducing him to the valiant heroes of the past such as Nestor and Menelaos as examples for him to follow.[57] Telemachos gradually overcomes each obstacle, including the plot of the suitors to murder him, and eventually attains "to the full measure of his manhood."[58] The reader of the epic witnesses Telemachos "learn the truth by listening to others" while discovering his own "spirit."[59] Eventually, the young man stands side by side with his father in the final combat with the suitors. Odysseus acknowledges his son's presence "where men do battle, and the best are put to trial."[60] Athena, still attending Telemachos in the appearance and voice of Mentor, witnesses the recipient of her guidance no longer behaving like a passive boy without knowledge of his true identity, but fighting as an active, self-possessed, man full of conviction.[61]

It is noteworthy that the origins of this transformative force are elusive in the epic tradition. Although the guidance that Telemachos receives appears to come from the mature Mentes or Mentor, its source is actually divine—Athena in disguise. The divine influence is given in mediated form, that is, humanly. Spiritual guidance is no less idealized or mysterious in other ancient Hellenic traditions regarding the mythic figure of Chiron the centaur. Chiron is best known as the early mentor of Achilles, the educator of the heroic Jason, or even as the instructor of Asclepius in the art of healing.[62] The offspring of the god Cronos and a mortal, Chiron uniquely embodied in his semi-divine nature knowledge curative of both body and soul. Well into the Hellenistic world, later orators could appeal to Chiron as an ideal example of the master trainer of soul and body who united in a single therapeutic art all medical and philosophical knowledge.[63]

The concern for the formation of the young present in mythic form in the epic tradition became a full-fledged discipline by the later fifth century BCE. Educators, who later came to be called sophists, presented themselves as professional guides for the young.[64] The instruction they offered was primarily an education to prepare students for success in public life.[65] The sophist Protagoras is said to have informed Hippocrates, a prospective student, "Young man, this is what you will get if you study with me: The very day you start, you will go home a better man, and the same thing will happen the day after. Every day, day after day, you will get better and better."[66] He continued by informing the young man that he would learn from him "sound deliberation, both in domestic matters—how best to manage one's household, and in public affairs—how to realize one's maximum potential for success in political debate and action."[67]

In a city where civic decisions were made in public assemblies or in courts of law, skillful public speaking was of central importance to anyone who hoped to exert influence in Athens. Virtuoso rhetoricians (for a fee) distributed performance texts to be used as educational tools by students. Such model texts were useful not only because they demonstrated how to make a weak case rhetorically stronger, but, more importantly, they functioned as collections of effective common topics that were reusable in other situations once they were mastered by the student.[68] The sophist Gorgias famously describes such learned speech as "a powerful ruler, which by means of the smallest and most invisible body brings about the most divine deeds. It is able to stop fear and to remove sorrow and to create joy and to augment pity."[69] He likens it to "the power of incantation" that "by conversation with the soul's belief enchants and persuades and moves it by sorcery."[70] Persuasive speech "molds ($\dot{\epsilon}\tau\upsilon\pi\dot{\omega}\sigma\alpha\tau\sigma$) the soul in the way it wishes" as it ably substitutes one belief for another. It is to the soul what drugs are to the body.[71] In contests of words, the speech that "pleases and persuades a large crowd" is not so much the "one spoken truthfully," but rather the one "written artfully."[72] If a teacher could pass on a skill this potent, why would an ambitious student pursue any other form of education?

In Plato's dialogue named after him, Gorgias argues for the supremacy of the rhetor by suggesting that if a doctor and an orator who was ignorant of medicine visited any city together and each tried to convince a gathered assembly that he should be appointed a physician, "the one who had the ability to speak well would be appointed." Gorgias contends that the rhetorician would trump any professional since a skilled orator is able to speak more persuasively on any subject than its practitioners.[73] Socrates then articulates for Gorgias the premise defining his rhetoric: "Oratory does not need to have any knowledge" of a particular subject matter, "it only need to have discovered some device to produce persuasion."[74]

Socrates' interlocutors in Plato's dialogues commonly are sophists who praise rhetoric as a discrete discipline and who underscore its sufficiency to bring human beings maximum fulfillment. Indeed, Socrates belonged to the same intellectual circles as the sophists and shared their concern for the formation of the young. He says to the Athenians in his *Apology*,

"I was always concerned with you, approaching each one of you like a father or an elder brother."[75] Unlike the sophists, however, he never charged a fee for his advice nor did he compose set rhetorical speeches to be imitated. Despite his association with the sophists, one finds in Socrates not only a radical questioning of the sophists' claim regarding rhetoric's ability to foster the good life, but also persistent worries about the effect of this kind of education on the formation of the young. The Socrates of Plato's *Gorgias* denies that rhetoric detached from knowledge is properly an art (τέχνη), "because it guesses at what is pleasant with no consideration for what is best." It "has no account to give of the real nature of what sort of things it employs, and so cannot state the cause of any of them."[76] Socrates claims that without such knowledge this rhetoric is nothing other than flattery, where orators are akin to mere pastry chefs catering to the tastes of the crowds. In this way, the rhetor who is most applauded is the one who in the most pleasant fashion reaffirms the cultural prejudices, unexamined opinions, and habits of a group. Later in the same dialogue, Socrates attempts to show Callicles how his oratory has been entirely co-opted by his desire to please the crowds. Socrates says to him, "You keep shifting back and forth. If you say anything in the Assembly and the Athenian *demos* denies it, you shift your ground and say what it wants to hear."[77]

Socrates suggests to Protagoras that there is need for an "art of measurement" because the "power of appearance often makes us wander all over the place in confusion, often changing our minds about the same things and regretting our actions and choices." Such an art "would make the appearances lose their power by showing us the truth, would give our souls the rest that comes from abiding in the truth, and would save our life."[78] In other words, this art of measurement would make conceivable "a distinction between moral and natural orders so as to de-reify the former" and make it mentally possible to distinguish "between what is naturally given and what is socially required."[79] Without such an art that is directed toward the truth to which language only points, speech becomes ingrown—reduced to nothing more than its own persuasive power.

Socrates' forceful critique exposing the futility of rhetoric detached from philosophy and its attendant deleterious social function is given mythological form in Plato's celebrated parable of the cave.[80] In the parable, the relationship between philosophy and rhetoric is set forth in imagery that becomes the common property of Plato's successors, who use the imagery to the point that it becomes ubiquitous in later literature.[81] Plato likens the visible realm to a dark cave where people have been shackled since childhood with bonds fastened so firmly that their heads are prevented from turning. He later explains that the bonds are those "of kinship with becoming, which have been fastened" to human nature "by feasting, greed, and other such pleasures and which, like leaden weights, pull its vision downward."[82] A fire with a long path along which objects are carried stands behind the prisoners. The only things they have seen since birth are the shadows cast by the objects on the wall in front of them, and the only voices they hear are from those who carry the objects. Plato points out that the prisoners "would in every way believe that the truth is nothing other than the shadows of those artifacts." Furthermore, if they could talk to one another, they would "suppose that the names they used referred to the things they see passing before them." He even imagines them awarding "honors, praises, and prizes among them for the one who was sharpest at identifying the shadows." Lacking the critical tools to discern the true nature of their cave-dwelling bondage, speakers inescapably employ a discourse that uses names detached from their proper reference. The more fluently they do so, and the more sufficient they make that discourse appear, the more they legitimate the social order and receive glory.

Plato then invites his reader to imagine what it would be like to have one's bonds loosed and to ascend from the darkness and shadows of the cave to the fully illuminated world. He describes a painful process where — over an extended period of time — all of one's judgments are reordered in such a way that actual objects began to be seen as real rather than their shadows, and the proper reference of words is shifted to no longer refer to shadows. He says that at first "shadows would be most easily seen, then images of men and other things in water, then the things themselves," until the sun itself is understood. Plato's "ascent," therefore, describes a shift in the mind's "mode of cognition" rather than "a passage from one world to another" as it begins to understand "reality in terms of the universal principles, the intelligible structures and natures, which appear and are exemplified in sense-experience."[83] A number of juxtapositions in the dialogues refer to this cognitive migration. On various occasions, Plato describes it as a movement from rhetoric to philosophy, from opinion (δόξα) to knowledge (ἐπιστήμη), and from appearances to truth. The one who has made this "ascent" thus no longer "assents" to beliefs that are contrary to those things that "are."[84] This is because unstable sources of knowledge such as phenomenal appearance, social custom, and sophistic rhetoric have lost their persuasive force.

Plato is keenly aware of the difficulty of such a conversion, as well as of the problems entailed in facilitating another person's "ascent." The task of guidance is especially complicated by what Plato calls the "double ignorance" that afflicts human beings. Not only are they "in the grip of ignorance" due to a lack of knowledge, but they are also, like those prisoners who have become experts at looking at shadows, convinced of their own wisdom.[85] Such double ignorance results in a crippling deformity of soul.[86] While Plato is anxious to correct these deformities, he knows that any attempt at "putting knowledge into souls that lack it" in any straightforward manner would not be sufficient.[87] Acknowledging that no simple method is adequate, Socrates laments, "If only wisdom were like water, which always flows from a full cup into an empty one."[88] In the shadow realm of words and meanings, communication is never simply informative, and truth cannot merely be passed on like a commodity from one person to another. In order to achieve his goals, Plato needed a more profound art concerned with "turning around" that "by which each learns."[89]

It is only after stripping away — as some thin veneer — rhetoric's expansive claims and laying bare its limited resources that Plato explores a theory of how rhetoric's artful manipulation of shadows can be of use in becoming acquainted with real objects. In his *Phaedrus,* Plato proposes an ideal rhetoric that is both supplemented by philosophy and put in service to it.[90] Plato's Socrates rejects any rhetoric that consists exclusively of techniques of persuasion or of decorating speeches. Instead, practitioners of this new rhetoric would use knowledge of the subtleties of persuasion not as an end in itself, but as a means to pursue wisdom. Indeed, Socrates attempts to convince Phaedrus that "unless he pursues philosophy properly he will never be able to make a proper speech on any subject."[91] In the dialogue between Phaedrus and Socrates, every attempt to find "some easier and shorter route to the art" fails and gives way to a long road of practice and preparation. Socrates declares, "No one can acquire these abilities without great effort — a laborious effort a sensible man will make not in order to speak and act among human beings," but "to speak and act in a way that pleases the gods as much as possible."[92]

Plato could still imagine a world where rhetoric's dubious manipulation of words would not be necessary. Socrates tells Phaedrus that in a less jaded time people "found it rewarding enough in their simplicity to listen to an oak or even a stone, so long as it was telling the truth."[93] In his time, however, truth could not present itself so plainly without encountering resistance. Just as inspired poetry requires the Muses (245a), truth needs a way of enchanting or charming the soul—an art which Socrates defines as "a certain psychagogy through words."[94] According to Plato's theory, this bewitching art, which guides souls toward truth by enchanting them, has the following primary components. First of all, unlike other orators, the practitioner of this art cannot be satisfied with "what will seem just to the crowd," or merely cater to the opinions of others, but instead will know the truth concerning the subject of the speech.[95] In order to communicate what is known persuasively, however, the speaker must have additional knowledge and ability. Just as medicine seeks methodically to determine the intricacies of the body in order to cure it, so psychagogic rhetoric, to achieve its therapeutic aim, must possess a thorough knowledge of that to which it pertains—the soul.[96] In theory, this means that the rhetor must learn the various kinds of souls, the different types of speeches, and then how each type of speech affects each kind of soul. In practice, the orator must be able to "discern each kind clearly as it occurs in the actions of real life" so that each speech may be carefully accommodated to the different kinds of souls in order to secure conviction in the listener.[97] This practice ensures that a "complex and elaborate speech is given to a complex soul and a simple speech to a simple one."[98] Moreover, the well-trained psychagogue will be as accomplished as any other orator in identifying the proper occasion for speaking and making the appropriate emotional appeals.[99]

Although articulated formally near the end of the dialogue, the psychagogic theory explains much of what is puzzling about the *Phaedrus*. Socrates' behavior at the beginning of the dialogue largely appears to be uncharacteristic of him. He is presented as "most out of place" (ἀτοπώτατος).[100] The urban-dwelling Socrates, devoted to the citizens of the polis, is led for the first time outside the city wall by Phaedrus. Additionally, the great dismantler of sophistry presents himself as such "a lover of speeches" that he can be led all over Attica simply by waving in front of him the leaves of a book containing a speech.[101] The one who famously committed himself to the examined life confesses his utter lack of self-knowledge: "I am still unable, as the Delphic inscription orders, to know myself. . . . Am I a beast more complicated and savage than Typhon, or am I a tamer, simpler animal with a share in a divine and gentle nature?"[102]

In the *Phaedrus*, Socrates not only articulates the psychagogic theory, but also dramatically enacts it throughout the dialogue. Socrates' fluctuating presentation is a result of his accommodation to Phaedrus, whose soul is overcome at the time by his love of Lysias' speech.[103] In the words of Elizabeth Asmis, "Acting as a 'psychagogue,' he [Socrates] associates Phaedrus with himself in search for self-knowledge, by guiding him to a holy place where Phaedrus may be healed of his evil enchantment."[104] Through this adaptation to Phaedrus, Socrates demonstrates the subtle psychagogic "art to lead others away from what is the case on each occasion little by little through similarities to its opposite."[105] Socrates strives, therefore, to lead Phaedrus gradually away from valuing eloquent speeches to loving the pursuit of wisdom.

In the justly famous second speech of the *Phaedrus*, Socrates seeks by means of words to lift Phaedrus' narrow vision away from his love of Lysias' speech in an ascent toward a higher love. Socrates begins by calling Phaedrus' attention to his own immortal soul. To speak of the soul, he resorts to the indirect language of myth, asserting that a more direct description would be "altogether a task for a god"—well beyond what Phaedrus could hear.[106] Socrates invites Phaedrus to imagine the souls of the gods and of human beings as charioteers. The gods ascend to the high ridge of heaven and gaze at "being that really is what it is, the subject of all true knowledge, visible only to intelligence." They delight in seeing reality as it truly is and are enriched by this vision, especially by the direct apprehension of Justice, Self-control, and Knowledge itself. The majority of human souls, however, struggle to rise as they are carried about in constant circular motion. They are distracted, "trampling and striking one another as each tries to get ahead of the others"—a marked contrast to the orderly vision and absence of jealousy found among the gods. These human souls fail to attain any stable perception of what truly is and consequently are left with only their opinions and beliefs to nourish them. They remain unsatisfied. Ideally a human soul can imitate the gods by loving what they desire and by rising to contemplate truth directly, even if only for a moment. This ascent requires developing means of lifting the mind's point of view, a painful process of growing "wings" that Socrates likens to the experience of a child "whose teeth are just starting to grow in."[107]

Of course, the gods do not philosophize because they do not yearn for a wisdom which they already possess.[108] Philosophy is reserved for human beings who compensate for their limited cognitive abilities with desire. Rather than the satisfaction and satiety of a stable product, philosophy yields a partial yet tantalizing perspective that whets the appetite and subjugates other affections to its service.[109] Socrates underscores that the most that can be humanly hoped for is a momentary glimpse over the roof of the world of becoming, as reality discloses its true nature only for an instant and just as quickly retreats into the memory. Discourse alone, then, remains as a mere image that can at best prompt the soul to remember what it perceived earlier. The perfection for which the lover of wisdom strives is the habitual use of such verbal and non-verbal images not as ends in themselves, but as reminders of the reality to which their existence points.[110]

In drawing Phaedrus' attention to his own soul, Socrates offers his own psychagogic words as a fragile ladder for Phaedrus to climb, as it were, with his mind. Socrates does so in the hope that the young man may, in a moment of insight, remedy the deficiency of perspective that informs his judgments. Having made such an ascent, even momentarily, Phaedrus may begin to contemplate his own immortal soul and to desire only what is worthy of it — food for its best part.[111] Influenced by this experience of insight, he would then no longer be satisfied with being a passive consumer of speeches which he can then reproduce when needed. Instead, desiring wisdom itself, he would commit himself, like Socrates, to the cultivation of his own soul (ψυχῆς παίδευσιν) and to the life of philosophy.[112] In the last third of the dialogue Phaedrus engages in dialectical discussion with Socrates and begins to philosophize himself under Socrates' guidance. The dialogue ends with Phaedrus returning to his beloved Lysias not to acquire another speech, but to sow seeds of philosophy in his soul as Socrates had sown seeds in his.[113]

Even as a concession to human weakness, Plato's psychagogic theory in the *Phaedrus* rehabilitates rhetoric and assigns it a strategic place in the complex process of guiding the soul to apprehend truth.[114] "Poetry and oratory" in the hands of such an able psychagogue then "can do more than make lies sound like truth. They are also means for making truth sound like truth — the only means, on many occasions, that are available."[115]

Plato's sharp critique of writing at the end of the *Phaedrus* is first of all an argument that the sophists' pedagogical reliance on written speeches falls short of the standards established by psychagogic theory.[116] Although a writer may have knowledge, the production of a written document will not communicate that knowledge effectively because of the intrinsic inadequacy of the chosen medium. Plato likens writing to a painting that may appear alive, but stands eerily silent as it continually presents the same image. Likewise, writing "continues to signify just the same thing forever." It is composed of words "as incapable of speaking in their own defense as they are of teaching the truth adequately."[117] Indiscriminate about its audience, a text "does not know to whom it should speak and to whom it should not." Speaking the same word over and over without explanation, writing can neither adapt itself to the state of the soul of the reader nor to the particularities of the occasion. Even the best of texts, therefore, are in need of oral supplementation. In the words of Plato's Socrates, each text "always needs its father's support." There is no substitute for "the living, breathing discourse of the man who knows, of which the written word can be fairly called an image."[118] Isolated from its author, a text is an insufficiently formative instrument to lead the soul to perceive wisdom itself. Plato judged "the dead word of the page" to be "unfitted to cope with the obliquity of man's affective disinclinations toward truth—truth which the written word, nevertheless, might embody in some measure."[119]

The philosophical use of rhetoric outlined in the *Phaedrus* clarifies the role of speech in the spiritual guidance found in other Platonic dialogues. For example, Plato's enlightened philosophers do not emerge from the cave to remain where they can see reality as it truly is. Even though Plato suggests that the prisoners in the cave would likely violently resist any efforts "to free them and lead them upward," those who have ascended and become free of their chains return to the cave "to guard and care for the others."[120] Each philosopher is told, "You must go down to live in the common dwelling place of the others and grow accustomed to seeing in the dark. When you are used to it you will see vastly better than the people there. You will know what each image is and of what it is an image, because you have seen the truth of things beautiful and just and good."[121] The prisoners would surely reject a forceful teaching that sought to impart knowledge like "putting sight into blind eyes."[122] Plato commends instead a gentle guidance that redirects human eyes toward the light. Plato notes that his prisoners' eyes are fully functional. They have only become too accustomed to darkness to tolerate sudden daylight. Similarly, rather than imparting knowledge, this psychagogic strategy promotes "conversion"—the gradual "turning around" of that "by which each learns" so that they acquire the skills and capacity to perceive wisdom for themselves.[123]

If Plato is right that the initial form of dark ignorance to be overcome has more to do with what one presumes to know than with what one does not know, then there is first of all the need for an exercise in self-scrutiny that reveals one's ignorance of self. Socrates' use of conversation as a tool to facilitate his interlocutors' reassessment of their core beliefs is perhaps what he was most remembered for.[124] In the *Laches,* Nicias reports that whoever begins a conversation with Socrates "must necessarily, even if he began by conversing about something quite different in the first place, keep on being led about by the man's arguments until he submits to answering questions about himself concerning both his present manner of life and the life he has lived hitherto."[125] Beginning with an "experiential judgment," Socrates' inquiry reveals the "more general propositions that constitute the basis of particular judgments passed" and by means of reflection eventually brings into view "the originally obscure assumption that lies at the bottom of the judgment on the concrete instance."[126] In this process, the professed beliefs of Socrates' interlocutors are used as evidence that reveals upon examination the real beliefs that inform their judgments. Through this joint inquiry, reflection is used "to lift the knowledge we already possess into consciousness."[127]

The Athenian visitor in the *Sophist* articulates this surgical method where one's opinions are collected, set side by side, and proven to "vary inconsistently":

> Doctors who care for the body think it cannot benefit from any food that is offered to it until what is interfering with it from inside is removed. The people who cleanse the soul . . . likewise think the soul, too, will receive no benefit from any learning that is offered to it until someone shames it by refuting (ἐλέγχων) it, removes the opinions that interfere with learning, and exhibits it cleansed, believing that it knows only those things that it does know, and nothing more.[128]

This procedure attempts to lead people to enough self-knowledge that they "lose their inflated and rigid beliefs about themselves."[129] The Athenian visitor sums up this description of the Socratic therapeutic method by asserting, "the refutation (ἐλέγχος) of the empty belief in one's own wisdom is nothing other than our noble sophistry."[130]

The Socratic *elenchus* ("refutation") provides a set of critical tools to refute false beliefs and bring into view deficiencies of self-knowledge. It is, nonetheless, largely a negative exercise with little positive content. Psychagogy is a broader term than *elenchus* since it includes the constructive task of spiritual guidance without excluding the critical one. In fact, *elenchus* and psychagogy overlap as one discards judgments that no longer accord with new learning, and vice versa.[131] In the Platonic dialogues, having the unarticulated beliefs that in fact guide one's actions and affections brought to the surface and made the subject of scrutiny does not generally lead directly to knowledge. Rather, the interlocutor is found to be in an aporetic state characterized by a "puzzlement and lack of passage" that is "closely associated with the awareness of one's own ignorance."[132]

Once unrealistic assessments of the true nature of oneself and one's place in the universe have been put in question, one is in a better position to begin to address one's ignorance of the truth concerning other things. The docility fostered by the first critical procedure creates room for positive guidance toward the apprehension of wisdom. As required by the psychagogic theory, speech encouraging the positive movement is accommodated to the state of the soul of the conversation partner. Its content is thereby limited by what the hearer is capable of listening to at any given time. For example, the cave prisoners, still only familiar with shadows, continue to understand words only insofar as they refer to the images they see. Lacking knowledge of reality, like the human souls in the *Phaedrus,* they dwell in the realm of belief and opinion. In such a situation, the psychagogic principle of accommodation demands that the one seeking to guide souls employ words familiar enough to the hearers so as to be intelligible, but use them in a novel way that would lead the hearers to recognize the true nature of their existence. This psychagogic speech, therefore, requires the use of words and concepts that are less than ideal as the guide descends into the murky water of opinions, judgments, and beliefs rather than knowledge.

As mentioned previously, in an ideal world Plato would clearly prefer a form of therapy that directly imparts sure knowledge. Merely believing the opinions of others is not as reliable a basis for actions as having direct personal knowledge for oneself. Unlike knowledge, beliefs can be false, and the maintaining of beliefs can be a form of ignorance.[133] Whoever begins with a false opinion (δόξης ψευδοῦς) has trouble ever attaining even a small part of the truth.[134] Plato states in the *Republic* that "opinion is concerned with becoming, intellect with being. And as being is to becoming, so intellect is to opinion, so knowledge is to belief, and thought to imagining."[135] Opinion carries with it all the instability of the fluctuating objects it considers.

Even with this commitment to certain knowledge, Plato believes, nonetheless, that the process of coming to full understanding for human beings includes intermediate steps involving belief. In the *Statesman,* it is asserted that it is utterly difficult "to demonstrate any of the greater subjects without using models" or "images" (μὴ παραδείγμασι) as intermediaries.[136] Inquiring how one might "care for" (θεραπείαν) the people of a city, Plato likens a statesman to an elementary language teacher who strives to teach students the skills of reading and writing. At first children learn to distinguish individual letters in the shortest and easiest syllables, but do not recognize them in other contexts. They are best "led" (ἀνάγειν) by using what they do recognize as models to be set beside what they do not. They gradually learn to recognize letters in larger and larger contexts knowing how each is both the same and different from the others. "The soul," analogously, "experiences the same process in relation to the individual 'letters' (στοιχεῖα) of everything" as it sometimes forms "correct judgments" (ὀρθῶς δοξάζει) about some things and is ignorant of the same things when they are transferred into the long "syllables" of other things.[137]

To guide souls to become literate in the "letters of everything" requires working with the opinions that they already possess. Opinion is an intermediate state darker than knowledge but clearer than ignorance.[138] Although opinion may be false, it may also be true. In such a case, "true opinion (δόξα ἀληθής) is as good a guide to rightness of action as knowledge."[139] True opinion falls short of understanding but it is no less true and is accessible to more people. Plato likens its usefulness to the correct directions given by a man to a place he has never been.[140] Directions given by one who has a reliable opinion produces similar results to that offered by a man who has been to the destination and led others there personally. True opinions, beliefs, and images, therefore, can be artfully employed to bring about "a single true judgment" in matters that would otherwise be inaccessible.[141]

It is due to his sophisticated understanding of the conditions necessary to lead other people to perceive the truth for themselves that Plato's Socrates is preoccupied chiefly with the opinions of his interlocutors and relies so much on the mythic form of expression. Phaedrus, in fact, teases Socrates saying that what he excels at is making up stories.[142] Although Platonic myths provide memorable stories and are entertaining, their real purpose is to serve as arguments in narrative form where the propositions are implied rather than stated directly.[143] Recall how Socrates resorted to the indirect language of myth to explain the soul in an attractive manner that would appeal to Phaedrus. In the human world, Socrates resorts to mythic imagery, knowing well that such language is by no means perspicuous; yet to describe "the ideal form" (ἰδέας) of the soul otherwise would be the "task of a god in every way."[144] For a mind not accustomed to the clarity of direct vision, it is the very obscurity of myth that adds to its intelligibility. Figurative language becomes psychagogically necessary insofar as it is accessible to those minds that may perceive the truth dispersed in the extended form of myth rather than more directly.

By adapting speech to the state of the soul of the hearer, the guide can bring false beliefs to the surface and offer truer ones to replace them. These new judgments, however, are not stable and may still "escape from the human soul." In order to abide in the soul they need to be "tied down," that is, transformed into knowledge through exercises of reasoning.[145] Beliefs and opinions, myths and images, are converted into stable understanding through exercises that help students acquire a certain set of skills that allow them to apprehend the truth for themselves. To develop these skills, Plato's Socrates advocates an extended program of training begun at an early age that moderates desire and strengthens both mind and body.[146] He details a decades-long educational process that culminates in the study of dialectic only after the student has mastered mathematics, geometry, astronomy, and harmonics. Such disciplines "have the power to awaken the best part of the soul and lead it upward to the contemplation of the best among the things that are." "Dialectical reasoning" secures the soul's conversion as it "gently pulls the eye of the soul buried in a sort of barbaric bog out and leads it upwards, using the arts we described to help it and cooperate with it in turning the soul around."[147] The singular purpose of this process is to cultivate a habitual mode of thinking that reasons from sense perception to universal principles, so as to be able to refer any sensate particular to the ideal form of which it is merely a particularized instantiation.[148] Ideally, then, internalizing this habit of mind enables one to distinguish the Good from lesser goods and to act accordingly as knowing and acting mutually condition one another.

Rather than marketing speeches that could be employed to secure success in conventional society, Plato founded an academy which, over an extended period of time, would foster a more deeply formative experience for his students. To be sure, this community of learning would use written texts, but supplement them with oral conversation and personal formation in the philosophic life. Associated with the guide's own quest for truth, the student would learn the practices of joint inquiry in a community that maintains philosophical reason as an authority higher than customary social norms. In a passage that echoes the *Phaedrus,* the Seventh Letter describes knowledge as best acquired "after long-continued association" between teacher and pupil. In this personal context, knowledge emerges "suddenly" out of "joint pursuit of the subject like light flashing forth when a fire is kindled. It is born in the soul and straightaway nourishes itself."[149] The mature student's eventual participation in public life would then be tempered by the awareness of norms transcending the merely customary.

It is questionable how many people, even with guidance, could make the ascent from the cave and gain a critical perspective on conventional norms by making use of the rational exercises. Indeed, Plato thinks that only a few can: "There remains only a very small group who consort with philosophy in a way that is worthy of her."[150] "The crowd," in fact, "can never be philosophers."[151] Lacking the requisite qualities of soul, the best that can be hoped for the majority is to accept and act upon true opinion that never amounts to understanding.[152] For the majority, making the truth one's own requires the experience of being enchanted by it. The survival of any society, thus, depends on its ability to make its laws appealing enough through psychagogic means that they are freely chosen by its citizens.[153]

In summary, Plato's rejection of sophistry did not necessitate a disregard of rhetoric as a tool of moral philosophy. One finds in the Platonic dialogues not only a thorough critique of rhetoric as such, but also intimations about what shape a philosophically informed rhetoric would take. Plato's "psychagogy" is a word connotatively similar to Gorgias' description

of the logos that "enchants and persuades and moves" the soul "by sorcery."
It is, however, a very different rhetoric from that which Plato characterizes
as succeeding only by catering to the tastes of the crowds, legitimating the
social order, and pleasing its prejudices. The oral resources of rhetoric
provided Plato with a more fluid medium than the written word—one
that could spontaneously vary words to suit widely divergent audiences
on any number of occasions. Plato imagined this rhetorically embellished
philosophy to be powerful enough to mend the deformity of souls lan-
guishing in ignorance. The beautiful words of the philosopher could se-
duce people away from that with which they were familiar toward an understanding of the true nature of themselves and the world. This process
entailed, first of all, a thorough, critical assessment of prior convictions
that as often as not led to their abandonment. This purification was then
followed by positive, constructive exercises that fostered skills of accurate
perception and evaluation to enable students to perceive wisdom on their
own, even when it was difficult to communicate in words.

Chapter Two

Hellenistic Refinements

The cures of the soul have been discovered by the ancients,
but it is our task to learn the method and the time of treatment.
—Seneca, *Ep.* 64.8–9

Cures for the Roman Soul

The influence of the Platonic dialogues continued to be felt well into the second sophistic.[1] An epitaph attested in the Hellenistic world refers to how Plato "healed human minds by letters. As the god's son Asclepius is a healer of the body, so is Plato of the immortal soul."[2] The exceptional popularity and influence of the *Phaedrus* has been well documented. Michael Trapp aptly observes, "As a treatise on rhetoric and dialectic, the *Phaedrus* was of obvious interest both to philosophers and rhetoricians; all the more so as, unlike its companion piece the *Gorgias,* it explicitly allowed for the possibility of a genuine science of rhetoric and offered prescriptions for its realization."[3] Much of Plato's recasting of rhetoric as psychagogy was taken up by later philosophers. Aristotle's own treatise on rhetoric is one example of what would become an ongoing movement to examine more thoroughly themes raised by Plato and to introduce more specific terminology toward that end.[4] Henri Marrou has described how, even though the rivalry between philosophy and rhetoric continued into the Hellenistic period, there was also "an inextricable interweaving, knitting the classical tradition into an ever-closer unity."[5] In spite of a profusion of schools and ideas, "philosophy in the Hellenistic age and under the Empire" was recognizable as "an entity and philosophers were a class falling under a specific rubric."[6] There was a degree of consensus such that, as A. D. Nock has observed, "any philosophy of the time" sought conversion of its practitioner's way of life by setting up "a standard of values" different from the "common ethic and values" of the "world outside."[7]

To be sure, the dogmatic commitments of any particular school of philosophy defined its identity, and such constitutive elements should not be set to one side in favor of purely formal considerations. Nevertheless, when the Hellenistic materials are reviewed with Plato's psychagogy in mind, his conception of a rhetorically embellished philosophy proves to be an ideal so remarkably flexible that its formal features could flourish even in communities rejecting most of Plato's doctrinal commitments. Representatives of the various schools of philosophy repeatedly employed similar metaphors and themes to describe the tasks and aims of philosophy as well as to specify its appropriate pedagogy. This is so much the case that Ilsetraut Hadot concludes, "The dogmatic foundations for overcoming fear of death as well as other fears and passions may vary greatly, but the methods employed by the spiritual guide to achieve this end are almost always the same."[8]

It is not surprising, therefore, that a Platonic handbook from the early centuries of the Common Era would paraphrase the psychagogy of the *Phaedrus* by commending that the philosopher acquire "an accurate perception of the faculties of the soul and the differences among people, and the types of discourse which are fitted to this or that soul, and when one perceives with precision which sort of person can be persuaded by what arguments and of what sort those are, such an individual, if he also picks the right opportunity for using the particular argument will be a complete orator."[9] Less expected, however, are the extant Epicurean writings which, despite the fact that they are far removed from Platonism philosophically, indicate that formal principles of psychagogy were employed in their communities. These writings testify to the wide dissemination of psychagogic traditions in the Hellenistic era. In a work known as *De libertate dicendi* (On Frank Speech), the Epicurean philosopher, Philodemus, preserved the substance of lectures delivered in Athens during the first century BCE by the head of the Epicurean school at the time, Zeno of Sidon.[10] Philodemus' lecture notes amount to a handbook offering "hypothetical questions and answers on aspects of psychagogic theory as well as reflections on psychagogic practice."[11]

Epicurus himself had described his philosophy as a therapy for the soul: "Vain is the word of the philosopher by which no human suffering is healed. Just as medicine confers no benefit if it does not cast out bodily disease, neither is there from philosophy if it does not drive away suffering from the soul."[12] Philodemus' handbook provides a number of guidelines clarifying the optimal use of speech by members of the Epicurean community in the cure of soul. Employing speech in a methodical fashion to call attention to another member's faults is likened to "applying a scalpel to those who are ill."[13] The ability to engage in self-criticism and be receptive to frank speech is praised as a necessary prerequisite for anyone who is to benefit from therapy.[14] The singular virtue of such communal frankness is that it enables members to "point out and persuade" one another of "the causes on account of which" they have "reasoned falsely" (Col. IXa). This is of great benefit since souls "unable to calculate what is advantageous suffer and do many opposing things" (Col. XXb). It is those who become "lovers of frankness" (φιλοπαρρησιάσται), rather than those who are vexed by it, who make progress in philosophy (Col. XVIb). Even the sages in the Epicurean community continue to "sting each other with the gentlest stings and acknowledge gratitude" for the benefits of such admonition (Col. VIIIb).

For frank speech to be effective, according to Philodemus, it must conform to certain standards and should be employed "neither at all times, nor directed indiscriminately against everyone, nor against every chance of error" (Fr. 79 = 81N). Its "suitable use" (Col. XIVb) is likened to the doctor's art of discerning illness from signs (σημειωσάμενον) and adapting treatment to specific cases.[15] Consequently, the treatise enumerates how treatment must be accommodated to the varying needs of a number of types of souls. Instructions are given regarding the particular qualities of, among others, the "strong" vs. the "weak" (Fr. 7, 10), those of high (Col. IVb, XXIIIa) or low (Col. Va) social status, women (Col. XXIIa–b), and the elderly (Col. XXIVa–b).[16]

Echoing Plato's guidelines in the *Phaedrus*, the handbook states that admonition is to be given "according to each" (καθ᾽ ἕκαστον) type of soul (Col. VIIa) and "at the appropriate moment" (κατὰ καιρόν [Col.

XVIIb]).[17] As a result, the sage's advice may appear inconsistent to those unfamiliar with the psychagogic art: "to those who will bring forward their errors, he will speak out with frankness, and to some he will speak on individual matters and with a view to being ingratiating, though the actions [in need of correction] are the same. And if one has needed frankness minimally, while another has been saved by means of this, then to the one he applies less, and to the other more of that through which he became perfect" (Col. VIb). To those aware of psychagogic principles, however, it is entirely clear that the wise teacher will not reproach a student for everything at once (Fr. 78 [= 80 N]), but will instead guide each one "little by little" (κατ᾽ ὀλίγον [Col. XIIIa]).

In addition to influencing the patterns of therapeutic speech in the Epicurean communities of the Hellenistic era, psychagogy supplied the essential presuppositions of the discourse of philosophically inclined orators. Its presence was often in the background, supplying the underlying form of public speeches and structuring them according to predictable patterns. For example, when Maximus of Tyre, a Platonist in the late second century CE, gave a series of orations in Rome, he informed his hearers that if they were merely looking for skill with words and sophistry, they would have no problem finding a teacher, since "the world is full of that kind of sophist. . . . Indeed, I would dare say that it has more teachers than pupils."[18] According to Maximus, a genuine teacher would "rouse young men's souls and guide (διαπαιδαγωγοῦντος) their ambitions" through instruction (λόγος) that is not "lax or slovenly or casual, but so combines appeals to both character (ἤθει) and emotion" (πάθει), that it compels them "to rise and share its fervor."[19]

Maximus described his own speech as a "treasury of eloquence" capable of appealing "to all ears and all characters, proficient in all styles of speech and all forms of training . . . freely available to all who can receive it."[20] He likens its beguiling quality to a song that charms listeners with "complex and musical harmonies."[21] Ordinary song, however, has only limited psychagogic value.[22] He claimed that his speech was inspired by a much stronger Muse—that of philosophy. Devotees of this Muse address the weighty subject of "human opinions and emotions, their causes and origins, and the factors that correct them (ἐπανορθώσεις) and preserve (σωτηρίαι) them."[23] In order to be effective, philosophical reason likens itself to "a skilled doctor" who attends to the changing needs of the body. Philosophy is always "adapting its tone to match the emotions of the moment" so as to care best for the human soul in its constantly shifting condition.[24]

Maximus told his hearers about a man who once kept birds that chirped as birds do — pleasantly enough but without a tune. The birds listened day after day to his neighbor play the pipe, and began to accompany him so that eventually their singing "was molded into tune with his playing." Maximus then exclaimed, "My audience is human beings, not birds, what they listen to over and over again is not inarticulate piping but rationally articulated speech which appeals to the intellect, stimulates its hearers, and is made for imitation. Who will answer my song?"[25] Maximus called out hoping that his hearers would respond in imitation, "Come, let philosophy step forward in the character of a lawmaker, bringing order (κοσμήσουσα) to a disorganized (ἄτακτον) and erring soul as if to a people."[26]

Maximus, and those like him, knew full well that responding to such oratorical virtuosity was only a first step in the cure of soul. To give assent to a true statement is not yet to live according to it. It is one thing to believe in philosophy; it is quite another matter to live philosophically. Maximus himself warned his hearers against any facile equation between knowledge and virtue, for

> this will prove a deceptive and dangerous thing to say, God knows, if people become convinced that mere qualities of theoretical knowledge (θεωρημάτων) and a handful of doctrines (μαθήματα) can bring virtue in with them when they enter the soul. If that were true, then sophists would be a truly valuable class of person, those garrulous polymaths stuffed with learning, trading in it, and selling to anyone who asks. They set up an open market in virtue, roll up and buy.[27]

During the Hellenistic period, philosophers, in this way, universally insisted that authentic philosophical inquiry necessarily altered one's way of life. Sublime ideas and beautiful words were no substitute for philosophically informed, embodied human activity. Maximus asserted that no philosophical orator "should find himself denouncing adulterers and rapists for crimes of which he too is guilty. He should be free of all such experiences, so as to make himself a candid scourge of wrongdoing."[28] Instead, ideally "there has to be a coincidence of word and deed," between λόγος and ἦθος, *sermo* and *uita*.[29]

To bridge this gap between words and deeds, there arose, particularly in the Hellenistic era, an intricate body of reflection on the relationship between knowledge and practice. Seneca's letters to Lucilius contain a wealth of information on Stoic practices of spiritual guidance in particular, but he often liberally borrows anything of use from other schools of philosophy.[30] Even as they promote Seneca's Stoic commitments, the letters echo psychagogic themes raised by Plato. He tells Lucilius that in writing these letters late in his life he is acting as a guide who helps others find the right path.[31] Fully aware of the limitations of writing in the task of spiritual guidance, Seneca intends his letters to be a vicarious conversation approximating his presence.[32] He varies his own self-presentation accordingly to suit the perceived needs of his intended readers—much like Plato's Socrates did to guide young Phaedrus.[33] He passes on "certain salutary admonitions" like a physician who prescribes "useful drugs" and states, "I have found them helpful in ministering to my own sores, which, if not wholly cured, have at any rate ceased to spread."[34]

Seneca's letters, nonetheless, go beyond Plato's explicit admonitions by advancing a more refined terminology regarding the problematic relationship between the beliefs and the emotions of those seeking to make progress in philosophy. His exposition of the nature of the links between philosophical doctrines, affections, and moral exhortation supplies important presuppositions for his practice of spiritual guidance. It is not always apparent how the speculative doctrines of the Hellenistic philosophical schools regarding such things as the nature of the gods and the universe fit with their practical concern for philosophy to be a way of life. By examining these connections, it becomes possible to understand why they would believe that abstract doctrines could have a therapeutic effect on the emotions, and that moral exhortation ought to be an essential feature of the teaching of doctrine.

Like Plato, Seneca and his philosophically inclined contemporaries considered the common antecedent acculturation that decisively shapes each person's affections and activities to be deleterious. He laments, "We are not allowed to travel the straight road (*recta uia*). Our parents and our slaves draw us into wrong. Nobody confines his mistakes to himself; people sprinkle folly among their neighbors, and receive it from them in turn. For this reason, in an individual, you find the vices of nations, because the nation has given them to the individual . . . the result is a vast mass of wickedness."[35] Human experience is filtered through cultural values that have been inculcated from our earliest days and have such force that nearly everyone passively conforms to them.

Due to the fact that we have had no conscious awareness to draw upon prior to this process of corruption, it is difficult even to be cognizant of it. Seneca asserts that unlike sickness of the body which often becomes more visible as the disease progresses, the sickness of the afflicted soul becomes progressively less perceptible: "For he whose sleep is light pursues visions during slumber, and sometimes, though asleep, is conscious that he is asleep; but sound slumber annihilates our very dreams and sinks the spirit down so deep that it has no perception of self. Why will no one confess his faults? Because he is still in their grasp; only he who is awake can recount his dream."[36] In such a situation, Seneca observes, fissures necessarily appear between one's words and way of life. He writes rhetorically, "You know that friendship should be scrupulously honored, and yet you do not hold it in honor. You know that a man does wrong in requiring chastity of his wife while he himself is intriguing with the wives of other men; you know that, as your wife should have no dealings with a lover, neither should you yourself with a mistress; and yet you do not act accordingly."[37]

Such breaches between knowing and acting are evidence of disease of the soul. Seneca defines disease as "a persistent perversion of judgment (*iudicium in prauo pertinax*) so that things which are mildly desirable are thought to be highly desirable."[38] Emotions such as "fear, anger, grief, and love are not blind surges of affect that push and pull us without regard to reasoning and belief."[39] They are instead capacities of the soul whose manifestation depends upon evaluative judgments about the meaning of experience. Seneca's contention is not that our feelings are without basis in biology, but that our experience of them is deeply malformed by social convention. Instead of emotions being naturally expressed, they have become, as it were, passionate.

The way that our individual experience of emotion is deformed by the commonly accepted value judgments of society is nowhere more evident than in Seneca's detailed examination of anger. In *De ira*, he argues that anger depends first of all on belief in the proposition "we have been wronged" or upon our anticipation that such a state of affairs will occur.[40] When this proposition is made the subject of scrutiny, it is shown to depend on false internal appraisals of external experience.[41] Once one becomes aware of the falsity of such a proposition, Seneca suggests that one will find other propositions to be more warranted such as "no wrong done to a great soul will make itself felt, being weaker than its object."[42] Ultimately, then, once the correct proposition is internalized, the state of soul of the one living according to this new belief will not be readily characterized by anger.[43]

Likewise, in a letter sent to a man grieving the loss of his son, Seneca concedes that it is natural to mourn such a loss, but seeks to persuade the father that his grief is excessive.[44] Grief derives its debilitating force not from the loss, but from one's beliefs about the loss. In other words, "we suffer more often from opinions than from reality."[45] Seneca suspects that the man is, in fact, conforming to the values "of the many, and observing what is customary rather than what ought to be done."[46] It is the misleading beliefs of the general populace that are actually driving his emotions and distressing his soul. Seneca remarks that the grieving father evidently shares the common belief that death is an evil to be avoided. He, furthermore, seems to believe that his son's death is somehow worse because it came early in life. Seneca reminds him that death is as natural as it is inevitable, and that the variations of human lifespans are minimal in the grand scheme of things.[47] Seneca rebukes the father, "Yours is not pain; it is a mere sting — and it is you yourself [on account of your beliefs] who are turning it into pain."[48] Seneca's admonition is consistent with his cognitive psychology which dictates that only when the father can "refer all these matters to reason" will he learn to "accept what is inevitable with a steady soul."[49] It is only through this practice that he will be able to follow in the footsteps of "countless men" who have buried sons in the prime of life "without tears" (*sine lacrimis*) and not allowed the funeral pyre to interrupt their public duty.[50]

The natural home of Seneca's highly cognitive analysis of emotion is the Stoic unitary account of the soul. Chrysippus, one of the early Stoic founders, is said to have equated emotions and judgments without remainder. The precise way that this intellectual analysis and the resulting therapy unfolded varied in the Hellenistic schools according to their different cosmological, anthropological, and psychological doctrines.[51] Platonists and Stoics, therefore, used this cognitive psychology differently due to their varying anthropologies. Platonists, and those influenced by them such as Augustine of Hippo, readily wrote of the negative effects of false evaluations of goods and the emotional consequences of such erroneous judgments of value. Notwithstanding their more complex account of the soul, Platonists employed this analysis quite naturally even when it over-lapped with Stoic commonplaces. Rather than equating emotions and rational judgments (like Chrysippus), Platonists understood belief in false propositions to result from combining weakness in the rational part of the soul with preexisting passion. False propositions are believed because the soul is in the grip of passion. Once they are believed, they, in turn, legitimate the passions. Since the passions are not reducible without remainder to cognitive judgments, but also have roots in the irrational lower parts of the soul, Platonists supplemented the cognitive work with other methods purposely designed to soothe the soul's irrational "horses" so that they would become amenable to reason's direction. As the lower parts of the soul are soothed through various practices, the cognitive exercise of acquiring true opinions can, in turn, strengthen the higher part of the soul in its task to govern the lower faculties and refute the false rationales fueling the passions.[52]

Despite these doctrinal variations between philosophical schools, Roman intellectuals such as Seneca were commonly convinced that if experience and emotions were to be wrested free of the cultural values that tightly bound them, it would only be by means of philosophy.[53] For this reason, Seneca advises the young Lucilius that "before all else" he needs to "strip things of all that disturb and confuse, and to see what each is in fact." Only then will he be able to "comprehend that they contain nothing fearful except the actual fear." He likens our typical emotional response to the way that children become afraid when their playmates appear wearing unfamiliar masks. In order to move on to maturity, "we should strip the mask, not only from human beings, but from things, and restore to each object its own aspect."[54]

If, as Seneca asserts, the cognitive content and emotional effects of cultural norms are so destructive that one needs to take such painstaking measures to be free of them, then does this not render ongoing participation in society problematic? Why not undertake a great exodus from the "vast mass of wickedness?"[55] In addressing this question, Seneca first explains how necessary it is to understand that we each hold citizenship in two overlapping commonwealths rather than one. On the one hand, there is our local citizenship, determined by the accident of birth and regulated by local custom. On the other hand, we belong to the global community of reason, which includes the gods as well as all human beings.[56] Rather than physical withdrawal from the local commonwealth, Seneca commends philosophical withdrawal and formation which will enable a person to continue to participate in corrupt local society without being defined by it. He counsels Lucilius neither to imitate nor hate the world, but to engage, instead, with Seneca in "a lifelong balancing act between two parallel sets of norms, philosophical and socio-political."[57] Thus, his social involvement will be tempered and guided by the critical distance supplied by philosophy. Seneca explains the balancing of philosophical commitment and social duty in the following way: "It shows much courage to remain dry and sober when the mob is drunk and vomiting; but it shows greater self-control to refuse to withdraw oneself and to do what the crowd does, but in a different way, thus neither making oneself conspicuous nor becoming one of the crowd."[58]

Conceding that Epicurus especially praised certain people who had found the truth without guidance, Seneca asserts that no one immersed in foolishness "has sufficient strength to rise above it, but needs a helping hand and someone to lead him out of it." He counts Lucilius and himself among those who stand in need of guidance.[59] He further suggests that each of us needs a guide who can "pluck us continually by the ear, dispel rumors, protest against popular enthusiasms," and give us such frequent admonitions that we are able to "reject the opinions which din about in our ears."[60] We each require "an advocate with an upright mind" who can help us mediate between the two norms "amid all the uproar and agitation of falsehood."[61] We may call upon this person to be "our preceptor in opposition to popular precepts."[62] Especially when we find ourselves among those "who glorify influence and power," our guide alone will commend to us the higher value of "a soul which has left the external and found itself."[63]

To serve this function effectively, the guide needs to be able to communicate persuasively not mere information, but true beliefs that become the ordering principles of the emotional life of the hearer. For Seneca, it is particularly important for the guide to have dexterity in skillfully relating the soul's emotions both to philosophical doctrines and to specific moral instructions. Seneca warns Lucilius against eccentric philosophers that either detach moral exhortation from philosophical teaching proper or limit their teaching to case-specific moral advice. In a technical discussion filling two lengthy letters, Epistles 94 and 95, Seneca contrasts the range and limits of two instructional methods that he terms most often as *decreta* (doctrines) and *praecepta* (instructions).[64] He tells Lucilius that *decreta*, *scita* (tenets), and *placita* (principles) all translate the Greek δόγμα and refer to broad global beliefs of general applicability such as those that are found in geometry or astronomy.⁶⁵ In contrast, the Latin word *praecepta* translates the Greek παραινετική and refers to instructions that are specific to particular situations. This category includes "all kinds of advice" including such rhetorical strategies as consolation, warning, exhortation, praising, and blaming.⁶⁶

Seneca criticizes two opposing positions that each see either *decreta* or *praecepta* as making the other unnecessary. The first, attributed by him to the unorthodox Stoic Aristo of Chios, contends that the doctrines of philosophy are sufficient in and of themselves, rendering further case-specific moral exhortations superfluous.⁶⁷ Admonitions to a particular course of action, according to Aristo, have no effect on diseased souls too weak to follow advice.⁶⁸ Once one has firm knowledge of ultimate philosophical principles, however, one already knows what actions ought to be undertaken or avoided in specific situations.⁶⁹ Any focus on the demands of mundane, specific situations distracts philosophy from its proper objective and occupies it with matters other than reason and virtue.⁷⁰ Seneca contrasts Aristo's rejection of paraenetic exhortation with a second position, which he attributes to "some," that considers the paraenetic branch of philosophy to be the only necessary one since philosophy, as the art of living (*ars uitae*), is sufficient to provide directions for correct actions.⁷¹ To transcend the concrete exigencies of human life and speculate on the universe as a whole needlessly "strays beyond the sphere of practical utility."⁷²

Rejecting each position as inadequate, Seneca contends that both instructional methods are necessary and mutually conditioning. He is skeptical whether one can, in fact, set doctrine aside since such an assertion is itself a doctrine. Doctrines are an inescapable feature informing human experience.⁷³ One is left either implicitly or explicitly with only good and bad doctrines. Seneca tells us that the "difference between philosophical doctrines and precepts" is the same "as there is between elements and members; the latter depend on the former, while the former are the source both of the latter and of all things."⁷⁴ He likens dogmas to the heart and precepts to hands. Dogmas are the hidden source of the hands' visible growth and motion.⁷⁵ Thus, particular moral instructions grow organically from doctrines and continue to be nourished by them.

Seneca, therefore, agrees with Aristo on the value and utility of doctrine. To drive out false opinions requires the full weight of larger convictions because "precepts by themselves are weak and, so to speak, rootless if they be assigned to the parts and not to the whole."[76] Giving particular moral instruction will be without effect "unless you first remove the conditions that are likely to stand in the way." Before being able to benefit from precepts, the soul must first be freed from mistaken judgments of value.[77] He maintains that "in order to root out our deep-seated belief in wrong ideas, conduct must be regulated by doctrines."[78] For example, the faulty presuppositions of those who have sanctioned the maltreatment of slaves will need to be undermined by the doctrine of the natural equality of human beings. Only then will they see that their slaves share their same dignity and ought to be dined with, talked to, and lived with.[79] Likewise, those who passionately pursue money assign excessive worth to it. In order to be free of greed, they will need to live according to the doctrine that teaches that wealth is in and of itself neither good nor evil, and believe that the securely happy person is not the one with worldly wealth, but the one whose entire good is in the soul.[80]

The limitations of precepts become apparent when they are cut off from doctrines. No matter how many precepts are given, "no one will do his duty as he ought" without knowing that to which each duty "refers" (*referat*).[81] Even when a person has been given good advice specifying the proper course of conduct in a given situation and acts accordingly, he or she will neither be able to persevere nor rightly apply such instruction in other contexts without knowing the reason for so acting. Precepts prescribe what ought to be done, but without a larger framework, falter on the subtleties of *how* things are to be done. Guided by precepts alone, a person makes decisions with "no rule (*regula*) in hand by which to regulate acts."[82]

Seneca likens particular moral admonitions to leaves that wither unless they draw sap from a living branch. In order to be vital, precepts "must be grafted" upon a body of doctrine.[83] Ideally, all actions and words should have the Supreme Good (*summi boni*) as their object (*finem*).[84] In this way, our actions will be "strengthened and supported" by doctrines of "the whole of human life (*totam uitam*) and the whole nature of things" (*rerum naturam*).[85] This gives the soul "unswerving decision" (*inflexibile iudicium*) and the assurance that comes when moral agents apprehend the deeper rationality informing their actions.[86] Just as precepts grow organically from doctrines, so doctrines ultimately depend on reason (*ratio*) as a kind of root system, which is in turn strengthened by the growths it produces.[87] It is on account of this view of the organic connections between reason, doctrines, and precepts that Seneca considers theological doctrines and even Platonic metaphysics to be of practical import for daily life.[88] One cannot but imply the others as doctrines have existential import and moral precepts presuppose doctrines. To be optimally effective, specific moral directives need to be integrated into a doctrinally articulated cosmic vision supported by systematic, philosophical reflection. Thus, for Seneca, real philosophical formation, the kind that strengthens the mind, heals emotions, and promotes responsible activity in the world, must at every stage be both theoretical (*contemplatiua*) and practical (*actiua*).[89]

Seneca, therefore, rejects Aristo's contention that doctrines are in and of themselves sufficient for philosophy. Seneca asserts unequivocally, "If we remove false opinions, insight into practical conduct does not at once follow."[90] Even when the false opinions that misshape affections are removed, correct action is still hindered by "lack of practice in discovering the demands of a particular situation." Our minds remain "inactive and untrained (*inexercitatum*) in finding the path of duty."[91] For example, although one may know the doctrine that "virtue is the only good," such knowledge will be of little help in specific moral contexts if one does not know how to apply it.[92] Without accompanying precepts, doctrines lack sufficient specificity for their implications to be clear in particular situations. It is as if certain truths lie scattered about in the soul "in various places, and it is impossible for the unpracticed mind (*inexercitata mens*) to arrange them in order."[93]

To overcome this deficiency, Seneca commends exercises to tone up the soul. Such practices, or "spiritual exercises," were to be taken as seriously as any physical training for athletic contests.[94] They were intended to compensate for the soul's unnatural passivity and lack of discipline in organizing sensation according to rational principles. By cultivating discipline, the soul participates in its own cure analogous to the way physical activity contributes to bodily health. Seneca would agree with the description of the rationale and goals of such training given by his Stoic contemporary, Musonius Rufus:

As the physician and the musician not only must master the theoretical side of their respective arts, but must also train themselves to act according to principles, so a man who wishes to become good not only must be thoroughly familiar with the principles (μαθήματα) which are

conducive to virtue, but must also be earnest and zealous in applying these principles. . . . Therefore upon the learning of the lessons
(μαθημάτων) appropriate to each and every excellence, practical training (ἄσκησιν) must follow invariably.[95]

Thus, "dogmas are not mathematical rules, learned once and for all and
then mechanically applied. Rather, they must somehow [through exer-
cises] become achievements of awareness, intuitions, emotions, and moral
experiences."[96]

In a similar manner, Seneca instructs Lucilius that philosophy is not
an endeavor to be engaged in sporadically or to be put aside in order to be
taken up again at another time.[97] Appealing to his own experience, Seneca
states that even after he has mastered a subject, it slips from his mind in
a short time. Consequently, he notes, "my mind needs to be unrolled [like
a scroll], and whatever has been stored away there ought to be examined
from time to time, so that it may be ready for use when occasion demands."[98] Even for the wise teacher, philosophical insight is always at risk
of either being lost to forgetfulness or merely overlooked. Unless it is kept
continually at hand, the mind tends to look past it when determining a
course of action. This poses a danger because anyone seeking progress in
wisdom is like "one who is convalescing from a severe and lingering illness for whom health means only a lighter attack of disease." Without constant care and attention "there is an immediate relapse."[99]

The mind, therefore, "must be exercised both day and night."[100] Lucilius is often told that he needs to rehearse specific thoughts every day,
toning and strengthening his soul in its effort to perceive each circum-
stance from the perspective of proper principles.[101] Even the clear idea of
the value of philosophy "must be strengthened and implanted more deeply
by daily reflection."[102] The exercises, therefore, have the repetitive quality
more characteristic of reminding and persuading than of teaching. They
are intended more to form than to inform the self as doctrines are continually rehearsed, reframed, and reapplied to new circumstances. Seneca
assures Lucilius that such exercises powerfully aid philosophy as it "molds
and constructs the soul, orders our life, guides our conduct, and shows us
what we should do and what we should leave undone."[103] Propositions
that are received into the soul in this manner are so formative that the
souls of the wise are said to be "metamorphosed (*transfiguratus*) into the
shape of that which has been learned."[104]

Those learning these practices do best under the supervision of a guide who can help them coordinate general rules with the demands of actual situations. Seneca appeals to the custom of physicians who do not prescribe medications without making a firsthand diagnosis of the illness to be treated.[105] The actual method of the philosophical therapist is initially most like an elementary language teacher who holds the fingers of students and guides them "so that they may follow the outline of the letters," and then "they are ordered to imitate a copy and base thereon a style of penmanship."[106] Through conversation, the guide will help each student traverse the itinerary back and forth between doctrines and practical precepts, always with an eye toward the effect the mind's beliefs have on the affections. In this way, particular admonitions both give doctrines their needed specificity and enlist our emotions so as to "engage our attention, rouse us, concentrate our memory, and keep it from losing its grip" on what we know.[107] In the interest of maximizing philosophy's therapeutic effect on the soul, all the psychagogic tools of rhetoric come into play.[108] Seneca describes the effect of this paraenetic speech as a kind of gathering together of experience into a coherent vision of the whole of life for the elevation of soul.[109]

As Seneca's metaphor of the elementary language teacher implies, the goal is for students to develop their own autonomous skills, vocabulary, and penmanship rather than to continue to depend upon guidance. Having not only learned doctrines but also having internalized them through daily exercises, students consequently have in themselves stable criteria by which to evaluate their experience and choices. For this reason, Lucilius is admonished to attain fluency in the language of philosophy and not to have his voice be one that merely "makes itself the mouthpiece of another's words, and only performs the duty of a reporter."[110] He should not be content repeating the informed opinions of the wise (not even Seneca's), but rather should "lean upon himself" and become wise himself.[111] His mentor wishes for him to own joy itself rather than borrow it.[112] Seneca probes, "How long will you be a learner (*disces*)? From now on be a teacher (*praecipe*) as well!"[113]

Ultimately, as Seneca recognizes, each student's progress is dependent on the quality of his or her personal involvement and participation in the maturation process. Indeed, "it is more than half, for the matter of which we speak is determined by the soul. Hence the larger part of goodness is the will to become good."[114] Seneca discounts anything he perceives that might hinder the student's sense of personal agency and self-responsibility. He admonishes Lucilius not to pray to the gods for virtue, because, rightly understood, it is within his own power to achieve it.[115] It will ultimately be up to him whether or not he is able to lay hold of "a single norm (*regulam*) to live by" that governs his whole life.[116] If he becomes so practiced in philosophy as to affect his own cure, he will be "high-minded, full of confidence, and unconquerable."[117]

The Psychagogic Value of Ancient Texts

One final defining characteristic of philosophical therapy in the Hellenistic era is its self-conscious indebtedness to the past and the texts inherited from it.[118] Hellenistic writers perceived themselves as living in a post-classical age and were constantly aware of the lingering presence of such towering predecessors as Homer, Socrates, Plato, and Diogenes.[119] When Maximus of Tyre begins his address on the subject of the nature of God, he expresses his mindfulness that he speaks on a subject that tested even Plato's incomparable eloquence and subtlety. He characterizes his own speech as an inferior spring when compared to Plato's mighty river.[120] In order to justify his continued speaking, he invokes another image to explain how his discourse remains derivative and dependent on Plato's. His hearers are miners of precious metals who are yet unable to discern for themselves what is or is not gold. The mine they excavate is Plato's dialogues. In order to benefit from their labor or do anything constructive with it, they need the assistance of fire to purify the gold. Maximus' own voice is one of assistance in finding and using the truth in Plato's teaching with the light of reason rather than with material fire.[121]

Maximus' posture is typical of an age when reasoning was increasingly situated within specific traditions and dependent on the interpretation of authoritative texts. To philosophize involved choosing a school, learning its received sayings and texts, and adopting its way of life.[122] Thus, when giving his advice to Lucilius, Seneca presupposes that "the cures of the soul have been discovered by the ancients." He writes as one benefiting from "the inheritance of many predecessors." His practice is one of striving to retrieve the remedies discovered in the past and making them usable in the present. He counsels Lucilius that although the ancients had discovered such cures, it is up to us "to learn the method and the time of treatment."[123]

This adoption of a mode of philosophy committed methodologically to the exegesis of ancient texts and traditions had difficulties with one particular set of authoritative writings—epic poetry. Plato's expulsion of Homer from the ideal philosophically ordered city is well known, and anyone familiar with his thorough criticism of Homeric passages regarding the gods and their deformative effects on the young may be surprised to find what appears to be a very different stance among his Hellenistic followers.[124] Even with its scandalous passages, epic poetry's great antiquity, cultural status, and persuasive force mitigated against its dismissal. Familiar to every educated Greek, it had to be engaged, and its relationship to philosophy was a pressing issue for those advocating the philosophic life.

Various methods (including allegory) for reading the poets were employed long before Plato's time. The manner in which each philosophical school in the Hellenistic era did or did not employ these methods is an area of continued research.[125] In terms of Hellenistic practices of philosophical therapy, Plutarch's treatise on the proper way to study poetry contains views that can be taken as representative of at least some of the methods used by those who wished to incorporate poetic texts into philosophical formation. Rather than avoid poetry or seek to replace it with new composition, Plutarch suggests that it should be used as "an introductory exercise in philosophy" (προφιλοσοφητέον).[126] He attributes poetry's appeal to the way it employs a kind of "sorcery" (γοητείαν) by mixing the true with the false rhetorically and fluctuating between them in an exciting manner. Truth's stable and predictable line drawings are not nearly as compelling as the poetic art's use of rich colors in its portrayal of the gods and mortals to create the illusion of plausibility.[127]

The very qualities that make poetry appealing pose danger to anyone unskilled in recognizing the difference between truth and falsehood. To adopt the false ideas of a poem uncritically is to make oneself vulnerable to the corrupt opinions that fuel passion.[128] Plutarch commends, therefore, that poetry be read with "proper guidance" (παιδαγωγίας ὀρθῆς).[129] Under these conditions, the student will learn that everything in poetry is not to be accepted without qualification because poetry "is an imitation of character (ἠθῶν) and lives (βίων), and of people who are not perfect or pure or unassailable in all respects, but pervaded by passions, false opinions, and sundry forms of ignorance."[130] The good and the bad are both depicted in poetry, and the reader must make choices regarding what is to be imitated or admired.[131]

Plutarch's guide will make use of the inherent psychagogic persuasiveness of the ancient poets in order to "convey the reader by poetry into the realm of philosophy."[132] By extending to the written word Plato's recommendations in the *Phaedrus* regarding the ideal oral rhetoric, Plutarch contends that it is the words of the poet that will correspond to the state of the immature reader's soul. As Plutarch notes, the young in all likelihood have already been not only introduced to the harmful falsehoods contained in poetry, but those corrupt opinions have also been solidified by parents and caretakers "who all beatify and worship the rich, who shudder at death and pain, who regard virtue without money and repute as quite undesirable and a thing of no worth." When these students then hear the words of the philosophers running contrary to what they have been previously taught, "they cannot accept or tolerate any such teaching."

Accordingly, in the familiar language of Plato's cave, Plutarch proposes that people who have resided in utter darkness can only come to see the truth in all its brilliance when they are introduced to it gradually. The truth, therefore, must be apprehended first in a "reflected light" where its brightness is "softened by combining truth with myths."[133] Immature readers then find in poetry language much more amenable to their souls than the austere words of philosophy. The philosophical teacher, thus, will use their very familiarity with the text and the values expressed in it to develop their powers of discernment and to train their affections. Plutarch states that through such reading, students can "habituate themselves (ἐθιζομένους) to seek the profitable in what gives pleasure, and to find satisfaction therein; and if there be nothing profitable, to combat such poetry and be dissatisfied with it."[134] Thus, Plutarch advocates developing critical skills so that each student "habitually exclaims with confidence 'wrong' and 'improper' no less than 'right' and 'proper.'"[135] At first this will likely require the voice of a guide who can "direct the young by use of criticism toward the better side."[136] But eventually, once students have been fully prepared in making correct judgments, their affections will follow such that they will "feel elation and a sympathetic enthusiasm over the good words and deeds" contained in the text "and an aversion and repugnance for the bad."[137]

Plutarch asserts that in order that they may make these discriminating judgments, young people should be "set against some upright standard of reason . . . guiding and guarding their judgment, that it may not be carried away from the course."[138] Philosophy supplies this standard. Plutarch suggests that whatever truth is found in the poets should be "amplified by means of proofs and testimonies from the philosophers," and that credit for its discovery should be given to the philosophers.[139] Clearly, then, the reading of poetry is not an end in itself, but is being used as an initiation into philosophy. Rather than a source of revelatory knowledge, it is an attractive exercise field for mental and spiritual training. To seek the meaning of texts is to engage in philosophy. For Plutarch, it is through this method of conjoining poetic statements with the doctrines of the philosophers that the poet's work is lifted out of "the realm of myth and impersonation," and "its helpful sayings invested with seriousness."[140] Philosophy, in this way, does not oppose the poetic and allegorical, but uses it "as a resource for understanding."[141] From this perspective, poetry, rightly understood, is a psychagogic mode of philosophy.[142]

The second-century CE satirist Lucian wrote a tribute to a philosopher named Nigrinus after he had been "moved" by his discourse.[143] Whether the account is a literary fiction or not, it is an apt conclusion of this chapter insofar as the above examination shows just how typical an account it is. Its elements are predictable because the logic of the account and its most conspicuous imagery are determined by the familiar cultural ideal with which it identifies Nigrinus. Lucian claims to have been in Rome seeking treatment for an eye condition, but stopped by to pay his respects to the Platonic philosopher. He first sees Nigrinus with a book in hand, surrounded by busts of the ancient philosophers and a reed globe that Lucian assumed to represent the universe.[144]

Once they began to converse, Nigrinus' persuasive speech in praise of philosophy had great effect upon him. It exceeded the appeal of Homer's Sirens.[145] Nigrinus proceeded then to refute all the things that are popularly considered of value (wealth, reputation, dominion, and honor). Lucian, at least as he presents himself in this work, admits that up to that moment these were what he valued as well, and he felt enormous grief at their downfall once he perceived for himself their little worth. As this grief gave way, he shortly found himself gazing out "of the murky atmosphere" of his past life "to a clear sky and a great light." His desire for improved physical sight, in fact, led gradually by degrees to the cure of his soul, which he had not yet realized was entirely bereft of vision.[146] Lucian goes on to recount how he then maintained an intentional practice of exercising his soul by recalling Nigrinus to his mind two or three times a day and rehearsing his words.[147]

Thus psychagogy provided not only norms and expectations for a certain kind of rhetoric in public venues, but also in the private relationships between older philosophers and young people seeking wisdom. The most famous practitioners of this art first received guidance themselves and typically attributed their spiritual health to the therapeutic practices of their own teachers. Seneca recounted to Lucilius how his encounter with the preaching of Attalus changed his way of life forever.[148] Epictetus told his students how his own teacher Musonius Rufus had such powers of discernment "that each of us sitting there felt that someone had gone to him and told him our faults, so accurately he touched upon our true characters, so effectively he placed each one's faults before his eyes."[149] Epictetus' own practice approximated what he first learned from Rufus. Epictetus asserted, "The school of the philosopher is surgery. You should not depart from it in pleasure, but in pain, for you are not healthy when you come in."[150] He described the philosopher's protreptic as showing "an individual or crowd the contradictions they are involved in, and that they care for everything rather than what they mean to care for; for they want the things conducive to happiness, but they seek them where they are not to be found."[151] Much as Epictetus extolled the teaching of Rufus, Epictetus' own student, Arrian, says that his teacher's words always aimed "to move the minds of his hearers toward the best."[152]

The cultural category of the orator who could cure souls in the same way that a physician cures the body not only preceded Christianity but held a prominent place in Greco-Roman society. While never becoming a single, coherent system in antiquity, psychagogic traditions constituted, in retrospect, an identifiable set of practices and strategies to influence the mental and emotional habits of others. The ancient concern for the formation of the young evident in the epic tradition became an intentional movement in the time of the sophists, especially with the stimulus of Socrates and Plato's own formulations. Even while the schools of Hellenistic philosophy disputed any number of first principles, the ideal of a rhetorically enhanced philosophy became widespread; namely, a philosophy that could, when necessary, manipulate souls to choose their own good. The Hellenistic schools developed and clarified the psychagogic traditions they inherited, especially by attending to the crucial links between philosophical doctrines, affections, moral exhortation, and the place of authoritative texts in instruction. Well before its motifs, ideas, and mode of expression made their way into the Christian community, psychagogy had proven both its usefulness and its flexibility in admitting the divergent doctrinal systems of the Hellenistic philosophical schools.

Although what Christians meant by the cure of souls differed from their philosophically minded contemporaries, classical therapy established the assumptions informing much early Christian preaching and spiritual guidance. Those who listened to those early sermons were already accustomed to hearing orations and brought with them assumptions and expectations about the nature of such speeches. Indeed, Christians preached down the street from their non-Christian peers.[153] Perhaps nothing is more telling of this cross-fertilization than the fact that for centuries it remained natural for Christians to send their most promising young people to study at Greco-Roman schools. Fourth-century bishops like Basil and Gregory Nazianzen studied in Athens with the same teachers as their future non-Christian opponents. Before John Chrysostom was ever famous for his Christian preaching, he studied rhetoric in Antioch with the pagan sophist Libanius.[154] Just as Platonists and Stoics accepted and adapted the classical traditions they inherited while maintaining the distinct identities of their schools, so also Christians received and reworked these same traditions. It would only be a matter of time before an aspiring rhetor in Northern Africa would learn them and transform them so thoroughly as to prove his mastery of them.

Part Two

Revising and Recontextualizing Classical Therapy

Chapter Three

Augustine's Early Formation

I was searching for signs whereby I might make my thoughts known to others . . .
and entered more deeply into the stormy society of human life.

—Augustine, *conf.* 1.6.10, 1.8.13

An Ambitious Young Orator

In the autumn of 384 CE, the prominent senator and prefect of the city
of Rome, Symmachus, was charged with making an appointment for the
chair of rhetoric in Milan. The city was the imperial residence and had
been the functioning capital of the Western Empire for nearly a century.
The person who would have the coveted chair would associate with the
most powerful figures in the Empire, would teach their sons the art of
rhetoric and letters prerequisite to the exercise of power, and give official
speeches before the royal court commemorating important events. Symmachus was also an ardent pagan and an accomplished orator himself.
Only months earlier he had given an eloquent appeal for the toleration
of paganism, the reinstitution of public subsidies for pagan cults, and the
restoration to the Roman Senate of the altar of the goddess Victory.[1] His
promotion of ancient pagan customs had brought him into conflict with
Ambrose, the influential local Christian bishop and staunch opponent of

any form of paganism.[2] It is not surprising that in making his appointment, Symmachus sought to locate a promising young man who would not be brought easily into the patronage of his Christian opponent. He found a relatively unknown North African named Augustine of Hippo.

Symmachus was familiar both with Africa—having previously held the proconsulship there—and with Augustine's Manichaean friends who appear to have arranged for his audition before the prefect. At that time, the young Augustine was a professor of rhetoric in Rome who had left the Catholic Christianity of his birth behind in favor of Manichaeism.[3] His parents had groomed him for the day that he might gain the attention of an imperial official. They sacrificed for him in hope that such a moment would come.[4] They ensured that he would be steeped in the literary traditions of classical Rome from an early age.[5] By the time that their son was fifteen they had sent him away to study literature and oratory in nearby Madauros, known as the home of the famous second-century Platonic philosopher and orator, Apuleius. Augustine would continue his studies in Carthage to prepare to be an advocate in the law courts. His natural talent would lead him to the top of his class in the rhetor's school.[6]

Augustine was a young man who in his own words was "impelled by the goads of ambition."[7] He returned to his hometown of Thagaste no longer a student, but as a teacher. In a short time, however, he moved back to the larger metropolis of Carthage to teach rhetoric for several years.[8] He continued there to deepen his knowledge of the classical tradition, including reading Aristotle's *Categories* and attempting to produce his own written work before leaving for Rome in search of better students.[9] He would later acknowledge that at that time he found secular success to "have no small sweetness."[10] He aspired to a life of "honors, money, [and] marriage" and hoped to "obtain preferment to public office"—at least a "minor provincial governorship" or the like.[11] He was a man whose ambition would lead him to set aside his long-time concubine in order to create the possibility of marrying a wife of higher status.[12]

An audition before Symmachus proved the young North African to be the man whose eloquence would decorate the imperial court. Augustine accepted the chair and its prestige. Within a few months he would give a panegyric in the presence of Emperor Valentinian II. Augustine gave the speech when the Frankish general Bauto was given the consulship.[13] One can imagine the applause when their new rhetor employed his exquisite skill to turn obvious faults and shortcomings into reasons for effusive praise.[14] The speech of such a rhetor would provide the audience with an image of themselves—not as they were in fact but as they wanted to believe they were. Sufficient eloquence could legitimate any imperial action and transform unremarkable deeds into works of eternal valor.

Some fourteen years later, the Christian bishop reflected back on his remarkable elevation from his parochial origins to the proximate edges of imperial power. He wondered how he came to seek "an arrogant success by telling lies"; how he came to put the good gifts of God to evil use.[15] He would describe his former self as "a seller of words" who was paid "in the markets of rhetoric" to tell lies persuasively especially when everyone knew he was lying.[16] He lamented, "I would tell numerous lies with the object of winning the good opinion of people who knew them to be untrue."[17] He was expected to teach his students to do the same as they were "giving their minds . . . to frenzied lies and lawcourt battles," and sought from his "mouth weapons for their madness."[18] Like Gorgias of ancient Athens, he was paid to teach others to imitate him in sweetly beguiling souls and swaying the minds of hearers by a kind of psychagogy.

From the perspective of the later bishop, the path to the imperial capital became available to him because he had been socialized into the aspirations of a civilization; he had imbibed its corporate longings and come to embody its ideal. He expected as a reward for it the glory, honor, and money associated with social status. For him this process was at work even in infancy when he—faced with his own vulnerability and dependence on others—sought to compensate by enfranchising others in his will. He needed, therefore, signs communicating his wishes. The search for effective signs led from primitive ones such as flinging limbs and crying to the discovery of words. He, nevertheless, could not establish for himself the meaning and usage of such words arbitrarily as some kind of private language. The meaning of words was already determined by customary usage. In order to articulate his wishes using linguistic signs in a way understood by others, he would need, therefore, to enter "more deeply into the stormy society of human life."[19]

He would do so under the guidance of teachers. As a boy, he was expected to observe the established conventions that governed the use of letters and syllables with the utmost care. Such linguistic rigidity resulted from his teachers' paramount concern to perpetuate the customs of that society. Other goods were subjected to this one to such a great extent that his own instructors were more embarrassed by committing a mistake in speech when describing their own bad acts than by the actions themselves. These values were quickly internalized by students so shaping their emotional lives that as a boy Augustine was more afraid of committing a barbarism than of envying those who did not.[20] Being formed in this way, he would seek success in the manner prescribed for him by his parents and teachers: in the study of eloquent speech. Augustine tells us that in the course of the regular curriculum a book of Cicero was assigned to him not for its content but as an example of eloquent Latin. Cicero's polished rhetorical skill and powerful use of it continued to be admired long after his lifetime.[21] Cicero once took up the defense of Ligarius after Caesar had resolved to prosecute him as an enemy. It was said that as Caesar listened to the moving speech, he was so affected by the sheer force of Cicero's rhetoric that his countenance changed and his body began to tremble.[22] Ligarius was acquitted.

The eighteen-year-old Augustine, aspiring to arm himself with Ciceronian Latin, began to read the *Hortensius*: a work that he would later describe as an "exhortation to philosophy."[23] Although it was assigned for its eloquence, what seized the ambitious young man was the subject matter.[24] Augustine confesses, "This book changed my affections, altered my prayers to be toward you yourself and made me have different purposes and desires. Every vain hope became empty to me, and with an incredible ardor of heart I thirsted after the immortality of wisdom, and began to rouse myself to return you. . . . How I did burn to fly from earthly things. . . . That love of wisdom is in Greek, philosophy, with which that book inflamed me."[25] In his reading of Cicero, Augustine was in fact encountering the well-established classical tradition of employing words in a particular manner to guide a student in the philosophic life.

Cicero, the orator, turned his attention to philosophy in his later life. Prior to his study in Athens and Rhodes, he had attended the philosophical lectures of Philo of Larissa in 81 BCE in Rome.[26] Philo is known to have shared the widespread opinion that the function of philosophy was best understood on the analogy with medicine. He taught that the initial task of both the philosopher and the physician was to "persuade the sick person to accept therapy" which for Philo belonged to the "argument of conversion" (προτρεπτικῷ). Once someone had been persuaded to accept therapy, "therapeutics" required "removing the causes of illness" and "installing what is productive of health." For the philosopher this entailed applying "argument to eliminate the false beliefs which have come about, due to which the soul's critical faculties have become ill, and then discourse to install beliefs which are sound." Once health was introduced, it was upheld by "principles" (θεωρημάτων) through which one maintained one's happiness.[27]

Similarly, Cicero promoted in his writings an ideal of a rhetorically informed therapeutic philosophy whose fundamental features were established by the Socrates of the Platonic dialogues.[28] Cicero, like others who turned to the philosophic life, paid tribute to Socrates as the one who "was the first in summoning philosophy down from the heavens. He placed it in actual human cities, introduced it into people's homes and compelled it to ask questions about life (*uita*) and behavior (*moribus*) and things good and evil."[29] The great Latin rhetor would eventually declare, "I confess that whatever ability I possess as an orator comes, not from the workshops of the rhetoricians, but from the spacious grounds of the Academy. There indeed is the field for manifold and varied debate (*sermonum*), which was first trodden by the feet of Plato."[30] He would not oppose philosophy to rhetoric, but to a sophistry that engaged style to the exclusion of substance. In his philosophical writings, Cicero was to play an important role as a transmitter of Greek ideas to the Latin world. He introduced into Latin a philosophical vocabulary that would become standard usage for centuries.[31] In so doing, he was a paradigmatic representative of what would be in the Hellenistic world not only "a flourishing bilingualism" but "a flourishing biculturalism as well."[32]

Augustine's description, in the early books of the *Confessions*, of his conversion from the sophistic rhetoric of his teachers to a philosophic one repeatedly echoes prominent Ciceronian themes.[33] Using language that we tend to associate with Augustine, Cicero laments:

> [A]s soon as we come into the light of day . . . we at once find ourselves in a world of iniquity amid a medley of wrong beliefs, so that it seems as if we drank in deception with our nurse's milk; but when we leave the nursery to be with parents and later on have been handed over to the care of masters, then we become infected with deception so varied that truth gives place to unreality and the voice of nature itself to fixed possessions.[34]

Cicero continues by describing how the whole educational process is infected with a "general tendency toward error" that confirms in us "vicious beliefs" that are unnaturally overlaid on nature. Since the affections have their ultimate source in beliefs, false beliefs give rise to disordered movements in the soul to which Cicero applies the term "disease" (*morbos*).[35] Moreover, this "revolt from nature" is complete when our "diseased" affections, informed by false beliefs, become directed toward an illusory object:

> We come to think that the clearest insight into the meaning of nature has been gained by the men who have made up their minds that there is no higher ambition for a human being, nothing more desirable, nothing more excellent than civil office, military command, and popular glory; it is to this that the noblest are attracted, and in their quest for the true honor which alone is the object of nature's eager search, they find themselves where all is vanity, and strain to win no lofty image of virtue, but a shadowy phantom of glory.[36]

Rather than exhibiting the health human beings have by nature, Cicero claims that we have "infected our souls" with the artificial customs of "escapism, luxury, inactivity, idleness, and inertia. We have enervated and weakened them by false beliefs and evil habits (*opinionibus maloque more*)."[37]

In describing their situation in these terms, Cicero admonishes his readers to subject all their received beliefs to deep scrutiny, to discover the foundations upon which they stand, to pay attention to the affections they foster, and to reject all those that prove not to be true, that is, those that prove to be purely human constructs with no basis in nature. This task requires, above all, the willingness to forsake the deepest convictions of the many — especially the desire to please them and to receive human glory.

By asserting that the human tendency toward error is so pervasive and damaging, Cicero's philosophical position risks sinking, as a consequence, into thoroughgoing skepticism. After all, how can those who have drunk in deception with their nurse's milk even realize that they have been deceived, let alone manage to learn the truth? Cicero, therefore, had to explain how it is possible for souls diseased with false beliefs to find effective medicines, that is, to find a critical point of reference from which it is possible to evaluate the various cultural options, discover truth, and act accordingly. Cicero finds this point of reference in philosophy. He asserts emphatically that since "the roots of folly go so deep," one must "be persuaded . . . that there will be no end to wretchedness unless the soul (*animus*) is cured (*sanatus*), and without philosophy this is impossible."

He, therefore, counsels us to put "ourselves into the hands of philosophy for treatment" (*curandos*) and see "how efficacious are the medicines (*remedia*) applied by philosophy to the diseases of souls" (*morbis animorum*).[38] Cicero holds forth the promise of a philosophy that can sift through the medley of false beliefs and become the "guide of life," the "explorer of virtue," the "expeller of vice," the destroyer of the "fear of death," and conferrer of "tranquility of life."[39]

Philosophy, therefore, cures the soul and stabilizes its affections. Through "disciplined thinking" people can "gradually realize the extreme falsity of their belief" and have the various diseases of soul "removed by the appropriate reasoning."[40] This process is difficult especially when the false beliefs in question have been hardened into habit and custom. For this reason, rhetoric becomes an indispensable art in service of philosophy by which persuasion is added to knowledge.[41] For Cicero, rhetorical "eloquence is nothing else but wisdom speaking copiously, which, drawn from the same class as that [virtue] which relates to reasoning, is more abundant and wider and more closely adapted to the passions and sentiments of ordinary people."[42] Accordingly, Cicero's rhetor will not only have facility in the concise definitions accessible to philosophers, but also will be able to present the truth with "greater fullness in a way better adapted to the ordinary judgment and popular intelligence."[43] In this way, Cicero argues for a rhetorically enhanced philosophy with a "critical" (the distinction between "nature" and "custom," etc.) as well as a "constructive" (a life guided by and oriented toward "wisdom") function.

The very eloquence that Augustine would need to achieve civil office could be found in abundance in the writings of Cicero. He would indeed find what he was seeking there—eloquent speech accommodated to the state of his soul. It would not, however, lead him toward civil office and popular glory because Cicero employed his mastery of the cultural idiom to point readers like Augustine to an ideal higher than the culture itself: "the immortality of wisdom." In this way, Cicero's psychagogy wooed Augustine, inspiring him to aspire to something higher than eloquence while exposing and refuting his previous (mis)estimations of value.

Augustine's "conversion" to philosophy, however, did not free him from his dependence upon human guidance. Neither would his love of wisdom lead him to the Catholic faith of his upbringing. Its scriptures appeared to him "unworthy in comparison with the dignity of Cicero."[44] He looked, therefore, for those who could speak of Jesus both eloquently and rationally. He hoped to find this among the Manichaeans because they had purged themselves of books written in a lowly style and filled with superstitious tales.[45] His association with them was not momentary but would last some nine years. Although he would later look back upon this period as a lapse into irrationality and superstition, it was at the time consonant with his newfound love of wisdom as advocated by Cicero.[46] Augustine's Manichaean friends were in all likelihood readers of Cicero and subscribed to the ideals presented in the *Hortensius*. Many of the basic Manichaean concerns were recognizable within the general discourse of the Hellenistic philosophical schools.[47] Mani had presented himself in the third century as "a doctor" (ἰατρός) from Babylon.[48] Through his teaching, he offered his followers knowledge of the universe and their place within it. Their experience was one that they shared with the entire cosmos in which good and evil had come to be literally mixed together as materials. Through certain therapeutic practices they could purify themselves, separate good matter from evil in their own bodies, and participate in the reordering of the entire universe.[49] Without such knowledge and practices, ordinary human living could only result in further contamination as the soul suffered additional pollution. Thus, not unlike the philosophical schools, Manichaeans furnished therapeutic doctrines and practices designed to bring their adherents' lives into harmony with the true nature of the universe.

The Manichaean materialist sensibility was one that abhorred allegory and figuration.[50] Their teachings and practices did not signify some further spiritual reality to be inferred indirectly. Their cosmic myths and rituals were meant to be taken literally and directly. Neither required further elaboration and interpretation. The promise of such literal truth apprehended by the senses appealed to Augustine's thirst for wisdom. As Augustine imbibed Manichaeism in all its explanatory power, he found it to be less convincing than what he had learned in his secular studies and came to question its claim to be wisdom at all.[51] He had hoped that his own ignorance of the full teachings of Manichaeism was the source of his troubles and that a sufficiently expert guide could remedy them. At Carthage he would await the coming of Faustus, a distinguished Manichaean orator with a reputation for being "most expert in all the disciplines and especially learned in the liberal arts."[52] When Faustus arrived, such a crowd assembled that Augustine was unable to ask him his questions. The young professor of rhetoric, nevertheless, was "delighted by the force and feeling he brought to his discourse and by the fitting language which flowed with facility to clothe his ideas."[53]

When Augustine was able to bring him his questions, he found that the knowledge possessed by Faustus was entirely conventional and that he was "ignorant of the liberal arts other than grammar and literature." Although he had read "some orations of Cicero," he fell short, in Augustine's eyes, of the Ciceronian ideal of knowledge speaking eloquently.[54] Augustine considered such ignorance entirely unfitting for one expounding the literal truth.[55] He came to see Faustus as another sophist with style but not substance, eloquence but not wisdom. Others thought him wise because "he charmed them by the way he spoke." Augustine's ears, however, "were already satiated" with this kind of rhetoric that did not seem to him better because it was "more elegantly expressed."[56] After this encounter, Augustine had no desire to advance further in the Manichaean sect.[57] He was left an unconvinced Manichaean still seeking wisdom yet unable to discard his ambition. He would continue as such in his secular career—equipped, not unlike Faustus, with more eloquence than truth— as he left Carthage for Rome and then to Milan.

Being Healed by Beautiful Words

When not teaching rhetoric or declaiming himself, Augustine says that he used to attend the preaching of Bishop Ambrose in Milan. He did so "testing out his oratorical skill to see whether it merited the reputation it enjoyed or whether his fluency was better or inferior than it was reported to be." He listened to Ambrose—assessing his rhetorical craft—as one professional hears another. His interest was in "the charm of his speech" and not at all the subject matter of the homilies.[58] He would realize only later, however, that while his ears were enjoying the bishop's rhetorical technique, his heart and mind were affected as well. Form could not so easily be severed from content even for one whose ears were well acquainted with rhetoric. "Together with the words" (*simul cum uerbis*), the "content" (*res*) insinuated itself into his mind. He would reflect, "While I opened my heart in noting the eloquence with which he spoke, there also entered no less the truth which he affirmed, though only gradually."[59] Ambrose's eloquence irrevocably shaped Augustine's notions of both Christianity and rhetoric as he witnessed time and again the bishop ministering a "sober intoxication" to his people that transported them by degrees toward divine truth.[60]

By all accounts Ambrose was one of the most able bishops of his time. Prior to becoming bishop of Milan, he had been its governor. At the death of the previous bishop such riots broke out that the governor needed to quiet the unrest. Upon seeing him, the crowd began shouting, "Ambrose for bishop."[61] He had been well educated in Rome as he prepared for a career in civil service.[62] He was not only familiar with the texts that orators were expected to know, but with philosophical ones as well. He had greater access than many of his peers to classical and contemporary texts since he was fluent in both Greek and Latin. Scholars have noted in his extant sermons ample evidence of his broad reading including Greek sources such as the Platonist Plotinus, Eastern Christian writers, and Philo of Alexandria as well as Latin ones such as Virgil and Seneca.[63] He produced his own writings and modeled one of them on Cicero's famous *De officiis*.[64] An early biographer asserts that upon being acclaimed bishop, Ambrose "determined to become a philosopher. But he was to be Christ's true philosopher."[65]

In his oratory, Ambrose combined an open antagonism toward pagan philosophy and rhetoric with an easy, familiar use of them. "Virtually all his remarks about philosophy were highly disparaging."[66] He tended to use the term polemically to refer to exclusively pagan intellectual traditions to which he would not concede any autonomous truth. Accordingly, he rejected such "worldly learning and wisdom" because it was "embellished with a great procession of words" (*uerborum*) rather than "relying on the real nature of things" (*rerum*).[67] Ambrose typically juxtaposed the "persuasive words of human wisdom" and the "false disputations of philosophy" to the "demonstration of the Spirit and power."[68] He admonished his congregation to follow neither "the traditions of philosophy nor those who gather the semblance of truth in the vain deceit of the arts of persuasion." Instead they should think "in accordance with the rule of truth (*regulam ueritatis*), which is set forth in the inspired words of God and is poured into the hearts of the faithful."[69]

Despite his Stoic bearing and Roman restraint, Ambrose promoted a specifically Christian rhetoric that was both sweeter and more potent than discursive reason alone. It was the Word of God that falls from heaven like rain and "inebriates mind and soul with its divine preaching."[70] Unlike the perceptual disorientation associated with the drunkenness of wine,

Ambrose insisted that the intoxication brought about by Christian liturgy and preaching produced a clear-sighted "sobriety of mind."[71] In the "darkness of this world" with its "many unseen pits and rocks" reliable guidance has been given in the sacraments of the Church as so many lights, especially in the "heavenly eloquence" of scripture which is fully capable of aiding the mind's "inner feet" to find their proper path.[72] All genuine learning "flows and streams" from the "speech and Word of God" as its "continual and ever-flowing source."[73] Any truth found in pagan philosophy is dependent on Christian authorities without which it would be entirely deficient.[74] In the Church is found "spiritual wisdom" that "truly possesses every domain that worldly knowledge falsely claims for itself."[75]

Despite the overt polemic against philosophy, those who heard Bishop Ambrose encountered philosophic notions and strategies. These ideas and methods, however, were attributed to ancient Jewish and Christian authorities rather than to pagan ones. In his sermons, the biblical patriarchs did not appear as the questionably moral people that the Manichaeans saw them to be. Instead they assumed their place in a procession of biblical sages living truly philosophic lives.[76] It was this way of life—visible in scripture for those who seek its spiritual meaning—that Ambrose contended was the proper subject of philosophy. The biblical narrative describing Jacob's effort to marry Rachel outlines the manner in which he partook of wisdom as his mind ascended by virtues the very steps he once saw in a vision (Gen. 28:12).[77] Ambrose's hearers were assured that David too found himself in a cave hiding from Saul and seeking wings for his soul to free him from his struggle.[78] The book of Jonah describes not "a bodily flight, but a mental ascent."[79] Although such readings of scripture were unmistakably influenced by Platonism, Ambrose was in fact using such terms and images to describe the life initiated in Christian baptism. Augustine preserves fragments from a lost work of Ambrose called *De sacramento regenerationis siue de philosophia.* It is not unlikely that in this work baptism and true "philosophy" were synonymous terms.[80]

His own writings clearly demonstrate that his pastoral theory was informed by classical philosophical views of the cure of soul. Whenever he describes the preaching of a bishop, Ambrose appeals to a number of metaphors that were commonplace in the psychagogic tradition. For example, in writing a letter of advice to a community seeking to choose a bishop, he states that a bishop is first of all a follower of Christ, "the type

of all priests," who as "the good physician" said, "it is not the healthy that
need a physician, but they who are sick" (Matt. 9:12). Therefore, the bishop
is one "chosen from among all to heal all."[81] On another occasion, he instructs a newly ordained bishop, Constantius, that speech "is a bandage
which binds up the wounds of souls, and if anyone rejects this, he shows
his recovery to be desperate. Likewise, with those who are afflicted by a
serious sore, use the oil of speech that you may soften their hardness of
heart; apply a poultice; put on a bandage of salutary precepts."[82]

Ambrose, accordingly, advises Constantius to cultivate his own preaching: "[L]et your sermons be flowing, let them be clear and lucid so that by
suitable disputation you may pour sweetness into the ears of the people,
and by the charm of your words may persuade the crowd to follow willingly your guidance." Ambrose encourages him to adapt his speech to the
condition of the souls of those hearing him so as to maximize the curative
effect of his preaching. Thus, Ambrose suggests that if there is any stub-
bornness or fault, some sermons should employ frank speech to "prod the
listener and sting the guilty conscience."[83] Other sermons, however, should
be like milk since "those who cannot eat stronger food develop from infancy by drinking natural milk."[84] Ambrose instructs Constantius further
that although "minds imbued with the poisons of infidelity" can only be
delivered from it "with difficulty," he ought to approach those who have
succumbed to a "harmful doctrine" (*mala doctrina*) like Arianism in the
manner of "skilled doctors" who wait for the "proper time" (*tempus*) before dispensing medicine.[85]

He explains to Constantius that in general greed "dulls human senses
and corrupts judgments so that people consider piety a source of gain and
money a sort of payment for prudence."[86] "Pious minds," therefore, will
need to possess "another scale" of value "by which the deeds of individuals are weighed."[87] For this to happen, the new bishop will need to admonish his hearers so as to "lift up their eyes to heavenly things with all the
intensity of their minds, to count nothing as gain except that which is
for eternal life."[88] He will need, as well, to live a life perfectly consonant
with his words so as to be an example to all.[89] In order to perform such a
ministry, Ambrose exhorts him, "Drink from Christ so that your sound
may go out."[90] Ambrose underscores that scripture's abundance is sufficient for these purposes. It is like a "sea" into which many rivers have entered. It "has within it profound meanings and depths of prophetic mysteries" as well as "good words like a honeycomb and pleasing maxims which

water the minds of hearers with spiritual drink and delight them with the sweetness of moral precepts."[91] Therefore, as one charged with the cure of souls, Constantius is first of all to read widely in the scriptures, that is, to "store up the water from many places" because the one "who reads much and also understands is filled."[92]

In his own practice, Ambrose continually directed his hearers to look to the psychagogic power of Christian scripture for wisdom. The bishop explained that while "every teacher seeks to enflame the affection of the listener," it is "the word of God (*sermo dei*) above all" that has the power to "penetrate to the place where joints are divided from the marrow of the bones" (Heb. 4:12).[93] Thus the soul is cured ultimately not by the skillful use of human eloquence or discursive reason but by "Christ's word": the "fire that purifies the mind and destroys error."[94] He instructed everyone to take on the reading of scripture as a daily spiritual exercise not unlike the way philosophers would read the sayings of the founders of their schools: "We should take up the daily practice of reading, having read we should meditate, and after meditating we should imitate what we have read."[95] Elsewhere he states that the "strength of the soul is enhanced by a course of exercises . . . we ought with our whole heart and soul to sift and polish for a long period of time the teachings of heavenly scripture in order that the essence of that spiritual food may suffuse the very depths of our souls."[96] He taught his hearers that the scriptures and sacraments were the food of the soul and should be eaten daily.[97] In this way, the Word of God would not be beheld from afar, but inscribed upon the heart.[98] Through such practices, one responds to the scriptural injunction to attend not "just to your money, possessions or physical well-being," but to "attend to yourself" (Deut. 15:9), that is, to "your soul and mind."[99] For Ambrose this meant acting "like a good farmer" who "cultivates his own earth with the plough and sickle of wisdom."[100] He suggested that such self-knowledge resulted in a sense of oneself as a mortal creature imbued with rationality who needs to accuse him or herself of failures, confess them, and turn continually toward God.[101]

Ambrose's Christian ministry with its philosophical acumen and rhetorical sophistication undoubtedly made a significant impression on the young Augustine. With his hopes raised once more, he sought—as he did with the Manichaean orator Faustus—to bring his questions to the bishop privately, away from the crowds, like a student in the intimacy of the philosopher's classroom. The busy bishop, nevertheless, seems to have had little individual time for him. Augustine would later remark, "I was excluded from his ear and from his mouth by crowds with arbitrations to submit to him, to whose frailties he ministered."[102] His hopes for a personal relationship with Ambrose appear to have never been realized.[103] Although not benefiting from the desired private guidance of Ambrose, the bishop's public ministry continued to affect him. Even without the hoped for personal attention, Augustine found himself being moved one step at a time as he gave his attention to the preaching.[104] He would later contrast his experience of hearing Faustus with that of Ambrose. While Faustus possessed a style of speaking that was in fact more witty and entertaining, there could be no comparison regarding substance. Each one possessed expertise in the art of persuasion. Ambrose alone taught "the sound doctrine of salvation."[105]

The contrast between the substantial truth of Christianity and mere words and appearances was one often put forward by Ambrose himself. He reminded Constantius that many people place their hope in "the empty and vain appearances" of the things which "come and go just as in sleep. They stop beside us, they vanish. They are near and they disappear. They seem to be grasped and are not." Christians, however, need not place their faith in such things because Christ himself came "to raise this life of ours from sleep, and to show that our use of life, in which there are various sorts of vicissitudes, was a dream with nothing solid or firm therein." In his own life Christ revealed how "seeing we do not see, hearing we do not hear, eating we are not nourished, rejoicing we are not made glad, and running we do not reach our goal." When Christians hear it said, "Awake, sleeper" (Eph. 5:14), they rise from their "dream of this world, and perceive then that all these things are false."[106] When compared to the substantial presence of truth in bodily form, even the accurate statements of philosophers appear to be so many "famous words, but mere words!" Ambrose boasted that among Christians "even maidens climb the steps of virtue mounting to the very sky with their longing for death."[107]

The effects of such preaching upon Augustine were exactly those that the psychagogic theory informing Ambrose's practice would suggest: it brought him into a process of gradual conversion where the convictions informing his life decisions at the time were first brought to mind with clarity and then whittled away. Ambrose attacked Manichaean doctrines directly and indirectly in his sermons and defended Catholic practices against their criticisms.[108] Augustine recounts how upon hearing Ambrose preach upon difficult passages of the Old Testament and interpret them figuratively, his Manichaean objections fell away one by one.[109] He came to discover that he "had been barking for years not against the catholic faith, but against the fictions of carnal thoughts."[110] Accordingly, he states, "I was confused and I was being turned around."[111] He found himself in an aporetic state where he "had not yet attained the truth, but was rescued from falsehood." When he later reflected on this critical moment in his passing "from sickness to health," he wrote that it was "through him [Ambrose] that I had been brought to the state of hesitancy and wavering."[112]

With his Manichaean worldview eroding under the force of Ambrose's preaching, Augustine resolved to leave a sect in which he could no longer be a member in good faith. He felt betrayed by their promise of readily apprehensible truth and grieved how his own commitment to truth had led him into falsehood. The memory of this experience of deception left a deep mark on him. He would never again facilely assume that truth was as easily available as the Manichaeans had indicated. The freer he became, the more shame he felt for how long he "had been duped and deceived by promises of certainty" and, as a consequence, "mindlessly repeated many doubtful things as if they were proven."[113]

In order to prevent himself from being deceived again, he would need to sharpen the critical tools that the writings of Cicero first encouraged him to acquire. He says that during this "period of skepticism" he preferred certain philosophers and "doubted everything" as his soul remained in "the fluctuating state of total suspense of judgment."[114] This posture was one for which Cicero himself had considerable sympathy.[115] While Hellenistic philosophical schools generally sought to replace false beliefs with true ones in order to ensure the health of the soul, Academic skepticism considered all such dogmatic commitments themselves to be the source of human problems. In its view, it was the very commitment to knowable truth that not only made people vulnerable to being deceived, but increased their anxiety as they consciously or unconsciously sought to preserve their beliefs and fend off whatever evidence would controvert them.[116] Protecting himself in this manner from all belief, Augustine would not yet give himself over to the Catholic faith of Ambrose. He, nonetheless, would purge himself of what he used to believe by endeavoring to refute Manichaean tenets.[117]

Augustine was not so persuaded by skepticism as to entrust the healing of his "soul's sickness" to its strategies. With critical tools in hand, he resolved to continue his inquiry into Christianity as a catechumen in the Catholic Church.[118] Unable to receive personal attention from Ambrose, he sought guidance from others familiar with the attractive ideas informing the bishop's preaching. In Milan there were other knowledgeable Christians besides Ambrose reading and translating Platonic texts, the writings of Eastern Christians, and the Jewish philosopher and exegete, Philo of Alexandria.[119] At this time Augustine seems to have had occasional conversations with Manlius Theodorus about the nature of God, the soul, and the best human life.[120] Theodorus was an impressive man himself who had already achieved much of what the young Augustine found so enticing. He was the former Praetorian prefect of Galliarum who had recently retreated from public life to Milan in order to use his eloquence to write books on philosophy.[121] It was Theodorus, or another person like him, who at that time introduced Augustine to texts written by Platonists.[122]

When Augustine began to read, he would have recognized continuities between what he saw in the Platonic books and the Hellenistic philosophy he had been initiated into by Cicero. In these books he would have found exhortations to turn away from worldly striving and, first of all, to attend to himself. Like Cicero's *Hortensius*, the books of the Platonists would have encouraged Augustine to take up philosophy as a way of acquiring self-knowledge and caring for his soul through philosophical exercises.[123] Plotinus' voice came to him as one saying:

> Go back into yourself and look; and if you do not see yourself beautiful, then, just as someone making a statue which has to be beautiful cuts away here and polishes there and makes one part smooth and clears another till he has given his statue a beautiful face, so you too must cut away excess and straighten the crooked and clear the dark and make it bright, and never stop 'working on your statue' till the divine glory of virtue shines out on you, till you see 'self-mastery enthroned upon its holy seat.'[124]

The Neoplatonic writings were not, however, as rhetorically charged as those of Cicero or Augustine's own speeches. Plotinus was certainly familiar with "rhetoric and music and all the class of arts which guide the soul (πᾶσαν ψυχαγωγίαν) that must be said to lead (ἄγειν) men to be better or worse by changing them," but such psychagogic arts of persuasion were not his primary interest.[125] He preferred a more restrained philosophic prose. His biographer, Porphyry, noted that Plotinus was free of the ways "of the sophists" because "in his writing he is concise and full of thought. He puts things shortly and abounds more in ideas than in words."[126] What made Platonic texts like those of Plotinus distinctive was not so much their advocacy of the philosophic life but their doctrinal content.

Augustine had been becoming increasingly discontent and disillusioned. His time was spent catering to ever more influential patrons.[127] Only months earlier, on his way to deliver a speech before the emperor, his anxiety was so great that his heart palpitated and his body was covered in perspiration. He was so much more prosperous than the destitute beggar he passed on the street who was drunk and laughing.[128] At the time, nonetheless, Augustine felt that the beggar may have been far better off than he was. The beggar could at least approximate happiness through drinking. The ambitious orator, however, was intoxicated with something that gave him no joy and was too debilitating to be able to sleep off overnight—personal glory. On account of it, Augustine's unhappiness weighed upon him as he was racked with fear and bereft of joy. He was without his long-time concubine because he had sent her away as a hindrance to marrying a wife of higher status. Unable to wait for the realization of such a prospect, he had recently begun a relationship with another woman because she could console him sensually right away.[129] Rumbling beneath the surface of his verbal virtuosity and subtle control of images was a persisting infirmity of soul. His outward learning and success were solid. Inwardly, he was far closer to slipping into the void than his outward appearance suggested.

His mind was incapable of soothing his anxious heart. His prior reading did not offer satisfactory answers to his questions. As a Manichaean he held that evil existed as a principle independent of goodness. He could attribute his experience of evil as suffering some alien intrusion for which he was not ultimately responsible.[130] Setting aside this explanation in favor of God's singular omnipotence, however, raised disturbing concerns about God's responsibility for the universe's troubles and the origin of evil.[131] Additionally, although Augustine was repulsed by the idea of God being in the shape of a human body, he also was not able to imagine how a reality that was not materially available to sense perception could be real.[132] At best he could visualize God as containing and filling the world as an immense sea does a sponge.[133] Finally, he remained puzzled about how the human will could be said to be free.[134]

Far from being mere distracting mental curiosities, such questions were integrally connected to the affective struggles he had in his own life. Augustine says that while his mind worried about the nature of the material world, it was his "heart that became heavy."[135] His eyes were restricted to seeing only material images, so also was his heart.[136] It was as if his heart were circumscribed by his implicit and explicit materialist beliefs. How could he become free of worldly ambition, worldly anxiety, and worldly consolation when he was unable to imagine anything qualitatively excelling them? His perceptions and feelings were limited to those that were possible within the world as he then conceived it and experienced it. He considered "simply non-existent anything not extended in space." As a result, he would eventually look back and confess, "I had no clear vision even of my own self."[137]

Platonism resolved these intellectual problems and eased his skepticism through its doctrines. In a passage that made a deep and abiding impression on Augustine, Plotinus writes that it is asking far too much of the material world to supply the soul with what it needs the most. The goal of human life is one that simply cannot be attained "on foot" for "our feet only carry us everywhere in this world, from one country to another." According to Plotinus, attention solely to matter yields a superficial encounter with the external surface of reality but no penetrating insight. He, therefore, advises, "Let all these things go, and do not look. Shut your eyes, and change to and wake to another way of seeing, which everyone has but few use."[138] Plotinus invited Augustine to see everything he had heretofore considered real to be an image or extension of a deeper, more primary immaterial reality.

Plotinus uses the example of an architect who assesses the quality of a house made out of materials by comparing it with the inner form of it in his mind. It is this inner form rather than its material realization which best functions as "a ruler" (κανόνι) to determine the house's beauty. "The house outside," after all "is the inner form dispersed by the external mass of matter, without parts but appearing in many parts." The house, then, is best seen by the soul which employs the data supplied by sense perception to see first of all the form "binding and mastering" the material and then "gather into one that which appears dispersed and bring it back and take it in, now without parts, to the soul's interior and present it to that which is within as something in tune with it and fitting and dear to it."[139]

In this way, Plotinus counsels those who "admire this perceptible universe, observing its size and beauty and the order of its everlasting course, and the gods in it . . . and the spirits, and all animals and plants" to "ascend to its archetypal and truer reality and there see them all intelligible and eternal in it, in its own understanding and life; and let him see pure Intellect presiding over them, and immense wisdom."[140] Those who follow this mental itinerary come to see the created world for what it is: an imperfect image of its superior invisible source. They still value the objects of sense experience as goods without allowing them to capture their exclusive attention. The material world for them is neither despised nor esteemed so highly as to have its own sufficiency. Matter is not evil in any absolute sense, but only in comparison to what is superior to it.[141]

When the intellect stops its inquiry prematurely and does not follow this mental itinerary, evil is the result. Evil then is a consequence of the human will exercising its freedom falsely by defining its own position in the continuum of being rather than accepting the good place it is given. It results when souls—ignorant of themselves and God—strive to compensate by acquiring autonomy and self-possession.[142] The deficit created by cutting themselves off from the whole necessarily involves identifying themselves with a part of the external world. The irony, according to this Plotinian analysis, is that the very effort to gain selfhood by pulling material things to oneself—as it were, materially enlarging the self—achieves the opposite effect. The effect upon the soul is that in actively seeking to become more substantial by accruing matter to itself, it becomes more passive as its natural capacities fail to come to fruition.[143] The inclining of the soul's affections toward non-being thus results in an unnatural dependence upon that which is inferior to it, and a corresponding decline in the functionality of human faculties. Far from a principle either independent of God or with the ability to constrain the will of souls, evil is a partial shadow of true substance which depends on goodness for any residual existence it continues to have.

For Plotinus, the human soul only flourishes when it can turn its attention toward its inner self without fear that doing so will increase its isolation. Rather than fostering narcissism or inviting solipsism, Plotinus contends that this self-attention leads to discovering one's true self that participates in that which is simultaneously present always and everywhere from which all things proceed as a single whole.[144] He likens this experience of turning one's attention inward to hearing a voice long forgotten that reminds us of who we really are.

> If then there is to be conscious apprehension of the powers which are present in this way, we must turn (ἐπιστρέφειν) our power of apprehension inwards (εἰς τὸ εἴσω), and make it attend (προσοχὴν) to what is there. It is as if someone was expecting to hear a voice which he wanted to hear and withdrew from other sounds and roused his power of hearing to catch what, when it comes, is the best of all sounds which can be heard; so here also we must let perceptible sounds go . . . and keep the soul's power of apprehension pure and ready to hear the voices from on high.[145]

Philosophy, according to Plotinus, is a discipline that trains the soul not to rely on what is inferior to itself for its well-being, but to follow the mind in its contemplation of that which is its true source. In his own words, "wisdom is an intellectual activity which turns away from these [ephemeral] things below and leads the soul to those above."[146] The soul's cure entails acquiring practices of thought that purify it of its inordinate attachment to what is beneath its dignity. Such practices entail first of all acquiring an awareness of the nature and faculties of the soul itself.[147] Through such mental exercises the soul discovers the sovereignty it has over the material world whenever it observes its proper reliance upon its immaterial source.[148] Indeed, the more it identifies with its higher faculties, the more it perceives its own kinship with the divine. The fluctuations and movements of the material world can then be understood within a larger procession outward of the whole from its immaterial and ineffable source.

Plotinus harshly objected to those who, like the Manichaeans with whom Augustine associated, propagated doctrines that did not require this transformation of mind and consequently obscured rather than illumined the soul's nature and its proper relationship to the material world. He worried that such teaching had adverse effects on those who heard it because it was able to show "neither how the soul can be cured (θεραπεύεται) nor how it can be purified" (καθαίρεται).[149] He thought that genuine insight into the true nature of oneself and one's place in the universe would reclaim, not eradicate, one's passions by wholly redirecting them toward their proper object. Plotinus explains that by "passing in the ascent all that is alien to the God, one sees with one's self alone That alone, simple, single and pure, from which all depends and to which all look and are and live and think: for it is the cause of life and mind and being. If anyone sees it, what passion will he feel, what longing in his desire to be united with it, what a shock of delight! . . . he laughs at all other loves and despises what he thought beautiful before."[150]

Since the soul's "ugliness" comes from its disproportionate attachment to what is inferior to itself, its beauty is regained when it "is singled out from other things and is alone by itself."[151] Thus, according to the Plotinian ideal, one's soul ought to be continually aware that it ultimately abides alone with the Alone. This very solitude yields the incomparable stability of knowing one's identity with that One who is the source of all things. Rather than pretentious assertion arising from a false freedom, it is the godlike serenity of the human soul that is entirely defined by its highest faculties.[152]

The more Augustine came under the sway of Platonism, the more he began to feel that his crisis of anxiety was connected to the way he had come to overvalue the success he was pursuing. The great hope presented by Platonism of finalities of meaning infused from beyond the limited sensible world qualitatively excelled anything of which he had previously dreamed. The true, the good, and the beautiful were not to be sought in the political and rhetorical decadence of public life, but were ideals perfect in themselves to which human life and the whole material world were but echoes. Although Platonism is often associated with a kind of dualism between the mind and body, Augustine found it remarkably healing in that it meant for him the *integration* of the self and the universe in terms of a single whole.

While Augustine had learned a good deal of Hellenistic philosophy primarily from Cicero prior to his reading of Platonic books, it is important to note that the dogmatic adjustments to his philosophical outlook bought about by Platonism did not cause him to set aside his earlier learning.[153] In fact, the Platonic books profoundly affected Augustine's reading of the Latin rhetorical tradition in which he was still professionally immersed. This is nowhere more evident than in his understanding of Cicero's characterization of the complimentary tasks of philosophy and rhetoric. Cicero came to be read by him not as a skeptical Academic but as an ardent Platonist who—in accordance with psychagogic principles—rhetorically concealed the more esoteric aspects of the truth. Thus, according to Augustine, Cicero and those representing the New Academy preserved the esoteric teaching of the Old Academy beneath the exoteric surface of their writings for those who had made sufficient progress to see it.[154] In this way, Augustine could maintain the Ciceronian ideal of wisdom speaking eloquently, but imposed upon it a (re)new(ed) Platonic telos. He never felt compelled to adopt the restrained prose style of Plotinus as something incompatible with Ciceronian fullness.[155]

It is also important to observe that Augustine's encounter with Platonism was construed by him *at the time* not as calling him to join a pagan philosophical school, but as making possible a new appreciation for Christianity. Neither did he see Platonism as a discrete tradition of thought that could be amalgamated into a new synthesis with Christianity. Platonism, for Augustine, served the valuable purpose of clearing away entire categories and dogmas that inhibited his apprehension of the truth. He would later sum up what he read in the Platonic books in the words of Christian scripture: "In the beginning was the Word and the Word was with God and the Word was God. . . . All things were made by him, and without him nothing was made. What was made is life in him and the life was the light of human beings. And the light shone in the darkness, and the darkness did not comprehend it" (Jn. 1:1–5).[156] While he was still encumbered by materialism, he found such texts to be utterly opaque. After Platonism helped him shed his prior presuppositions, the truth that had been present in the Bible all along became more visible to him. He asserts, "I began reading [scripture] and found that all truth I had read in the Platonists was stated here."[157]

Having become acquainted with the doctrines found in the Platonic books, the young rhetor still struggled with his personal and public life. The more his new learning qualified his ambition for worldly honors, the more burdensome his public duties felt.[158] Augustine had once before contemplated withdrawing from public life with a group of friends so that they would have the leisure to devote themselves entirely to the love of wisdom.[159] They, nevertheless, soon discarded the whole idea and "returned to sighs and groans following the broad and well-trodden ways of the world."[160] Even though Augustine had since acquired from the Platonic books a much clearer idea of the philosophic life he desired to live, this pattern continued.[161]

As he had at other times, he would again seek out a guide for his soul. He found Simplicianus—an "old man . . . of much experience and learning" whom he knew Ambrose to love as his own father in the faith.[162] Augustine told him of his past "wanderings" and that he had been reading "some books of the Platonists which had been translated into Latin by Victorinus."[163] Simplicianus greeted the news that Augustine was now reading Platonic books with approval and then took the opportunity to lay before the young rhetor the example of the very man who had translated the books he was reading. Augustine heard how Victorinus "was tutor to numerous noble senators," had a statue of himself placed in the Roman forum, and had employed his tongue for years to defend pagan cults before crowds. He heard how Victorinus—an orator of African origins who became philosophically learned—came to feel that "there was no salvation in the rhetoric which he had taught." He also heard how after a period of hesitancy, Victorinus converted to Christianity and resolved to use his rhetorical gifts to confess the Christian faith publicly.[164] Eventually, he abandoned "the school of loquacious chattering" and preferred to cling to the "word" which makes "skilled the tongues of infants."[165] Simplicianus hoped that Augustine would follow Victorinus' example.[166]

Augustine received from Simplicianus no new doctrines, but personal kindness and paraenetic exhortation designed to overcome his opposition to the way of life implied by the doctrines he had read. Through this narrative medium Simplicianus sought to help Augustine see for himself the beauty of such a life. He instructed the younger man's imagination, as it were, regarding how he could live differently if only he would fully internalize and live out the doctrines his mind had already begun to grasp. This paraenetic exhortation set in motion events where Augustine's anxious striving—indeed his whole past—would loosen its grip on him.[167] Not long after that, Augustine read the words of St. Paul inspiring in him a security that could be found neither "in riots or drunken parties, nor in eroticism and indecencies, nor in strife and rivalry" (Rom. 13:13).[168] These human words, ones with which he was long familiar, became beautiful to him and were the means by which divine grace penetrated him deeply enough to become the core of his future identity.[169]

Chapter Four

Christianizing Classical Therapy

The healing of the soul, which is brought about in distinct steps by
God's providence and ineffable kindness, is most beautiful.
                                        —Augustine, *uera rel.* 24.45

Christian Philosophy and the Cure of Soul

The Milanese public learned in 386 CE that their municipal orator had
retired for a time from his duties on account of ill health.[1] To recover his
strength, he had retreated to an estate at Cassiciacum lent to him by the
local grammarian Verecundus. What Augustine was actually doing must
be inferred from the writings he produced at the time. He wrote from Cassiciacum to his long-time patron, Romanianus, saying, "philosophy now
nourishes and sustains me" in "retirement" (*otium*).[2] He boasted of gathering "fruit from a generous retirement" (*otium liberale*).[3] In his writing,
Augustine described how he hoped to find in philosophy a kind of safe
tranquil harbor away from the storms in which he had been previously
caught.[4] If Augustine's later description of his secular career is reliable,
then the very people who paid him to lie persuasively to them and teach
their sons to do the same were now expected to receive him as a philoso-

pher in search of the truth.[5] Thus, Augustine had something to prove if he were no longer to be merely a "seller of words."

A superficial reading of the Cassiciacum writings could give the impression that Augustine was in the process of renouncing rhetoric and separating himself entirely from the willful manipulation of language for political effects. Pervading these writings is an intense concern with the use of words (*uerba*) and a steady subordination of them to reality itself (*res*). Augustine affirmed Cicero's declaration that the wisdom which philosophy seeks is not ultimately found in words, but in the "knowledge of things (*rerum*) human and divine."[6] He lamented how "rare and extremely difficult" it is for any human being to hold to the "order of things" (*ordinem rerum*).[7] Whenever one pursues wisdom, words interpose themselves, thus, complicating the whole search.[8] In a very odd statement for such an able rhetorician, Augustine wrote, "I ask that you bear with my inability to speak" and "with quick minds grasp the things themselves" (*res ipsas*).[9]

Rather than perceiving it to be an act of irresponsibility, the citizens of Milan would have seen Augustine's retreat in terms of respected earlier cultural precedents. It has been shown that Augustine's presentation of "his life at Cassiciacum as a life in *otium*" placed him "firmly within a venerable social and literary tradition": a "time-honored tradition of genteel intellectual retreat, which had taken shape in the Late Republic, [and] had lost little of its vitality as a cultural ideal."[10] It had been twelve years since he first read Cicero's *Hortensius* and first longed for the philosophic life. Cicero had written the work during a period of time when he had retired from public life in order to pursue philosophy.[11] Perhaps Augustine hoped that leaving political life aside would enable him to devote himself to philosophical matters as it had for Cicero, Marius Victorinus, and his contemporary Manlius Theodorus. In retrospect, it is apparent that Augustine would never again return to public office or seek imperial preferment. At the time, however, this would not have been at all clear.[12] Just as Cicero himself returned from his *otium* to public life, Augustine could have as well.

This indeterminacy contributed to what Augustine described as the "huge mountain" that loomed over the "harbor of philosophy" found at Cassiciacum and threatened its very existence. Augustine told himself and those with him that it was this mountain that "must be greatly feared and must be avoided with all caution." This mountain, whose towering presence he felt so keenly, was made of ambition—what he called "the proud pursuit of empty glory."[13] He was all too familiar with how this mountain was outwardly "resplendent and clothed in such a deceiving light that it presents itself as a dwelling place not only to those who are arriving and have not yet landed and promises to satisfy their desire for the happy land itself, but it also frequently attracts those from the harbor itself, and often it holds those who, through their delight in its sheer loftiness, take pleasure in looking down on others." He also knew from experience that it had "nothing substantial or solid within, and, with a crackling of the ground-crust beneath, it plunges down and swallows up those who are walking above, puffed up with themselves, and, as they tumble headlong into darkness, it takes from them the glittering home which they had just barely seen."[14]

As he attempted to navigate around this looming mountain of ambition through an "extremely narrow" (*angustias*) passage to Cassiciacum, Augustine supported himself there by teaching Romanianus' son and three other pupils.[15] In his retirement, he experimented with something of a "school" where he would (still) be the "teacher" but the subject matter and its goals would have changed entirely.[16] Thus, rather than retiring from teaching *per se*, Augustine was in the process of renouncing his occupation of selling sophistic skills. His school would no longer be one that supplied students who aspired to worldly glory with what they needed to attain it. Words would no longer be weapons to attain personal victory, but tools for inquiry into the nature of things as they stand apart from contests of human cultural construction. His teaching would less resemble Gorgias' training for maximal success in public life than the "surgery" that took place in Epictetus' classroom. Thus, Augustine used his own attempt to become free from the cultural values he propagated in his former profession to provide an education that would lead his students to renounce those same values and convert them to an alternate way of life. He was "gathering" his friends "to that harbor" of philosophy.[17] He would teach them to turn away each day from the very striving that so effectively distracts the soul from itself. "They should train the mind to be at home with itself."[18] In becoming members of his school, they were in effect being initiated into the values of a new community.

Augustine's writings at the time, nevertheless, show—more than anything—the utter difficulty and complexity of attaining such freedom from the cultural constraints governing our use of words. Thus, when an argument erupted between two of his students, in which Licentius insisted that Trygetius' incorrect answer become part of the written record, Augustine harshly rebuked Licentius and then noticed Trygetius' resultant happiness. Witnessing such apparently normal school behavior, Augustine exclaimed, "Oh, that you could see, even with as bleary eyes as mine, in what dangers we lie, and what heedlessness of ills this laughing indicates! . . . Unhappy boys, do you know where we are? To have their minds immersed in darkness—that is the common lot of all the foolish and unlearned."[19] When Licentius continued to be perturbed—this time over the matter that it was being recorded that he was rebuked—Augustine further admonished them, "Do you not yet even acknowledge your fault? You do not know that I used to be sorely vexed in that school [of rhetoric in Milan] because boys were motivated, not by the advantage and beauty of learning, but by the love of paltriest praise. . . . You are, nevertheless, trying to introduce and spread the contagious disease of corrosive rivalry and empty boasting—the lowliest of contagions, yet even more harmful than all the others—into philosophy and into the life which I rejoice to have finally made my own."[20]

Thus, behaviors that were customary in his former school were now for Augustine signs of his students' distorted affections. He sought to "deter" them from such "disease and falsehood."[21] He warned them of how much we are "overburdened by the weight of perverse habits of life and buried under the shadows of ignorance."[22] To speak to them frankly about this, nevertheless, was risky. He worried that if he extinguished their "burning desire for vainglory" too quickly through frank speech, it would not promote in them an active love of wisdom, but would rather make opportunity for them to lapse into passivity "growing cold in the sluggishness of inertia."[23] If Augustine were to succeed in wresting his students away from their deeply entrenched values and lead them toward the truth itself, if he were going to move them from words (*uerba*) to things (*res*), he would need to draw on the very rhetorical arts which sat so uneasily with his evident commitments to philosophy. He would need to undermine one rhetoric by means of another rhetoric. For his students' own good, he would appeal not only to their reason, but also to their non-rational faculties. If truth were to refrain from coercion, it had to make itself desirable enough to be freely chosen. Augustine would adorn the truth with such beautiful garments that its real, natural beauty would gain the attention of his students. In other words, philosophy at Cassiciacum became a certain psychagogy that used words (*uerba*) to lead its adherents to things (*res*).

Augustine meditated deeply on the relationship between words and things and struggled to perfect a rhetoric that would lead beyond itself to the truth. As the remainder of this chapter shows, Augustine gradually unfurls his christianization of classical psychagogy in his early writings, but his insights into the complex relationship between words and things continued to deepen for decades. His earliest writings were dialogues similar in form to Cicero's philosophical prose.[24] Augustine's choice of genre was deliberate and perfectly suited to his goals. He was explicit about writing within the tradition of using words for philosophic ends: "I have imitated them [the Academics] as far as I was able, rather than overcome them, which I am completely unable to do."[25] The characters in his dialogues, much like those in Cicero's works, circle through multiple opinions as their author leads readers indirectly step by step to question their own assumptions while only hinting at the actual truth of the matter. Rather than the revered heroes of the Roman Republic, Augustine's characters, nevertheless, were the very people present with him at Cassiciacum, a gathering of Christians of various abilities and educational levels. Augustine the writer was using words to point to a present reality outside of the texts he composed.

With none of the reticence of Bishop Ambrose, Augustine's earliest writings extol "philosophy" in language worthy of the *Hortensius*. Philosophy is "our true and unshakable abode."[26] It is "philosophy" that "promises that it will clearly display the true and hidden God, and now and again deigns to show us a glimpse of him, as it were, through transparent clouds."[27] "Genuine philosophy" teaches "what is the First Principle of all things—Itself without beginning—and how great an Intellect dwells therein, and what has proceeded therefrom for our welfare, but without deterioration of any kind."[28] Wisdom is said to admonish people "to bear with the physician and to permit themselves to be healed" since by submitting "to the physician's injunctions" they could "be restored to the condition of the healthy and to the light."[29]

Augustine does not use the term "philosophy" in the same manner as Ambrose, partly because for him it was not synonymous with "the philosophy of this world" that he knew Christian scripture to warn against.[30] Rather, during his time at Cassiciacum, his use of the word was informed by a particular view of the development of Hellenic philosophy and Christianity's relationship to it. Augustine explained to his students and readers: "Plato added the knowledge of natural and divine matters, which he had diligently acquired from those I have mentioned [Pythagoreans], to Socrates's ethics with its wit and subtlety. He brought these components together under dialectic as their organizer and judge, since dialectic either is wisdom itself or that without which there cannot be wisdom. Plato is thereby said to have constructed a complete system of philosophy."[31] Thus, in this way the diverse classical philosophical traditions had a unity about them for those capable of understanding it—a unity most clearly visible in the writings of Plotinus. Augustine wrote of "this Platonic philosopher" that he "is considered to be so like Plato" that "Plato should be thought of as coming to life again" in him.[32]

For Augustine to believe that this tradition had resources to care for the soul is not to say that it was capable of doing so independently of Christianity. Although classical authorities appear continually in the Cassiciacum dialogues like familiar friends, their author had a psychagogic task in mind. Augustine invited his students and readers into not unfamiliar philosophical controversies such as the nature of divine providence, human happiness, and knowledge. As he strove to improve their thinking about such things by philosophical argument, he did so implying that such an exercise led to Christianity.[33] Indeed, Augustine contended of Christianity, "Regarding erudition, doctrine, and morals—all of which care for the soul—there is, in my opinion, one system of really true philosophy."[34] Whereas Greek philosophical schools fractured into schisms without number in their pursuit of truth, Christianity, at the appointed time, perfected the tradition that each of them witnessed to more or less. Augustine, however, would not yet linger directly on uniquely Christian matters. He concealed them as if they were the esoteric teachings of the Old Academy. For all his praise of Platonic authorities, he asserted in his first published work, "I am resolved not to depart from the authority of Christ on any score whatsoever: I find none more powerful."[35] He felt free to engage the thought of the Platonists as long as he sensed that whatever he found there would not "be opposed to our Holy Scripture."[36] By associating readers with his own quest for wisdom, Augustine sought to lead them to the same conclusion.

Augustine imitated a Cicero that he believed had put forward his philosophy in dialogic form as a way of persuading the readers of his day gradually without alienating them by disclosing more than they were prepared to receive. In Augustine's view, Cicero sought to loosen the grip the prevailing materialism had upon his contemporaries. A shift in times, however, would demand a shift in content. Augustine worried that what was appropriate in Cicero's day "for eradicating the deepest errors might now begin to be an obstacle for the inculcating of knowledge." To be accommodated to the state of the souls of his contemporaries, speech needed to be crafted to meet different demands. It needed a new aim, namely, "that human beings should be led back to the hope of discovering truth."[37]

Augustine, thus, believed that truth was best pursued conversationally as in a Ciceronian dialogue "by question and answer" (*interrogando et respondendo*). He recognized, however, that it is "hard to find anyone who would not be ashamed to be defeated in an argument. The almost inevitable result is that a subject for discussion which is well begun is driven out of mind by the unruly noise of self-opinion, accompanied also by wounded souls (*laceratione animarum*) which are usually concealed but are, at times, laid bare."[38] For students (such as Licentius and Trygetius) to be able to benefit from guidance and enter the safe port of philosophy, the shame of being defeated in argument would have to lose its power over them. This could only happen if they came to love the honest pursuit of truth more than the exhilaration derived from verbal victory.

Rather than incurring the risks involved in confronting his students frankly and directly, Augustine more often chose to maneuver carefully around his students' complex motives and sensitive souls. He drew on a metaphor which the psychagogic tradition employed to explain the spiritual guide's adaptation of speech to the state of the hearers' souls. Augustine portrays himself at Cassiciacum as catering meals "not only for our bodies but also for our souls."[39] He invited his students to come, dine with him, and eat the meal prepared specifically for them.[40] He knew that—even if his students' souls were healthy—his efforts would be in vain if he tried to feed them against their will.[41] Accordingly, he enticed them with dishes served in small amounts,[42] apportioned to their appetites, "made and seasoned, as it were, with scholastic honey."[43] Such sweetened discourse, nevertheless, in no way guaranteed success because souls sufficiently "sick" (*aegri*) refuse and spit out even food that is carefully prepared.[44] Augustine solicited his students' involvement in the conversation as if they were helping him serve a feast prepared by God.[45] At one point, Navigius responds to his teacher's offer of "sweets" saying, "Such things will surely cure (*sanabunt*) me, for the dish which you have set before us, concocted and spiced in some way or other, is, as that writer [Cicero] says of Hymettic honey, sharp in its sweetness and does not bloat my stomach. Therefore, even though my palate has sampled only a little, I swallow it all gladly insofar as I am able."[46]

Adapting his discourse, in this way, to his students' taste and enriching it so that it was sweet to the palate placed Augustine's practice at Cassiciacum uncomfortably close to that of his former school of rhetoric in Milan. There was no bright line between philosophy and sophistry. At one point, Augustine asks his students why he continued to use "copious and ornate language . . . as if I were still engaged in that school from which I am glad that I have in some measure escaped."[47] Even if the psychological distance Augustine traveled exceeded the physical distance between Milan and Cassiciacum, during his retreat he sought to invest truth rather than lies with charms to win the attention of human hearts and not awaken their resistance. "Because," he explained,

> the unwise generally follow their own senses and habits rather than the most genuine truth which the rare soul sees, it was necessary that they not only be taught to the extent of their ability, but also frequently and strongly aroused as to their emotions. To the portion of itself which would accomplish this—a portion more full of necessity than of purity, its lap heaped high with charms (*deliciarum*) which it would scatter to the crowd so that the crowd might deign to be influenced for its own good—to this portion, it gave the name rhetoric.[48]

What he sought to banish from Cassiciacum was not rhetoric, but the pretensions, cultural ambitions, and affective distortions it had in the late Empire.

In imagery reminiscent of Plato's description of the mind's cave-like captivity to images once it turns from the truth, Augustine reflected upon the human eye's need to have extraordinary health to be able to look upon the sun. Lacking such strength, it develops an affinity for darkness and begins to construe its limited capacity to be actual health. He says, "In this the mind is often mistaken." The human experience is one where "we think we see how much progress we have made, but it is not granted to us to imagine or know how deep we had sunk or how far we had risen. Therefore, in comparison with more serious sickness we think that we are healthy." Beauty in all its radiance, however, knows how to reveal itself in a specific manner even to eyes such as these: "It performs the office of the physician (*medici*) and it knows which ones are healthy better than they themselves do who are being healed" (*sanantur*).[49]

Augustine notes that there are different kinds of people each with differing capacities and needs. There are a fortunate few whose "eyes are so healthy and vigorous that they can fearlessly turn toward the sun as soon as they are opened." Finding their source of health in the light, they require at most some reminding rather than teaching. "Others, however, are dazzled by the very luster which they so ardently desire to behold and they gladly turn back to the darkness without having seen the light. To these, even though they can rightly be called healthy, it is dangerous to wish to show them what they are not yet capable of seeing. They are, therefore, first to be trained, and, for their own good, their love is to be usefully redirected and nourished."[50]

He describes this process of educating the affections in the following way. Since people are accustomed to what is most easily seen, their attention should be directed toward those very things—"some things which do not shine with their own light but which may be seen only by means of light, such as a garment or a wall or something of that kind." Next their eyes should be drawn to "something which, though it does not shine with its own light, yet glitters more fairly by means of that light, such as, gold, silver, and the like, which, yet, are not so radiant as to hurt the eyes." Then, guiding their vision sequentially toward ever brighter objects, "this earthly fire perhaps should be carefully shown them, then the stars, then the moon, then the splendor of the dawn and the radiance of the brightening sky." Augustine comments that it is precisely "through these things that, each one growing more proficient according to his own strength, either through all the steps or leaving out some of them, sooner or later will behold the sun without flinching and with immense delight." Augustine concludes, "The best teachers do something like this with those who are most desirous of wisdom, and who can see, though not yet clearly. For it is the duty of good teaching (*bonae disciplinae*) to arrive at wisdom by means of a definite order" (*ordine*).[51] Since he believed that for the vast majority of people, the soul's health was best restored through a gradual therapy understood as this kind of affective ascent, Augustine did not directly pass on to his students the philosophical conclusions to which he had come. Neither did he convey the truth in propositional form or follow a linear outline in his teaching at Cassiciacum.

Instead, during his philosophical retreat, Augustine psychagogically led souls gently to apprehend truth for themselves. He engaged his students in conversations whose outcome he claimed not to know in advance.[52] For this reason, Augustine's representation of himself in the dialogues is not straightforward historical reporting. The "Augustine" in the dialogues is very much a character whose real historicity is used for the purposes of the author of the dialogues. Every purely historical reconstruction — including this one — must make judgments about the author on the basis of the character. The historical Augustine often knows a great deal more than the character "Augustine." The ongoing misperception of the early dialogues as immature or merely philosophical has a great deal to do with the success of Augustine's own rhetoric! The more one becomes aware of the manner in which Augustine manipulates his own self-representation for psychagogic purposes, the more one comes to appreciate the maturity and literary artistry of the dialogues themselves. The subject of inquiry for any given day was approached indirectly in digression-filled discussions that only eventually circled back around to their primary topic. When Licentius began to retreat from a contention he had been advocating, Augustine admonished him, "You still should not abandon your position on that account, especially since we have engaged in this discussion of ours to train you (*exercendi*) and to incite you to cultivate your mind."[53] Augustine describes engaging his young men in conversations "where philosophy itself freely played along with us, so to speak."[54] Indeed, even when Augustine sought to renew his students' interest in dogmatic rather than skeptical philosophy, he thought this best accomplished through "play" rather than indoctrination.

The reading and interpreting of texts were integral components of the spiritual exercises at Cassiciacum. Augustine's students read Virgil daily.[55] In seeking to turn the souls of his students to ever brighter things, texts were convenient objects to be used in exercises because they did not shine of their own light but could be seen by the light that gave them meaning. In the midst of debate, appeal was made to Cicero's *Hortensius* as a text they had surely read.[56] Teacher and student quoted in turn verses of Terence.[57] As Licentius composed his own poetry, his teacher hoped that "philosophy might gain and retain a larger share of his mind."[58] Augustine worried that Licentius' love of poetry would, like other worldly cares, become an impenetrable wall between himself and reality.[59] How pleased his teacher must have been when Licentius confessed that he had come to see "philosophy" as "more beautiful than . . . all such loves of every kind."[60]

Although this teacher of Christian philosophy recognized the power of the resources for the care of soul handed on by the Hellenistic schools, he also saw an obvious limitation. He, along with his students and readers, believed that only the elite few could benefit fully from such philosophical exercises. Indeed, he acknowledged that it was the "rarest class of men" who were "capable of using reason as a guide to the knowledge of God or of the soul."[61] The highest truths were "easily perceived only by those who purify themselves of all vice and adopt a different way of life, one that is more than human."[62] "Knowledge" was something "cultivated rarely and only by a few" on account of the "many different upheavals of this life . . . some thickness or laziness or sluggishness of dulled minds, or our despair of finding [wisdom] . . . or the common error that people, having found a false opinion, do not search diligently for the truth if they search at all."[63] Consequently, "they are few and far between who arrive" in the port of philosophy.[64]

For the soul to benefit from philosophy, aside from possessing the requisite ability and favorable circumstances, it would need to follow a definite order of study accompanied by personal discipline. Augustine warned, "If anyone dares to rush into knowing these things rashly without the due order of the branches of learning, he becomes not studious but [merely] curious, not learned but credulous, not circumspect but ready to discredit everything."[65] Although the five senses that people customarily rely upon in fact provide reliable information regarding what they perceive, problems arise when they are ascribed a sufficiency that they lack. They only have access to what constantly changes and thereby lack a critical principle by which to assess either themselves or to organize their impressions into a hierarchy of value. Under his teacher's guidance, Licentius exclaims, "Whoever knows only those things which the senses of the body contact seems to me to be not only not with God, but not even with himself."[66] Exclusive reliance on sensation leads to a darkness of the mind that does not perceive the true nature even of the material world. "Human authority" is no more reliable since it "for the most part fails."[67] To perceive truth transcending the fluctuations of sensation, words, images, and human authority requires skill and training beyond what is available to the majority of people. To gain at least some knowledge of oneself it is necessary to acquire "a constant habit of withdrawing from things of the senses and of concentrating thought within and holding it there."[68] Augustine writes that it is "philosophy" that "teaches, and teaches truly, that nothing whatsoever that is discerned [outwardly] by mortal eyes, or that any of the senses comes into contact with, should be worshipped. Instead, everything of the sort must be despised."[69] Being led step by step by his teacher, Trygetius observes, "It happens that those who narrow-mindedly consider this life by itself alone are repelled by its enormous foulness, and turn away in sheer disgust." Nevertheless, they will "find nothing unarranged, unclassed, or unassigned to its own place" who are able to find an alternate mode of perception; namely, raising the eyes of the mind, broadening their field of vision, and surveying "all things as a whole."[70]

This habit of mind that continually rises above ordinary experience and perception must be carefully cultivated for it to have the desired effects. Augustine states, "This they alone succeed in doing who either cauterize through solitude the wounds of opinion which the course of daily life has made, or heal them by means of the liberal branches of learning."[71] Thus, every sense impression and experience is to be scrutinized and categorized in terms of a prior scale of value that intervenes and defines each of them. What mainly separates the wise from those who merely seek knowledge is that they have so internalized wisdom that it has become for them "a fixed possession," that is, a "*habitus.*"[72]

To develop this disposition, Augustine suggests engaging in daily learning that "rears for philosophy a soldier, or even a captain, so competent that he sallies forth wherever he wishes and leads many others as well, and reaches that Supreme Measure, beyond which he desires nothing else."[73] Augustine's hope was one that would have been recognizable to representatives that he admired from the classical philosophical tradition. They each believed that the soul could remedy its infirmities by availing itself of the services of the potent captain of learning. Augustine explained to his students that through the study of such things as music, geometry, the movements of the stars, or the fixed ratios of numbers, they could learn to perceive the larger order of the universe, or at least be led to it.[74] Filling the heart and mind with musical harmonies and mathematical proportions would yield a more harmonious and proportionate soul; a soul that became more orderly the more it conformed itself to the order of the universe.

When the knowledge of such things is fully integrated in the soul, it excludes all behavior and desires not in keeping with it. Augustine asserts,

"For, to the soul that diligently considers the nature and power of numbers, it will appear manifestly unfitting and most deplorable that by virtue of this knowledge it should write a rhythmic line and play the harp, and that its life and very self—which is the soul—should nevertheless follow a crooked path and, under the domination of lust, be out of tune by the clangor of shameful vices."[75] Augustine encouraged Zenobius to conform his individual life to the very cosmic order that was the subject of the treatise dedicated to him.[76] In short, Augustine imagined that through such spiritual exercises the souls of at least the few capable of benefiting from them could attain in microcosm the stability, solidity, and wholeness of the cosmos itself.

Refashioning the soul in this manner so that one's security and happiness derive only from eternal wisdom produces a kind of invulnerability where at least one's inner life is bounded off—no longer subject to the whims of chance. Augustine explains,

> [N]o soul, being perfect, is in need of anything; and, while it takes whatever seems necessary for the body if it is at hand, if it is not at hand, the lack of such things will not crush it. For every wise man is brave and no brave man fears anything. Therefore, the wise man does not fear either bodily death or sufferings for whose repelling or avoiding or deferring he would need those things that he is capable of lacking.[77]

He continues, "How will anyone be unhappy to whom nothing happens contrary to his will, since he cannot wish for anything which he sees he cannot attain? For he has his will set on very definite things so that, whatever he does, he does solely in accordance with some precept of virtue or divine law or wisdom, and these things cannot be taken from him in any way."[78]

Those things that intrude upon less philosophical souls—around which they bend their emotional lives like water does around a massive submerged rock in a river—a soul possessing wisdom rises above. Augustine queries, "[H]ow will any burdens, dangers, scorns, or smiles of fortune disturb a just man?" By loving only true beauty, the wise are able to refer each experience to its ideal form and understand that "in the intelligible world, every part is as beautiful and perfect as the whole."[79] In this way, although the wise may suffer outwardly, they will not be diminished inwardly by it. Their souls are no longer being battered about as they grasp after separate things, but have gathered inward strength by finding their "one center by which the other parts are mutually measured."[80]

In reading Augustine's published writings of the time, one is led to believe that he and his students experienced this ideal in their philosophical leisure. Augustine tells of eating material food without being distracted for a moment by its taste from thoughts of the soul's nourishment. They were eating, as it were, without eating, thus engaging in many of the same activities yet doing so differently.[81] His student Licentius' soul rose above bodily necessity while urinating as he chanted "joyously and with gusto" from the Psalter, "O God of hosts, convert us, and show your face; and we shall be saved" (Ps. 79:8).[82] Augustine himself would turn over in his mind philosophical thoughts during his sleep. His students would often find sleep not interrupting their contemplation.[83] Not even witnessing the spectacle of cockfighting lured them down from their philosophical vantage point.[84] Such combat was the very thing that less philosophical minds found irresistible in the gladiatorial spectacles of the time. Alypius' earlier experience was more typical. When he then witnessed such events, his soul was so enthralled that Augustine describes it as being more wounded than the body of the contestant.[85] This time, however, even as the cocks ripped feathers from each other's necks, neither teacher nor student was so engulfed by it as to lose track of their philosophical conversation.

In this way, Augustine taught Christian philosophy at Cassiciacum and greatly opposed all efforts to secure one's well-being externally either through imperial preferment or sophistic skill. He felt little tension between Christianity and Greco-Roman philosophical traditions that sought to overcome the same cultural tendencies. His teaching at this time manifested not only formal continuities with the psychagogic tradition as he adapted his speech to the souls of his hearers and commended spiritual exercises, but also embraced its material aims as he idealized the invulnerable life of the wise. In letters to friends written after his philosophic retreat, Augustine writes of his own "striving to love nothing which can be taken from me against my will."[86] Using language that could have come just as easily from Seneca, he says that "those who are most truly wise, and whom alone it is right to pronounce happy," maintain that those things beyond their control should "neither be the objects of fear nor of desire."[87]

Augustine, however, portrays himself as struggling to realize this invulnerable life personally. He labored to possess through philosophy a happiness bounded off both from the external intrusions of chance or the flaring up of internal passions. He knew that philosophy's healing remedies were only for the few, but he was, after all, one of the rare souls that apparently had all that was thought necessary. He was a free man at leisure possessing the prerequisite skills and resources needed for the therapy to be effective. As he reflected to himself about the progress of his soul, his own "Reason" pointed out to him the persisting disharmony between his affections and his professed beliefs:

> Are you not aware how confidently we had announced yesterday that we are now liberated from all defilement, that we love nothing but wisdom, and that we seek or desire other things only for wisdom's sake? How vile, how detestable, how shameful, how dreadful did we consider the embrace of a woman, when we were making an inquiry between ourselves concerning the desire for a wife. Yet that same night while we were lying awake and going over these things once more in our minds, you realized how differently from your claims those imagined caresses and their bitter sweetness excited you.[88]

In seeking by philosophical means to cure his soul, Augustine found it to be not so pliable as to be easily molded into shape. His soul was more recalcitrant than he thought, more difficult to domesticate, and harder to fashion into a perfectly ordered form. It felt to him at the time like he was failing to persuade his innermost self sufficiently. Augustine exclaimed, "How happy are those who are persuaded, either by themselves or someone else, that death is not to be feared even if the soul perishes! But wretched as I am, no philosophical reasoning (*rationes*), no books, have been able to persuade me."[89] He even longed for a more desperate instrument, "a poem" that he believed Zenobius to have written in his leisure, "in which the fear of death is cast out by an incantation (*excantatus*), and the soul's torpor and coldness, hardened like long-standing ice, is driven away."[90]

Augustine's situation was less a failure of belief than of internalizing what he already believed deeply enough to penetrate the depths of his soul. He felt that as a Christian he did have the most important truths given to him by the Church. Plato had written of how only a few could see for themselves the truth about things. Others, who could not apprehend the truth itself, nonetheless, would best know it by believing, as it were, the true opinion of another. Augustine knew that this other avenue of knowledge was available to him, but he yearned to be one of those who not only believed the right opinion but also understood it himself. He acknowledged that Christianity's "venerated mysteries, which liberate people by a sincere and firm faith," teach philosophic truths.[91] Contemplating his upcoming baptism, he knew the truth was "being delivered to us so secretly and steadily by the sacred rites into which we are now being initiated: therein the life of the good is easily purified, not indeed by the circumlocution of disputations, but by the authority of the mysteries."[92] As he inquired into philosophical wisdom, he did so placing his confidence in that "divine authority which not only transcends all human capacity in signs perceptible to the senses," but also condescended to use that limited capability in order to bid people "not to be confined by the senses . . . but to soar upward to the intellect."[93]

Augustine had no doubt that Christianity communicated openly and effectively what would otherwise be lost on all but the most elite minds. On this score, Augustine was well aware of his mother's lack of formal education. He, in fact, uses Monnica's lack of formal training in his dialogues to undermine the pretensions of traditional rhetorical education. He has Monnica, the woman who has never read the *Hortensius,* state in her own words the truths articulated in it.[94] As Augustine notes, such a woman was not usually present in the philosophical tradition he was self-consciously working in at the time.[95] Although Augustine depicts himself in the *Soliloquies* struggling to advance even with the benefits of philosophical learning, Monnica is portrayed consistently as making progress without the aid of philosophical training. Augustine praises his mother's love of wisdom and states that she has advanced so far in the philosophic life as to attain what is difficult for "even the most learned," a position that all acknowledge to be the very "citadel of philosophy"—fearing neither chance discomfort nor even death itself.[96] Monnica had traveled another road toward the good life. She is the only one present in the Cassiciacum conversations who has been baptized. Her words were not from Cicero, but emanated from the wisdom she had garnered from her faithful participation in the ordinary Christian mysteries.

Augustine was fully aware that there were those like his mother who were "content to follow authority alone" and were unable to make an "account of the liberal and fine arts" or be "instructed in them." They were the ones who cared for their souls by applying "themselves constantly to right living and holy desires." At this time in his life, nevertheless, Augustine confessed his own ambivalence; "I know not how I could call them happy as long as they live among human beings."[97] This was because souls not "trained in any studies," souls that "have not drunk at all from the fountain of the liberal arts" were accounted by him "hungry and famished as it were . . . suffering from a kind of barrenness and hunger of soul."[98] It was as if authority alone was unable to penetrate, shape, and heal the soul as deeply and thoroughly as the experience of seeing the truth for itself.

As Augustine contemplated his own state of believing the truth while still falling short of its full realization in his own life, his reason intervened and assured him inwardly, "What you seek is something which can be seen only by one who is most pure, and you are poorly trained (*parum es exercitatus*) for the vision of such a thing. We have labored for no other purpose in these digressions (*per istos circuitus*) but your own training (*exercitationem*), so that you may be capable of seeing this."[99] Thus, Augustine attributed the lingering weakness of his soul to insufficient effort, discipline, and learning. Further study and more effort would be needed to shore up the remaining fissures in his soul and still his yet undisciplined passions. The gap between his affections and beliefs could still be bridged. It would require perfecting his spiritual exercises and philosophical discipline.

At this point in his life, not coincidentally, Augustine conceived a plan to compose a comprehensive course of education in the liberal arts believing that such studies completed in the proper order under the proper conditions would lead to the good life.[100] He would perfect the learning that he had earlier told Zenobius both "cleared" the mind of obstructions and "cultivated" its faculties.[101] He says, "At the time that I was about to receive baptism in Milan, I also attempted to write books on the liberal arts, questioning those who were with me and who were not averse to studies of this nature, desiring by definite steps, so to speak, to reach things incorporeal through things corporeal and to lead others to them."[102]

The singular purpose of this process of training was to cultivate that habitual mode of thinking that reasoned from sense perception to universal principles so as to be able to refer any sensate particular to the ideal form of which it was merely a particularized instantiation. He advised readers of the final book of his *De musica* that he had lingered in the first five books "childishly in those number-traces belonging to time-intervals" so that whoever reads them "might with reason guiding be torn away, not quickly but gradually, from the fleshly senses and letters that it is difficult not to cling to, and adhere with the love of unchangeable truth to the one God and Lord of all things."[103] In book after book, Augustine was to examine each area of human life methodically and trace it back from the sensible to the intelligible. This "order of the studies of wisdom" (*ordo studiorum sapientiae*) would make its practitioners fit to understand the true "order of things" (*ordinem rerum*).[104] Ideally, in carrying this work to completion, he would acquire for himself this habit of mind and be able to recognize lesser goods as such, transcend the cognitive restrictions placed upon him by relative cultural constructions, organize the data yielded by the senses properly, and act accordingly.

By putting such effort into the curative potential latent in the liberal disciplines for shoring up the souls of at least the few, Augustine had worried comparatively less about the resources available in the Christian mysteries for the same. He knew Christian scripture and liturgical acts from an early age, but their potential would not be fully exploited by him as long as he was attending to his career or possessed the leisure to pursue philosophy in a more traditional manner.[105] Augustine, however, set his ambitious educational project to one side for a time in order to be instructed in the Christian mysteries by the revered Bishop Ambrose whose sermons had caught his attention when he first arrived in Milan.[106] This, thus, brought his philosophical retreat to an end.

Returning to Milan, Augustine resigned from his chair of rhetoric, the prestigious post he had occupied for two years.[107] He would never again teach rhetoric to the Empire's most promising young people. He also broke off the marriage plans that had been arranged to further his political career. He requested by letter that Ambrose recommend to him what he should read from the Bible in order to prepare properly for baptism. The bishop suggested that he read the prophet Isaiah. Augustine found the opening passage of the book utterly opaque and had no reason to believe that the rest of it would be any more accessible. It would be set aside as well until he "had had more practice in the Lord's style of language."[108] The full integration of scripture into his already forming convictions about the soul's guidance and cure would have to wait for his own initiation into the Christian mysteries.

Christ's Inner and Outer Rhetoric

Although Augustine had already benefited from Ambrose's public preaching for some time, he was customarily dismissed with the rest of the unbaptized after the sermon.[109] Augustine now had the opportunity to participate in the full liturgy. The bishop of Milan took responsibility personally for initiating those about to be baptized into the Christian mysteries.[110] In the Lenten weeks preceding his baptism during the Easter Vigil of 387, Augustine most likely heard daily sermons on "the deeds of the patriarchs or the precepts of the book of Proverbs" so that he would be "educated and instructed by these things, grow accustomed to treading the paths of our ancestors," and "obey the divine commandments."[111]

A week before his baptism, Augustine was given the Creed summing up scriptural doctrine in a brief form that would enable him to have the dogmatic tenets of his faith in hand.[112] His bishop likely admonished him never to write it down, lest its truth fall into the hands of those not properly prepared.[113] Instead, he should "daily meditate" upon it, repeating it to himself "inwardly."[114] In this way, it would be "a spiritual seal" and an ever-present "guard" for his soul.[115] Ambrose told his hearers that they should understand those "ancients" who put the Creed in its current form to be "physicians" who had witnessed such "sickness of mind" that they furnished a medicine that would "add health to sickness." He assured them that such medicine continued to be sufficient and required no alteration.[116]

During the week following his baptism, Augustine would have continued to be instructed each day as the bishop explained to him baptism, Eucharist, and the Lord's Prayer in the context of the liturgy itself. Along with the other newly baptized, Augustine would have worn new white garments to fully impress on him the new life he was beginning.[117] Ambrose likely challenged him saying that he had been anointed as an "athlete of Christ, as if to contend in the contest of this world."[118] His struggle was one that required equal training, dedication, and effort. Ambrose likened the Roman social world into which his new Christians would venture to a sea with "heavy waters and severe storms." Having been recently submerged in the baptismal waters, they were now to be like fish who swim undaunted amid the tempests.[119]

Augustine had been admonished in Ambrose's public sermons to train his mind not to stop at the obvious meaning of the scriptural text, but to press on until he could perceive its spiritual meaning. Now he would learn that participating with the faithful in worship would require the same skill. Ambrose imagined an interlocutor standing before the baptismal waters protesting, "I see [only] the water that I am accustomed to seeing every day."[120] And even, "Is that all?" Ambrose conceded, "Yes, this is all, truly all."[121] The bishop told his hearers, however, "Consider the eyes of your heart." Previously, they had seen "the things that are corporeal with corporeal eyes." The "things that are of the sacraments" they "were not yet able to see with the eyes of the heart."[122] They had "seemed before to have been blind in heart." Now they had begun "to see the light of the sacraments."[123] Ambrose exhorted his new initiates, "You ought not, then, to believe solely with the eyes of your body. What is invisible is more completely seen, because the other is temporal, whereas this is eternal. What is not grasped with the eyes but perceived by the spirit and the mind is more completely viewed."[124]

Likewise, upon first viewing the eucharistic bread, Ambrose anticipated someone thinking, "My bread is ordinary bread."[125] Ambrose, nevertheless, exhorted his hearers, "[R]ecognize what you have received."[126] He instructed them that by sharpening their perception and seeing with the eyes of the heart, they may now come to see that what they eat and drink "is not, therefore, bodily food but one that is spiritual."[127] They were to confess within their minds and acknowledge in their hearts the truth they had affirmed by saying "Amen" after hearing Christ's words pronounced over the sacrament.[128] He assured them that "the heavenly and venerable sacrament" was "medicine" for their wounded souls. They, accordingly, ought to "receive daily what is of benefit daily."[129]

Augustine welcomed the Milanese bishop's call to be Christ's athlete.[130] He received not only Christian instruction from Ambrose, but witnessed firsthand an episcopal ministry informed by the rhetorical and philosophical traditions that he taught and admired. Ambrose did this while being biblically informed and actively engaged in public life. Ambrose's formidable image remained with Augustine as a "definite model" of a possible vocation.[131] At the time, however, Augustine appeared to be a different man from the bishop of Milan. He yearned to continue his retirement away from the city and resume the intellectual endeavors begun at Cassiciacum. He and his friends resolved to move back to North Africa and live together in community there.[132] That enterprise would be delayed by a civil war. He was, nevertheless, intent upon "doggedly pursuing his great intellectual program."[133] He did so temporarily in Rome until the following year when travel had become safe once more.

As he waited in Rome, Augustine composed an extensive treatise on the soul in which he contemplated how the soul could know itself since it was given to only a few to be able through reason to see the soul, as it were, by means of the soul itself.[134] Like his earlier works it takes the form of a classical dialogue, this time with his student Evodius. It is crucial to realize that in the dialogue it is Augustine's artful *words* that are the essential means by which Evodius is to be led beyond words to see the soul by means of the soul. Augustine admonishes Evodius verbally that he should delight more in "reality (*rerum*) than in words (*uerborum*)."[135] Throughout this dialogue, Augustine maintained that the Church in its liturgy and scripture taught the truth about the soul authoritatively. Like a mother, the Church nourished her children in perfect health by the milk that the apostle Paul described giving to little ones.[136] Augustine tells Evodius that there is no shame in being content with this, since the safest path for the majority of people is "to trust a most reliable authority and to shape their conduct according to it." If, however, he shares his teacher's desire not only to believe the truth, but to perceive it for himself "by reason," Augustine counsels him that he must "be prepared" to tread "many long, circuitous" ways as he pursues the path "where reason leads."[137]

As one would expect from the author of the Cassiciacum dialogues, Augustine promotes "studies" to "train the mind (*exercet animum*) to perceive more subtle matters" so that it will not be so "dazed by their light" that it retreats to "the very darkness it desired to escape."[138] Reason will function fully "only if lovers of the truth will dare to follow its guidance most consistently and respectfully" over paths made "difficult" because we are unaccustomed to traveling them.[139] Augustine's dialogue is itself such an exercise through which he guides students and readers as they train the very souls into which they inquire. When Evodius expresses discomfort with his teacher's critical judgment of his opinions, Augustine tells him that he perceives his own role to be like an attorney whom Evodius has retained to confute and instruct him in private so that he is well prepared for his appearance in open court.[140] In the treatise, Augustine notes that although we look to the body's bulk and growth in years to assess its strength, they are often not as determinative as the "training and formation of its members."[141] Augustine observes that exercise is so important that it is generally agreed that a man who lifted a little calf every day could hold it even when it had become a bull since he had adapted to the little weight it gained each day.[142] Size and age provide even less evidence of the soul's growth. One should look rather at the virtue which it develops naturally from "studies that are calculated to promote the good and happy life."[143]

The greater a soul's training, the greater its potency is to act.[144] In a detailed passage, Augustine leads his readers in an analysis of the soul's powers and the progressive stages indicating its maturity. He begins with the soul reduced to its most basic functions that it has in common with plants and ends with it in a state "freed from all disease, cleansed of all its stains" and dwelling in full "vision and contemplation of truth."[145] Augustine's chief concern, however, is with the crucial fourth stage of development because it is during this stage that the soul acquires virtue.[146] According to Augustine, it is here that "goodness begins as well as esteem for all true things." It is here that "the soul dares to rank itself not only before its own body . . . but before the whole material world itself." It is here that the soul compares the world's goods with "its own power and beauty" and judges them insufficient. Consequently, the more the soul values its own nature, the more it is free to withdraw from "baser things" and "cleanse itself." This process of purification, however, involves "a hard and bitter fight" against "the vexations and enticements of the world."[147] In the higher stages, the soul becomes increasingly stable in its virtue. The highest functioning of soul is indeed reachable by "great and peerless souls."[148]

While conversing with Evodius, Augustine gives high praise to a line of Horace in which he describes one truly wise as "strong, and contained entirely in himself; all smooth and round."[149] The soul of Augustine's Christian was to be as virtuous and invulnerable as any soul of classical antiquity. He wrote, "I reserve the term 'wise' for those who truth demands should be called wise, those who have achieved peace by placing all inordinate desire under the control of the mind."[150] One should not, however, believe that Augustine imagined this invulnerability achieved through human efforts alone, as if by a kind of autonomy. On the contrary, the soul only became free from all intrusions from below itself on account of the help of divine providence. The careful training and strenuous exercises commended to human agents in their "reformation" in no way excluded "the mercy of Him whose goodness and power are the cause of human formation."[151]

After his time of making arrangements and writing in Rome, Augustine succeeded in establishing his community in his native Thagaste.[152] Once again, his activities and interests have to be reconstructed from his literary efforts. Augustine continued to pursue similar questions, but in these works there is not only a playfully concealed psychagogic practice, but also an articulated psychagogic theory that is unmistakably Christian.[153] Notably, Augustine made his first foray into a new genre: biblical commentary, this time interpreting the opening chapters of Genesis. Augustine described how divinely created human beings in their natural state received knowledge from God as if from an interior spring, and therefore had no need for "words from the outside." Instead, in the human soul "the truth welled up from its interior."[154] The fall described in Genesis is taken as the human soul's satisfaction with its own power and quest for autonomy, as if it had "no need of interior light."[155] This resulted in human beings "clothing themselves in falsehood," that is, in their speech becoming purely external as it was severed from what gives it truth. This gap between words and reality resulted in a loss of knowledge both of self and the world.[156] Thus, the fall described in Genesis was a fall into external signs, a fall into a world where the only way toward the inward spring of truth was by means of external signs. The quest for truth ever since has been labor under the curse, a toiling with verbal signs akin to Adam's tilling of thorn-laden soil.[157]

As he wrote his first Genesis commentary, Augustine analyzed the problematic nature of postlapsarian teaching in a dialogue with his son Adeodatus.[158] When father and son reflected together, they considered how teachers naturally seek to accomplish their task with words as a kind of "external sign of the will."[159] In fact, teachers have no other resources since in a world reduced to outward appearances "nothing is taught without signs."[160] Cut off from the inner spring and unreceptive to inner teaching, signification remains the only medium available for their purpose. This presents the grave difficulty, however, that words only have meaning to the extent that the hearer already knows the thing to which the word refers and can connect the sign to its referent.[161] If hearers lack the requisite knowledge, they learn only signs from the signs expressed. From words, therefore, all they learn is the "sound and noise of words."[162] Teachers can vocalize words, but these bare sounds in no way convey understanding of the things to which they refer. If the external words are not met with inward comprehension, they remain nothing but sound. The external word itself cannot, as it were, teach from inside. Without clear firsthand knowledge of the realities to which words refer, one can only batter words about rhetorically—an enterprise "as entangled as interlocking one's fingers and rubbing them together, where hardly anyone but the person doing it can distinguish the fingers that itch from the fingers scratching the itch."[163]

The former rhetor declared somewhat surprisingly to his son, "Most of all I am trying to persuade you, if I shall be able to, that we do not learn anything by these signs called words."[164] Neither a sophistry concerned only with words nor naïve claims of transferring knowledge from one person to another can rightly be called teaching at all. If Adeodatus was to have access to truth itself rather than to signs about the truth, it would not be because someone else was ever able to communicate truth directly to him. No human teacher, not even his adept father, would be able through words or other forms of signification to exhibit truth to him as a kind of commodity. After searching, Augustine never uncovers "anything that can be exhibited through itself—except speaking."[165] As Augustine wrote his dialogue, he placed no more stock than Plato did in the efficacy of written words since they were properly understood to amount to nothing more than "signs of words rather than as words."[166] Augustine intended the reader of *De magistro* to perceive the utter futility of all human rhetoric. On its own it never amounts to more than the sound and noise of words.

Even as Augustine set out to discredit human language as a means of attaining the truth about anything, his dialogue with his son is framed by a discussion of Christ the teacher. Near the beginning of the dialogue, Augustine asked Adeodatus, "Does it not trouble you that when the supreme teacher (*summus magister*) was teaching his disciples to pray, he taught them certain words (*uerba*)?" Adeodatus responds that this fact did not disturb him at all because Christ "taught them not the words (*uerba*) [alone] but the things themselves (*res ipsas*) by means of the words (*uerbis*)."[167] While many of the propositions in the dialogue are asserted only to be overturned, this one never is. By the end of the dialogue, Augustine expects Adeodatus to understand why "we should call no one on earth teacher (*magistrum*), since there is one in heaven who is the teacher of all (*omnium magister*)."[168] Thus, to understand Augustine's dialogue the reader must discern how Christ was able to teach things by means of words rather than merely spouting sound and noise.

Once again, Augustine's commentary on Genesis sheds light on the matter. There, in figural language, he describes how the lack of the knowledge proceeding from inner springs creates the human need for external water. The earth needs "rain from clouds, that is, instruction by human words" so that in its parched state it may become green and flourish. According to Augustine, the external water that becomes inward water is Christ himself who "deigned to assume the cloud of our flesh and poured out most generously the rain of the holy gospel. He promised that anyone who drank of his water would return to that inner spring and no longer need to seek rain externally."[169] In this way, divine rhetoric overcomes the futility that afflicts human rhetoric. In *De magistro,* we understand something only when we consult "the Truth that presides within over the mind itself." In fact, as the mind ascribes meaning to words, it only understands truly that to which the words refer insofar as divine reason discloses it within.[170] Christ, the "supreme teacher" (*summus magister*), is the only teacher who teaches simultaneously without and within. He is both the external rain and the internal well of truth.

Augustine discredits human rhetoric as a means of attaining the truth only to bring it back again in a new form. As he leads his own son to recognize Christ as the only teacher, Augustine suggests to him that it is Christ who "prompts us by means of external signs through the instrumentality of human beings to turn to him internally and be instructed."[171] Human rhetoric functions properly when it directs attention to the divine rhetoric. In his own artfully constructed dialogue, Augustine modeled a type of instruction that was neither preoccupied with words alone in a sophistic manner nor naïve about their use and limited capacity to communicate the truth directly; a manner of teaching that redeems words by leading souls to apprehend the truth of the very things that invest them with meaning. Rather than teaching as it is conventionally understood, Augustine suggests that we would be better off idealizing the manner of speech that priests employ "for the sake of signifying what is in their minds: not that God might hear, but that in doing so, people might by remembering, with one accord, be raised to God."[172] Augustine recounts how "it often happens that someone denies something when questioned about it, and is brought around by further questions to admit it." This person's original judgment was mistaken on account of a "weakness of discernment" that is unable to "consult the light regarding the whole matter." One commonly observes how this weakness becomes less pronounced when she or he is prompted "part-by-part when questioned about the very parts that make up the whole." Leaning on the external assistance of such a guide, the one who is questioned "learns within, corresponding to his ability to do so."[173]

Guidance, thus, expands the student's partial perception not so much by offering words as the object of vision as by using them to direct attention to "the unchangeable power and wisdom of God, which every rational soul consults, but is disclosed to anyone, to the extent that he can apprehend it."[174] In this way, words "have force only to the extent that they remind us to look for things; they do not display them for us to know."[175] This force is by no means negligible. It is "a necessary but not sufficient condition of learning."[176] Augustine considered rhetoric's external words to be an essential external prompting that guides the soul where to direct its vision. It is an external mode of persuasion that strives to elicit participation in the learning process and invites the hearer to turn toward the truth "that presides within over the mind itself."[177]

Without the mediation of signs that lead the mind out of its isolated, self-satisfied inwardness, nothing can be learned. Without sufficiently attractive external objects of representation upon which the mind may gain its cognitive footing, it cannot find its own path to the real. As he conversed with Adeodatus about signs, in a conversation itself resembling the image of entwined fingers, Augustine paused and noted that it may appear that he has set up some detour by inquiring into signs rather than things. He admonished his son, nonetheless, that even though such conversation is indeed playful, it is by no means childish. It is playing with words, "not for the sake of playing around, but to exercise the mind's strength and sharpness, with which we are able not only to withstand but also to love the heat and light of that region where the happy life is."[178] By means of this very psychagogy, this enticing exercise in signs, he hoped that he and his son would be led to the truth, ultimately, not by his own art, but by "the guidance of God, the Truth itself, via stages" adapted to their weak steps.[179]

While Augustine completed his first writings in his native North Africa, his confidence was growing and he composed a work in which positions he had hitherto been content merely to allude to emerge boldly in full color. Augustine wrote that the "chief concern" of religion was "the dispensation of divine providence in time," that is, the manner in which God orchestrates creation for "the renewing and restoring of the human race."[180] The "Christian religion in our times" is nothing other than God's employment of "mutable creation . . . to remind the soul of its original and perfect nature," thus coming "to the aid of individuals, and indeed of the whole human race."[181] This creaturely psychagogy is necessary, according to Augustine, because of the human inability to distinguish truth from falsehood. The common human experience is one of being immersed in a kind of futility (*nuga*) of jests (*ioci*) and games (*ludi*) in which deception (*ficta*) delights us rather than truth (*uera*). Rescinding from the "primal objects of beauty" (*primis pulchris*) that structure reality itself, we embrace instead our own "fictional imaginings" (*phantasmata*).[182] The divine rhetoric is nothing less than God's subversion of our "futile and deceptive games" (*nugatorios et deceptorios ludos*) by means of a "truly liberal and noble game" (*uere liberali et ingenuo ludo*).[183] Providence itself has deigned to make for us steps to "teach us by means of sound and letters, by fire and smoke and cloudy pillar, as by visible words. So with parables and similitudes in a fashion God played with us when we were children, and sought to heal our inward eyes by smearing them with clay."[184]

God's providential ordering of creation is most visible in the fleshly rhetoric of the incarnation where God "showed carnal people, given over to bodily sense and unable with the mind to behold the truth, how lofty a place among creatures belonged human nature, in that he appeared not merely visibly . . . but as a true man."[185] Much as Augustine had theoretically set aside rhetoric only to have it reclaimed by divine Wisdom, the five bodily senses are given a role by divine providence as means of perceiving the "works of God" (*opera dei*), that is, the incarnate suasions of divinity.[186] In this way, rather than a speculative science only, God offers in Christianity "a kind of temporal therapy" so that we may "strive, by means of the carnal forms which detain us, to come to know those of which carnal sense can bring us no knowledge."[187] By means of this psychagogy of material creatures, God influences creation while doing "nothing by violence, but everything by persuasion and admonition."[188] It is this "art of God's ineffable medicine that turns even the foulness of human vices into something that has a beauty of its own."[189]

Having emphasized the priority of God's rhetorical economy, Augustine argued that Christian religious rites and methods of instruction should be preferred to all others since they were effective in bringing about the very ideals to which the most venerated classical philosophers aspired but failed to attain. Christianity has more resources than previous traditions in that it is no mere school philosophy, but the religion of the Wisdom of God that has become incarnate in human nature and thereby liberated it.[190] Christian teaching derives its effectiveness from its inclusion within the broader divine economy which continually seeks "to heal souls" by adopting "all kinds of means suitable to the times."[191] However much the teaching of the philosophical schools in antiquity differed from one another, Augustine contended that they had in common that none of their teaching made enough of an impact to cause any of the philosophically educated to cease to participate in the common religious rites. What they "observed along with the people in the way of religious rites was something quite different from what they defended in private, or even in the hearing of the people."[192] Socrates, although bolder than the others, "venerated images along with his people." Augustine contended that neither he nor Plato were ever able "to change the minds of their fellow-citizens and convert them from idolatrous superstition and worldly vanity to the worship of the true God." The great founders of the philosophical schools ultimately did "not dare to preach to the people." They "yielded to popular custom" rather than bring the populace over to a more enlightened form of thinking and living.[193] However noble and true were the ideals of the Greek philosophers, they lacked an effective psychagogy to incarnate those ideals and truly heal the fissures troubling soul and society.

According to Augustine, Christians suffer from no such fissure between their cognitive and religious lives. Indeed, they do not separate "philosophy, that is, the pursuit of wisdom" from "religious rites" at all. The one is so deeply implicated in the other that Christians are unable to share their sacramental rites with those whose doctrines they do not approve.[194] Rather than saying one thing privately and doing another publicly, Christian priests liturgically expound the precepts of Christianity "every day in the churches." "Multitudes" have as a consequence entered "upon this way of life from every race."[195] "In cities and towns, castles and villages, country places and private estates, there is openly preached and practiced such a renunciation of earthly things and conversion to the one true God that daily throughout the entire world the human race makes response: Lift up your hearts to the Lord."[196] Augustine argued that the rise of Christianity was opening up in his day a conspicuous gap between the "timid conjectures of the [philosophically enlightened] few and the obvious salvation and correction of whole peoples."[197] Christianity, moreover, offers a "natural discipline" that is "worthy of the complete faith of less intelligent

Christians, and for the intelligent it is free from error." True to the best classical traditions "it teaches partly quite openly and partly by similitudes in words, deed, and sacrament. It is accommodated to the complete instruction and exercise of the soul."[198] "Great and spiritual men" of the Catholic Church "earnestly feed the multitude of those who are weak and needy with copious supplies of milky food." The "few who are wise they feed with stronger meats," speaking "wisdom among the perfect" while withholding what is not yet digestible for the "carnal and psychics."[199]

Given what divine providence has wrought, Augustine contended that the Christian calling was nothing less than "to perfect human nature as God made it before we sinned."[200] He imagined that if the founders of the classical schools were given the opportunity to view Christianity's noble aim along with its comparatively more effective and sophisticated methods, they would "change a few words and sentiments" and "become Christians, as many Platonists of recent times have done."[201] Christianity offers the very security imagined in their philosophies but unrealized in their lives as God's guidance ably turns the hardships of life to human advantage.[202] Augustine concedes, "We want to be unconquered and rightly so, for the nature of our mind is unconquerable though only as we are subject to God in whose image we are made."[203] He knew, as well as the philosophers did, the difficulty of achieving such invulnerability. He pointed out that one need only to witness one's emotional life for a few moments to know the soul to be as mutable in time as the body is in space.[204] To counter such instability, Augustine appealed to a hallowed Platonic metaphor saying that in order to rise above such things it is necessary for the mind to take command of this situation like a charioteer—"let him get back into his place in the chariot, and take control of the reins, and tame his horses and rule them more cautiously."[205]

Accordingly, to reach "our pristine and perfect nature" requires us to "resist carnal custom" and "hate" the carnal features of relationships to such an extent that we would be able to show no more preference for our own children than we do for others because we love in them not our own personal advantage but the rational souls they share with us.[206] In this way, one can never lose what one loves, because what one loves most in others, one already possesses in oneself.[207] Augustine assures his readers that it is human beings who "love what cannot be taken from them" that are thereby "rendered unconquerable and perfect."[208] They are able to help others without needing them. The needs of a man like this are met by God alone, and by this love such a man flourishes. No vicissitude can take this from him. He, then, becomes "most truly and certainly an unconquerable man (*inuictus homo*)" not "to merit any extra good thing, but because nothing but clinging to God is itself good."[209]

As Augustine pondered such things from the safety of his community in Thagaste, he exchanged letters on philosophical topics with his friend Nebridius. Nebridius had been with him in Milan and sought (unsuccessfully) to persuade Augustine to carry his enterprise away from his hometown to Carthage. In one of the letters, Augustine entertains the possibility of "growing godlike in retirement."[210] He concedes that there are a "few" administrators of the Church who are able to carry out their duties while remaining free from anxiety. As for himself, he writes that he finds it "impossible without the aid of such carefree leisure to taste and love that only true good."[211]

In a short five years after his conversion to Christianity, Augustine had both permanently abandoned his teaching of secular rhetoric and thoroughly revised the very traditions he used to teach by systematically integrating them into a particularly Christian understanding of the universe. However much he may have wished to enjoy this moment of personal and intellectual maturity, death robbed Augustine both of his friend Nebridius and his nineteen-year-old son, Adeodatus.[212] It had not been long since he had lost his mother Monnica. When the news of his mother's death spread, people came to comfort a man that appeared to rise above such a loss and showed no signs of grief—neither shedding a tear nor even changing the expression on his face.[213] He later confessed, nevertheless, that it felt like his "soul was wounded" and his life was "torn to pieces." Feeling deep grief, he was ashamed of what "power these human frailties" still had over him after all his laborious training. Tears flowed later, but only when he was alone.[214] It was not these heartrending losses alone, however, that would shatter his philosophical leisure forever. It was yet another crisis beyond his control. After that seismic event, there would never again be a protected retreat in which to grow godlike and entertain notions of invulnerability. Rather than lifting him above the human condition's suffering and grief, the desire for God would lead him further into it.

Chapter Five

A New Context for
Classical Therapy

*If these problems disturb you as they disturb me, discuss them
with some kind doctor of the heart (cordis medico), whether you find one there
where you live or when you go to Rome every year.*

—Augustine, *ep.* 95.6

Ordination Crisis

While in Rome in 388, prior to his departure for North Africa, the recently
baptized Augustine wrote a treatise extolling the superior way of life found
among various groups of Catholic Christians. The active life of bishops,
priests, and deacons is depicted by him as "exceptionally difficult" (*difficil-
limus*) since it is lived out under circumstances that make it problematic
"to hold to the best way of life, and to maintain tranquility of mind." They
have "under their care, not only the healthy, but those in need of cure, and
the vices of the crowd must be borne with in order that they may be cured."
In contrast to those Christians who live their lives in other forms of community more friendly to the virtuous life, the ordained live like physicians
in the midst of a "plague."[1]

His awareness of the difficulties and dangers of ordained ministry combined with his love of philosophical leisure gave him ample incentive to do his utmost to avoid ordination. In a later sermon given on the anniversary of his ordination he reminisced, "So much did I dread the episcopate, that since I had already begun to acquire a reputation of some weight among the servants of God, I would not go near a place where I knew there was no bishop. . . . I came to this city to see a friend. . . . It seemed safe enough because the place had a bishop. I was caught, I was made a priest, and by this grade I eventually came to the episcopate."[2] Augustine was publicly overwhelmed with tears at his ordination to the priesthood. Possidius recounts that some of those present thought that he was crying because he really wanted to be a bishop and not a mere priest. Instead, Augustine's tears "bemoaned the many great dangers to his way of life that he anticipated would come crowding in on him."[3]

He would now spend the rest of his years as that physician of souls living amid the epidemic raging among the diseased. Now for him, the "safe harbor of philosophy" was replaced with unending pastoral tasks.[4] Rather than days filled with pleasing discussions of what cultivates human flourishing, he arbitrated lawsuits, interceded for prisoners, and ransomed those who were kidnapped.[5] This transition from the philosophic retreat begun at Cassiciacum to the priesthood, and eventually to the episcopate, however, amounted to something more than an anguished move from a life of contemplation to one of action. Augustine's means of coping with this crisis was to make his new life a subject of inquiry. "His intellectual interests" persevered, but were "transformed by his new duties."[6] Rather than causing him to reject his earlier learning or ideals, his forced ordination made possible the recontextualizing of his previous work. He would bring his years of reflection on spiritual guidance and personal reform to an arena they were never imagined to serve. Indeed, soon after his ordination to the priesthood, he wrote a letter to his bishop, Valerius, that makes clear that experience in ordained ministry only confirmed his earlier belief that "nothing in this life, especially at this time, is more difficult, more laborious, or more dangerous than the office of bishop or priest or deacon."[7] He contended that as a priest he had "learned much, very much more" than he had expected; the priesthood had especially exposed the limits of his previous "skill and strength" and showed him his "weakness."[8] He proceeded to inform Valerius that although he knew and held with firm faith all that is necessary for his own salvation, he was still inquiring how "to make use of this for the salvation of others."[9] To do this he requested a time of retirement to study "all [of God's] remedies in the scriptures" so that he could be better prepared for his new duties armed not merely with his own skill, but rather with "the most salutary counsels" of the scriptures.[10]

After this retreat seeking "all [of God's] remedies in the scriptures," Augustine's mature reformulated psychagogy emerges most visibly. Soon after his ordination, he wrote to Honoratus, a friend from his days as a Manichaean auditor who had not followed him into the Catholic Church. In the treatise produced from this situation, *De utilitate credendi,* Augustine mounts a striking attack on the guidance that persuaded him and Honoratus to become Manichaeans and contrasts it with the Catholic guidance he had come to believe was superior. He outlines to Honoratus his view of the complexity "of finding and retaining truth," admitting that "nothing is easier" than "not only saying but even thinking that one has found truth, yet how difficult it is to realize in reality."[11]

He recalls that in those days as auditors they were striving to form opinions that were truer than those generally held by "the crowd of believers."[12] Indeed, he says to Honoratus, "[Y]ou know that for no other reason did we fall in with such people than that they kept saying . . . that they would lead to God any persons who willingly listened and free them from all error." What made this promise especially seductive to Augustine and his young friends was the assurance given them that such enlightenment could be attained without being forced to submit to any external authority. Their Manichaean teachers would lead them to the truth by rational explanations alone.[13] Conceding that "the human soul naturally rejoices at this promise [of reason]," Augustine queries, "Who would not be enticed by these promises?"[14] Having been seduced by such beguiling words, how could they have known that what they were being subjected to was in fact the "false promise of reason" (*false pollicitatione rationis*) that would eventually amount to nothing more than "untold thousands of fables?"[15]

Catholicism, burdened especially with scandalous tales in the Old Testament, appeared far less sophisticated than Manichaeanism. Augustine recounts how Honoratus "knows well" a favorite strategy of the Manichaeans where they would find fault with the Catholic faith, "disturbing the unlearned chiefly by tearing apart and shredding the Old Testament." Augustine concedes that this strategy is effective because there are certain things in the Old Testament that appear offensive to the uneducated majority. These passages "can be attacked from a popular point of view," especially because there are few who can defend them "on account of the mysteries which they contain." The "very few" who understand and can defend them usually "have no love for public and much advertised contests of debate, and, for this reason, they are little known except to those who seek them out most urgently."[16] This Manichaean rhetorical strategy was made all the more persuasive by its accompanying argument that the Catholic Church's commendation of the Old Testament is indicative of the general problem that "it commands its adherents to believe," that is, it promotes faith rather than rational understanding. The Manichaeans, by contrast, "do not impose the yoke of believing on their followers, but rather reveal the source of their teaching."[17]

Augustine introduces the contours of his alternative to Manichaean guidance, and its justification of faith as a necessary mediator of the mind's rational apprehension, by retracing autobiographically the steps that led him to Catholicism. He tells Honoratus that after they had parted, he began to doubt the Manichaean promise of a directly rational apprehension of truth. He confesses that after his disappointing encounter with "that man" who possessed "a certain eloquence" but could not solve his difficulties, "often it seemed to me that it [the truth] could not be found, and the mighty waves of my thoughts were carried on to favor the Academics."[18] Instead of remaining in skepticism, however, he decided that it was the *way* of seeking the truth that was unavailable to his mental perception rather than the truth itself; therefore, the way to truth would have to be revealed by some divine authority.[19]

His newfound convictions that truth existed and that an authoritative intermediary would provide the entrance to it were, nevertheless, of limited use since they provided no basis for discriminating between the contradictory claims of competing authorities. As Augustine says, amid "such great disagreements" where "everyone promised to deliver" the truth, "there grew up before me a forest yielding no way of escape."[20] His incapacity to discern the way to the truth left him "with nothing but to appeal to Divine Providence" with "tearful and piteous cries."[21] It was eventually "some arguments of the Bishop of Milan" that created in Augustine the desire to inquire, of all places, into many things concerning the very authority upon which he used "to invoke curses," the Old Testament itself. After his encounter with Ambrose's homilies, he decided to become a catechumen in the Church. Augustine concludes his autobiographical reflections on the way he came to the truth by exhorting Honoratus that if he has any "care for his soul" that he ought similarly to follow "the path of Catholic teaching."[22]

It is important to observe that Augustine describes his personal turning from Manichaeanism to Catholicism not as simply the replacement of one body of directly apprehended truth claims with another. Quite deliberately he invites Honoratus to join him in following *a path* of inquiry. Even as a priest, Augustine does not offer to Honoratus the truth as if it were some kind of possession. Instead, echoing Plato's metaphor of the cave, Augustine describes his current state:

> Night and day I try to gaze upon Him, and, with the eyes of my soul damaged, both because of my sins and because of my being habituated to the plagues of spiritless opinions, often with tears I recognize my own weakness. It is like what happens after a long period of blindness and darkness. The eyes are barely opened and they still refuse the light, blinking and turning away from it, even though it is what they desire — especially if anyone tries to show them the sun itself. This is what is now happening to me, for I do not deny that there is a certain ineffable and singular good of the soul which is seen with the mind, but with sighs and tears I confess that I am not yet fit to contemplate it.[23]

Augustine, the priest, presents himself to Honoratus as *one of the guided* rather than as the *guide*.[24] Augustine does not offer himself as a guide who is capable of delivering the Catholic equivalent of the Manichaean promise of reason. Instead, he invites Honoratus to join a Christian community engaged in a disciplined seeking after wisdom that remains tempered by its awareness of its continuing weakness.

Augustine's alternative to Manichaean guidance is firmly grounded in the classical philosophical tradition, especially in the manner in which it employs the finite mediations of human guidance to extend the cognitive operations of the mind and the yearning of the human spirit. He tells Honoratus of the utter necessity of finding a reliable spiritual guide: "As long as we are fools" who are seeking a good and religious life "nothing remains to us except to seek out the wise."[25] The wise who are to be sought are "those in whom there is, as much as humanly possible, a solid comprehension and knowledge both of human nature itself and of God, and a life and habits that accord with this knowledge."[26] Every life that falls outside this definition, including Augustine's own, is numbered by him among the fools. Just as Augustine was left with nothing but his own incapacity after he had become disenchanted with Manichaeanism but before he had come to see the truth of the Catholic faith, so also the not-yet-wise have no resources to recognize wisdom even when it is found. Without wisdom one is in need of a guide, yet unless one is already wise, one cannot recognize who it is that is wise. As Augustine says, "I do not at all see" how the foolish "can clearly distinguish and recognize" the wise, for "there are no signs whatever by which they can recognize something, unless they know the thing itself of which these are the signs."[27] Consequently, under the influence of Manichaeanism, Honoratus attacks scriptural books that are "holy and full of divine things." Augustine asserts, "If anything appears there which seems absurd, you, like all foolish people, do not find fault with yourself for being slow and having a mind corrupted by the filth of this world, but rather find fault with those books which, perhaps, are simply unintelligible to minds such as yours." According to Augustine, the wisdom of such authoritative books appears "absurd" to Honoratus because he attacks them "without a guide" (*sine duce*), and dares "to pass judgment upon them without a teacher!"[28]

Augustine points out that Honoratus would not take up a difficult author such as Terentianus Maurus "without a teacher." Indeed, he says that to understand any poet, grammarians such as "Asper, Cornutus, Donatus, and countless others are consulted."[29] Not even Virgil would appear praiseworthy without the "recommendation of our forebears" and teachers with understanding.[30] Accordingly, he counsels Honoratus, saying, "You should seek out someone both good and learned, or one who would be considered such by common consent, that through his teachings you might become better and more learned by his instruction." He continues by asserting that even though such a guide is not easily found, every effort should be expended upon the search, even if it necessitates travel by land or sea to faraway places.[31]

The unguided reader of the Old Testament will not understand it because she or he will judge it by pre-established standards of rationality that have been uncritically accepted. Without guidance anyone is vulnerable to being deceived by superficial teachers who rely exclusively on the impressions and images supplied by the five senses. According to Augustine, even when they claim access to truth not dependent on the senses, they inevitably think that they can "accurately measure the ineffable mysteries of truth" by what turns out to be "the fatal and utterly false standard" (*mortifera et fallacissima regula*) supplied by the impressions and images given them by sensation.[32] The uncritical acceptance of such a standard leads the reader to evaluate the Old Testament as "apparently of no value," or even worse, to spurn it as "old wives' tales" in favor of the specious promise of "pure and open truth."[33] This error leaves one with what Augustine calls, "your reason," and by that he is not referring to the universal reason that orders the universe, but a purported rationality that amounts to nothing more than a particular social construct.[34]

Just as Plato's Socrates argued that passing on wisdom was not "like water, which always flows from a full cup into an empty one," so Augustine insists that the Manichaeans do not have an adequate view of what it takes to lead a soul that is "immersed and entangled in error and foolishness" into wisdom.[35] In this way, Augustine builds upon his early dialogues' complex epistemic explorations of rhetoric's limited capacity and inescapable necessity. He portrays the Manichaean promise "to guide us by means of reason" (*ratione ducturos*) as a kind of sophistry that tempts the human soul that has not considered its own strength and health to try "to get the food of the strong, which is prescribed harmfully except for the strong," and thereby "rushes right in to the poisons of the deceivers."[36] Augustine had come to see Manichaean guides as differing little from Plato's Protagoras who would sit in the marketplace bragging, "Young man, this is what you will get if you study with me: The very day you start, you will go home a better man, and the same will happen the day after, and the day after that."[37]

For Augustine the priest, in accord with the traditions of philosophical therapy he inherited, the apprehension of wisdom was far more indirect than being taught straightforwardly the "pure and open truth."[38] Just as one has to come to appreciate the persuasive force of Virgil with a skilled teacher in a community that commends this text, a similar incremental process is at work where the student comes to find truth compelling. Augustine states that although nothing "is more pleasant and familiar to our eyes than the light of day," after "prolonged darkness they cannot bear or endure it." In such a situation, the extreme difficulty of the task of seeing itself "exercises the mind of the inquirer (*mentem quaerentis exercet*) to grasp and display what it finds."[39] Augustine suggests that the dynamics involved in learning the truth are fundamentally the same as gradually regaining one's sight or, for that matter, recovering from any illness. It simply does not suit the human condition to be fed strong food immediately. While the sick are convalescing, they are "restrained and prevented from indulging in the full portions of the healthy," so that "by means of the food itself," they do not bring harm on themselves and "relapse into the very disease which caused them to repudiate it."[40]

Augustine proposes that we learn from the form of instruction given by Christ to his followers. He observes that what is seen there is not a "showing to fools a complete disclosure of reason as it concerns God," but a Christ whose "first and greatest wish was to be believed" because those with whom he was dealing "were not yet fit to receive the divine secrets." Indeed, according to Augustine, Christ worked miracles "for no other reason than that he might be believed." In this way, "he guided fools by faith" applying "the medicine which was to heal the most corrupt customs."[41] Augustine defines a miracle as "anything that is so difficult or extraordinary that it appears to be beyond the expectations or abilities of those who marvel at it. Among events of this kind, there is nothing better suited for the populace and for fools in general than what affects the senses." Since it is not easy for the foolish in need of guidance to recognize the wise through reason, it was necessary to present certain miracles to the very eyes that fools readily use. Christ's miracles were a means by which "divine authority" adapted itself rhetorically to the ordinary perception of the foolish to "turn the wandering souls of mortals to itself."[42] Faith in the reports of their own physical eyes about Christ's external acts would grow in his followers so as to purify their "lives and habits" and promote in them a further ascent eventually beyond ordinary perception toward real intellectual and spiritual understanding. Christ's incarnation was for Augustine precisely the paradigmatic miracle that makes possible the mind's traveling through ordinary perception toward greater insight. Augustine questions, "What could have been done more kindly and generously by God than that the very Wisdom of God, pure, eternal, unchangeable, to whom we must cling, should condescend to take on human form?" The very Wisdom of God that cannot presently be perceived directly by human beings took on flesh, adapting himself to the weak powers of human sensory perception, so as to "suffer those things which deter us from following God," and to entice us positively to fall in love with God.[43] Unlike a merely human guide, who strives to live a life in conformity with wisdom while being most careful "that hope be not placed in him," the incarnate

Wisdom is itself "the healthiest authority" and the "first way of uplifting our minds from their dwelling on earth." It alone makes possible "the turning (*conuersio*) to the true God from the love of this world."[44]

Thus, for the recently ordained Augustine, Catholic Christology supplied the logic legitimating genuine therapeutic practice. Appropriate guidance is defined christologically as divine Wisdom adapting itself to the weak perceptive powers of human beings who lack both wisdom and the criteria by which to recognize it. Catholics teach that the Old Testament is to be believed because scripture is understood analogously to Christology. In the Old Testament as well as in the incarnation, truth appears, to the mind that is entangled in error and dependent on ordinary sense perception, in a form accommodated to that condition. Describing the Old Testament as "something lofty and divine," Augustine says, "Truth is there entirely, and a discipline best adapted to the renewal and restoration of minds, which is so simply ordered that everyone can draw from it what is sufficient for his needs if only he comes to partake devoutly and faithfully as true religion demands."[45]

Rather than measuring the Old Testament by a "fatal and utterly false" preunderstanding of truth, Augustine invites Honoratus to receive it as an authoritative text whose purpose is to exercise the mind and purify it of its habitual misperception of itself and the world. In so doing, the truth can then eventually disclose itself through its mediations to the prepared mind. He states that faith "in those things which we do not yet grasp" liberates the believer from a life based on mere "opinion."[46] Augustine implies that passages that readers find offensive should be understood as accommodated speech conforming to psychagogic ideals. He asks, "What if those matters which are seen to offend those unpracticed in these same scriptures were put there for this purpose, that when there should be read matters abhorrent to the feelings of ordinary people, not to speak of the wise and holy, we should much more diligently look for an inner signification?"[47] Just as faith in the fleshly life of Christ could become the path to understanding and loving his divinity, so also the letter of scripture provides the opportunity to turn to a purer understanding.

The Manichaean rejection of the Old Testament is therefore, according to Augustine, clear evidence of deep-seated misunderstandings both of the workings of the human mind and the divine economy. By assuming that human beings can be guided directly "by pure and simple reason," they fail to see the salvific value of the psychagogic speech of scripture.

The pretense of a purely rational guidance apart from the God-given authority of the full scripture only leads to further deception because such a promise leaves the student insufficiently critical of ordinary experience and language. Honoratus has not been led by them into the depths of his own experience, and, therein, "to find fault" with the "slowness and worldly corruption" of his own "mind."[48] In this way, Augustine argues that the "rational" religion of the Manichaeans, in fact, never passes beyond a superficial, carnal reasoning process. Contrary to its promise, it never actually succeeds in teaching how to form opinions truer than the general crowd of believers. By over-leaping Reason's mediations in their coarsest Old Testament form and promising in their place the subtle, rational "food of the strong," Manichaeism deprives itself of the very therapeutic exercises necessary to purify the mind.

Augustine's worry that unaided human reason will be insufficiently critical of customary experience leads him to qualify the more classical model of "reason for the few" and "belief for the many." He argues, first of all, that for those who accept this model there is no safe way to proceed as long as they assume that they belong to the few who are capable of a rational apprehension of God. Even if such gifted people exist, they would have no way of ensuring that they were not deceiving themselves under the pretense of rationality: "There is scarcely anyone who accurately assesses his own abilities."[49] Second, he explains to Honoratus that no one else could confirm for him that he was one of the few, since "as a human being, you would not be able to disclose to another the inner recesses of your soul so as to be completely known."[50] Finally, even if one could know, or another could know, those taking such a path to the truth would be socially irresponsible, since others of lesser ability would be harmed when tempted to imitate their example. For these reasons, Augustine informs Honoratus that pursuing an elitist path to reason is to be "a source of danger to yourself and an example of rashness to others."[51]

Instead, Augustine proposes a single road for all types of persons to travel. He expects Honoratus to agree with him that the many unlearned are "brought gradually by certain steps to those innermost mysteries" and will "in no other way attain to pure truths" than by coming to them "with the mind of a suppliant, obeying certain important and necessary precepts, and completely purging himself by a certain way of life." Augustine, nonetheless, contends that, even for the few, there could not be a "more healthful way than first to become fitted for the reception of truth by accepting in faith those things which have been divinely appointed to prepare and to cultivate the mind." The learned few and the unlearned many are guided along the same path as they "go the indirect way (*circuire*) where it is safest to enter."[52] Rather than the learned and the unlearned engaging in two different types of exercises, reason and faith, Augustine proposes a single progressive exercise for all types of souls beginning with faith and striving for understanding.

In summary, Augustine's polemic against Manichaean guidance amounts to an argument that their spiritual direction—by being unable to accommodate itself to the psychic states of all hearers—falls short of therapeutic imperatives established since classical antiquity. Catholic guidance, however, especially in its use of the Old Testament, not only meets the classical standards, but perfects them in an unprecedented manner. Christians find in scripture, as in the incarnate Christ, authoritative truth adapted to their weak perceptive powers. Rather than the province of the rational few, belief in such accommodated truth makes possible for the many both a critical reassessment of customary judgments and the positive yet gradual ascent "to those innermost mysteries."

Controversies over the Cure of Soul

During his episcopacy, Augustine engaged opponents in unrelenting, decades long, verbal conflict that included public debates and exhaustive treatises. There can be little doubt that through these polemics he sought to influence the shape of both Christianity and the Roman Empire. It is gravely reductive, however, to construe Augustine's concern for orthodoxy and the Catholic Church only as means of extending his own authority and that of his colleagues. If the man and his ideas are to be grasped in their complexity, it is necessary to discern why he felt so strongly that the beliefs he argued for (and not others) were true and the very ones that contributed to the well-being of individuals and communities.

Although deeply formed by the instruction he received from others early in his life, as he matured Augustine was in a large measure self-taught. He was known to have remarked that he not only read Aristotle by himself, but also understood him.[53] One suspects that much of his reading of the Platonic books was also alone. He was a man who had in fact come quite far relying on his own inner resources in ordering his life and in acquiring an understanding of himself and the world. When the public first read the *Confessions* of the bishop of Hippo, they were introduced to a man who exclaimed, "See, I do not hide my wounds!"[54] Rather than extolling the future progress to be made in the philosophic life, this writer confessed past failures and claimed not to know which temptations he could resist and which ones he could not.[55] He asserted that when his conscience made confession, it had to rely daily on God's mercy rather than on its own integrity.[56] From his earliest writing, Augustine was a man who had emphasized the human soul's ongoing dependence upon divine grace for both its survival and flourishing, but he now no longer believed that grace would produce in him wholeness and self-sufficiency. He came to believe, instead, that it was this very dependence upon grace that freed the soul to embrace its limits and be its insufficient self. Only when the heart was "aroused by love" to delight in the "sweetness" of grace, did the soul find the strength it has in weakness.[57]

As he reflected upon the manner in which he had been overwhelmed with grief at his mother's death, he felt the need to fend off critics who would "arrogantly" (*superbe*) interpret his tears as falling short of some ideal of self-control. The bishop suggested that they would be better served by weeping themselves.[58] He lamented that the quest of philosophers had led them by "the arrogance of their learning" to "inflate their chests rather than beat their breasts."[59] Instead of promoting further exercises to augment the mind's sovereignty, Augustine now sought to become proficient in exercises that trained the mind to find its happiness by subordinating itself to God.[60] It was God alone who was able "to exercise rule without pride."[61] One wonders if those early readers noticed how different this man was from the one who had imagined freeing the soul from its dependence on the external world by cultivating its rational faculties to such an extent that everything necessary for happiness would be possessed internally?

As a bishop, Augustine continued to believe that passion and sin often go hand in hand whenever the soul's non-rational, lower faculties failed to follow its higher ones. He, nevertheless, came to identify the soul's sin less with a loss of self-control than with its active grasping to impose an order of its own making upon itself or others. Thus, not only passionate excess but also philosophic asceticism could be equally misguided as attempts to cure the soul of what ails it. In one of his most widely read works, he described the perfectly modulated self of the Stoic sage as a kind of "stupor."[62] He openly criticized the effects of the boundary carefully constructed by Stoics between the self's pure, internal, rational functioning and the haphazard mixture of external experience. Augustine worried that in seeking by such means to achieve "tranquility" they had in fact lost their "humanity."[63] He pointed out that "insensitivity is no guarantee of health" and perhaps should be considered itself a state of moral deformation.[64] He asserted that if our philosophical ideals imply "a condition in which there is no fear to terrify, no pain to torment, then it is a condition to be shunned in this life."[65] The attempt to become, as it were, "grounded in oneself" was for him not health, but a proud and "perverse kind of exaltation."[66]

If such strategies succeed in insulating the self from the intrusions of chance, how do they not also exclude divine love that transcends both one's expectations and capacity to grasp it? Augustine's mature works imply a sense of identity as substantial as anything that he achieved by philosophical means, but one that was more permeable and open as well. It would be a life filled with "fear and desire, pain and gladness in conformity with the holy scriptures and sound doctrine." In short, a life "exhibiting all those emotions" flowing in the right way.[67] He had a new ideal of embodied wisdom: a man whose tears shed over Jerusalem in no way diminished his perfection; a man whose "weakness resulted from his power."[68]

Augustine not only questioned the desirability of the human ends promoted by philosophy, but also the efficacy of the means employed to achieve them. He came to believe that purely cognitive interventions in the cure of soul were insufficient in themselves to free us from habits whose connections were woven in many cases prior to cognitive development. As discussed in the previous chapters, Augustine was not the first to consider the limitations of philosophical methods and strategies. The philosophical tradition that he inherited generally qualified its claims by stating certain preconditions for their effectiveness: namely, the necessity of a certain amount of early training, education, leisure, intelligence, etc. Cicero remarks unabashedly that the wise man "must be of outstanding intelligence; for virtue is not easily found to go with sluggish minds."[69] Such figures recognized the potential gap between one's knowledge and behavior, but contended that it could be crossed by effort, education, and training, as the soul was strengthened and the truth was internalized through exercises. After years of effort, Augustine believed that the gap between wisdom and lived experience was as intractable as ever, even when the best philosophical methods were employed under optimal conditions. After his philosophical leisure at Cassiciacum, he suspected that even among the elite philosophy could not produce what it intended. Philosophical learning alone could not accomplish all that Cicero promised. It would not single-handedly lead us from the darkness of opinions to the light of truth and through its exercises give us the ability to live accordingly. As a bishop, he continued to point to the inconsistencies in the lives of Plato and the Platonists to confirm this assessment.[70]

Little more than a decade after their composition, Augustine looked back on his writings from his Cassiciacum retreat and said that "they still breathe the spirit of the school of pride, as if they were at the last gasp."[71] He eventually felt that he had given too prominent a place to the liberal arts in the reform of soul. There were many people who had become saintly while knowing little of them and many who knew them well that had never reached sanctity.[72] The mature Augustine conceded that certain Platonic philosophers "have been able to direct the keen gaze of their intellects beyond everything created and to attain, in however small a measure, the light of unchanging truth." He asked, "What good does it do a man to gaze from afar on the home country across the sea?"[73]

Human knowing and willing were beset with such ignorance and difficulty that one did not necessarily follow from the other.[74] His understanding of the soul came to focus less on the mind's struggle to order unruly passions and desires than upon the effects its social nature had upon it. He came to imagine the character of Adam's temptation in the garden to be most fundamentally about defective companionship. Death, immoderate pleasure, and destructive lusts followed as a consequence of joining a community turned toward itself, bounded off from God. Augustine remarks poignantly that Adam fell to Eve's suggestion because "they were so closely bound in partnership." Adam became a "captive to sin" when he — out of love for "his life's companion" — joined her "in a companionship in sin."[75] Adam's failed attempt to preserve intimacy with Eve, thus, introduced a novel disjunction in the human soul — one in which human eros was tragically turned in on itself and isolated from its own perfection in its ultimate divine object. For the mature Augustine, sin derives its power less from individual weakness than from the manner in which our souls are embedded in the deeply flawed communities to which we owe our physical existence. It is thereby an unavoidable feature of our social lives and formation. Amid the complexity of such a situation, "we simply are not possessed of the power Plato supposed" to amend ourselves.[76] Neither is renewal to be found in isolating ourselves from others. This withdrawal would only perpetuate the same condition. The mature bishop believed that the healing process began by becoming incorporated into the Church: a remedial community not turned in upon itself, but turned toward Christ as the head of his broken body.[77]

Augustine, nevertheless, lived in a world where ideals more in accord with classical antiquity often co-existed happily with Christianity. Christianity could be seen as the very thing necessary to achieve in this life the Christian equivalent of pagan virtue, self-reliance, and autonomy. Although the bishop of Hippo no longer admired such a sage, others did. It is no surprise that he had misgivings when he read a well-written letter composed by a Christian teacher named Pelagius that exhorted the young virgin Demetrias to commit herself "to complete moral perfection" and "a heavenly life."[78] Pelagius begins the letter warning her that "the mind" tends to "become more negligent and sluggish in pursuit of virtue" the less confident it is "in its ability to achieve it, supposing itself not to possess something simply because it is unaware that it is present within." Pelagius continues by asserting that to begin "a holy and spiritual life" she will need to "recognize her own strengths." It is "the best incentive for the mind" to teach it "that it is possible to do anything which one really wants to do: in war, for example, the kind of exhortation which is most effective and carries the most authority is the one which reminds the combatant of his own strengths."[79]

Pelagius draws Demetrias' attention to the fact that "many pagan philosophers" have been "chaste, tolerant, temperate, generous, abstinent and kindly, rejecters of the world's honors as well as its delights, lovers of justice no less than knowledge." He tells her that if pagans could accomplish so much "without God" how much more should be achieved by those who have been instructed by Christ and aided by divine grace.[80] He admonished her, however, that "the ordering of a perfect life is a formidable matter, formidable, I say, and dependent for its success on a considerable degree of effort and study."[81] She will therefore need to engage in daily spiritual exercises as if in a gymnasium.[82] Doing the will of God follows naturally from knowing it, which takes precedence in time but not in terms of merit.[83] Pelagius encourages her that by doing this she will avoid "the broad path which is worn away by the thronging multitude" and enter upon "that narrow path to eternal life which few find."[84] She can in this manner "embellish her virginity with moral purity," knowing that the "only good possessions are those which we neither find nor lose at any time save by the exercise of our own free choice"[85]

Augustine's struggle with "Pelagianism" was no small controversy, because Pelagius was not wrong in seeing that there was an easy fit between the late antique quest for virtue and calls to Christian holiness. Pelagius— not without justification—claimed that his teaching was supported by Catholic leaders of no less stature than Ambrose of Milan and even Augustine himself in his earliest works.[86] As Pelagius called Christians to perfection, memories still lingered of times when Christians were so dedicated to their faith that they readily died for it. Augustine, nonetheless, believed that this call to a renewal of Christian effort was no remedy for the soul. It was something that would only worsen its condition. He saw Pelagius propagating a "cure" that appealed to the very pride and egotism that he had come to believe were the root of the soul's problems.[87]

While commenting on the appeal of Pelagius' instruction, Robert Markus situates it within "the crisis of identity which afflicted Western Christians in this time of mass-Christianization of Roman Society." According to Markus, Pelagius' teaching "offered a means of establishing one's Christian identity" through a moral migration from society. "Pelagius wanted his Christians to be as clearly defined and as distinct a group in society as the ascetics were in the Christian Church."[88] Pelagius wrote of the Church: "God wanted his people to be holy and averse to all contamination by unrighteousness and iniquity. He wanted it to be such, so righteous, so godly, so pure, so unspotted, so sincere that the gentiles might find nothing in it which they could criticize but only what they could admire."[89] There would, thus, be a perceivable social boundary defining the identity of the Church in a time when the boundaries were less than clear. The internal boundary within the self would provide an external boundary as well, distinguishing the Christian community from those whose behavior indicated that they did not belong to it.

Augustine's reaction to the ascetic elitism of Pelagius and his followers may well have been so virulent because of his continuing rejection of the rigid boundaries set by the form of Christianity that dominated North Africa during his upbringing. Augustine's family belonged to the minority of

North African Christians who remained in communion with the Roman Church while the majority, whom he referred to as the "Donatists," sought to separate themselves strongly from the Roman world. The "Donatists" were so well established in North Africa that for a number of years during Augustine's ministry in Hippo it was a town with two altars, divided households, and marriages.[90] Their concern for the purity of Christian ministry led them to reject the Catholic Church and its clergy as irretrievably compromised by its extensive participation in Roman governmental affairs and society. The Donatists strongly identified with the Church of the martyrs and sought to preserve that identity not so much by means of an internal boundary accompanied by Christian behavior, but by erecting a spatial boundary setting them apart from the Empire.[91] As Frend observes, "To become a Donatist . . . entailed the complete renunciation of pagan literature, knowledge, and way of life. One finds plenty of quotations from the classics in Augustine, but none in the works of Petilian and Emeritus, and almost none in Cyprian. . . . No wonder Donatists urged their Catholic compatriots to 'become Christians.' Nothing illustrates better the clash of ideas between the two Churches than their respective attitudes towards the Imperial Government and classical civilization."[92]

The Donatist bishops associated Catholics not with the martyrs, but with the *traditores:* those Christians who during the era of persecutions had handed the scriptures over to the Roman authorities intent on destroying them.[93] Catholics who joined their congregations would be rebaptized since the baptism they received from a polluted Catholic clergy was considered by them invalid. In joining the pure Church, Catholics needed to establish their new identity by being properly cleansed. This sense of pollution appears to have been so keenly felt by the Donatists that there are reports of them ritually scouring reclaimed church buildings with salt water, including washing the walls.[94] In response to the Donatists' linkage of the efficacy of baptism to the purity of its minister, Augustine exclaimed, "For I believe, not in the minister by whose hands I am baptized, but in Him who justifies the ungodly!"[95] He asserted, "No difference is made to the sanctity of baptism by the demerit of the individual who receives or confers it."[96] Augustine elaborated, "The baptism which is consecrated by the words of Christ in the Gospels is holy, even when conferred by the polluted, and on the polluted, however shameless and unclean they may be. This sanctity is itself incapable of contamination, and the power of God abides in his sacrament."[97] Moreover, "even when a sheep, which has wandered outside, has received the Lord's branding at the hands of dishonest robbers, and then comes into the security of Christian unity, it is restored from error, freed from captivity, and healed of its wound."[98]

Augustine felt that the Donatists and the Pelagians each shared a concern for Christian purity that was not so much entirely wrong as it was being asserted prematurely.[99] Augustine exhorted the Donatist bishop Petilian to "judge nothing before the time the Lord comes, who both will bring to light the hidden things of darkness and will make manifest the deliberations of the heart."[100] The Christian task in the present age was not, first of all, to avoid pollution and contamination. After all, the quest for such purity was the primary aim of the Manichaeans. Augustine had long insisted that our infirmities were not so much purged or split off from ourselves as *healed*.[101] Augustine saw the Church not as an island of holiness in a profane sea, but as a field spread throughout the world in which wheat and tares grow side by side awaiting the final harvest in which God will separate them on the threshing floor.[102] Rather than oppose the Church and Empire, Augustine preferred to think of two entwined communities spanning them both, "interwoven and intermixed in this era and awaiting separation at the Last Judgment."[103]

Augustine's valuing of the civil order provided by the Empire is evident in his response to the sack of Rome by Alaric in 410. The three days of pillaging of the Empire's first city was an event that threatened not so much the Church, but raised fears about the crumbling of civil order throughout the Empire. As refugees from Rome drifted into Carthage, Augustine traveled there to assure them and the Christians at Carthage that the secular order had not fallen: "The city that gave us birth in the flesh remains standing, thank God!" "Carthage remains" as well.[104] He pressed them, nonetheless, to examine their fear, "Why panic, just because earthly kingdoms crumble?"[105] Is it that they believed Virgil when he fictitiously had Jupiter promise the Romans a city with "no bounds of space or time, dominion without end?"[106] What was it that caused them to be deceived by words that were never intended by Virgil to be anything but flattery? Augustine explained that an informed reader knows that even Virgil believed that all earthly kingdoms were doomed by finitude, even the one founded by Romulus. What was shaken, then, according to Augustine, was not the Empire, but the arrogant pretensions and lies upon which it had come to rest.

As he spoke, Augustine strained to convince his hearers that they should not consider his unflinching description of the limits, finitude, and vulnerability of Rome an insult to the great city.[107] He was, rather, interceding for its redemption, expressing his longing for its spiritual birth, and its passing over into eternity.[108] He argued that Christianity was not the source of the Empire's vulnerability. In fact, far from weakening the fabric of society, Augustine argued that Christian faith, above all, made it possible to embrace the hard truth about the precarious nature of our political life and still to carry out responsibilities in the world. He contended that by not falsely locating their security in an eternal dominion that never was to be and anchoring instead their hope in faith, each of his hearers could live without despair or evasion as a fish that is "not broken or dissolved by the waves" it swims upon but "lives in the waves."[109] Augustine thus exhorted his hearers not to take these tragic events as reasons for despair, but, in fact, as portents of hope, for "nothing is so inimical to hope than to place it in things that are passing away."[110] On account of this faith, they could fulfill their duties to the broader society while maintaining a realistic assessment of its limitations and finitude.

Indeed, Augustine told his Christians that "in a sense we still belong to the old city" and are called by God "to make our passage over to Jerusalem," so that we have in the end one single homeland, one *patria*.[111] This ideal community, this "City of God," is "the perfectly ordered and completely harmonious fellowship in the enjoyment of God, and of each other in God."[112] Its final establishment, nevertheless, awaits a future age. No amount of human effort or ingenuity can bring it about. In the meantime, its norms leak back in history, exposing the ways contemporary civic life falls short of transcendent ideals, but also providing daily hope in the full reality of those ideals. Thus, in their affections, Augustine's Christians will be a community of exiles (*peregrinam societatem*) who are called out of all nations and whose identity is not reducible to Roman citizenship (their geographic home), but is determined more fundamentally by the object and quality of their love. This higher allegiance will not, however, mandate that they destroy local "practices, laws and institutions." In fact, insofar as these traditions have a place in the peaceful ordering of civil society and do not conflict with worship, Christians will "make use of earthly peace" and, for the time being, defend it for the preservation of human life.[113] Moreover, according to Augustine, the earthly state makes use of the faithful to be "its good citizens and its magistrates, its judges, generals, governors, and kings," even when this requires "a better person keeping faith with someone less good, in the knowledge that he or she will have to be in servitude for a time."[114] Augustine concedes that this "mixing together in the present age" sometimes brings it about that those who in no way belong to this exilic community wield temporal authority over it, that is, "certain persons who belong to the city of Babylon are in charge of affairs that concern Jerusalem."[115] In this way, Augustine eschewed simple dichotomies between Christian and non-Christian, between Church and Empire. He had come to imagine the Christian Church and every Christian soul to be less bounded, more permeable, and more ambiguous than did either Pelagius or Donatus.

In his deferral until the eschaton of the perfect ordering of human society and of the individual soul, appraisal of all perfectionist claims as a proud triumphalism, and emphasis on a prolonged process of healing grace, Augustine was a champion of the ordinary Christian and the ordinary means of grace available to all.[116] Near the end of his life, some monks of Hadrumetum worried that the logical conclusion of Augustine's teaching excluded human initiative. In this case, more specifically, they worried that Augustine's emphasis on the priority of divine grace excluded the usual paraenetic methods intended to prompt the soul toward amendment such as admonition, teaching, frank speech, and exhortation. Augustine paraphrased their objection: "[S]ince the will itself is prepared by the Lord, why do you admonish me when you see me unwilling to do His commands? Why do you not rather ask Him to effect in me the will to do them?"[117] Thus, at least one group among Augustine's first readers wondered whether his mature theological reflections had made the human teacher obsolete, along with the highly evolved methods of the classical tradition. Prayer, then, would always be more appropriate than guidance.[118]

The elderly bishop contended that anyone drawing this corollary from his theology of grace was mistaken. In his treatise, Augustine argued expansively for "both precept and prayer."[119] It is a fundamental theological misunderstanding of God's relationship to the world to see divine agency as competing in history with human agency and art. No matter how robust one's notion of divine grace is, its transcendent quality prevents it from being a simple substitute for human effort. The presence of the Divine

Word does not reduce the human voice to silence. It makes it possible to speak and understand. Augustine rhetorically pressed for the ongoing necessity of all pastoral methods with his interlocutor:

> For you are unwilling to have your faults pointed out to you; you are unwilling to have them lashed and to experience a salutary pain that would make you seek a physician. You are unwilling to have yourself shown to yourself so that you may see your own deformity and seek one to reform you and beg him not to leave you in your ugliness of soul. . . . One who is unwilling to be admonished (and who says, instead: 'Pray for me') is for this reason to be admonished, that he may himself act. As a matter of fact, the pain, which makes him displeasing to himself when he feels the sting of admonition, stirs him to desire more prayer. . . . This is the usefulness of admonition, administered more or less severely according to the diversity of sins; it is health-giving when the heavenly physician looks upon its administration.[120]

In this way, Augustine defended methods of spiritual guidance that sought to further self-knowledge and proper action as in no way incompatible with the work of the heavenly physician. He reminded the monks of Hadrumetum that the same one who out of his great love for the weak "made himself weak for the sake of all, and for the sake of all was in his weakness crucified" advocated the use of frank speech in the Christian community (Matt. 18:17).[121] For many years, Augustine himself had cared for the weak, nursing them with milk rather than feeding them solid food. In doing so he found his methods of spiritual guidance not to be at odds with the ongoing work of divine grace upon which they depended for their efficacy. He, in fact, devoted two theoretical treatises to improving Christian methods of the cure of soul so as to maximize the therapeutic potential latent in Christian scripture and liturgical traditions. These treatises are the subject of the following chapter.

Chapter Six

Signs Eliciting Love

There is nothing that invites love more than to be loved first.
—Augustine, *cat. rud.* 4.7

Exegetical Integration

In *De doctrina christiana* the contours of Augustine's mature psychagogic theory are worked out with the most precision and applied with the widest purview. Over the course of thirty years, Augustine came to write a book revising the very psychagogic tasks enumerated by Plato in the *Phaedrus*; namely, how one discovers truth (*modus inueniendi*) and passes it on to others (*modus proferendi*).[1] Although composed over such a span of time, *De doctrina christiana* is a unified work in which the salient topics of classical psychagogy are addressed in the form of instructions regarding methods of reading scripture fruitfully and communicating the results to others.[2] In it, the reading of scripture in an ecclesial context has become the primary avenue toward progress in the Christian life.[3] Psychagogic traditions continue to provide the structural features of Augustine's mature theory even as they have been transformed and put in service of his new context.

In the prologue, the bishop likens himself as the author of the book to an elementary language teacher who passes on skills of reading·that enable students to gain sufficient fluency to "be able themselves to apprehend the hidden meaning of a passage without any error."[4] He anticipates that some could oppose such an enterprise in principle. One objection comes from "Christians, who rejoice over their knowing the holy scriptures without human guidance" (*sine duce homine*).[5] Apparently, such objectors held an ideal such as the one exemplified by "the holy and perfect" Antony, who "is said to have memorized sacred scriptures simply by hearing them, without any training in reading, and understood their meaning."[6] Is not Christian knowledge simply "a divine gift" (*diuinum munus*) given directly rather than something so laborious and indirect as to be facilitated by rules and exercises such as those Augustine proposes?[7]

The bishop replies that scripture itself indicates that Christian knowledge is given in mediated form. He notes that although St. Paul had been "struck down and instructed by the divine and heavenly voice" itself, he was still "sent to a man to receive the sacraments and be joined to the church." Although the centurion Cornelius had spoken directly to an angel, that very angelic voice sent him to Peter for instruction.[8] The eunuch, perplexed at a passage in Isaiah, was not sent an angel; instead, Philip was prompted by God to be his exegetical guide, and "in human words and human language opened up to him what was hidden in that passage of scripture."[9] Augustine concedes that God surely could instruct every person directly, but explains that God, by responding to human beings through "human temples," dignifies the human condition by having "his word administered to human beings by other human beings."[10]

The bishop states that his opponents must at least grant him that they were taught by human beings the alphabet from an early age.[11] They had learned a language that was not just any one, but the particular one that they heard constantly spoken.[12] Therefore, their knowledge of sacred scripture is at least mediated by the very language it was written in and influenced by the human teachers that taught them to speak. Augustine's prologue alerts the reader to a feature of *De doctrina christiana* that informs it throughout: its attention to the effects of inherited traditions of human instruction; or, as it were, the cultural mediation of knowledge.[13] The prologue indicates that Augustine construes the human teacher who seeks to discover truth by reading the scriptures and to pass it on to others as an essential part of God's providential order, as well as his awareness that

Christian instruction occurs in a particular cultural context that power-fully influences the perception of both the guide and the student.

This positive affirmation of the necessity of human guidance in the di-vine order stands in tension with a rather severe view of the mixed quality of human influence in general on the formation of the individual. Al-though the dependence of human beings upon one another for instruc-tion is a good created by God, it also makes humans vulnerable to being deceived by each other. This vulnerability is especially pronounced since Augustine continued to view the ordinary governors of human conduct—social custom and habitual behavior—as untrustworthy, pernicious guides in life.

For example, in the first book of *De doctrina christiana,* the bishop writes that our bodies are "being dragged along by the chains of habit (*per consu-etudinis uinculum*), which have grown into a kind of law of nature (*natu-rae lege*), being rooted in the inheritance derived from our first parents."[14] Human beings are likened to exiles, who, although they can only be truly happy in their native country, become so "perversely captivated" along the way that they lose interest in it.[15] Their road back is blocked by their "love of inferior things."[16] Those who habitually set their affections on what is secondary and changeable, Augustine likens to the blind who do not perceive the sunlight enveloping them. "The sharpness of their minds" is "blunted by growing accustomed to the dark shadows of the flesh" so that they are "beaten back from their home country, as it were by the con-trary winds of crooked habits, going in pursuit of things that are inferior and secondary."[17] John Rist, among others, describes the manner in which Augustine began "to emphasize that we are habit forming creatures, for good and for ill, but more readily for ill; we live under the dominion and constant threat of 'carnal custom,' which forms a 'second nature.'"[18]

By not only rejecting the customary guides of human conduct, but also labeling them as harmful, Augustine, like his philosophical predecessors who did the same, needed to provide an alternate guide. At this point, they appealed to the speech of the philosopher that was adapted to the state of the hearer that would facilitate the hearer's own construction of a proper scale of value in the mind. Through this process the student would find a stable criterion of critical judgment from which it would be-come possible to evaluate the various cultural options, discover truth, and act accordingly. Having come to believe that a purely human guidance has proven incapable of effecting this needed reorientation of the human person, Augustine is unable to follow his predecessors by appealing to philosophy *per se,* or to the refined skills of the philosophical guide. Augustine, instead, asserts that divine Wisdom will gain the attention of those far from it through its own active expression in the flesh of Christ and in the scriptures and sacraments that tell of Christ. Augustine exclaims, "Wisdom itself" took on the qualities of the ideal psychagogue deciding "to adapt itself even to such infirmity as ours, giving us an example of how to live in no other mode than the human one."[19] Seeing that the "road of the affections" was "blocked" by the "ill will of our past sins," Wisdom deliberately became "the way along which we could return home . . . and being crucified for us to root out the firmly fixed barriers blocking our return."[20] In this way, "Wisdom adapted its healing art to our wounds by taking on a human being" and becoming "itself both the physician (*medicus*) and the medicine (*medicina*)."[21] Christ becomes our way by humanly signifying his divinity, being himself both sign and Signified.[22]

Thus, Augustine does not call into question the psychagogic tradition's contention that human beings need a non-conventionally determined wisdom that is fully adapted to their condition to guide them gradually to apprehend Wisdom itself. Rather, he concludes that philosophy lacks the resources to carry through its own assessment. He contends that although philosophy itself has never been able to escape the limited mental imagining, emotional stultification, and habitual errors that afflict human collective life, it can find in Jesus Christ, the crucified Wisdom of God, both a stable criterion of critical judgment and an effective psychagogue whose healing remedies are fully adapted to our condition.[23]

After outlining the debilitating effects of disordered loves hardened by habit, and their cure only in the crucified Christ, Augustine provides in the remaining three books of *De doctrina christiana* instructions on how that cure comes in the context of the Christian community's reading and preaching of scripture. As he had in the past, Augustine says that the cure of soul is like an ascent of the heart or mind.[24] What distinguishes the following passage in *De doctrina christiana* from earlier works is that the interpretation of scripture is theoretically integrated into the ascent to Wisdom. He says that the reader of scripture needs "above all else" a fear of God, that growing discomfort with what has come to be the routine ordering of one's life. It is this fear that "shakes us with thoughts of our mortality . . . and nails our flesh and fixes our stirring of pride to the wood of the cross."[25] When this fear is supplemented by a modest piety that believes that what is written in the scriptures "is better and truer, even if its meaning is hidden, than anything we could think of by ourselves," the reader is ready for the critical third stage of progress.[26]

Augustine states that the third stage is about "knowledge" (*scientia*), and it is important to determine what kind of knowledge he highlights in this stage of personal development.[27] He says that one is not going to find anything else in the scriptures but that "God is to be loved on God's account, and one's neighbor on God's account . . . that is to say, that one must refer (*referatur*) all the love of one's neighbor, as well as oneself, to God."[28] The truths of Christian teaching, then, are neither naked objects of vision nor simple verbal propositions, but the truth of things as they are known through an ongoing hermeneutical struggle that orders that knowledge toward the love of God and neighbor. According to Augustine's exposition of Christian *doctrina,* all Christian knowledge of actual things is a knowledge of how to refer things to their proper referent. Since the human experience of knowing is necessarily bound up with mediating signifiers, thought and emotion deeply inflect one another. If the mind's vision is to be accurate, it must correctly value or order the objects mediating its perception. For this reason, Augustine introduces technical vocabulary to describe the human subject's relationship to the presenting objects of desire. In his words, a "just and holy life requires one to be capable of an objective and impartial evaluation of things; to love things, that is to say, in the right order" (*ordinatam*).[29]

The process of thought requires distinguishing what things are to be "used" (*uti*) from those to be "enjoyed" (*frui*). Use (*uti*) is differentiated from enjoyment (*frui*) by its "reference."[30] The great temptation is to receive the good things in the world and turn their goodness to evil use by loving them wrongly; that is, seeking to enjoy (*frui*) them while not referring them to God, in whom all things are to be used (*uti*) for God's sake. It is this misdirected love that Augustine describes as a "perverse sweetness" where we make the subject of our intention the things on our journey rather than our homeland itself.[31] Learning to love in the proper order involves a cognitive migration where one refrains from making the objects of experience ends in themselves, but travels with them as on a "road" that does not extend "from place to place," but is traversed "by the affections."[32] By probing the ultimate reference of human love, Augustine draws attention to the emotional distortions that derive from mistaken judgments of value and the customary beliefs that inform them.

With this stage, namely of acquiring a particular form of "knowledge" (*scientia*), Augustine asserts that "every serious student of the scriptures has to exercise himself" (*se exercet*). Far from something passively acquired, this "knowledge" entails the "work and labor" of active learning.[33] In keeping with the aims of classical interpretive practices, Bible reading is not simply ideological construction, but part and parcel of the quest for truth. To understand the biblical signs for what they are requires, among others things, knowledge both of their linguistic form (including Hebrew and Greek languages) and of the material objects to which they proximately refer. Consequently, a large portion of *De doctrina* is taken up with parsing those areas of the liberal arts necessary for scriptural interpretation.[34] The liberal arts as they are learned in the context of biblical interpretation, however, are relativized insofar as they have been made a part of the believer's ascent. According to Augustine, by means of this learning "one first has to discover oneself in the scriptures as tied up in love of this world (*amore huius saeculi*), that is, of temporal things, and far removed from such love of God and such love of neighbor as scripture itself prescribes."[35] This "knowledge" ultimately discovered, when combined with fear of God and reverence for scripture, leads to mourning and prayer for divine help.

Knowing one's true condition and grieving over it frees one to enter the fourth stage where with fortitude "one extricates (*extrahit*) oneself from all deadly delight in passing things, and turning away (*auertens*) from that, one turns (*conuertit*) instead to love of eternal things, namely to the unchanging unity which is at the same time a Trinity."[36] In subsequent stages of ascent, those who make progress are perfected in this rightly ordered love until they ultimately "cannot be diverted from the truth" enjoying "wisdom" (*sapientia*) in "peace and tranquility."[37] Having made knowledge the third of seven stages of ascent, Augustine ensures that knowledge is never self-referential. It can never rest in its own discoveries or become proud in its power of self-determination since it is formatted by the Wisdom of divine love whose paradigmatic expression is none other than the humble Christ crucified.

Just as the first-century Stoic, Musonius Rufus, maintained that philosophy was a most difficult discipline since those who approach it have previously internalized habits contrary to the truth they will be taught, so Augustine says that those making this ascent to wisdom do so in an environment where "many base and evil things" that should be "shunned and detested" have been presented with "the most eloquent persuasion" by "base and wicked" people.[38] This situation is worsened by the popular assumption that supposes that those who speak eloquently are also speaking the truth.[39] If in the struggle to know and to love one happens to encounter the truth, one may well not be fully persuaded by it because people "are able both to act and not to act upon what they know."[40]

Not believing that truth intrinsically has sufficient force to persuade those whose affections are habitually driven by mistaken judgments of value, Augustine appeals to a Ciceronian ideal of wise speech made persuasive through rhetoric.[41] He explains that "there is a certain similarity between eating and learning; so because of the disdain of the majority, even those nutrients without which life cannot be supported need to be made appetizing."[42] He, therefore, commends to anyone who seeks to pass on Christian knowledge an eloquence whose "universal task . . . is to speak in a manner that leads to persuasion."[43] In order for hearers to be fully persuaded by speech, Augustine insists that the Christian rhetor must not only speak with an eloquence that gives pleasure to those listening, but also address them in such a way that their very delight in the speech ultimately assists them in enacting the good promoted by it.[44]

In keeping with this ideal not merely to cater to the tastes of those listening, the bishop asserts that the "interpreter and teacher of divine scriptures, the defender of true faith and vanquisher of error" must take on a twofold task: "to communicate what is good (*bona docere*) and eradicate what is bad" (*mala dedocere*).[45] Thus, in addition to offering positive, constructive guidance, Augustine's homilist has a responsibility to evaluate critically what has been customarily accepted, even if it is beliefs and values that have been in unreflective use. Augustine cites as an example the prophetic speech of Jeremiah, exclaiming: "Oh what eloquence, all the more terrifying for being so plain, and all the more forceful for being so genuine! Oh indeed 'an ax splitting the rocks' (Jer. 23:29)! For that is what God himself, through this very prophet, said that his word is like, which he has pronounced through his holy prophets."[46]

He imagines that, in his time, it is the interpreter of Christian scripture who does this task most effectively. Augustine describes the first work of scripture in terms similar to the Socratic *elenchus* outlined above.[47] The style of scripture is deliberately adapted to the human condition so that it bewilders the mind lacking the skill of properly referring signs (*signa*) to that which they signify (*res*). Those who read scripture lightly "are liable to be misled by innumerable obscurities and ambiguities, and to mistake one thing for another, while in some passages they find no meaning at all that they can grasp at, even falsely, so dense and dark is the fog that some passages are wrapped in. This is all due, I have no doubt at all, to divine providence, so that pride may be subdued with hard labor."[48] Scripture, then, is written in such a way that it exposes our accustomed habits of reference. As examples, the bishop relates two families of mental habits that occlude understanding of scripture and amount to a kind of subjugation to signs rather than a free use of them. The first is a "Jewish" pattern. By "Jewish," Augustine intends anyone who has "observed the signs of spiritual things" as "things in themselves" and remains "unaware to what they should be referred."[49] This failure of reference is "the wretched slavery of spirit" that renders one "unable to lift up the eyes of the mind above bodily creatures to drink in the eternal light."[50] It can become a second nature to be in "bondage" to those very signs designed to raise them up to spiritual realities.[51] The encounter with scripture rightly interpreted seeks to expose the "Jewish" mind's habit of stopping prematurely or superficially at the sign, and cultivates a disposition that intentionally reasons through to that reality which extends beyond what is contained in the sign's appearance.

The second pattern is a "Pagan" one. Augustine claims it is worse than the "Jewish" one for it takes signs that are themselves worthless for the things themselves. In this case, even if one were to refer them properly to that which they signify one would still be weighed down with "a servile, carnal burden." Scripture ideally exposes the system of signs these kind of people employ to navigate the world to be "useless" and indeed mere "human constructions" (*simulacra manufacta*).[52] Augustine states that the effect of "Christian liberty" is to "cut out the slave labor under such signs" and even "the signs themselves." Moreover, scripture, in turn, offers a set of efficacious signs for "exercising their minds in the spiritual understanding of them" so that they can be "converted from the corruption of a multitude of false gods . . . to the worship of the one God."[53]

If readers approach scripture from either of these two families of mental habits that subject the mind to signs, the exercise of reading the scripture provides insight that they are "tied up in the love of temporal things, far from love of God and neighbor."[54] The reading of scripture, therefore, yields knowledge of self—even though this knowledge at first takes the form of admitting one's customary habits of reference are carnal, and one's ignorance of the true meaning of biblical signs. In order for self-knowledge and knowledge of scripture to mutually condition one another, Augustine suggests that "it is good practice" for the one who interprets biblical signs to use the opportunity presented by difficult passages of scripture "to refute such objections as may occur." It is "the teacher's responsibility not only to open what is inaccessible and to unravel knotty problems, but also while this is being done, to anticipate other problems that may arise."[55]

In this respect, the sign theory articulated in *De doctrina christiana* provides critical tools for learning that one's *customary* judgments of value are exactly that, and not necessarily natural.[56] Augustine furthers this analysis by articulating the manner in which various aspects of human society are entwined with significations that ultimately involve our affections (he emphasizes *signa data,* those signs which include an "intentional" quality that involve others in the will of the signifier).[57] He draws attention to the ways each human individual is thoroughly embedded in systems of signification that are deeply formative and have been internalized at an early age.[58] He warns the reader of *De doctrina christiana* not to take signs as merely a given, but contends that they are in fact "given" by some agent, and are subject to being infected by the disordered loves of those signifying them. In order to understand the variegated signs of scripture, one must discern who the "giver" is that instituted any particular sign. In this way, Augustine instructs the reader to acquire knowledge of signs, to subject them to evaluation, to scrutinize the intentions of those signifying, and the habit of mind that particular constellations of signs foster.

With such critical tools in hand, Augustine is able to subject customary social practices to criticism by examining their signification. The bishop is particularly critical of socially inscribed systems of signification that do not present their own relativity as pointing to God. This means for him that they shape their participants in such a way that they suffer a premature closure of vision, a stasis where the signs themselves have lost their proper referent beyond themselves. Furthermore, the participants become involved in the disordered affections intrinsic to these patterns of signification.[59] This process of critical assessment is, according to Augustine, not without its own pleasure for those involved. He says that "even falsehoods give delight when they are convincingly laid bare and revealed to an audience. It is not because they are false, you see, that they delight, but because it is true that they are false, the speech by which this is shown to be true also gives delight."[60]

Once the true commitments of those listening are made manifest, there is room for a more positive guidance. Amid varying systems of signification vying to pattern our affections, there is a great need to develop a habit of mind that constantly refers every particular *signum* to its proper *res*. Signs, properly understood, are not freestanding or self-referential. They naturally convey a content that exceeds their material appearance such that every "sign is a thing (*res*) which, besides the impression that it presents to the senses, causes some other thing to come to mind."[61] Augustine commends scripture as the means by which we can strip the objects of our experience of their artificial cultural overlay and restore them *in ourselves* to their natural state within God's providential ordering of the universe. This exercise of discovering the words of scripture to be signs is the same process as the more fundamental one of discovering the quality of signification inherent in all material things.

By means of scripture "so many diseases of the human will are cured" because it offers an alternative system of signification that involves one in the intention of its givers—God and the human authors' will to discover God.[62] Since this intention is properly ordered, the more deeply one is involved in these given signs, the more one's affections begin to conform to those of the givers. The more fluent one becomes in this properly ordered sign system given by God, the more adept one becomes in recognizing the relativity of human customary signs and their systemic misuse. One begins to perceive that all the *signa* of scripture refer to Christ who is the ultimate pattern of a properly ordered love.[63] Indeed, it is the love of the Crucified for us that is able to overcome our resistance to traveling the road to our native country. It is what liberates our affections from their "perverse captivity" and makes it possible to delight in the eloquence of reality itself and enjoy all things in God.[64]

Placing so much of the burden of the cure of souls on the process of interpreting scripture creates a potential problem for Augustine—misreading. Augustine worries that readers may in fact force scriptural signs to conform to their own preconceived prejudices, thereby blunting their transformative influence. He states,

> The human race, however, is inclined to judge (*aestimare*) sins, not according to the gravity of the evil desire involved, but rather in reference to the importance attached to their own customs (*consuetudinis*). So people frequently regard only those acts to be blameworthy which

in their own part of the world and their own time have been customarily treated as vicious and condemned, and only those acts to be approved of and praised which are acceptable within the conventions of their own society.[65]

Consequently, "if scripture either commands something which does not accord with the customs of the hearers, or censures something which does not fit in with them, they assume they are dealing with a figurative mode of speech." In this way, someone "already in thrall to some erroneous opinion" (*erroris opinio*) will not realize "that these things are written down for a useful purpose, to enable people of good conscience to see, for their own spiritual health, that a practice which they reject can have a good application, and that a practice which they embrace can be damnable."[66] In order for scripture to realize its critical potential it must not be normed by custom, but call custom to conform to its own standard that is not subject to variation.[67]

One purpose of Augustine's "rules" is to prevent the Bible from being co-opted by cultural factors that will eventually render it impotent. He advocates reading scripture on its own terms, that is, reading it through a hermeneutical framework given by scripture itself. For Augustine, the interpretive norm given by scripture is the twofold commandment of love of God and neighbor. He famously states that anyone who has "understood the divine scriptures or any part of them in such a way . . . that does not build up the twin love of God and neighbor" has "not yet understood them."[68] Amid the instability and fluctuation of human experience, scripture offers a trans-cultural, normative principle of which Augustine states: "'What you do not wish to be done to you, do not do to another' (Tob. 4:15) can suffer no variation through any diversity of national customs. When this maxim (*sententia*) is referred (*refertur*) to love of God, all shameful conduct dies, when to love of neighbor, all crimes."[69] Such a principle is not merely a procedural guide of human conduct, but involves giving oneself over to an ontological order of value made by God where the Trinity is of supreme worth and rational souls in the image of the Trinity are second. Scripture is understood when each portion of it is interpreted in a way that it conforms to the natural order intended by the Creator rather than forcing scripture to yield to an alternate order discontinuous with the divine will deriving its substance from human custom.[70]

As an illustration of the powerfully transformative potential of a Christian preaching that adapts its eloquence to the needs of those hearing, Augustine recalls once being in Caesarea of Mauritania and attempting to dissuade its inhabitants from participating in an annual ritual resembling civil war. They were in the grip of a "monstrous custom, handed down from their fathers and grandfathers and remote ancestors, which was laying hostile siege to their hearts, or rather, was in full possession of them." Augustine states that he sought by his speaking "to root out such a cruel and inveterate evil from their hearts and habits and rid them of it." He reports that his preaching brought the crowd to tears, evidently mourning their condition once its true nature became visible. Subsequently, finishing his sermon, he redirected their hearts and lips to giving thanks to God. As of his writing, the bishop notes that no such custom had since reappeared in Mauritania.[71]

In summary, according to *De doctrina christiana*, those who hear or read scripture encounter it assuming that they understand the world, yet they then find the text impossible to understand, since it does not conform to their customary habits of interpreting signs. They find that they cannot account for the gaps they perceive in scripture by their own constructions — that is, not merely their private, individual prejudices, but the larger hermeneutical frameworks they inhabit and to which they appeal when trying to make sense of their experience. This then leads toward an aporetic state as the text whittles away the confidence of the reader to interpret signs. The "second law of nature" gradually begins to lose its force as one discovers that it is what has been preventing understanding of the inspired text. As those reading persevere, they begin developing new habits of reference that increase their understanding of scripture and influence their judgments of value in the world.

Scripture, therefore, provides "constructive" guidance in addition to its "critical" perspective as the soul of the reader gradually becomes rightly ordered in love of God and neighbor. The skills one develops to read scripture properly are the very ones needed to act morally.[72] Love is the hermeneutical criterion in both overlapping spheres. This overlap between the hermeneutical and the moral drives Augustine's reformulated psychagogy. Habits of reading and habits of acting imply one another as misinterpretation indicates moral failures and moral failures cause misreadings. The reader and moral agent continually strives to cultivate the ability to reason from any particular *signum* and refer it to its proper *res* within the order established by God.

As a result, in Augustine's mature theory the inquiry into the signs of scripture is an encounter with the divine reason psychagogically adapted to the human condition. Scripture presents us with a point of reference not determined by custom and it is in the reading of it that our affections become ordered. Scripture serves its critical function not because it is revealed in an "a-cultural" way, so that it stands above other merely human constructions. Scripture is not privileged in this manner. In fact, Augustine underscores in the prologue that scripture itself is a limited set of human cultural traditions—"the words of God in human words." Thus Augustine's case does not amount to a bald fideism vis-à-vis this text. Rather it is based on a view of God's providential ordering of the particular cultural history of those writers of the Bible. When one encounters scripture, one is encountering a culture where its signs have already been made subject to God. Scripture, then, can function critically as a privileged set of cultural traditions that set the standard for how signs should be ordered in any other culture.

Augustine's insight into the massive cognitive and affective distortions that afflict all people—no matter how disciplined or classically educated—has a leveling effect regarding which students he believed could profit from psychagogy. In a late letter, the bishop advises an aspiring rhetor to tell his potential critics in Milan that there is a way to attain a happy life based on "a sure and unalterable truth, not on some wrong or rash opinion," without the arduous intellectual exercise of the schools.[73] Convinced of the effectiveness of divine resources, Augustine would call even the poor and illiterate of Hippo to make progress (*proficere*), "for those of you who have not been schooled in what they call the liberal arts, of much more value is the fact that you have been brought up on the word of God."[74] On another occasion, while commenting on the scripture stating that God's Spirit rests "upon one who is humble and quiet and trembles at my words" (Isa. 66:2), Augustine states pointedly, "At these words Peter trembled, Plato did not. Let the fisherman keep what the great and famous philosopher lost. 'You have hidden these things from the wise and the knowing, and have revealed them to the little ones'" (Matt. 11:25).[75]

Therefore, on the one hand, Augustine's dark realism about the intransigence of evil in human life and his perception that even our best intentions are brought to naught through weakness of will, bring him to view classical therapy as ultimately unable to effect human happiness even in the best of circumstances. On the other hand, his belief in divinely given tools of scripture and sacraments leads him to make available his reformulated psychagogy to an ecclesial body that included even those sorts of people lacking the skills thought necessary to benefit from the classical tradition. Hence, to whatever degree that Augustine's perception of the human condition was bleaker than that of his philosophical interlocutors, he had proportionately greater confidence in the healing efficacy of the tools available to human beings for the amendment of life.

Such Augustinian confidence, nonetheless, does not obscure the limits of his own reformulated psychagogic theory. In the end, after encouraging the spiritual guides who follow him to be as sophisticated as possible in refining their skills and "learn all the things that are to be taught, and acquire proficiency in speaking, as befits a man of the Church," he states that even the most eloquent speaker "should not be in the slightest doubt that . . . it is more the piety of prayer than the ready facility of orators that enables him to do so; by praying then both for himself and for those he is about to address, let him be a pray-er (*orator*) before being a speaker (*dictor*)."[76] Even when every pastoral method is mastered, the ultimate success of guidance in individual cases depends on divine involvement. He states,

> This is why even with the ministry of holy people, or indeed of the holy angels, nobody properly learns the things that pertain to a life with God, unless, through God, he becomes responsive to God. . . . Just as physical medicines, applied by humans to other humans, only benefit those in whom the restoration of health is effected by God, who can heal even without them . . . so too the benefits of teaching, applied to the soul through human agency, are only beneficial when the benefit is effected by God.[77]

Furthermore, the guidance offered does not in this life culminate in the direct vision of God, but in a fluency in regard to the humble, broken speech of scripture.[78] The biblical signs are never transcended in this life; they, along with all created things, remain precisely signs pointing beyond themselves.[79] The ultimate good of the human soul is deferred until an eschatological consummation. As he says of those ascending to Wisdom, "we are walking more by faith than by sight as long as we are on our journey through this life."[80]

Through this deferral, Augustine maximizes his psychagogic theory's critical capacity by excluding under any circumstances the one condition that would exempt something or someone from assessment: the full equation between the transcendent and a particular instantiation of it. He would view any such purported objectification as yet one more false finality, another premature stopping on the way, and the very thing that makes one chronically vulnerable to pride. This exclusion pertains to any cultural feature that does not continually demonstrate its own relative and qualified existence, as well as any use of material or verbal signs which obfuscates their limitations as the finite, contingent vehicles they are. As with every other cultural project, interpretations of Christian scripture never are to acquire autonomy from the very text they claim to explain. In this way, the text never becomes fully subjugated to the meaning established for it by its readers. Resisting absolutizing their own theorizing about scripture and the temptation to rest in the security of their own perfected reading, Augustine directs readers toward a lifelong process of inquiry and discovery that gives form to human knowing, longing, and suffering without fully resolving them.

Since God's love shed abroad in our hearts does not cure us in the sense of realizing perfection in this life, Augustine's mature theory softens all such striving and pretensions.[81] Instead, God's love results in an owning of creaturely finitude and flaws, and frees us from the anxious striving and negative consequences of seeking to achieve a security of our own making. In setting aside this aspiration as ultimately false and utopian, Augustine hopes that we would receive God's love for us as we are, and that our love for God would then not be merely a function of our ambitious quest for personal wholeness. Augustine contends that the reception of this love as it is given is what frees us to love other human beings as they are rather than doing so as a way of enfranchising them into our own efforts to achieve well-being. In this way, love of neighbor springs less from the surplus that arises from the prior alleviation of personal pain than from its ongoing integration into the self-understanding of the imperfect soul in the process of being cured by God.[82]

Teaching the Uninstructed

De doctrina christiana presents a panoramic vision in which the divine rhetoric, through the orchestration of human words, awakens in us a love for its beauty that is so powerful that it revises our relationship to everything else. This vision, nevertheless, was an Augustinian ideal that even he fell short of in specific ways, namely in his lack of fluency in the Greek and Hebrew languages.[83] After completing the first books, but long before bringing *De doctrina christiana* to completion, Augustine responded to a request from an otherwise unknown deacon named Deogratias in the form of a treatise sometime between 399 and 405, *De catechizandis rudibus,* on teaching those not yet instructed in the Christian faith. Unlike the earlier treatise, in *De catechizandis rudibus* Augustine is not so much working out the global details of his own pastoral theory as he is applying that theory to a specific situation. It therefore provides the opportunity to demonstrate the great extent that his mature psychagogic theory informs his own episcopal directives about how souls are to be cared for in the context of the Catholic congregation. Augustine's ability to distil his psychagogic theory into a treatise that appears on the surface to be simplistic and lacking philosophical underpinning only underscores his mastery of the art.[84]

In describing the work of the ideal catechist, Augustine rehearses the conventional topics of the classical therapeutic tradition. He reminds Deogratias how necessary it is to discern the various types of students. After all, "the same medicine is not to be applied to all."[85] He says that it matters whether the person to be instructed is "cultivated or a dullard, a fellow-citizen or a stranger, a rich man or a poor man, a man having some official authority, a person of this or that family, of this or that age or sex, coming to us from this or that school of philosophy, or from this or that popular error." To guide various types of souls requires a versatile director that is "in travail with some, becomes weak with others; is at pains to edify some, dreads to be a cause of offense to others; stoops to some, before others stands with head erect; is gentle to some, and stern to others; an enemy to none, a mother to all."[86] The majority of the theoretical advice in the treatise, therefore, is occupied with practical strategies on how to adapt one's discourse to the needs of different types of inquirers: especially singled out are those who arrive with an education in the liberal arts,[87] those who have an ordinary rhetorical education,[88] and those who are altogether without previous instruction.[89] Furthermore, one finds themes similar to those argued for so strongly in Augustine's prior treatises: namely, that the soul comes gradually to truth as it purifies itself of error, guidance is necessary in this process, the human Christ is the Wisdom of God adapted to our weak powers of perception, the reading of Christian scripture is a training of the soul, etc. In *De catechizandis rudibus*, it becomes clear both how well suited these themes are to Augustine's ecclesial context and how helpful they are in offering concrete and practical advice to one who seeks to guide inquirers in the context of the Catholic congregation.

Addressing, among other things, Deogratias' concern that he was "almost always perplexed to discover how suitably to present that truth, that belief that makes us Christians," Augustine begins by introducing factors that limit and complicate instruction.[90] He confesses, "I am nearly always dissatisfied with my discourse," for "my powers of expression come short of my knowledge." He continues by saying that although what he seeks his hearer to understand is like "a sudden flash of light," his "expression of speech is slow, drawn out, and a far different process." Even as "speech is being formed, intellectual apprehension has already hidden itself in its secret recesses" stamped upon the memory. It is, nonetheless, from these impressions that the catechist constructs "those audible signs called language." Therefore, the instructor cannot assume that by speaking, he or she is presenting anything "parallel to the open and evident expression of the face." Rather, discourse is far more indirect. "It does not resemble even the memory impression." Twice removed from direct perception, it "differs" much from "that instantaneous flash of intellectual apprehension."[91]

Augustine advises Deogratias that he should take into account that even he in all likelihood cannot perceive what he teaches as fully as he desires. "For who in this life sees except as 'in a dark manner (*in aenigmate*) and through a glass?'" (1 Cor. 13:12). Augustine declares that "not even love itself is so mighty as to rend asunder the gross darkness of the flesh and pierce to that eternal clearness (*aeternum serenum*) from which even transitory things derive their radiance, such as it is." Augustine nevertheless urges Deogratias not to consider his efforts "fruitless" (*infructuosum*) since it is by means of human teaching that "the good progress from day to day toward that vision of that day which knows neither revolution of the heavens nor onset of night."[92] In this way, Augustine prefaces his remarks regarding how to present the truth with the qualification that the speech of the catechist is not only far removed from human perception, but never fully captures its subject matter and is no substitute for the personal participation of the catechized.

Once Deogratius fully recognized how much his apprehension of the truth differed from the Truth itself and how impossible it was for him to transfer his own spiritual experience to others, one wonders why he would not consider his catechetical attempts to communicate knowledge to be "fruitless" endeavors. If Deogratius had been a reader of Augustine's treatises, he may have thought of Augustine's earlier conversation with his son where Augustine contended, "We do not learn anything by these signs called words."[93] Much like that earlier conversation, Augustine invites Deogratius to reframe the whole process of catechism. Deogratius' efforts will not be in vain if he establishes more proximate goals than directly conveying either his own perception of truth, or the Truth itself. Instead, the bishop tells Deogratias that his instruction should be a "narration" instructing the beginner from the text, "'In the beginning God created the heavens and the earth' down to the present period of the church."[94] The instructor, therefore, ought to make the primary task the presentation of passages of scripture, and to do so not "as a rolled up parchment and at once snatch them out of sight, but we ought by dwelling somewhat upon them to untie, so to speak, and spread them out to view, and offer them to the minds of our hearers to examine and admire."[95] In this way, Augustine suggests that a homily is most "fruitful" when composed of compelling scriptural images and interpretive exercises instead of offering a straightforward description of reality. For this reason, he says that from among the scriptural material, the catechist should choose "certain of the more remarkable facts (*mirabiliora*) that are heard with greater pleasure and constitute the cardinal points in history."[96] Thus, the psychagogic discourse is adapted to appeal to minds that are accustomed to gain pleasure from the fluctuating images of sense perception rather than from the singular beauty of divine truth.[97]

This preference contrasts with that of the more mature instructors who are "more delighted and enthralled by that which we perceive in silence in our minds, and do not wish to be called off from it to the babble of words which fall far short of reproducing it." Nevertheless, even though no longer wishing to move "with any pleasure in such well-trodden and, as it were, childish paths," the catechist continues to do so out of the desire for others to enjoy "what is offered them for their salvation."[98] Augustine describes this ministry of the catechist as an imitation of the Christ who "became weak to the weak that He might gain the weak" and "became a little child in the midst of us, like a nurse cherishing her children." Every spiritual guide, according to the bishop, is invited by the love of Christ to learn how pleasurable it is "to murmur into the ear broken and mutilated words," as "men wish to have babes for whom they may do this," or to be like that mother who finds it more pleasurable to chew "morsels small and put them into her tiny son's mouth, than to chew and consume large morsels herself."[99] He instructs the deacon that when he feels discouraged by his duty he should remind himself of the surpassing value of the service he offers. Since human flourishing requires so much more than mere bodily nourishment, it is more important "to instruct the mind of the one who feeds on it with the word of God" than "to fill the belly of the hungry with bread."[100]

Accordingly, Augustine writes that one objective of the catechist is to strive to "direct" (*transferenda*) the "attention" (*intentio*) of the inquirer away "from the guidance of wonders or dreams" to "the more solid path and the more trustworthy oracles of the scriptures." The task is to persuade the hearer that "walking in the way already provided in the holy scriptures" is the path of "greater safety and security." The inquirer whose thoughts have been thus redirected, for whom the interpretation of scripture has accordingly become the priority, would then no longer have the need to "seek visible miracles but become accustomed to hope for those invisible" and be admonished "not when sleeping but when awake."[101] This "transference" involves nothing so straightforward as the mere reception of the authority of the biblical text. Rather, in being initiated into the Christian community, the inquirer is taught to become an interpreter of the text, and to have his or her perceptions shaped by this ongoing task. It is important to note how and why Augustine instructs Deogratias to teach inquirers to interpret scripture themselves. In spreading out the biblical materials for view and "offering them to the minds of our hearers to examine and admire," the catechist is handing to the inquirer as much a certain set of predetermined problems as a set of solutions.[102]

The bishop observes that the humble style of scripture poses a problem especially for people who have received training in rhetoric.[103] For those "who surpass all others in the art of speaking" to interpret scripture is to call into question a whole constellation of cultural values and preferences. It is the duty of the catechist, therefore, to warn them "to clothe themselves in Christian humility, and to learn not to despise those whom they know as shunning more carefully faults of character than faults of diction; and they should not even presume to compare with a pure heart the trained tongue which they had been accustomed even to prefer." By being "taught to listen to the divine scriptures," their preferences are to be trained in such a way "that genuine eloquence (*solidum eloquium*) not seem inferior to them merely because it is not pretentious."[104]

By cultivating this affinity for the humble style of scripture, and training hearers to desire a pure heart rather than rhetorical skill, the catechist helps them to perceive the true nature of the sacred text. Then they can believe that "the words and deeds rolled up and concealed in fleshly coverings" are to be "unfolded and revealed so as to be understood." Augustine contends that this process of discerning the meaning hidden in the obscure text "effectively sharpens love for the truth and shakes off the unresponsiveness induced by their aversion for it."[105] He suggests that such people "must have this shown them by actual experience when something which failed to move them when set plainly before them" elicits such an effect "by the unraveling of some allegory." By being guided in the ascent from the obscurity inherent in the literal reading toward the greater spiritual clarity in the figurative, the inquirer learns to value "meaning more than words just as the spirit is esteemed more than the body," and "to prefer discourses more for their truth than their eloquence, just as they ought to prefer to have wise rather than handsome friends."[106]

A second set of problems for inquirers is raised when they are offended by what they hear. First of all, Augustine states that if the catechist is speaking "rightly and truly," it may merely mean that the listener has misunderstood. Nevertheless, offense can arise when something is said that "from its very novelty is harsh because it is contrary to the opinion and custom of a longstanding error" (*contra opinionem et consuetudinem ueteris erroris*). In this case, the catechist should seek to "cure" the hearer "without any delay, by an abundance of authorities and reasons. If, however, the scandal is unseen and secret," the catechist is left to believe that "God's medicine (*dei medicina*) is able to remedy it."[107]

A special instance of the ordinary perception of the hearer being offended occurs when a passage of scripture is the cause of the scandal. The bishop instructs Deogratias that since this will happen it is necessary "to admonish" the hearer "that if he hears anything even in the scriptures that has a carnal ring, he should believe, even if he does not understand, that something spiritual is therein signified (*significari*) that pertains to holy living and the life to come." Augustine says that the inquirer needs to learn this so that "whatever he hears from the canonical books that he cannot refer (*referre*) to the love of eternity, and truth, and holiness, and to the love of neighbor, he may believe to have been said or done with a figurative meaning, and endeavor so to understand as to refer (*referat*) it to that twofold love."[108]

In this way, scripture, by its very nature, challenges the hearer to "endeavor so to understand" the proper reference of what it signifies. Augustine asserts that it is necessary "to keep in view the goal of the precept, which is 'love from a pure heart, and a good conscience, and an unfeigned faith'—a standard to which we should make all that we say refer" (*referamus*). Moreover, he states that it is toward this standard that "we should also move and direct the attention of him for whose instruction we are speaking."[109] To understand the problematic passages of scripture, the hearer learns to refer the signs of scripture to that love that conforms to the divine order where the supreme value is God and the rational souls created by God, namely, neighbors. Insofar as the hearer is accustomed to love another way of ordering the world, he or she will be scandalized by scripture by being unable to determine the suitable reference of its signs.

The obstacle obscuring understanding is that habituated love of an alternate order to the one established by God which Augustine calls pride. He says that "nothing is more opposed to love than envy, and the mother of envy is pride."[110] Neither the skill of the catechist nor the problems providentially posed by scripture overcome this obstacle. Indeed, the catechist's artful exposition of scripture can amount to nothing more than a salutary spur prompting hearers to apprehend for themselves the solution to their disorder. That remedy, according to Augustine, is the "Lord Jesus Christ, God-Man, at once the disclosure of divine love towards us and an example among us of human lowliness." Christ's humble divinity confronts "our swollen conceit, great as it is, so that it might be healed (*sanaretur*) by an even greater antidote (*contraria medicina*). For the misery of human pride is great, but the mercy of God's humility is greater."

The bishop counsels the catechist who is concerned about the cure of souls to have this crucified divine love continually set forth "as the end to which you may refer (*referas*) all that you say."[111] Ultimately, "there is nothing that invites love more than to be loved first."[112]

The bishop's instruction that catechetical discourse should not depart far from the exposition of scripture accords with the conviction that it is ultimately Christ's love that cures the soul, since "whatever has been committed to writing and established by divine authority tells of Christ and counsels love."[113] The whole law and prophets depend on the commandments to love God and neighbor and foretell the coming of the Lord. In this way, the catechist is proficient who guides hearers to understand scripture on its own terms so that they learn "to refer" everything narrated there "to that end of love from which in all our actions and words our eyes should never be turned away."[114]

Like the philosophic guide who ideally displays complete harmony between speech and deeds, Augustine pays as much attention to the character of the instructor as he does to the catechetical tasks. He warns Deogratias that we who guide others should not "despise a remedy" when it is offered not for the salvation of our neighbor, but for ourselves.[115] As we lead others, the bishop suggests that it is a mutual process where "they, as it were, speak in us what they hear, while we, after a fashion, learn in them what we teach."[116] Having set out one primary objective of catechism as cultivating love for the order created by God, he reminds Deogratias of his own need to conform himself continually to God's providential order:

> But if anything unavoidable happens to disturb our order, let us bend readily to it, lest we be broken; so that we may make our own that order which God has preferred to ours. For it is more proper that we should follow his will, than he ours. . . . Why then do we chafe that God, who is so much more excellent, should take precedence over us, who are but men, so that we desire to be rebels against his order through our very love for our own order.[117]

Likewise, if the exposition of scripture is to elicit the love of the hearer for what is of the highest value, the instructor's affections should be similarly kindled. Augustine, therefore, states that "our chief concern must be how to bring it about that one may take pleasure in catechizing."[118] He goes so far as to commend strategies for the catechist to be so prepared for the task that what is said "bursts forth readily and cheerfully from the rich abundance of love," and can be "drunk in with enjoyment." There should be such harmony between the affections of the catechist and words spoken that it would be as if "love itself says them to us all, that love which is poured into our hearts by the Holy Spirit."[119]

After beginning the treatise by pointing out how impossible it is for one person to "rend asunder the gross darkness of the flesh" for another and "pierce to that eternal clearness from which even transitory things derive their radiance," and having then established more proximate goals for spiritual guidance around the interpretation of scripture, the bishop continues to underscore that even with such a strategy firmly in hand the sermon will have "an uncertain outcome."[120] Although the catechist hopes for the inquirer "to make progress in morality and knowledge and to enter upon the way of Christ with eagerness," Augustine insists that the one making progress must "not venture to ascribe the change either to us or to himself, but will love both himself and us . . . in him and for his sake, who loved him when he was yet an enemy." In the end, any progress brought about through the work of the catechist is ascribed to the manner in which the inquirer was "listening to God through us," rather than placing "hope in a human being."[121]

To recapitulate, in *De catechizandis rudibus,* Augustine has adopted psychagogic traditions such as adapting speech to the various types of students to lead them gradually to perceive wisdom for themselves and re-contextualized them by applying them to the local needs of Catholic congregations. Of special note is the manner in which the guidance he describes is especially one that centers on initiating inquirers into the Christian community and its practices of reading its sacred text. The proficient catechist described by Augustine is one who guides souls by spreading the text out to view in such a way that the interpretation of scripture poses predetermined problems for the hearers that expose the obstacles inhibiting their spiritual progress. The catechist ultimately lacks the ability to cure anyone. That alone is ascribed to Christ's salvific power and humility. The catechist can, nonetheless, be involved in the process by re-directing each hearer's attention away from competing authorities toward a sacred text divinely arranged in such a way that the very exercise of interpretation that is required for understanding it involves the reform of the mind and the retraining of desire.

Twenty-one years later, when the elderly Augustine resumed writing *De doctrina christiana,* a work whose composition thus spanned the course of his ministry, he began by appealing to the classical topos that ultimately it is one's manner of life that is more compelling than even eloquent words.[122] Only three years later the bishop lay on his deathbed as the end of Roman rule in North Africa approached.[123] As narrated by Possidius, Augustine requested that penitential psalms be placed on a wall he could face while lying in bed. Possidius states that "when he was very weak, he used to lie in bed facing the wall where the sheets of paper were put up, gazing at them and reading them, and copiously and continually weeping as he read."[124] The tears of this bishop were not shed by a man dying the death of the Stoic sage who had already achieved tranquility through philosophical therapy. Possidius draws attention, moreover, to Augustine's manner of death not as evidence of despair or a loss of composure, but as the culmination of a life in harmony with his theological reflections. On his deathbed lay a man that had long ceased from striving to transcend the human condition by attaining through philosophy the perspicuous vision of divine wisdom. Neither was the struggle any longer compelling to legitimate the sufficiency of any particular humanly constructed sign system. The bishop dies abiding in a brokenness that for him was the only true openness of a creature who is content in the givenness of the divine order. It was this openness that had gradually liberated him from concepts, beliefs, and practices he had earlier hid behind to insulate himself from God and the world. It was this openness that freed him from striving to unify his experience into a closed coherent whole.

Augustine's life remained open and vulnerable to the intrusion of suffering; security remained only in the divine promise.[125] There was no other fixed point (philosophical, social, or religious) to provide the self with its footing. Whereas Augustine had in all likelihood been taught by Ambrose years earlier that physical death was a good whose only evil has to do with our mistaken beliefs concerning it, Augustine had come to see the matter quite otherwise.[126] One sees in his death not the claim to a fully cured soul that sees the true signification of all things and has moved beyond needing daily exercise in scripture. Instead, the spiritual progress of the venerable bishop is seen in his fluency in the humble, broken speech of scripture. His death was the cessation of a lifelong convalescence. The cure of soul, then, is not so much the binding up and making whole of the flawed human being; rather, given the analysis that much illness is due to the compulsion to impose our own order on the world, health has more to do with the difficult task of letting go of this responsibility, residing in creaturely finitude, and awaiting a not-yet realized completion of existence. The cure of soul amounts to perfecting in life the studied imperfection of scripture.

For all the confidence the mature Augustine had in God's "remedies in the scriptures," he believed that those medicines were most effective when the sacred text was given a voice in the context of the Christian liturgy.[127] In the same way that *De doctrina christiana* remained incomplete, from his perspective, until he added a fourth book more directly on homiletical concerns, so Augustine's psychagogic theory required enactment in life.[128] This can be found with precision and innumerable variation in his own homilies which are the subject of the following chapter.

Part Three

Augustine's Homiletical Practice

Chapter Seven

The Christian Rhetor

What after all am I, but someone needing
to be set free with you, cured with you?
                    —Augustine, *s.* 9.10

Continuity amid Discontinuity

Sometime in the middle of the second century, a sizable crowd gathered in a theater in Carthage to witness the rhetorical performance of the celebrated sophist and author Apuleius. The speaker drew attention to the large numbers in attendance and congratulated the city "for possessing so many friends of learning among her citizens."[1] He then dazzled his audience by declaiming successively in Latin and in Greek.[2] This feat was accomplished by the same man who was known to show off his versatility by accepting requests to give speeches without any preparation, testing his ability to adapt his style moment by moment to suit the taste of his hearers.[3] The citizens of Carthage eventually showed the extent of their appreciation for Apuleius' talent and North African origins by erecting a statue to him there.[4]

Apuleius regularly claimed Socrates as his "forefather" and described himself as "a Platonic philosopher."[5] He informed his audiences that

Socrates spent his days conversing with others because he believed that without speech people were, in a sense, invisible. Socrates, accordingly, relied upon the eye of the mind rather than upon bodily vision to make judgments. Apuleius exhorted his hearers that to do otherwise risked rendering human beings inferior to animals. After all, compared to eagles, "we cannot see things far removed from us or things that are very near us. All of us are blind to a certain extent. If you confine us to the eyes alone with their dim earthly vision . . . a cloud, as it were, is spread over our eyes and we cannot see beyond a stone's throw."[6]

When he had been accused at an earlier time of using, among other things, his eloquent mastery of Greek and Latin to charm the wealthy widow he had married, Apuleius argued that his fluency had been overestimated while—in perfect sophistic manner—quoting Homer in Greek.[7] He related to audiences how he had benefited not only from the customary literary and rhetorical education, but also from an extended philosophical formation in Athens during which time he had imbibed encyclopedic knowledge like wine while cultivating "all nine Muses with equal zeal."[8] Philosophy bestowed on him an eloquence that he claimed excelled even that given to birds. Their brief song occurs only at certain times, while "the wisdom and eloquence of the philosopher is ready at all times, is heard with reverence, is profitable for understanding, and is musically of every tone."[9] As a result of his philosophical formation, he came to "value gold and precious stones no more than pebbles or lead."[10] He warned his hearers that a soul without virtue was like "a barren inheritance of stony fields, mere heaps of rocks and thorns." Lacking its own fruit, such poverty of soul leads one to "go forth and steal the fruits of others and rifle through their gardens."[11]

If Apuleius had walked the streets of North Africa some two centuries later, he would have found that the populace's hunger for rhetorical performance had not diminished. The statues dedicated to him were, in all likelihood, still standing. His literary works were still prized. On a certain day, he could have seen all kinds of people, Christians and non-Christians, learned and unlearned, rich and poor, flocking to witness yet another display of eloquence. So great was the fame of this orator that whenever he traveled he would be asked to speak in town after town on his way.[12] Boseth was likely one such town.[13] This time, however, the crowds gathered at a Catholic church rather than the theater. The speaker they came to see was no longer a professional orator but was now the Christian bishop of Hippo.

Aside from the shift in location and the public reading of a series of biblical texts, the scene would have been largely familiar to Apuleius. He would have recognized the orator's art of speaking without notes so that the hearers could witness the speech's creation before their very eyes. Apuleius would have known, nonetheless, how much preparation such apparent spontaneity required. The speech would have appeared to him to have taken a rapid philosophical turn as the orator announced that his subject was neither "some sort of color or light with which the eyes are acquainted," nor "some sweet sound in which human ears usually delight," nor any of the senses with which the body is familiar. Instead, the orator was to inquire into the meaning of the text addressing "what eye has not seen nor ear heard, nor has come up in the heart of man" (1 Cor. 2:9).

The bishop told his hearers that such a text is difficult to understand because one is not ordinarily asked to "think of any good thing" except in the manner in which one has been "in the habit of seeing or hearing or encountering with some such sense perception."[14] He contended that even their loftiest thoughts are only amplifications of what they have perceived physically through their senses. When asked to imagine paradise, they picture "a pleasant garden" where small trees merely become bigger ones and a circumscribed meadow acquires "limitless immensity." Likewise, the God who "dwells in light inaccessible" (1 Tim. 6:16) is construed as a very bright light rather than one "of a totally different kind"—one "not of eyes but of minds."[15] The bishop advised his hearers that if they were to become "capable of bearing that intelligible and immortal light," they would need to cleanse not the "eye of the flesh" but the "eye of the mind and heart."[16]

Having heard the beginning of the speech, Apuleius and the others present would then observe Bishop Augustine pause to inquire into the meaning of the word "man" in the text under consideration. As an aside, the bishop acknowledged that those present who knew the scriptures would already understand and "be running ahead" in their thoughts toward what he was about to say. He then explained to those less familiar with scriptural language that "'men' is what our scriptures, by a certain signification, call those who are still fleshly minded," that is, all of us "born in this mortal life" and carrying in us that "wound of the inner eye."[17]

If they are to cease being "men" in this sense, they will need to purge their minds of the patterns of thought to which they have become accustomed.[18] Whenever they apprehend anything, they will need to say to themselves, "This is not my God, it is the work of my God."[19] This process is no less necessary when the mind regards itself. Much as Apuleius did, Augustine described the greatness of the human soul by contrasting it to the frailty of the human body whose abilities are so often exceeded by animals. It is only by the power of reason that human beings distinguish themselves from animals. The soul, however, is as invisible as it is great.[20] It is not as easy to discern as the body, especially because of the manner in which we have been "habituated to the senses of the flesh" such that the mind seems to us akin to "air or fire, or perceivable light."[21] In order for the mind to understand that its true nature "surpasses all bodily things," it needs to transcend all the objects of the physical universe. It climbs, as it were, every material object eventually to arrive at a vision of itself. It only fully perceives itself, however, when, while apprehending its true nature, it can exclaim, "This is not yet my God."[22] Accordingly, Augustine admonished his hearers, "Pass beyond even your mind!"[23] Even though the mind "surpasses all bodily things," it is itself inconstant. It remembers and forgets, is wise one moment and foolish in another, is angry and calms down.[24] To ascend to a security beyond the mind itself, those listening would need to engage in a critical process of unlearning, or, as he states more positively, to "become ignorant of God in order to be worthy to find him." Those present were assured by him that such cultivated ignorance was itself superior to the falsehood that usually passes for knowledge.[25]

They should harbor no illusions, however, that such a process would be free of pain. He warned them that giving up things in which they are "in the habit of finding enjoyment" will create in them a painful "hunger."[26] Rather than exhorting them to harness their strength and apply themselves wholly to such a task, the bishop suggested that the best place to begin was to ask God to give freely the very thing desired. He told his hearers that such asking was itself a spiritual exercise commended by the one who said, "Ask and you will receive, knock and it will be opened to you" (Luke 11:9). "Knock as you stand in front of the door, knock insistently. The one who is keeping it shut is not turning you away, he wishes to exercise (*exercere*) the one knocking. So knock then, go on knocking, not with the hand of the body, but with the affection of the heart."[27] He argued, furthermore, that truly to love and experience "what eye has not seen, nor what ear has heard, or what has come into the heart of man" requires, first of all, not knowledge, but belief.[28]

Augustine continued by drawing on familiar material from the psychagogic tradition to depict the soul's plight in terms of a physical malady and medical cure. He asked his hearers to imagine a man bereft of sight "perhaps from the very beginning of his life, so that now he does not even know what is being seen by those who can see." Any physician treating such a patient will first need to "arouse" in him "a desire to see what he does not know, wishing to cure him so that he may be able to see what he cannot see now." Augustine's hypothetical patient objects, nevertheless, saying, "You will not cure me, unless you first show me what I am going to see." The bishop observes that any doctor, as a matter of course, would explain that one must first "be cured in order to see, not see in order to be cured." Indeed the physician admonishes the blind man saying, "I beg you, let yourself be cured. . . . I mean, you hear about light, color, lightning flashes; you hear these words. These words signify certain things, the things themselves (*res ipsas*) you cannot see. . . . So then, endure a little pain as the price of great joys." Augustine contended that any man who resists this curative treatment proves to be "the enemy of his own health."[29]

According to the bishop, the "healing doctor who has come to us" is "our Lord Jesus Christ." Christ is the one who "found us blind of heart."[30] During his ministry, Christ was the physician of souls who administered "an especially bitter cup to a patient swollen and blown up with pride; he himself came in humility, and suffered every conceivable humiliation from proud individuals."[31] Augustine described how Christ's patients were made so frantic by their disease that they killed their healer. Unlike other doctors, however, Christ was able "to prepare a remedy" for his patients' disease "from his very death."[32] The bishop argued that when Christ's murderers heard the proclamation of the disciples and "sensed that he was alive, the one they had ridiculed as he was dying," their consciences were "wounded more painfully than when they had seen him hanging on the cross." The "crucifiers" were themselves "cut to the heart."[33] Augustine understood his own oratory as echoing that apostolic proclamation which first drew attention to the healing work of the crucified physician.[34] He told those listening to him that the "humility of Christ" was, in this way, the "remedy" for the pride that was the root cause of their distress.[35] The "art of the doctor" was written down in the same Christian scriptures that allow them to "listen to the doctor as he hangs on the cross; looking round at the frantic crowd raging against him."[36] Christ offered in himself a cure that was bitter because it was adapted to our condition. Otherwise, it would have been "beyond human imitation."[37] The treatment prescribed for our souls is one that Christ the physician endured himself before our very eyes.[38]

Augustine imagined his hearers objecting to such a doctor saying, "What sort of God am I going to have? One who was born, suffered, was smeared with spittle, crowned with thorns, hung up on a cross?" He asserted that although those raising this objection rightly perceive the "lowly humility of the doctor," they are unable to notice the tumor of their own pride. He directed their attention to the magnitude of their very displeasure and maintained that its disproportionate nature was an indicator of disease—"the remedy the doctor is giving you is displeasing to your disease," that is, to your "pride."[39]

By contrast, those who are being treated by Christ do not find such a physician unseemly. These people have found written in their sacred scriptures that "God chose the weak things of this world to disconcert the strong, and he chose the low-born things of this world and the things that are not like those that are, that the things that are might be brought to nothing" (1 Cor. 1:27–28). In this spirit, the physician came "to give the cup of humility and to cure pride," and as a result "did not gain a fisherman through an emperor, but an emperor through a fisherman."[40] They have found in Christ's medicine no mighty panacea that renders them whole and reality transparent, but a modest course of treatment that purifies the heart as it travels the path of faith. Although they continue to be "not yet whole," they take comfort in the fact that they "are still being cured." Augustine sought to persuade his hearers that at the present time, "Your health, your salvation, lies in hope, not yet in reality."[41] Their souls will one day be completed by a vision of truth so direct that it will fulfill and realize their deepest desires. To insist arrogantly on leaping over the healing process in order to begin with vision itself inhibits the soul's cure. With hearts opened up by hopeful longing, they should "persevere under the doctor's treatment" and "put up with his precepts as with strong ointments."[42]

Augustine remarked that those who continue to object to Christ are "astonished at the way the human race is converging on the name of the crucified and streaming together."[43] The very one "who was crucified and scorned on the cross" has "subdued the nations—not with ferocious steel—but with a scorned piece of wood."⁴⁴ This "cup of humility" is a cure offered to all "from kings to those dressed in rags. No age is passed over, no manner of life, no school of thought. It is not the case, you see, that the unlearned have believed and the learned have not, or that the low-born have believed and the high-born have not, or that women have believed and men have not, or that children have believed and old people have not, or that slaves have believed and free persons have not." The bishop portrayed his hearers that were not yet Christians as some of the "few who have remained outside, and still go on arguing." He pleaded with them to "wake up" and notice the whole world shouting at them.⁴⁵ He declared, "Let them condescend to be humble, let them now recognize their medicine, let them come and believe."⁴⁶ "Let them believe, then they will see."⁴⁷ Let them "be joined together" both with the physician bringing their medicine "and with each other as parts of the body" of which Christ is the head.⁴⁸

The last words Apuleius would have heard from the speaker that day were, "Any who are here that have not yet come to believe, well, here we are, here is the church; if they wish, they can become believers. If they think it is to be put off . . . let them give up their places to those who are about to celebrate the divine mysteries." At that, the pagans, along with any of the unbaptized remaining, left the room.⁴⁹ What would Apuleius have been thinking as he witnessed such an oratorical display as familiar as it was foreign? The bishop's use of rhetoric for psychagogic ends, his counsel to care for the soul as a physician does the body, his belief that this requires a shift of perspective to gain critical insight into customary experience, his mention of spiritual exercises, and even his appeal to ancient texts supplying paradigmatic norms would have all been standard topics for the philosophically informed sophist. Apuleius may have even been amused by the rhetorical challenge of making someone who was crucified appear beautiful: a task at least as daunting as Dio's famous attempt to prove that Troy was victorious in the battle that bears its name.

Despite Apuleius' familiarity with Augustine's rhetorical strategies, how could he have been anything other than bewildered by his canon of authorities? Exercising the mind by inquiring into enigmatic passages of Homer's classic text is one thing. So also is contemplating how heroic Odysseus could be said to be wise. It is quite another to exercise the mind in the interpretation of the Christian Old and New Testaments and to train it to see a crucified Jew as the embodiment of wisdom. One suspects that Apuleius would have known that it was no longer his century. It was, according to Augustine, a time when "a professional orator wins great acclaim if he is able to understand the fisherman [Peter]."[50] Although representatives of the educated elite attended Augustine's sermons, on the whole the audiences which Apuleius congratulated for their erudition were far more impressive in this respect than those that gathered in churches to hear the bishop of Hippo.[51] It was now baptism rather than education or status that qualified one to participate in the divine mysteries.

That Augustine would become the most celebrated orator in North Africa since Apuleius was recognized soon after he was ordained a priest. In fact, Bishop Valerius put him in the unusual situation of preaching as a presbyter. In 393, a plenary council of the African Church was held in Hippo. It is remarkable that during that meeting, the young priest found himself explaining the tenets of the Creed to the assembly of bishops.[52] Many of the bishops likely heard for the first time that day a voice that would echo through the region for nearly four decades. He told them that faith required not only the service of the tongue, but of the heart as well. In doing so, he reminded them of Paul's statement: "With the heart one believes unto righteousness, and with the mouth confession is made unto salvation" (Rom. 10:10).[53]

He explained to them that the Creed is a kind of non-rhetorical core of truths derived from scripture itself. The other biblical texts are rhetorical extensions providentially designed to foster reception and internalization of the core truths. Thus, "the Catholic faith is made known to the faithful in the Creed who have learned it by heart in as few words as the great subject permits." This enables "beginners and infants who have not yet been strengthened by knowledge of the divine scriptures and the most diligent spiritual interpretation of them" to have what they believe in hand. This belief, then, can be a foundation enabling them to profit from the "faith being expounded to them at greater length as they make progress and ascend to divine doctrine." They progress "by knowledge of the divine scriptures and the most diligent spiritual interpretation" to a deeper understanding of the creedal propositions they have been impressing on their hearts daily.[54]

In this way, as the former rhetor preached on the Creed, he introduced the gathered bishops to the first points of a Christian rhetoric that endeavored to engage both the heart and mind. This was a rhetoric that sought adherents "found worthy not only to accept and believe the Catholic faith as set forth in the words of the Creed," but also who "possess a knowledge and understanding of it."[55] In the course of his exposition, Augustine explained to the bishops that even though they beheld "these truths in the present life 'in part,' as it is written, and 'in an obscure manner'" (1 Cor. 13:12), they would be unable to make anyone else see them who was "hindered by defilement of heart."[56] Although entirely unnatural, sin has infected human experience through the power of custom (*consuetudo*).[57] In such a situation, even the soul can be called "flesh" because it has been corrupted by immoral living, setting its affections on the visible flesh.[58] The Christian faith, however, is one that proclaims not only "a renewal of soul" but also the "resurrection of the body."[59] This truth about human transformation is so profound, and so far removed from customary experience, that for someone to understand it, he or she would need "to be guided to the faith step by step."[60] Such a task was worthy of the episcopate, an office that Augustine could advise at this time, but not exercise.

Van der Meer observed perceptively some time ago that Augustine "made his sermons deliberately artless" to such an extent that "the average sermon of Augustine makes such a disorderly impression that his unpretentious manner seems almost to suggest downright carelessness." He suggested that the source of this impression lies in the manner in which Augustine deliberately veiled the rhetorical framework of his sermons while simultaneously showing "positive genius in his strict observance of all artistic rules." One is thus left with "no sign in Augustine's sermons of a rigidly laid out plan being strictly adhered to."[61] Anyone attempting to reconstruct from the homilies themselves the principles informing Augustine's preaching gets the sense of working at cross-purposes with their author. The more effective his artistry, the more elusive its underlying principles become.

The bishop's art, nonetheless, did not preclude him from providing his hearers and readers with instructions about how to profit from his homilies. In fact, there are many explicit statements in the homilies where he tells his hearers what he is and is not hoping to accomplish with his preaching. Although far removed from his school of rhetoric in Milan, and even from the school of Christian philosophy at Cassiciacum, those who came to his church at Hippo were informed by Augustine that they had come to a school (*schola*) in which "we learn something everyday. We learn something from commandments (*praeceptis*), something from examples (*exemplis*), something from sacraments" (*sacramentis*).[62] In the Church, these commandments, examples, and sacraments become for us "remedies for our wounds, material for our studies."[63]

Even as he described the Church as a school whose studies cure the soul, Augustine denied being a teacher. He contended, "It is Christ who is doing the teaching. . . . His school is on Earth, and his school is his own body. The head is teaching his members, the tongue talking to his feet."[64] He told those who came to hear him that in spite of the fact that he was preaching, "we are all hearers."[65] Although the congregation heard his voice, it was God who instructed.[66] Likewise, Augustine explained that his task was not to expound his own opinions, but to interpret the scriptures.[67] He portrayed himself as one who was giving the text itself a voice by saying "listen to holy scripture preaching."[68] Accordingly, as he preached, Augustine claimed to be receiving instruction along with his hearers, "we are walking along the way with you."[69] His hearers were really his "fellow students in the school of the Lord."[70] He told them that as he preached, he attended to himself as well because "one is a futile preacher of God's word outwardly if one is not also inwardly a listener."[71] When he did admit to teaching, he qualified the assertion by saying that he strove to teach in such a way as not to be unteachable himself.[72] He shared publicly his worry that his ministry of speaking outwardly exposed him to the danger that he would cease listening inwardly to the voice that he was charged merely to relay.[73]

Augustine admonished his hearers never to be content with belief in his human words or anyone else's for that matter. Rather, they should strive to apprehend directly the truths to which the words refer. He told them flatly, "Do not think that anyone learns anything from a person." Reliance upon external words yields only "useless sounds."[74] His own voice was at best one that offered superficial "aids and suggestions," a kind of external prompting that was nothing more than empty sound.[75] His hearers should employ this external aid to acquire the skills necessary to hear the "Interior Master": one who teaches in the deep recesses of the heart rather than while standing at one's side.[76]

Augustine encouraged them to look upon him as a hired hand who cultivates trees from the outside, but lacks all ability to make them grow or produce fruit. They should know that his labors would have no effect at all apart from their response to the one who "dwells within through faith and the Holy Spirit."[77] He was for them a basket in which the sower had placed seeds that he wished to broadcast abroad.[78] They should not look at him as the physician of their souls; he was, instead, one seeking to be cured along with them.[79] As evidence of the limits of his art, he drew attention to the fact that, although he addressed everyone with the same words, not all were persuaded by or even understood him.[80] If they were to profit from his homilies, they could not be content with passively appreciating his eloquent words. They needed to press beyond them actively to apprehend wisdom for themselves.

Given the above qualifications, Augustine contended that "the Catholic Faith" was something "which must be preached to all." He believed, however, that openly commending spiritual truth to those whose carnal minds cause them to treat it with disdain was irresponsible.[81] To prevent this misstep, he appealed to New Testament texts, informed by psychagogic theory, which counseled teachers to temper their aims with rhetorical principles. He knew well that St. Paul wrote to the Corinthians about feeding them with milk rather than solid food because he could not speak to them about spiritual things so long as they remained carnal.[82] He also read the exhortation in Hebrews that stated that while milk is for infants, "solid food is for the perfect, for those who by habit have their senses exercised to separating good from evil."[83] He, therefore, advised his hearers, "Do not be in a hurry, then, to hear what you cannot yet take in, but grow up so that you may become capable of it."[84] He explained to them that their understanding depended on the degree of development their souls possessed: "in the mind, that is, in the inner man, one grows in a certain kind of way, not only so that one may go from milk to solid food, but also so that one may more and more take solid food itself. But one does not grow in the expansion of size, but in the enlightenment of intellect; for in fact the solid food itself is intellectual light."[85] To perceive profound truth required becoming a profound person.

By the time of Augustine's episcopal preaching—as one would expect from his theoretical reflections discussed in the previous chapters—he worried that this strategy, as well as the New Testament texts supporting it, would be used not to inform the public ministry of the Church, but to justify private esoteric teaching for the elite few in the name of Christianity.[86] In his own practice, he defined these texts so that they would be used only in service of formal methods of spiritual guidance. He openly opposed any material polarity between the milk given to his little ones and the solid food of the mature. The bishop taught his congregation that

there is "no need that certain [esoteric] secrets of doctrine be kept silent
and be hidden from the immature faithful, [only] to be uttered separately
to the mature, that is, to those with more understanding." In fact, both
groups "hear the same message."[87]

In Augustine's view, the milk with which the apostle says that he nourished the little ones was "the crucified Christ himself": the same crucified who is "made of God for us wisdom and justice and sanctification
and redemption."[88] His flesh "is both milk for those suckling and [solid]
food for those advancing."[89] The "solid food" of spiritual things "is not
incompatible with this milk, even so much that it itself turns into milk
whereby it can be suitable to infants."[90] The more mature do not hear any
other words than the immature. They understand more — not because
they receive private instruction that differs from what is available to all —
but on account of their greater capacity to do so. The bishop therefore
exhorted all of his hearers, regardless of their spiritual maturity, to "make
progress toward the solid food of the mind, not the stomach." He told
them that it was by "adhering" to Christ more and more that they would
be "freed from evil" — a process whereby evil is not merely removed from
the soul spatially, but is "healed in you."[91]

In a similar fashion, Augustine explained Jesus' instructions regarding
the Spirit who would guide his congregation in apprehending the "many
things" that he could not teach them because they were not yet capable
of understanding them. Noting that Jesus did not say what these things
were, the bishop insisted that this saying could not pertain to "some very
cryptic secrets or other that, though they could be said by a teacher, could
not be borne by a student."[92] He warned them to distrust anyone claiming to possess such knowledge because this life is so limited that even if
the "interior teacher would now wish to say these things, that is, to open
and show them to our mind, human weakness could not hear them."[93]
Jesus did not pass on this knowledge through words because it could not
be humanly possessed either then or under the current conditions.[94]

The bishop also cautioned his hearers not to expect to learn such truths
from him, "who of us would dare to say that he was now capable of apprehending the things that those men were not strong enough to apprehend?"[95] Even if their bishop were so great to grasp them himself, he
would not be able to communicate truth to them that was too profound
for them to understand. Neither could they expect to acquire such direct
insight from reading scripture as if the truth Jesus spoke of could be

equated with what was later written down by the apostles.[96] Those things that the Lord was reluctant to say in fact cannot be learned by "exterior teachers" in the form of "readings and discourses presented from the outside."[97]

He counseled those who came to hear him that the only way they could come to a fuller knowledge would be to grow in the love that they already have received, the love poured forth in their hearts by the Holy Spirit. "By this very love a better and fuller knowledge is affected."[98] Augustine contended that only by being "afire in the spirit and loving spiritual things" could the soul make progress in understanding "not by some sign apparent to the eyes of the body, or by some sounds making a loud noise in the ears of the body, but by the interior sight and hearing, the spiritual light and spiritual voice that the carnal cannot bear."[99] It is "the Holy Spirit himself" who "now both teaches believers, as far as each one can apprehend spiritual things, and inflames their breasts with a greater desire if each should progress in that love by which he both loves what is perceived and longs for what is to be perceived."[100] The most profound truths are "taught of God" so that "by the very mind itself" one "may have the ability to discern these very things."[101]

Even as Augustine admonished his hearers to seek the guidance of the Holy Spirit in their efforts to apprehend spiritual truth directly, he also taught them that what they did experience would amount to no more than a "pledge" toward the "fullness" of the Spirit that is "reserved for us in another life." Whatever things the soul now "to some extent perceives" are "not yet known as they are to be known in the life that neither eye has seen nor has entered into the human heart."[102] As the faithful labored in the half-light of human existence, Augustine cultivated in them a longing to emerge from the shadows even while reminding them that they would never do so in this life. He assured them that, at the dawning of the redeemed future, they would discover that what they then perceived directly was not discontinuous with what had been revealed to them as a shaft of light amid the former shadows. In this way, Augustine enjoined those listening to his homilies to yearn for perfect understanding without ever forgetting that they perceive the truth only to the extent that their capacity permits. They were pilgrims through time, whose Christian identity was not yet fully revealed even to themselves, who had knowledge without complete understanding and love without the possession of all that they loved.

Augustine's influence upon Roman civic life was due more to his persuasive ability than to his social status or imperial rank. He was never able to wield political power comparable to that of a figure like Ambrose. Neil McLynn comments that "the real power-holding elite remained beyond Augustine's reach."[103] Peter Brown notes how "we do not hear" in the sermons "the voice of a man confident that, as a Catholic bishop, he had been called to rule an entire society."[104] His preaching reveals, instead, "an Augustine struggling with all the rhetorical and didactic resources at his disposal to keep the Christian congregation from being absorbed back into a world in which Christianity had by no means yet captured the cultural high ground."[105] In his sermons, Augustine used the medium with which he was most comfortable to pass on both the critical skills required to form a distinct Christian identity and the constructive guidance necessary to sustain it.

Critical Skills

Augustine was keenly aware that those who gathered to hear him had elected to turn their attention away from the sundry forms of entertainment available in Roman cities. At times, the surrounding cultural events were so attractive to his hearers that the bishop felt compelled to comment on them in his homilies. He told his hearers that the spectators at the stadium had gone to cheer for the uncertain victory of someone other than themselves. In doing so, they were already "defeated by the very fact of their running off there."[106] He explained to those who gathered to hear him that in forgoing the games they had not disdained shows altogether, but were choosing instead the better spectacle.[107] They had come to witness "the shows truth puts on" rather than the "shows put on for the flesh."[108] It was the kind of "spectacle" Christ himself provided as he subdued the minds of those who nailed his body to the cross.[109] The spectacle they came to witness was one for which they would never need to feel shame. On the contrary, this was a spectacle where they themselves would be the victors. Augustine encouraged his listeners to tell their friends who had run off to the stadium about the delightful display they had missed. His hope was that as more of his listeners' friends realized how much the other spectacle "cheapened themselves," the more it would "grow cheap" in their eyes.[110]

One reason that people chose to attend the bishop's homily was that Augustine's preaching was itself a spectacle worth watching. As he railed against the secular games, he gave an extended sermon during which they could watch him wrestle with the meaning of biblical passages that they had heard read earlier. He paused in the middle of the struggle to admire the scriptural mystery saying "to my mind it tastes delicious."[111] He preached without notes, although there are indications that he mentally prepared in advance his explications of the day's readings. Whenever the lector inadvertently read a different text, Augustine was known to delight his hearers by accepting the challenge presented by providence by preaching on whatever was read.[112]

The manuscripts of many of the sermons end abruptly, often with the unfinished concluding exhortation "turning to the Lord . . ."[113] This common conclusion suggests the manner in which Augustine intended his homilies to facilitate the ongoing conversion of those who heard him. Their choice to hear him was not just a matter of the location of their bodies, but of the state of their hearts. It was a choice that Augustine hoped would foster a growing awareness of their innerselves as well as of their mode of participation in Roman society. Attaining this critical perspective was an integral component of the cognitive and emotional reorientation of the self that Augustine promoted.

The bishop, however, was not one to understate the difficulty of this task. He believed that "every human being, wherever he or she is born, learns the tongue of that country, or district or civic community, and is imbued with the customs and way of life proper to that place." He queried, "How, for instance, could a child born among the pagans avoid paying cult to a stone idol, when his parents have trained him in that form of worship? In that milieu he heard his earliest words; he sucked in that falsehood with his mother's milk."[114] Augustine told his hearers that it was common for those who are sick to have every confidence in their good health and not to know how dangerously ill they are.[115] He warned the faithful, "There are things in a person which are hidden from the person in whom they are."[116] Deep character flaws can lie fallow in their souls without ever becoming subject to scrutiny. For example, Augustine cautions that "the horrid depths of avarice are hidden from our eyes, all the while they are seething in our souls."[117] He explained how "every sin becomes trivial with habit, till you come to treat it as practically nothing."[118] Lacking the perspective necessary to see itself, the soul turns toward outward things and falls in love with its own ability to manipulate them. In the process, the soul loses track of itself and becomes incapable of accurately assessing its own actions. Instead, it "justifies its iniquities. It grows insolent and proud in self-will and self-indulgence, in positions of rank and authority and wealth, in vain and empty power."[119] It resists having its bonds broken because it does not see them as restrictive. In fact, it considers its chains attractive and a source of pleasure.[120]

In whatever city he preached, Augustine continually exhorted those listening to attend primarily to themselves rather than to continue to be distracted by concern for outward things. He admonished them, "How long are you going to go round and round creation? Come back to yourself, look at yourself, inspect yourself, discuss yourself."[121] He told them that this distraction resulted in a kind of "external wandering"—an "exile" from oneself so severe as to lose track of oneself altogether.[122] The more accustomed they became to this exile, the more they would resist change. The preacher thus chides, "You are unwilling to see yourself as you are! You blame others, you do not look at yourself; you accuse others, you do not think of yourself; you place others before your eyes, you place yourself behind your back."[123] He believed that his hearers would not succeed in finding a good larger than themselves so long as they looked for it apart from themselves.

Augustine deliberately crafted his sermons to involve his hearers in a reflective process whereby the heretofore unperceived blockages that inhibited their self-perception were brought to the surface and articulated. He exclaimed, "I take you from behind your back, and put you down in front of your eyes. You will see yourself, and bewail yourself!"[124] Such reflection served to show the soul to itself as it was. What had been believed implicitly had to be subjected to scrutiny before it could be explicitly denied. The very act of articulating propositions weakened their persuasive force. According to Augustine, when the soul sees itself "it is dissatisfied with itself, it confesses the ugliness" it has accrued through its defective loves; it confesses how it has diminished itself by neglecting the One by whom it was made, and it "longs to be beautiful" itself and to possess a satisfying love.[125]

The seasoned rhetor knew well, however, that frank speech showing the soul its unvarnished self was not sufficient to affect the hoped-for reorientation. It was a kind of radical surgery resulting in such excessive pain for the patient as to render it an ineffectual treatment. It was a light so bright that to look at it would result in total blindness. To be sure, the soul needed to acquire an accurate assessment of itself, but for it to profit from such insight it would need gentle guidance — a poultice rather than surgery, a lamp rather than the sun, milk rather than solid food.[126] He advised his hearers, therefore, not to rush forward prematurely, but to accept the breast of the Church knowing that its milk would bring them to the stage of eating the food that they could not yet manage.[127] He explained to them that "the Word became flesh, so that we little ones might be nourished on milk, being babies still in respect to solid food."[128]

He informed his hearers that, if truth is to reach us in the present life, it will do so as a shaft of light traveling a winding and oblique path to hearts filled with shadows.[129] Augustine readily invoked the words of Peter, who exhorted his readers to attend to the word of prophecy as to "a lamp burning in a dark place until the day dawns and the morning star rises in your hearts."[130] Those finding themselves in the dimness of the present life need to find "lights in a dark place." The Christian scriptures they hear read in church partially illumine the opacity of their own hearts and the murkiness of Roman social life.[131] The scriptures burn as "lamps for us in the night of this world that we might not remain in the darkness." Only by attending to such lamps will their eyes be illumined. The more they accustom themselves to this light, the more their own "little flame" will burn: a flame whose light burns brightest when placed upon the cross of Christ as upon "a great lampstand."[132] In place of the harsh and bitter experience that direct confrontation poses for the soul, "we are given the sweetness of the scriptures to help us endure the desert of human life."[133] The bishop regularly exhorted his hearers to use the opportunity of hearing scripture read and proclaimed as a gentle means of acquiring the needed self-knowledge. Thus, he instructed those listening to "begin by seeing our own faces in those words. For as the reader intoned them we had a kind of mirror held up to us in which we could inspect ourselves, and inspect ourselves we did. Inspect yourselves too."[134]

True to his theoretical works (from every period of his life), Augustine endeavored in his sermons not only to state the truth, but to persuade; that is, to see the content enacted in the lives of hearers.[135] He recognized that persuasion was exceedingly difficult because successful persuasion requires an active change in the life of the hearer rather than passive assent. Much of the challenge of preaching, then, becomes employing a *form* that inculcates the *content* of the homily, that is, a form that educates the mind and trains the soul.[136] It is for this reason that explicit propositions, even if they are true, do not cultivate the necessary *habitus* involved in reforming the self. Scripture is an effective medicine because it is administered to readers in a pedagogical form that allows them to identify and overcome the obstacles preventing them from understanding and applying its truth to their lives.

To take one example, the bishop began homily 32, as he often did, by providing instructions to his hearers about how to participate in the homily. Augustine said that the Lord had just provided "many medicines from the holy scriptures" during "the divine readings" to "heal every ailment of the soul." He states that his task in preaching is "to apply these medicines to our wounds." He categorically denies being the physician himself. He does not present himself as a spiritual guide seeking to cure the soul with philosophical knowledge and rhetorical skill. Instead, the soul is cured by the medicine provided in the scriptures, not by Augustine. Indeed, he explicitly includes himself as one of those "in need of treatment."[137]

Augustine could have expressed the core *content* of the sermon in the following three succinct propositions: pride is a form of self-reliance that ultimately proves to be an illusion; humility, pride's opposite, entails relying on God and is a truer way of life; the task of the Christian is to put off pride and to put on humility. Succinct propositions, however, are exactly what the bishop did not present. It is not that he was incapable of putting forward a straightforward argument. The man who bragged of reading and understanding Aristotle's *Categories* could have easily spun an argument of perfect syllogisms, but he deliberately chose not to express himself this way in the sermons.

Rather than outlining propositions, in his sermons Augustine typically invited his hearers to join him in a shared inquiry into the meaning of Christian scripture. This inquiry ideally would lead to self-knowledge and personal transformation. The vast majority of his homilies take the form of an inquiry into the meaning of specific biblical texts.[138] He would say, "I am prompted by the Lord . . . to tackle together with you this text that has been read, and find out what it really means."[139] He taught others to value the act of biblical questioning. He could remark accordingly, "If you have seen the question, you have seen no small thing."[140] Augustine exhorted those who came to hear him not just to listen, but to search actively with him: "Join in the work with me"; "help me knock at the door";

"I am your fellow worker"; "Let both of us, therefore, seek; let both knock"; "Listen to me, or rather, listen with me; let us both listen together, both learn together."[141] Rather than rushing to conclusions, they were to learn to "inquire peacefully, without strife, without contentiousness, without altercations, [and] without hostilities."[142]

In this manner, the bishop inquires of each section of Psalm 144, "Who is the speaker?" Augustine solicits his hearers' participation in such an inquiry. Who is it asking in verses three and four, "What is man? His days pass by like a shadow." Who is it saying in verse nine, "I will sing a new song to you, O God; on a ten-stringed harp I will play to you." And why is this psalm entitled, "*Ad Goliam*" as if it were a smooth stone aimed at Goliath's head? Augustine promises his hearers that the psalm "contains hidden secrets of great importance" since God has put such things in the scriptures "in order that [those listening] may be exercised in seeking" the meaning. He assures his hearers that those who often come to hear the scriptures "know who Goliath is" because they have practiced learning its language, while for others the meaning of the name is less apparent.[143]

While engaging in this interpretive exercise, Augustine and his hearers discover that there are two speakers in Psalm 144: David and Goliath, each signifying "two kinds of life"—the "old" life of the Philistine who is driven by pride and the "new" life of the Israelite who holds a humble faith solely in God.[144] For Augustine, Goliath's outward actions on the day of battle reveal the inner disposition characterizing his whole way of life: "Goliath is bursting with pride, and proud in such prosperity, issues his challenge to the contest: 'Who can match me? Who will dare me?'"[145] Goliath, convinced of his own strength, takes "upon himself the entire responsibility for the victory of his whole side."[146] Augustine queries whether a man like Goliath does not "feel like this every day? He has to some extent more than his neighbor has. Does he not say, 'Who can match me?' or, 'If this neighbor of mine does me wrong, will I not just show him?' See if Goliath is not challenging to the contest like this."[147] As Augustine's hearers realize that Goliath is speaking in the psalm, they also see their own similarities to the giant—namely, the struggle for self-sufficiency and for a safe way of being in the world based on their own strength and skill—in a new light.

Augustine points out that David, in contrast to Goliath, eschews all worldly armor and weapons. He enters into battle "completely unencumbered," with his hope "in the Lord, not himself, armed not with steel but with faith" enacted in "love."[148] Like Goliath, David acts in a manner that reveals his inner character. David's actions, however, proceed from a genuine humility that is shown to be stronger than Goliath's unwarranted pride.[149] The battle reveals what David already knew to be true, that the head raised up in pride would be brought low by the head "marked with the humility of the cross of Christ."[150] "What is man?" is what David "chanted like a spell" (*incantat*) against Goliath to lay the giant low. Augustine suggests that in discerning the voice in the text to be that of Goliath, his hearers have found their own to be that of the Philistine's self-reliance. He admonishes them, "[H]umble yourself under the flood of grace . . . trusting not in yourself, stripping yourself of Goliath, [and] putting on David."[151]

Augustine considered the hearing and delivering of the sermon itself to be a similarly humbling exercise.[152] The bishop's continual reminder to his congregation that the sermon is a shared inquiry was not mere rhetorical posturing. He purposefully constructed sermons as exercises in which both he and his congregation participate in order to develop for themselves habitual skills of reading and living. Interpretive choices and life choices did not fundamentally differ. Failures in understanding the meaning of a biblical text revealed fissures in one's moral life and vice versa. In the words of *De doctrina christiana* discussed earlier, the sermon itself was a "traveling down the road of affections" for the speaker and the hearer.

Augustine's attention to signification is integral to the homily itself. He articulates the message in a form that facilitates its internalization in the souls of his hearers. In other words, the formal characteristics of the homily are deliberately constructed to further its material content. The form of the homily cultivates a *habitus* that fosters the life described in its content. If Goliath were to devote himself to the humbling task of understanding the Bible, he would not be able to understand it until he discarded his basic orientation toward the world, which was a prideful closure to the world of signification that did not refer to himself.[153] He would need the faith to live in a world not centered on his own strength and skills, a world where he was dependent on the faithfulness of another for victory. For this reason, the homily's focus on the difficulty of understanding scripture is intimately related to its moral exhortation against pride. Pride's expansive pretensions stand in sharp contrast to its actual limiting effects. Augustine remarks that "the real Philistines are those who assume that the only perfect well-being is to be found here and now."[154]

The humble, sometimes difficult, speech of the Bible is stronger than pride. Scripture is a God-given field of exercise upon which souls can be persuaded as they give themselves to the task of interpreting it and becoming practiced in discerning its meaning. As the bishop says, "[T]his psalm, which is aimed *at Goliath,* claims your attention."[155]

The experience of Augustine's hearers was often one in which the scriptural text came to them like the psalm whose words were intended to fell Goliath. The bishop told them that if they felt like the word of God was their adversary, they were right.[156] He explained, "As long as you are your own enemy, you have God's word as your enemy."[157] It was a word that challenged behaviors and judgments which enjoyed widespread cultural approval—ones with which they themselves were deeply identified. For example, Augustine observed that it was common to treat the infidelity of husbands more lightly than that of their wives, making what was equally sinful seem more innocent when committed by a man. Indeed, he believed that this custom had taken on the force of a law.[158] Although such a practice was socially accepted, it did not fare well under the critical scrutiny of divine truth. Augustine suggested to his hearers that they were now confronted with an adversary possessing such authority that it would be in their best interest to seek to come to an agreement with it rather than oppose it.[159] They should, therefore, behave more like patients who agree to be cared for by doctors, trusting that any painful treatments would be aimed at their disease rather than themselves.[160] To do this would require conforming their hearts to the very standard that first showed them that they were "all warped and twisted."[161] The bishop assured those listening that making peace with the word of God results in making peace with oneself, since it is our enemy only insofar as we are.

The word of God is an adversary of the false propositions that have such deep roots in the heart that they shape emotional responses and behaviors. These are propositions that often lie hidden, yet deeply influence one's perception of oneself and the world. Augustine's indirect exegetical argument does not appear to be threatening to the hearer, at least not at first. In the course of the inquiry into the meaning of the scriptural readings, however, the divine word makes its presence felt as the implications of passage after passage gradually become apparent. In this way, the preacher articulates the divine word's claim upon its hearers. As a fellow learner, he gives voice to their various responses to the divine word, including outright opposition to the scriptural insight. Those listening were free to identify or not with the objections raised. Augustine was confident that this practice of biblical inquiry was so potent that even prior to any answers, the very act of questioning was often enough to expose and discredit falsehood.[162]

Augustine sums up the work done by his hearers one day in the following way: "You have dug very deep to pull up hatred of your enemies from your heart."[163] He had brought before them texts enjoining forgiveness and love for their enemies. As he spoke, Augustine was attuned to his hearers' responses and emotional participation in the homily. He directed them to attend to themselves as well.[164] If they were really free of hate, why was this a word that bothered them so? Why would they fear, unless they were coming to see that they were "riddled with hate" and really asking "what is wrong with a man hating his enemy?"[165] If they were not "crippled with disease," why would they desire revenge?[166] When listening to such a homily, hearers discover that their emotional responses to the text offer better evidence of the implicit propositions that guide their lives than their own public statements (which have been shown to mask their true inner commitments). Emotion is an indicator of the basic doctrines of the soul. The bishop admonished them that if they want to quarrel with their enemies, they would be better off quarreling with their own hearts.[167] The "strife of the heart" is as much a barrier to understanding as any lapse of the intellect.[168]

Day after day, Augustine struggled to root out false propositions, one at a time, from the inner field of hearts, like so many weeds. He believed that the impediments inhibiting the progress of soul were both affective and intellective. In one homily, Augustine was explaining the following verse of the Psalter: "I said, Lord have mercy on me; heal my soul for I have sinned against you" (Ps. 41:4). He portrayed his hearers as being suspended between God's "good doctrine" in the scriptures and the "evil persuasions" of the devil. He was concerned that beliefs in such things as luck and fate obstructed the understanding of the truth expressed in the psalm. He challenged them openly, "Get rid of all this stuff and nonsense, whoever of you say such things, because luck in this connection is just human self-deception and fate is just illusion."[169] To be rid of such beliefs required turning away "from this twisted perversity," and to begin "contradicting yourself" as one doctrine is rooted out and replaced with one more suited to human flourishing.[170] Healing one's soul required gaining a sense of one's own agency and purging oneself of beliefs obscuring it. In doing so, they would come to see that the responsibility implied in the psalmist's confession held the promise of freedom as well.[171] Accordingly, the bishop exhorted them, "Purify your habits again and again, with the help of God, to whom you make your confession."[172]

Augustine contended that all this uprooting, all this clearing and overturning of habitual patterns, rather than being a purely negative process, made room for positive growth. He likened scripture's critical effects on his hearers' beliefs to the way that adults wrest harmful amusements away from children so that the young would entertain themselves with what would be of benefit to them.[173] The openness brought about by this deprivation made it possible for new "scales to be built in the heart."[174] Scriptural texts were providentially given to serve constructive purposes as well. When a difficult text such as the first verse of the gospel of John was read, Augustine reassured his hearers that they were not wrong to feel that it was "incomprehensible." He suggested, however, that "it was not read in order to be understood, but in order to make us mere human beings grieve because we do not understand it, and make us try to discover what prevents our understanding, and so move it out of the way, and hunger to grasp the unchangeable Word, ourselves thereby being changed from worse to better."[175] If they made enough progress to long for a positive apprehension of the truth, he counseled them, "for the time being, treat the scripture of God as the face of God." They should "melt in front of it" as it burned away the human constructions they had overlaid as a veneer upon God's natural creation.[176]

Constructive Guidance

While Augustine was teaching at Cassiciacum, he imagined that those with the requisite skill and leisure could remedy their souls' infirmities through proper training. Accordingly, he advocated a set of daily practices for fostering the ongoing formation of the soul. Internalizing the fruits of such studies would yield a stronger and more harmonious soul that could discipline its passions and rise above adversity. It would not be deceived by the fluctuations of sense perception, but would ascend toward

the singular and unchanging good in which its happiness was found. In
the sermons as well, Augustine encouraged all who came to hear him to
adopt a set of therapeutic practices for the good of their souls.

Not unlike his earlier self, or the Hellenistic philosophers, he advised
his hearers that they needed to engage in such spiritual exercises daily
if they expected them to be sufficiently formative. They were to receive
the word of God as "our daily food on this earth."[177] The Christian needs
most of all "a regular discipline of listening to the word of God."[178] Augustine instructed his congregants that his labor of preaching was to be
accompanied by equal effort on their part. Sweat should appear on the
faces of both preacher and hearer as both struggle to interpret the word
of truth.[179] The daily practice of listening to scripture functioned as much
to remind or retrain the soul as to bring it new information. He said,
"These readings that are read to you, this is not the first time they have
been read to you, is it? Are they not repeated every day? Well, just as readings of God's word have to be repeated every day, to prevent the vices
of the world and thorns from taking root in your hearts and choking
the seed which has been sown there, so too the preaching of God's word
has to be repeated to you always."[180] Through this ongoing engagement,
they were to internalize the language of scripture and be so formed by
it that they would "hear with Catholic ears and perceive with Catholic
minds."[181]

Augustine explained to his hearers, "I think, brothers and sisters, that
when we speak about these things, when we reflect upon them, we are
training ourselves."[182] Regular participation in liturgical practices involving the Christian mysteries was intended to be a curative experience. He
contended:

> Brothers and sisters, what calls for all our efforts in this life is the heal-
> ing of the eyes of our hearts, with which God is to be seen. It is for this
> that the holy mysteries are celebrated, for this that the word of God is
> preached, to this that the Church's moral exhortations are directed,
> those, that is, that are concerned with the correction of our carnal de-
> sires, the improvement of our habits, the renunciation of the world,
> not only in words but in a change of life. Whatever points God's holy
> scriptures make, this is their ultimate point, to help us purge that
> inner faculty of ours from that thing that prevents us from beholding
> God.[183]

In this way, the discrete liturgical acts were expressions of the divine economy. Scripture and preaching, baptism and Eucharist were all means by which the Holy Spirit captivated minds and healed hearts by re-ordering their affections.

The bishop employed common Platonic imagery to describe the desired effects of his Christians' participation in such exegetical and liturgical practices. In a formulation as daring as any in Plato's *Phaedrus,* Augustine likened the seductive quality of the Christian message to the magic spell the snake charmer uses to lure the snake out of its dark hiding place into the light.[184] This experience of being psychagogically drawn out of a cave-like existence through Christian practices is ultimately the work of the divine physician:

> When we train ourselves in ourselves and are again, so to speak, bent back by the weight of these ordinary ideas, we are such as are the weak-eyed, when they are led out to see light, if, perhaps, they did not at all have sight before and they begin some way or other through the vigilance of the doctors to recover their sight. And when the physician wishes to test how much healing has come to them, he tries to show them what they desired to see and could not when they were blind. And when the sight of the eyes is now returning to some extent, they are led out to the light; and when they have seen, they are, to a certain extent, repulsed by the very brightness, and they reply to the physician who is showing them the light, "Just now I saw, but I cannot see." What, then, does the physician do? He resumes the usual treatment, and he adds a salve, so that he may nourish the desire for that which was seen and could not be seen and from this very desire a cure may be effected more fully.[185]

Augustine, thus, likens his congregation to those who have indeed been led out into the light, but whose still weak eyes are not yet strong enough to see clearly for any amount of time. They say, "Just now I saw, but I cannot see." He advises them to continue the "usual treatment," — the conversation about the scriptures in the context of the eucharistic liturgy — even if it stings, to cultivate a love for the light, and constantly to entreat the physician to cure them.

In their ecclesial experience, the faithful were given the opportunity to identify with their predecessors who called out from a distant age through their writings saying, "We shall go to the house of the Lord" (Ps. 122:1).[186] Augustine encouraged members of his congregation to find their own voice in these words of scripture "let each of you be this singer."[187] Through such songs they were invited to ascend with the preacher "not with our feet, but by our affections."[188] This would mean ascending "in heart, in holy desires, in faith, hope, and charity, in the desire of eternity or of life without end."[189] Augustine hoped that his hearers would make such an ascent even as he preached. He remarked, "If I am getting anywhere, if my sweat and toil are not proving unprofitable, you are ascending to the heaven of the divine scriptures, I mean the understanding of them, by means of our preaching."[190]

The bishop of Hippo assured his hearers that each soul that ascends in this manner discovers that it has a pair of wings and "flies with them, that is, with the two commandments of the love of God and the love of neighbor."[191] The more proficient it becomes at flying with these wings, the more it realizes its true identity.[192] Augustine never tired of reminding his hearers that the love of God was something that was infused into their hearts by the Holy Spirit.[193] It was this love that was the source of human renewal.[194] This love was "the soul of the scriptures, the force of prophecy, the saving power of the sacraments, the fruit of faith, the wealth of the poor, the life of the dying."[195]

It is important to note that scripture is no *deus ex machina* in this process of renewal, as if it could mechanistically cure the soul as a kind of efficient cause. In Augustine's homiletic practice, scripture maintains a necessary place within the organic whole of God's larger economy, which includes the entire ecclesial life of the Church. God's Word extends its curative presence into the world through the Holy Spirit's use of the whole sacramental life of the Church, which includes baptism and Eucharist.[196] Scripture's efficacy in healing the affections of the heart derives from the Holy Spirit's use of it.[197] Augustine preached to his congregation, "We cannot love God except through the Holy Spirit." "Since the Holy Spirit is God, let us love God with God."[198] He explained, "To love God is even a gift of God. . . . Through this Spirit we love both the Father and the Son, and this Spirit we love together with the Father and the Son."[199] The only unforgivable sin was to resist the Spirit's persuasion, to reject this love.[200]

When Augustine preached on an especially obscure text or point of doctrine, and he sensed that the members of his congregation had reached the limit of their understanding, he commonly exclaimed, "Lift up your heart!"[201] For those who knew, this was the very phrase drawn from the eucharistic canon that Augustine would intone as he stood in front of the bread and wine calling the faithful to elevate their minds and see in these elements the body and blood of Christ. In the same way, when faced with the common letters of scripture, Augustine called the faithful to lift their vision up and see in these words the realities to which they referred. He told them that if they could discern Christ in the scriptures, what they read would become wine for them. It would become not only "savory," but also would "intoxicate, shifting the mind away from the body [of the text], so that . . . you stretch yourself forth to those things that are before you."[202]

If the text could become wine, other sacraments could become "visible words."[203] Baptism was "the bath of water in the Word."[204] The interpretation of scripture and the participation in the other mysteries each cultivated the same habit of mind, or formation of soul. Both of these practices called one to ascend mentally and emotionally from the "words" to that to which they refer and in which they cohere. This formation of soul, carefully cultivated through liturgical practice, was intended to pervade the rest of the Christian's life. Thus, Augustine explained metaphorically:

> No one who has heard or heeded the invitation, "Lift up your hearts," can have a bent back. An erect stance characterizes one who looks to the hope stored up for us in heaven, especially if we have sent our treasure there ahead of us, whither our heart looks to follow. Those who, by contrast, are already so blinded that they have no understanding of our hope in the life to come can think only of affairs here below; and this means that their backs are bent.[205]

Through the regular liturgical discipline, sacramental "words" are taken up again and again as an ongoing training of perception that shapes actions as it re-awakens and re-orders love. This is a therapeutic process that begins to heal the affections by elevating the soul's occluded vision and persuading it gradually to move toward integration in a stable love. It begins to see providentially given external signs such as words, water, bread, and wine transfigured by the singular love from which they derive their being. Rather than separating the soul from externalities by training it to depend on its own inner resources, Augustine told the faithful, "We are nourished by outward signs that we might be able to come to the endur-ing realities themselves."[206] Instead of buttressing the boundary between the self and its external circumstances, these practices strove to mend the breach by establishing a healthy relationship between the inner person and the outer world.

Even as he encouraged his hearers to ascend in their affections toward God, Augustine increasingly thought that the experience of soaring high above worldly attachments paradoxically served to reveal the extent of one's identification with them. He taught those who came to hear him that to belong to "Israel" (by etymology, to "those who see God") is for "the one who acknowledges that he is not what God is."[207] The closer they approached the eternal divine grandeur, the more it became clear that "there is nothing more fragile than our soul situated amid worldly temp-tations."[208] Rather than strengthening their souls so that they could with-stand the hardships presented by the world, Augustine counseled them to realize that they were more fragile than glass.[209] They were to be pilgrims whose every experience of momentary safety in the present world would lead them all the more to appreciate the enduring happiness of their home country.[210] It was this very mentality, nonetheless, that would allow them to receive each good available in the present world as a gift rather than crushing it under the weight of their own search for happiness.

The ascent of these travelers is, therefore, characterized not by affirma-tions of their increasing strength, goodness, or autonomy, but by their con-fession of the very divine goodness that continually exposes their human vulnerability.[211] Augustine frequently drew the attention of his hearers to Jesus' parable of the Pharisee and the tax collector (Luke 18:11–14).[212] He wanted them to see that it was not the Pharisee's sin that prevented him from receiving anything further from God, but his reliance on his uncontested good deeds such as fasting and tithing. In other words, the Pharisee "had come to the doctor to be cured" but then only showed the physician sound limbs while "covering up his wounds." By contrast, the tax collector could be cured because he confessed his need.[213] Augustine coun-seled the faithful to remember that they, too, had already fallen through evil desire and could not truly ascend by their own strength. They would "ascend by clinging" to Christ, who came down to us.[214]

He repeatedly warned them not to confuse the strength cultivated through human discipline with the true strength of heart that could only be received as a gift.[215] In sermons addressing philosophical therapies designed to promote human happiness, Augustine argued that those who seek to find it in excellence of soul are far better off than those who seek to find it in the body.[216] Augustine conceded that there was much to admire in the principled life trained in virtue advocated by Stoic philosophers: "a virtuous mind is something very praiseworthy, sagacity, telling the difference between bad things and good, justice, distributing to all what is theirs by right, moderating, curbing lusts, courage, imperturbably enduring trials."[217] He told his hearers that through such ideals, "the Stoics present themselves as the bravest of the brave, and it is not because of the body's pleasure but on account of the mind's virtue that they cherish not being afraid for the sake of not being afraid."[218]

He argued that however excellent such personal achievement may be, or for that matter, however excellent the cultural art is that promotes that achievement, it results in a closure to the world beyond their carefully constructed selves. Accordingly, the Stoic philosophers' virtue endangers their health to the extent that they rely on their own efforts to cure their souls.[219] He cautioned his hearers that in this life, "many have grown so hardened that they do not feel their own bruises."[220] Their quest for vitality had inadvertently lulled them into a kind of deadness that feels neither passion nor the pricks of pain. Augustine warned those who heard him that it makes all the difference whether one is free from pain because of health or because of numbness. He reminded them that "healthy flesh feels pain when it is pricked."[221]

Without setting aside notions of excellence, Augustine contended that they "who have been made sons" by God have "regained the sense of pain" in the process.[222] If Augustine's Stoic locates human happiness in human virtue, Augustine's Christian receives it as a gift of God.[223] It is a happiness that comes *to* us, rather than *from* us, as love poured into our hearts by the Holy Spirit. The mature bishop, nevertheless, reminded his hearers when they heard scripture portray the Spirit as a dove that it was no placid animal. This was the Dove that "fights for its nest with beak and wings, it expresses anger without bitterness . . . love expresses anger."[224] This was the Dove that comes into the world to convict the world of sin (John 16:8), that is, to undo Christians in order to heal them. In this way, Augustine taught the faithful that the work of the Spirit was less to free Christians from pain than to use it for God's purposes. In his own words, he says:

Yes, he [the Psalmist] says to God, "you shape our pain as your pre-cept" (Ps. 93[94]:20), you fashion pain (*dolore*) into a precept laid on me. You give form to my pain; you do not leave it shapeless but mold it to your purpose, and this carefully formed pain inflicted on me will be for me a commandment from you, so that you may set me free. You form pain, scripture says, you shape our pain, you mold our pain. . . . As an earthenware pot is so called because it is the potter's work, so do you like a potter mold our pain into shape.[225]

Thus, instead of responding to an emotion like fear by spiritually ascend-ing, as it were, above it by means of a deliberative process that ultimately proves that the feeling lacks a rational basis, the bishop exhorted his hearers: "Let fear occupy your heart that it may lead to love." He assured them that if they could feel the fear, God would use it like a physician uses a scalpel.[226] They would discover such emotions not to be lingering bonds to the external world that need to be transcended, but rather to be ongoing indicators of their finite existence and consequent receptivity. Their pain would not, then, be alleviated in this life. It would not be re-moved from them, but it would be integrated into their souls and made part of their creaturely identity until the final day when it would be trans-figured along with the rest of creation.

As the faithful placed themselves, day after day, amid so many mys-teries, Augustine called out to them, "Remind yourselves what you are."[227] He wondered at the difficulty they had in seeing how truly valuable they were, even in their wayfaring state.[228] They would not be able to under-stand the meaning of any Christian sacrament without revising their own perception of themselves. About the consecrated-yet-broken bread of communion, he instructed them, "It is the mystery of yourselves that has been placed on the Lord's table; it is the mystery of yourselves that is what you receive."[229] They needed to "recognize in the bread what hung on the cross, and in the cup what flowed from his side."[230] As they labored with the benefit of such an external sign to discern what it meant for them-selves, the bishop admonished them, "Be what you see and receive what you are."[231] Participating in their own transfiguration in the sacramen-tal consecration of the bread and wine, the faithful realized their member-ship in Christ's body that was broken by his love for the world. Just as the eucharistic offering was not reducible to individual acts of willing or to the distinctive achievements of priests, but was most essentially the Holy

Spirit's gift, so also they were to experience the Spirit's work in their lives most essentially as a gift. The Spirit's therapeutic love was not one that insulated them from the travails of the Roman Empire, but was one that made it possible for them to love and hope amid the insecurity, pain, fear, and grief of Roman political life. Indeed, communion in Christ's long-suffering desire for the world was, for Augustine, the basis of the only solid, life-giving, politics. It was that which led each Christian to discover his or her true citizenship in that final communion of love that Augustine called the heavenly city.

Chapter Eight

Therapy and Society

The art of God's ineffable medicine turns even the foulness
of human vices into something that has a beauty of its own.
—Augustine, *uera rel.* 28.51

The Incarnate Word and Community

Others have noted that although Augustine remains known for his forceful critique of a Roman Empire that had too often come to see its hege-
mony as eternal in duration, he never anticipated the extent to which
classical institutions, especially those concerned with education, would
decline soon after his death.[1] The great irony of Augustine's reception
and transformation of classical traditions of philosophical therapy is that
his sermons and treatises presuppose to a remarkable degree the very classicism that he endeavored to qualify. As he worried about how Christians
could maintain a distinct identity while participating ever more deeply
in Roman society, he self-consciously employed resources derived from the
very culture from which he sought to distinguish the faithful. In this way,
the more one appreciates the extent to which Augustine remained immersed in the vital traditions of antiquity, the more one sees that it is in his
critique of Roman culture that his classical humanism is most evident—

198

a humanism that reclaimed precisely those elements of culture that he saw slipping into decadence.[2] Perhaps this is not a surprising legacy of a man who taught that it was not the origin of cultural materials that was morally relevant, but the use to which they were put by the human heart.

This peculiarity of Augustine's work is nowhere more visible than in his use of classical rhetoric. Even as he inveighed against fundamental elements of Roman culture on a daily basis, he did so by reviving Cicero's retrieval of classical philosophical rhetoric in opposition to pragmatic sophistry. Margaret Atkins has observed that by the early fifth century, "classical texts needed digesting to be of use" either to pagans or to Christians. Ironically, "Cicero's ideas took on new life" for Augustine in ways that they did not for many of Augustine's pagan contemporaries.[3] Cicero had explained to Augustine the origins of rhetoric in the following manner:

> There was a time when people wandered here and there in the fields like animals and lived on uncultivated food; they did nothing by the guidance of reason, but relied chiefly on their physical strength; there was as yet no institution of worship nor of social obligations; no one had yet seen lawful marriage, nor had anyone looked upon children known to be his own, nor had he accepted what usefulness just law had. And so, on account of error and ignorance, desire, the blind and rash mistress of the mind, exploited to its satisfaction physical strength, the most pernicious of accomplices.[4]

According to Cicero, human beings only came to differentiate themselves from the beasts when a great man harnessed the power of words to gather them together.[5] "Through reason and eloquence" such an orator gave the human race what it needed to become civilized and no longer live like animals.[6] Civilization came into existence through eloquent words, ordering what would otherwise be chaos. Cicero's narrative advances the classical notion that human flourishing requires a certain formation of soul that gives it the capacity to order its instincts by words. Civilization is, as it were, a rhetorical achievement and rhetoric is a civilizing force.

The orator is the hero who embodies this ideal and consequently excels other human beings as much as they do the animals.[7] Stories of sophists such as Dio Chrysostom calming mutinous armies by the sheer power of persuasive speech were repeated because they personified the deepest aspirations and fears of a civilization. It is worth remembering that "citizens of the Roman Empire at its height, in the second century A.D., were born into a world with an average life expectancy of less than twenty-five years. Death fell savagely on the young. Those who survived remained at risk. Only four out of every hundred men, and fewer women, lived beyond the age of fifty."[8] The food available fluctuated perpetually between scarcity and famine.[9] Human survival and flourishing were closely allied to the cultural mechanisms that made them possible. Cicero held that it was through the peculiarly human combination of reason and eloquence that "many cities have been founded, that the flames of a multitude of wars have been extinguished, and that the strongest alliances and most sacred friendships have been formed."[10]

When Plato imagined the need of a philosophical orator that could lead souls from darkness into the light, he was worried about the survival of the Greek city whose future was in doubt. If human beings were to have a more stable life than the animals, they could not make their decisions the same way animals do; appearances and instinct prove too often vulnerable to deception and prejudice. Social life would need to be informed by enduring standards of truth that at least the elite few were able to perceive for themselves. Through speech adapted specifically to the souls of the many, such people could then seek to liberate others from the very falsehood and subsequent passions that held them in chain-like bondage. This practice would require using rhetorical theory for a philosophic end: that is, carefully adapting speech to the state of the souls of the hearers, beguiling them, so to speak, away from their customary behavior and habitual thought patterns.

Teachers—even those that Augustine had and harshly criticized in his *Confessions*—were part of a larger enterprise of evolving ever more complex methods of using oral speech and written words to form the young into proper citizens. Augustine's parents, like those across the Empire of his time, yearned above all else for their son to study with cultivated human beings who could develop his art of speaking. If Cicero's mythic orator brought social chaos into order with words, teachers like Seneca and Epictetus did so one soul at a time. Students first underwent a kind of moral surgery where they acquired the critical skills necessary to strip themselves of cultural fads and prejudices before moving on to exercises helping them gradually to perceive wisdom for themselves. Seeking to understand true doctrines was an exercise in moral formation for the soul analogous to the legal ordering of society.[11]

By internalizing such wisdom, by inscribing it, as it were, on the soul, students who acquired virtue were able to regulate their own emotions and were less dependent on the actions of others for happiness. Seneca's advice that Lucilius not pray to the gods for virtue did not stem from impiety.[12] This advice was typical of the larger tradition he represents, which believed that Lucilius needed to see that his happiness was dependent on his own art (τέχνη) of self-mastery rather than left to the whims of fortune (τύχη).[13] Rightly understood, it was within his own power to achieve. He would never succeed to the extent that he believed that his flourishing was out of his control or beyond the range of his individual choices. Instead, he needed to learn to "lean upon himself" and attend to his own decisions and virtue.[14] In doing this, his own agency would be realized in a wholeness of soul that would enable him to participate in all aspects of society without being compromised by it in the process.

Augustine and other Christians of his time received as part of their own self-understanding basic classical presuppositions about the relationship between human reason and society, words and emotions, as well as the soul and its cure. Augustine, Basil, and Gregory Nazianzen were students of this educational system and public oratory before they were ever bishops. During his secular career, Augustine acquired mastery of a cultural idiom that idealized the effects of eloquent speech on impressionable human beings. This professional experience, and the intellectual formation that made it possible, permanently marked him. Augustine's earliest preserved writings, produced during his retreat from public life at Cassiciacum, recount the first steps he made not as a teacher of rhetorical techniques alone, but as one who used rhetorical techniques in service of the philosophically informed Christian life. From his early experiences as a teacher of Christian philosophy at Cassiciacum to his late episcopal ministry, Augustine made his own the basic tasks of classical therapy, namely, of finding a non-conventionally determined scale of valuation, the need for critical tools to do so, and of constructive guidance that adapts language to the state of the soul of hearers and strives by means of rational and non-rational arguments to lead them gradually to apprehend wisdom for themselves.

One does not need to read far into the treatises or homilies from any period of his life to notice the standard developmental metaphors and concerns of the psychagogic tradition. Augustine was alert to the cultural associations of this language. He often likens the soul's progress to an ascent from darkness to light, moving from milk to solid food, an education in letters, a medical cure, or the training of an athlete. The continuity of vocabulary and imagery, however, obscures sub-continental shifts in meaning. The distinctive vocabulary and formal assumptions provided by classical psychagogy persist in what becomes for him an exegetical endeavor in the context of the Christian liturgy. The well-known methods of the psychagogic tradition were themselves shaped by his use of them in an ecclesial context. Augustine perceived his responsibility as a teacher to pertain primarily neither to the passing on of reliable information nor to the exercise of his own eloquence, but to the guiding of his hearers in spiritual practices that foster in them the skills necessary for them to live the Christian life. Beginning and advanced Christians each engaged in the same exercises because these practices were themselves flexible enough to challenge all types of practitioners and potent enough to become the basis of a shared humanizing project. In the hands of the bishop of Hippo, philosophical rhetoric is subsumed within the larger economy of God's psychagogic wooing of creatures by means of the dark and shadowy instruments of the world. For the faithful, this meant that their experience of providentially given external signs would become both the means to acquire self-knowledge and the impetus for positive spiritual growth. In both his post-ordination theoretical writings and homiletical practice, the stock metaphors of the psychagogic tradition refer to the healing medicines of Christ persuasively administered in the Christian congregation.

The manner in which Augustine's mature psychagogic theory fully integrates central elements of the ecclesial life of the Church, especially Christian scripture, distinguishes it from his earliest practice. The formal characteristics of his use of scripture were prepared to some extent by Hellenistic philosophers who adopted a mode of inquiry methodologically committed to the exegesis of authoritative texts and traditions. Augustine's sermons were typically framed as a shared inquiry into the biblical text where he invited his hearers to join him in seeking to discover the true meaning of a specific passage within the larger context of scripture. This indirect quality of the sermons is a feature of a homiletical practice that struggled to persuade hearers without raising their emotional resistance. Those listening would find, in due course, that they could not account for the gaps in their understanding of scripture in terms of their prior perceptions. To grow in understanding required them to begin to question not only their own personal prejudices, but also the larger hermeneutical frameworks to which they turned when trying to make sense of their experience. As they inquired into the text, they were brought into contradiction with themselves. Over time, they were to come to love wisdom and find new trustworthy precepts facilitating awareness of the true nature of the world. Augustine's objective, therefore, was not met simply by having his congregation memorize scripture, or even by their being able to repeat his interpretation of it. Rather, they were to make their own judgments about it and, thereby, develop the capacity to reason theologically.

With Cicero, Augustine believed that there was an innate affinity between society and the cultural art that made it possible. The soul fashioned by philosophical rhetoric was an image of the regimen that cured it. The inner life of Cicero's philosophical orator was to be as orderly as his speech was eloquent. The soul's formation as a final product was, so to speak, integrally related to the process that brought it about. To hear a Ciceronian speech was to admire the way its copious treatment of the subject gave the impression of sufficiency and completeness. Versed in Ciceronian style, Augustine himself had found Christian scripture distasteful and wanting, and likewise loathed his own passions and weakness. When Augustine's suppositions were in accord with his classical learning, he believed that the soul was best reformed by training it in the liberal arts. As these assumptions shifted, they necessitated a corresponding shift of method. Rather than philosophy embellished with verbal artistry, Augustine argued that it was another kind of speech altogether that would best gain the attention of passionate human beings and reorder their instincts: namely, the divine speech itself, the incarnation of the Word in Jesus Christ, a word spoken rhetorically, adapted to the human condition and meant to become the object of our desires. He contended that the eloquence of this humble word spoken by God in Jesus Christ subdued "not with ferocious steel but with a scorned piece of wood" as it created a community that took its character from the very speech that constituted it.[15]

It may well be true, nonetheless, that the shift in method preceded the shift in Augustine's sense of the cure of soul since he applied himself to learning "the Lord's style of language" as a consequence of being ordained to the priesthood and being required to teach not only the privileged elite but also the poor and the illiterate. He was charged with the responsibility of caring for a congregation that was a community of interpreters of the very canonical texts he once rejected as morally and stylistically inadequate. Many of those who heard him could not read. He taught them, nonetheless, to listen to the text speaking, to internalize its words, and to understand them. Others who heard him could read the scriptures themselves. The authoritative texts, however, appeared crude to the refined tastes of many of these learned people. Augustine strove to help them appreciate the humble style of the scriptures and begin to see it as genuine eloquence as opposed to the illusory rhetoric of speechmakers. To learn to appreciate "the words and deeds rolled up" in the biblical texts and "concealed in fleshly coverings" was an exercise analogous to apprehending the flesh of the incarnate wisdom expressed in the humanity of Jesus.[16] It was to understand that truth presents itself in this humble form on account of our weak perceptive powers. Indeed, the form of presentation was inseparable from the content because it taught us much about ourselves and our capabilities. The text lacked stylistic perfection because it was itself incomplete apart from its perfection in the eternal Word from which it derived its meaning. Christian scripture is filled with enigmatic and obscure passages that call the mind to seek an understanding that ultimately leads beyond the text itself. In his mature oratory, Augustine strove not to sidestep the apparent failings of scripture, but to draw attention to them as if to a kind of virtue. This being so, rather than oppose the spirit of the text by translating it into a more compact non-rhetorical form, the task of Augustine's preacher was to extend the text further and follow its lead.

The results Augustine aimed for in his practice were integrally related to the regimen of care he advocated. In the same way that Augustine sought to teach others not to find fault with the lowly style of the biblical text, he counseled them to admire a humble life: a life whose weakness and passion, much like the enigmas of the canonical scriptures, led it beyond itself to the eternal Word from which it derived its existence. The soul being cured in this life, therefore, would not seek to transcend such creaturely imperfections. Instead, it would follow them as a kind of path, remaining with them and discerning their meaning.[17] Augustine did not imagine, however, that the irrational parts of the soul possessed wisdom that the rational faculties could appropriate and articulate rationally. What the god-like rational faculties have to learn from the irrational "horses" is what they are least likely to discover on their own. The irrational "horses" communicate nothing other than their firsthand experience of desire, hunger, and pain—in other words, their raw need. If in Stoic therapy, the irrational motions of the soul recover their inherent rationality, in the

Augustinian version, the irrational "horses" are recognized for what they are and are thereby soothed in such a way that they become capable of following reason (christologically defined). On account of the utter primacy of the biblical form for the cure of soul, Augustine believed that the scriptural readings were irreplaceable. No dogmatic system abstracted from them could substitute for the scriptural materials themselves. In its final form, the scriptures were psychagogically necessary, holding an irreplaceable, providentially given place within the divine economy.

Augustine's mature view of the cure of soul had broad social implications. The therapeutic practices he advocated incorporated people into an ecclesial community itself in need of cure. The bishop told the faithful that they should understand their experience as Christians in terms of the patriarch Jacob.[18] They too would wrestle with God in this life and ask for a blessing. They would find, however, the effects of this struggle to be the same that Jacob found them. They would discover that the touch of God was both "chastising and life giving."[19] Augustine reminded the faithful that as Jacob was blessed, one limb of his body withered that left him limping. The bishop explained to his hearers that even as the body of Christ puts one foot down firmly, it drags another one behind it. Even as the faithful "are blessed through the flesh," the Church would not be whole in all its members. It would limp amid the nations anticipating its future redemption.[20]

Critics of the social effects of Augustine's teaching have worried that it blunts this-worldly striving and limits political action.[21] Far from being an idealism that flees the difficulties and perplexities of public life, Augustine's spirituality was, in fact, a means of gaining cognitive purchase on the real. Hillary Armstrong noted some time ago, "Plato himself shows how other-worldliness can be combined with an intense concern for the reform of the human city."[22] Augustine's social thought was only "otherworldly" to the extent that he insisted that the temporally conditioned institutions which order human life are subject to a divinely established, natural order of things. Much as rhetoric can become enamored with its own persuasive power rather than with the truth it is responsible to communicate, so also individuals, states, and churches can lose track of their instrumentality and become myopically self-regarding. For Augustine, if human beings are to materially flourish, they will need a means to find their way through the dense fog of their own cultural power to the fundamental truths that they did not make.

Augustine's teaching that the present material world ultimately provides the soul with no lasting city did not depart from the goal that he shared with his educated contemporaries who sought by means of philosophy to give the soul a stable identity that enabled it to participate in society without being compromised by it.[23] Even as he received such a goal from his philosophically inclined predecessors, Augustine transformed it particularly in regard to the way he construed such an identity. According to Robert Dodaro, "[I]t becomes clear that what is at stake for Augustine's conception of civic virtue is nothing less than a reformation of the Roman heroic ideal away from the illusions of moral victory and self-possession which it promotes."[24] He believed that such moral heroism was an ideal as dear to Pelagian ascetics and Donatist Christians as it was to Stoic philosophers. He worried that it fostered individuals who, in rising above their circumstances, left behind important features of their humanity. This abridgment of the self resulted in individuals and communities who were not open to possibilities exceeding their own technical skill (τέχνη) because the very thing that ensured their health was their success in maintaining boundaries and preserving purity. On both a communal and individual level, this limited the range of human possibilities to experiences of their own fashioning rather than ones open to grace. In an Augustinian word, it was an ideal that substituted pride for love.

The fundamental distinction between God and the world entailed for Augustine an *a priori* rejection of every human claim to know the truth directly in an unmediated manner. In this life, there was no cure for the human condition, no final solution to the question of the self. For Augustine, all such "cures"—be they philosophical, political, or religious— were the work of human pride rather than the truth. Truth, for Augustine, could never be possessed in this way. It could never be made the object of direct vision. It could only be loved. This very rejection of material finalities resulted not in the disparagement of physical matter, but, instead, in the valorization of the limited objects mediating perception: the ordinary language of texts and speeches, liturgy and sacraments, Church and Empire. Truth's mediated presence in the world, its flirtation as it were, was the only real rhetoric. Augustine's hearers and readers were to assess their own health in terms of their sensitivity and openness to this divine rhetoric rather than in terms of their perfection or wholeness or mastery. Anchored by this rhetoric, the identities of Augustine's Christians would thus be both stable and permeable, remaining open to each reminder of creaturely finitude. Their identities would remain secure not because of the success of their own efforts, but through the love of God infused in their hearts. The faithful would form a community whose identity was defined more by its steadfastness in love than in its success in either separating itself from the world or rising above it.

Conclusion

It has been widely recognized that "Plato helped to set the form of the dominant family of moral theories in our civilization."[25] In terms of the subject at hand, Plato's analysis of the challenges human beings face in acquiring their own moral agency amid the pressures and duties of social life and his proposed solution of curing the soul with beautiful words has had a long history. Plato's influence was certainly not limited to the direct effects of his own writings. These writings were transmitted by later readers so that many of his leading thoughts took on their own life and influenced far more people than actually had read a Platonic dialogue. Augustine's contribution in this regard over the thousand years following his death is incomparable. Platonic ideas were often transmitted to the West in their Augustinian form.[26] The manner in which the bishop of Hippo subjected these traditions to severe assessment and at times modified them dramatically was not always evident. It has been left to readers ever since to discern where Augustine supplements his classical inheritance and where he supplants it.

Augustine revises classical psychagogy for much the same reason and in the same ways as he revised classical philosophical and political thought. In each of these other areas, he deeply felt that classicism lacked the means to realize its highest ideals.[27] Augustine invigorated classical rhetoric by reorienting it to Christian purposes. The importance of this achievement was recognized in his own lifetime. He commonly received requests for written copies of his sermons and sent them as models for others to imitate.[28] That so many of them were preserved over the centuries testifies to their perceived value. As a consequence of this study, the formal structure of the homilies as homilies becomes more transparent. Pierre Hadot remarks, "We often have the impression when we read ancient authors that they write badly, that the sequence of ideas lacks coherence and connection. But it is precisely because the true figure escapes us that we do not perceive the form that renders all the details necessary . . . once discovered, the hidden form will make necessary all of the details that one often believed arbitrary or without importance."[29] Making explicit the "hidden" psychagogic form that makes necessary the details of the sermons constitutes at least a beginning to assessing the homily as a discrete task with its own explicit criteria for effectiveness.[30] The unstated psychagogic principles informing their composition are responsible for the characteristic qualities of the homilies—even their digressive and repetitive features. On account of the great extent to which it informs pastoral theory and practice, awareness of psychagogic methods is especially important for understanding the dynamic interaction between preacher and audience. Other bodies of late antique Christian homilies and other literature are due a similar assessment as well.

Such methods also have import for understanding the interpretation of scripture in late antiquity. Augustine's interpretations can appear to be arbitrary or uncritical to contemporary readers.[31] This can have the unfortunate result of making it more difficult to appreciate the value of the homilies (since they constantly concern scriptural interpretation). His exegesis is more intelligible when the philosophical and theological assumptions informing it are made clear. Augustine's interpretation of scripture in the homilies is explicitly guided by psychagogic traditions as he describes the text as medicine adapted to our condition or as a lamp shining in the darkness. Augustine is, perhaps, at his most innovative in his creative interweaving of hermeneutics and soteriology.

Augustine's mature psychagogy developed amid the social dynamics of Christianity's complex relationship with the Roman Empire. The legalization of Christianity accompanied by the Theodosian myth of a Christian Empire created a great deal of confusion in the North African Church about the place of a rigorous Christianity in relation to a culture where being a Christian had become respectable, populating the churches with folks with less than ideal motives. Imperial patronage brought with it access to power and its corrupting influence. Although the favor of the Empire allowed for unprecedented participation in all aspects of Roman society, it also exerted an assimilative pressure threatening to reduce the Church to a purveyor of imperial ideology. Augustine resisted the manner in which the Donatists responded to this situation by erecting a social boundary between the Church and the world that separated the pure from the impure. Instead, he endeavored to supply a vigorous Christian identity that did not follow the Donatist solution. Augustine sought to construct a thick ecclesial practice for the faithful of Hippo that would enable them to continue to participate in corrupt society without being defined by it. The approximately 1,000 extant sermons from Augustine's thirty-nine years of public preaching are a remarkable testimony both to the complexity of this endeavor and to the utter seriousness of Augustine's commitment to it. His sermons provide evidence of the way in which he employed the best philosophical tools available to him to offer solid guidance without prematurely establishing, from his perspective, an arbitrary social boundary of his own making.[32] Not unlike his Stoic predecessors who were determined to construct a critical philosophy that would both engage society and act as a counterbalance to imperial ideology, Augustine sought to further a Christianity that could account for such cultural intermingling without so diminishing the critical edge of Christianity that it became merely "cultural."

Notes

Translations of cited works have been modified as necessary.

Notes to the Introduction

1. Peter Brown asserts, "The surprisingly rapid democratization of the philosophers' upper-class counterculture by the leaders of the Christian church is the most profound single revolution of the late classical period" ("Late Antiquity," in *A History of Private Life*, vol. 1: *From Pagan Rome to Byzantium*, ed. Paul Veyne [Cambridge, MA: Harvard University Press, 1987], 251).

2. See Averil Cameron, *The Later Roman Empire: AD 284–430* (Cambridge, MA: Harvard University Press, 1993), 66–84.

3. See Claudia Rapp, *Holy Bishops in Late Antiquity: The Nature of Christian Leadership in an Age of Transition* (Berkeley: University of California Press, 2005); Peter Brown, *Power and Persuasion in Late Antiquity: Towards a Christian Empire* (Madison: University of Wisconsin Press, 1992), esp. 3–70; Henry Chadwick, "The Role of the Christian Bishop in Ancient Society," in *Protocol of the Thirty-Fifth Colloquy of the Center for Hermeneutical Studies in Hellenistic and Modern Culture*, ed. E. C. Hobbs and W. Wuellner (Berkeley, 1980), 1–14; Rowan A. Greer, "Who Seeks for a Spring in the Mud: Reflections on the Ordained Ministry in the Fourth Century," in *Theological Education and Moral Formation*, ed. Richard John Neuhaus (Grand Rapids, MI: Eerdmans, 1991), 22–55; Brian E. Daley, "Position and Patronage in the Early Church: The Original Meaning of 'Primacy of Honour,'" *Journal of Theological Studies*, n.s. 44 (1993): 529–53.

4. Peter Brown, *Poverty and Leadership in the Later Roman Empire* (Hanover, NH: Brandeis University Press, 2001); idem, *Power and Persuasion*, esp. 71–117; idem, "Augustine and a Crisis of Wealth in Late Antiquity," *Augustinian Studies* 36 (2005): 5–30; Claude Lepelley, "Facing Wealth and Poverty: Defining Augustine's Social Doctrine," *Augustinian Studies* 38 (2007): 1–17; Richard D. Finn, *Almsgiving in the Later Roman Empire: Christian Promotion and Practice (313–450)* (Ox-

ford: Oxford University Press, 2006); Boniface Ramsey, "Almsgiving in the Latin Church: The Late Fourth and Early Fifth Centuries," *Theological Studies* 43 (1982): 226–59; Brian E. Daley, "Building a New City: The Cappadocian Fathers and the Rhetoric of Philanthropy," *Journal of Early Christian Studies* 7 (1999): 431–61; Susan R. Holman, *The Hungry Are Dying: Beggars and Bishops in Roman Cappadocia* (Oxford and New York: Oxford University Press, 2001).

    5. Timothy S. Miller, *The Birth of the Hospital in the Byzantine Empire,* 2d ed. (Baltimore, MD: Johns Hopkins University Press, 1997), esp. 68–88; Andrew T. Crislip, *From Monastery to Hospital: Christian Monasticism and the Transformation of Health Care in Late Antiquity* (Ann Arbor: University of Michigan Press, 2005); Brown, *Poverty and Leadership,* 33–35.

    6. Rapp, *Holy Bishops,* 242–52; J. C. Lamoreaux, "Episcopal Courts in Late Antiquity," *Journal of Early Christian Studies* 3 (1995): 143–67; Noel E. Lenski, "Evidence for the *Audientia episcopalis* in the New Letters of Augustine," in *Law, Society, and Authority in Late Antiquity,* ed. Ralph W. Mathisen (New York and Oxford: Oxford University Press, 2001), 83–97; K. K. Raikas, "*Episcopalis audientia*: Problematik zwischen Staat und Kirche bei Augustin," *Augustinianum* 37 (1997): 459–81; Peter Iver Kaufman, "Augustine, Macedonius, and the Courts," *Augustinian Studies* 34 (2003): 67–82; W. Waldstein, "Zur Stellung der *episcopalis audientia* im spätrömischen Prozess," in *Festschrift für Max Kaser zum 70. Geburtstag,* ed. D. Medicus and H. H. Seiler (Munich: Beck, 1976), 533–56.

    7. Brown, *Power and Persuasion,* 96; Rapp, *Holy Bishops,* 228–32; William Klingshirn, "Charity and Power: Caesarius of Arles and the Ransoming of Captives in Sub-Roman Gaul," *Journal of Roman Studies* 75 (1985): 183–203.

    8. See especially, Gregory Nazianzen, *Oratio* 2 (SC 247: 84–240), trans. Charles Gordon Browne and James Edward Swallow, NPNF 2.7: 204–27; John Chrysostom, *De sacerdotio* (SC 272), trans. Graham Neville, *Saint John Chrysostom: Six Books on the Priesthood* (Crestwood, NY: St. Vladimir's Seminary Press, 1984); Ambrose, *off.* (CCL 15), trans. Ivor J. Davidson, *Ambrose: De Officiis* (Oxford and New York: Oxford University Press, 2002); Augustine, *doctr. chr.* (CCL 32: 1–167), trans. Edmund Hill, *Teaching Christianity,* WSA 1.11; Jerome, *Ep.* 52 (trans. F. A. Wright; LCL 262: 188–228).

    9. In an edict of June 17, 362, which was, in turn, rescinded in 364 by Julian's successor. See Rowland Smith, *Julian's Gods: Religion and Philosophy in the Thought and Action of Julian the Apostate* (London and New York: Routledge, 1995), esp. 179–218; Robert Browning, *The Emperor Julian* (Berkeley: University of California Press, 1976), esp. 169–74; Glen W. Bowersock, *Julian the Apostate* (Cambridge, MA: Harvard University Press, 1978); Robert A. Markus, *The End of Ancient Christianity* (Cambridge: Cambridge University Press, 1990), 27–43.

    10. Julian writes, "It seems that our own oracles are reduced to silence, submitting to the cycles of time. Surely our humane master and father, Zeus, observing this, has given us the possibility of inquiring by means of the sacred arts, with

which we may find enough help to answer our needs" (*Gal.* 198C–D [trans. Wilmer C. Wright; LCL 157: 72]). See Johannes Geffcken, *The Last Days of Greco-Roman Paganism,* trans. Sabine MacCormack (Amsterdam and New York: North-Holland, 1978); Pierre Chuvin, *A Chronicle of the Last Pagans,* trans. B. A. Archer (Cambridge, MA: Harvard University Press, 1990); and the dated but classic work of E. R. Dodds, *Pagan and Christian in an Age of Anxiety: Some Aspects of Religious Experience from Marcus Aurelius to Constantine* (Cambridge: Cambridge University Press, 1965).

11. Tertullian, *Praescr.* 7; *Apol.* 50.13. For Tertullian's attitude toward Roman culture, see T. D. Barnes, *Tertullian: A Historical and Literary Study* (Oxford: Clarendon Press, 1971); Robert D. Sider, *Ancient Rhetoric and the Art of Tertullian* (Oxford: Oxford University Press, 1971); D. E. Groh, "Tertullian's Polemic against Social Co-option," *Church History* 40 (1971): 7–14; Jean Claude Fredouille, *Tertullian et la conversion de la culture antique* (Paris: Études Augustiniennes, 1972).

12. Rufinus, *Apol. adu. Hier.* 2.11 (CCL 20: 92.19); trans. W. H. Fremantle, NPNF 2.3: 434–82. He also objects to the fact that secular authors appear even in Jerome's works where he "addresses girls and weak women" (*Apol. adu. Hier.* 2.7 [CCL 20: 89.17–18]).

13. Rufinus, *Apol. adu. Hier.* 2.11 (CCL 20: 92.11–12).

14. Jerome, *Apol.* 1.30 (SC 303: 84): *uerborum copia, sententiarum lumen, translationum uarietas;* trans. W. H. Fremantle, NPNF 2.3: 482–541. Aside from the polemical context, Jerome did worry about his own love of classical literature (see his *Ep.* 22.29–30 [LCL 262: 120–28]).

15. See William S. Babcock's description of how Christianity in North Africa "emerged with a sharp sense of the boundaries between the Christian and the non-Christian, the church and the world" ("Christian Culture and Christian Tradition in Roman North Africa," in *Schools of Thought in the Christian Tradition,* ed. Patrick Henry [Philadelphia: Fortress Press, 1984], 39).

16. Peter Brown, *Augustine of Hippo: A Biography,* 2d ed. (Berkeley: University of California Press, 2000), 221. Markus writes of efforts in the fourth century to "resist the tide which was sweeping Christians towards wholesale assimilation of the secular culture of their society" (*End of Ancient Christianity,* 30).

17. Babcock, "Christian Culture and Christian Tradition," 42.

18. Jaroslav Pelikan, *Divine Rhetoric: The Sermon on the Mount as Message and as Model in Augustine, Chrysostom, and Luther* (Crestwood, NY: St. Vladimir's Seminary Press, 2001), 59. Likewise, Gerald A. Press observes, "The art in the use of language . . . that he acquired from his pagan education and traded upon in his early profession became the hallmarks of his activity as a Christian preacher and writer" ("*Doctrina* in Augustine's *De doctrina christiana,*" *Philosophy and Rhetoric* 17 [1984]: 106). Carol Harrison concludes, "In Augustine's own personal history and identity, and in his work and preaching," he "did not leave his past behind, as it were, and try to root out any traces of it in his new Christian identity; he was too

well aware of the futility of such a task, and of the pervasiveness, importance, and usefulness of secular culture, even for Christianity, to make such an attempt" ("The Rhetoric of Scripture and Preaching: Classical Decadence or Christian Aesthetic?" in *Augustine and His Critics: Essays in Honour of Gerald Bonner*, ed. Dodaro and Lawless, 228). See also Marie Comeau, *La rhétorique de Saint Augustin d'après les Tractatus in Ioannem* (Paris: Boivin, 1930) and Maurice Pontet, *L'exégèse de saint Augustine prédicateur* (Paris: Aubier, 1946), 196.

19. Philip Rousseau, "'The Preacher's Audience': A More Optimistic View," in *Ancient History in a Modern University*, vol. 2, ed. T. W. Hillard et al. (Grand Rapids, MI: Eerdmans, 1998), 391.

20. Possidius, *Vit. Aug.* 31 (PL 32: 64); trans. (altered) Frederick R. Hoare, *The Western Fathers* (New York: Sheed and Ward, 1954). On the historical accuracy of Possidius, Bastiaensen concludes, "In a general way we may state, while the details in the *Vita Augustini* in some cases need correction, the substance of the information is reliable ("The Inaccuracies in the *Vita Augustini* of Possidius" *Studia Patristica* 16.2 [1985]: 483), but see now Erika Hermanowicz, *Possidius of Calama: A Study of the North African Episcopate in the Age of Augustine* (Oxford: Oxford University Press, 2008).

21. James J. O'Donnell, *Augustine: A New Biography* (New York: Harper Collins, 2005), 137. Counting the 205 *Enarrationes in Psalmos*, 124 *In Iohannis euangelium tractatus*, 10 *Tractatus in epistolam Iohannis ad Parthos*, the *Sermones ad populum*, which are more problematic to number, but amount to some 559 (see Hubertus R. Drobner, *Augustinus von Hippo: Sermones ad populum* [Leiden: Brill, 2000], 3), and the "new" sermons in François Dolbeau, *Vingt-six sermons au peuple d'Afrique* (Paris: Institut d'Études Augustiniennes, 1996).

22. James J. O'Donnell, *Confessions* (Oxford: Clarendon Press, 1992), 2.350.

23. His comment includes Augustine's letters as well (J. J. O'Donnell, "Augustine: His Time and Lives," in *The Cambridge Companion to Augustine*, ed. Eleonore Stump and Norman Kretzmann [Cambridge: Cambridge University Press, 2001], 23).

24. "On looking back, I think that I had given undue weight to the formidable clarity of Augustine's formal theological works, and that I had not paid sufficient attention at that time to his sermons and letters" (Brown, *Augustine of Hippo*, 446). Basil Studer writes that scholars have come to recognize "that they must not limit themselves to the principal works of Augustine but must take his other writings into account, especially his sermons" (*The Grace of Christ and the Grace of God in Augustine of Hippo: Christocentrism or Theocentrism*, trans. Matthew J. O'Connell [Collegeville, MN: Liturgical Press, 1997], 10).

25. Hubertus Drobner concludes, "Unfortunately, not a single one of all the *Sermones ad populum* can definitely be dated by day, month, and year. The maximum we have are firmly established *termini ante quem* and *termini post quem*, which, if they both apply to the same sermon, determine a reliable time range" ("The

Chronology of St. Augustine's *Sermones ad populum,*" *Augustinian Studies* 31 [2000]: 212). In Peter Brown's assessment, "The most elusive element in the reconstruction of a life of Augustine remains the chronology of his sermons" (*Augustine of Hippo,* 483).

26. Peter Brown, *Augustine of Hippo,* 249–50, 258.

27. Those who recorded them, nonetheless, were capable stenographers (*notarii*), see Michele Pellegrino, "General Introduction" (WSA 3.1: 16–18).

28. Pierre-Patrick Verbraken, *Études critiques sur les sermons authentiques de saint Augustin* (Steenbrugis: Abbatia Sancti Petri, 1976). Hubertus Drobner has produced a helpful guide to the literature associated with the sermons (*Augustinus von Hippo: Sermones ad populum*). Especially noteworthy are the important collection of texts and studies by François Dolbeau, *Vingt-six sermons*; Pierre-Marie Hombert, *Nouvelles recherches de chronologie augustinienne* (Paris: Institut d'Études Augustiniennes, 2000); and Adalbert G. Hamman, "La transmission des sermons de Saint Augustin: Les authentiques et les apocryphes," *Augustinianum* 25 (1985): 311–27.

29. See William Harmless, *Augustine and the Catechumenate* (Collegeville, MN: Liturgical Press, 1995); Geoffrey G. Willis, *St. Augustine's Lectionary* (London: SPCK, 1962).

30. Numerous studies examine a particular topic in a body of sermons. See the recent volume, *Augustin Prédicateur (395–411): Actes du Colloque International de Chantilly (5–7 Septembre 1996),* ed. Goulven Madec (Paris: Institut d'Études Augustiniennes, 1998); Pontet, *L'exégèse de saint Augustine prédicateur*; Christine Mohrmann, *Die altchristliche Sondersprache in den sermones des hl. Augustinus* (Nijmegen: Dekker, 1932); Pasquale Borgomeo, *L'Église de ce temps dans la prédication de saint Augustin* (Paris: Études Augustiniennes, 1972); Marie Comeau, *Saint Augustin exégète du quatrième Évangile,* 3rd ed. (Paris: Gabriel Beauchesne, 1930); Coleen Hoffman Gowans, *The Identity of the True Believer in the Sermons of Augustine of Hippo: A Dimension of His Christian Anthropology* (Lewiston, NY: Edwin Mellen Press, 1998). Suzanne Poque has provided a useful survey of the common images employed by Augustine in the homilies (*Le langage symbolique dans la prédication d'Augustin d'Hippone: Images héroïques,* 2 vols. [Paris: Études Augustiniennes, 1984]).

31. Along these lines, for example, Jaclyn L. Maxwell uses late antique sermons to illumine the relationship between elite and non-elite Christians (*Christianization and Communication in Late Antiquity: John Chrysostom and His Congregation in Antioch* [New York: Cambridge University Press, 2006]).

32. Pauline Allen and Wendy Mayer, "Through a Bishop's Eyes: Towards a Definition of Pastoral Care in Late Antiquity," *Augustinianum* 40 (2000): 345–97.

33. Allen and Mayer, "Through a Bishop's Eyes," 359–60. They warn, quite aptly, that "to view pastoral care [in late antiquity] as directed exclusively towards the individual is to overlook those forms of care, such as preaching, liturgical pro-

cessions, letters of encouragement . . . which are directed towards all or part of a community" (395).

34. See, for example, Peter Berger's discussion of the legitimating function of religious discourse (*The Sacred Canopy: Elements of a Sociological Theory of Religion* [Garden City, NY: Doubleday, 1967], esp. 29–51) and Averil Cameron's important study of Christianity's construction of a "totalizing discourse"—especially in the fourth century—to secure the "cultural system" it "implied" (*Christianity and the Rhetoric of Empire: The Development of Christian Discourse* [Berkeley: University of California Press, 1991], 123, passim). Thomas Habinek likewise asserts, "If early Christians drew on Greek rhetoric to articulate key aspects of their new system of belief, equally did they employ rhetoric instrumentally as a means of securing the identity of their emergent community and advancing its interests" (*Ancient Rhetoric and Oratory* [Oxford: Blackwell, 2005], 88). In this school of thought, the "curative" function of sermons is much the same as contemporary psychoanalysis or "talk therapy." They are each "universe maintaining conceptual machinery" (Peter Berger and Thomas Luckmann, *The Social Construction of Reality: A Treatise on the Sociology of Knowledge* [Garden City, NY: Doubleday, 1966], 112–14).

35. J. J. O'Donnell remarks that Augustine's sermons and letters "have been mined for facts that fit the pre-determined structure of biographical narrative, but have received far too little attention for their literary and philosophical content" ("Augustine: His Time and Lives," 23); Gowans observes that "very few scholars have attempted to treat the *Sermones ad populum* in their own right" (*Identity of the True Believer*, 13).

36. Pierre Hadot, "Forms of Life and Forms of Discourse," in *Philosophy as a Way of Life: Spiritual Exercises from Socrates to Foucault*, trans. Michael Chase (Cambridge, MA: Blackwell, 1995), 61.

37. P. Hadot, "Forms of Life," 64.

38. A. D. Nock, *Conversion: The Old and the New in Religion from Alexander the Great to Augustine of Hippo* (Oxford: Oxford University Press, 1933), 177. Frances Young has highlighted the continuity between schools of rhetoric and later Christian models ("The Rhetorical Schools and Their Influence on Patristic Exegesis," in *The Making of Orthodoxy: Essays in Honour of Henry Chadwick*, ed. Rowan Williams [Cambridge: Cambridge University Press, 1989], 196).

39. George Kennedy, *A New History of Classical Rhetoric* (Princeton, NJ: Princeton University Press, 1994), 237. A. Cameron writes, "The seemingly alternative rhetorics, the classical and the pagan and the Christian, were more nearly one than their respective practitioners, interested in scoring off each other, would have us believe" (*Christianity*, 20).

40. Graham Anderson, *The Second Sophistic: A Cultural Phenomenon in the Roman Empire* (London: Routledge, 1993), 203. Anderson observes, moreover, "the phenomenon of the Christian sophist or the sophistically trained Christian

father serves to underline the adaptability and resourcefulness of late antique rhetoric and its practitioners" (42).

41. Anderson, *Second Sophistic*, 205–6, referring to Lucian's comment of Christians "worshipping that crucified sophist" (ἀνεσκολοπισμένον ἐκεῖνον σοφιστὴν) (*Peregr.* 13 [trans. A. M. Harmon; LCL 302: 14]).

42. Anderson, *Second Sophistic*, 206. Robert Browning remarks that by the time of Julian's prohibition of the teaching of classical pagan literature by Christians, "a whole generation of Christian men of letters had grown up. The rules of rhetoric were observed in the pulpit as much as in the theatre or the law-court" (*Emperor Julian*, 174). See also Cameron's discussion of "the capacity of the great [fourth-century] Christian preachers and writers to accommodate themselves to the modes of discourse that already prevailed" (*Christianity*, 121).

43. Abraham J. Malherbe, "Hellenistic Moralists and the New Testament," ANRW 2.26.1 (1992), 301. Paul Rabbow uses the term to refer to "that system of ancient spiritual guidance (*Seelenleitung*) and cure of soul" (*Seelenheilung*) practiced in a period of time that he characterizes as "the epoch of the methodical leading of the soul" (*Seelenführung: Methodik der Exerzitien in der Antike* [Munich: Kösel-Verlag, 1954], 17). Wayne A. Meeks describes how "Christian letter writers and, presumably, the local prophets and teachers freely adapted the topics and methods that characterized a long tradition in the Greek and Latin worlds of *psychagogia*, the guidance of souls" (*The Origins of Christian Morality: The First Two Centuries* [New Haven, CT, and London: Yale University Press, 1993], 102).

44. Research has confirmed the widespread presence of philosophical traditions of guidance in the work of St. Paul. See Clarence Glad, *Paul and Philodemus: Adaptability in Epicurean and Early Christian Psychagogy* (Leiden: E. J. Brill, 1995); Abraham J. Malherbe, *Paul and the Popular Philosophers* (Minneapolis, MN: Fortress Press, 1989); idem, *Paul and the Thessalonians: The Philosophic Tradition of Pastoral Care* (Philadelphia: Fortress Press, 1987); Stanley Stowers, "Paul on the Use and Abuse of Reason," in *Greeks, Romans, and Christians: Essays in Honor of Abraham J. Malherbe*, ed. David L. Balch, Everett Ferguson, and Wayne A. Meeks (Philadelphia: Fortress Press, 1990), 253–86.

45. Abraham J. Malherbe, "Hellenistic Moralists and the New Testament," 304. Clarence Glad states at the outset of his study, "I use the term 'psychagogy' or the 'guidance of the soul' to describe a mature person's leading of neophytes in an attempt to bring about moral reformation by shaping the neophyte's view of himself and of the world. Such reshaping demands in many cases a radical reorientation through social, intellectual, and moral transformation. Psychagogic discourse attempts to effect such a transformation" (*Paul and Philodemus*, 2).

46. Ilsetraut Hadot, "The Spiritual Guide," in *Classical Mediterranean Spirituality: Egyptian, Greek, and Roman*, ed. A. H. Armstrong (New York: Crossroad, 1986), 455. Robert Wilken has examined continuities in the practices of the Chris-

tian teachers in Alexandria and the Hellenistic philosophical schools ("Alexandria: A School for Training in Virtue," in *Schools of Thought in the Christian Tradition,* ed. Patrick Henry [Philadelphia: Fortress Press, 1984], 15–30). It should also be noted that centuries earlier Greek-speaking Jews had allowed these classical traditions to inform their synagogue homilies and scriptural exegesis. Consequently, these traditions appear to have been available even to the earliest Christians. Graham Anderson observes, "The Jewish assimilation of the techniques and outlook of the Hellenistic schools would already have had a long history by Philo's time" (*Second Sophistic,* 205). See also Folker Siegert, "Homily and Panegyrical Sermon," in *Handbook of Classical Rhetoric in the Hellenistic Period 330 B.C.–A.D. 400,* ed. Stanley E. Porter (Leiden: E. J. Brill, 1997), 421–43.

47. Roos Meijering, *Literary and Rhetorical Theories in Greek Scholia* (Groningen: Egbert Forsten, 1987), 8.

48. Meijering, *Literary and Rhetorical Theories,* 9. Playing on both meanings of the word, Aristophanes portrays Socrates as "conjuring souls (ψυχαγωγεῖ) from the lake below" (*Au.* 1555 [trans. B. B. Rogers; LCL 179: 272]).

49. This is acknowledged by the studies relying on the term. Glad observes, "Embedded in the meaning of the term 'psychagogy' is a tension between 'beguilement' and a more neutral 'guidance'" (*Paul and Philodemus,* 17). Throughout his study of Paul, Glad shows quite well how the psychagogue's methods of persuasion can be assessed either as positive guidance or negative beguilement. For further notes on usage, see Elizabeth Asmis, "*Psychagogia* in Plato's *Phaedrus,*" *Illinois Classical Studies* 11 (1986): 153–72, Judith Kovacs, "Divine Pedagogy and the Gnostic Teacher according to Clement of Alexandria," *Journal of Early Christian Studies* 9 (2001): 14, and the discussion of classical psychagogy in the next chapter.

50. John Locke (1689), *An Essay Concerning Human Understanding,* 3.10.34, ed. Peter H. Nidditch (Oxford: Clarendon Press, 1975), 508.

51. See Hans Armin Gärtner, "Cura," *Augustinus-Lexikon,* ed. C. Mayer, vol. 2 (Basel: Schwabe, 1986–94), 171–75.

52. See John T. McNeill, *A History of the Cure of Souls* (New York and London: Harper and Row, 1951).

53. Paulinus of Nola, *Ep.* 45.4 (CSEL 29: 382.20–21).

54. Augustine himself viewed the doctrine of predestination and perseverance as "an insurmountable bulwark" (*insuperabili munitione*) for the doctrine of grace (*perseu.* 21.54 [PL 45: 1027]).

55. Stephen J. Duffy, *The Dynamics of Grace: Perspectives in Theological Anthropology* (Collegeville, MN: Liturgical Press, 1993), 75–76.

56. Augustine, *conf.* 13.15.18 (CCL 27: 252.47–48): *attendit per retia carnis et blanditus est et inflammauit, et currimus post odorem eius* (a reference to Song of Songs 2:9); trans. Henry Chadwick, *Confessions* (Oxford: Oxford University Press, 1991). Marianne Djuth argues similarly that the more one notices the extent to which

Augustine places "the incarnation at the center of his thought," the more this insight "subverts the conventional view of Augustine's works as being primarily theological in nature" ("Philosophy in a Time of Exile: *Vera Philosophia* and the Incarnation," *Augustinian Studies* 38 [2007]: 282). For a useful survey of the problems afflicting study of Augustine's Christology in modern scholarship, see Joanne McWilliam, "The Study of Augustine's Christology in the Twentieth Century," in *Augustine: From Rhetor to Theologian*, ed. Joanne McWilliam (Waterloo, Ontario: Wilfrid Laurier University Press, 1992), 183–205.

57. This is the fundamental theological theme that emerges in the following chapters. See, for example, Augustine's description of the manner in which Wisdom made a lamp out of Christ's flesh (*caro Christi*), that is, out of earthen clay, to become the object of our delight (*deliciae*) and, thereby, make the night radiant with light (*en. Ps.* 138.14 [CCL 40: 2000.28–35]). On a more general level, Augustine writes of the "divine eloquence" (*diuina eloquentia*) that orchestrates events in the material world (see *ciu.* 11.18, *ep.* 102.33, *uera rel.* 10.19, 16.30, *trin.* 1.1.2). This theme is an organizing principle also in monographs by Robert Dodaro, *Christ and the Just Society in the Thought of Augustine* (Cambridge: Cambridge University Press, 2004); Jean-Michel Fontanier, *La beauté selon saint Augustin* (Rennes: Presses Universitaires de Rennes, 1998), esp. 151–67; and Carol Harrison, *Beauty and Revelation in the Thought of Saint Augustine* (Oxford: Clarendon Press, 1992). Augustine's lack of involvement in the major christological controversies that occurred primarily in the Greek East and the consequent absence of any systematic treatise devoted to the subject on his part has generally resulted in Augustine's distinctive Christology being pushed to the margins of presentations of his life and thought (see Brian E. Daley, "A Humble Mediator: The Distinctive Elements in Saint Augustine's Christology," *Word and Spirit* 9 [1987]: 100–17; Goulven Madec, *La patrie et la voie: Le Christ dans la vie et la pensée de Saint Augustin* [Paris: Desclée, 1989]; Tarsicius J. Van Bavel, *Recherches sur la christologie de saint Augustin* [Fribourg: Éditions Universitaires, 1954]; Lewis Ayres, "Christology as Contemplative Practice: Understanding the Union of Natures in Augustine's Letter 137" and Rowan Williams, "Augustine's Christology: Its Spirituality and Rhetoric," both in *In the Shadow of the Incarnation: Essays on Jesus Christ in the Early Church in Honor of Brian E. Daley, S.J.*, ed. Peter W. Martens [Notre Dame, IN: University of Notre Dame Press, 2008]).

58. Anderson, *The Second Sophistic*, 240.

59. Augustine, *cat. rud.* 15.23 (CCL 46: 148.42–45); trans. Joseph P. Christopher, *S. Aureli Augustini: De Catechizandis Rudibus* (Washington, DC: Catholic University of America Press, 1926). See also his famous advice that "eloquence will come more readily by reading and listening to eloquent speakers than by poring over rules of eloquence" (*doctr. chr.* 4.3.4 [CCL 32: 118.16–18]), echoing Cicero, *De Orat.* 2.22.90 (trans. E. W. Sutton and H. Rackham; LCL 348: 246).

60. See, for that matter, John Dillon and Anthony A. Long's observation that "it is only in the last generation or so that the study of Hellenistic philosophy has

come into its own, and its exciting features have ceased to be overshadowed by the towering figures of Plato and Aristotle" ("Introduction," in *The Question of "Eclecticism": Studies in Later Greek Philosophy,* ed. John M. Dillon and A. A. Long [Berkeley: University of California Press, 1988], 3). This change reflects a general reappraisal of the period as a whole which has come to be characterized as a time in which a vibrant late antique civilization came into existence rather than as one bringing about the so-called decline and fall of Rome (see Glen Bowersock, "The Vanishing Paradigm of the Fall of Rome," *Bulletin of the American Academy of Arts and Sciences* 49.8 [1996]: 29–43).

61. Peter Brown describes how in Augustine's reading, ideas "were thoroughly absorbed, 'digested' and transformed. . . . He made his masters his own to such an extent, he picked out their main preoccupations with such uncanny perceptiveness, that he felt he could elaborate their thought in very different terms" (*Augustine of Hippo,* 86). Brian Stock remarks, "Augustine reshapes everything that he reads" (*Augustine the Reader: Meditation, Self-Knowledge, and the Ethics of Interpretation* [Cambridge, MA: Harvard University Press, 1996], 4). See also John M. Rist, *Augustine: Ancient Thought Baptized* (Cambridge: Cambridge University Press, 1994).

62. Harald Hagendahl, *Augustine and the Latin Classics,* 2 vols. (Gothenburg: Acta Universitatis Gothoburgensia, 1967); Pierre Courcelle, *Late Latin Writers and Their Greek Sources,* trans. Harry E. Wedeck (Cambridge, MA: Harvard University Press, 1969); J. J. O'Donnell, "Augustine's Classical Readings," *Recherches augustiniennes* 15 (1980): 144–75. Brian Stock offers numerous comments on Augustine's sources throughout his *Augustine the Reader.*

63. See Pierre Hadot, *What Is Ancient Philosophy?,* trans. Michael Chase (Cambridge, MA: Harvard University Press, 2002); Martha Nussbaum, *The Therapy of Desire: Theory and Practice in Hellenistic Ethics* (Princeton, NJ: Princeton University Press, 1994); A. A. Long, *Hellenistic Philosophy: Stoics, Epicureans, Sceptics,* 2d ed. (Berkeley: University of California Press, 1986); A. A. Long and D. N. Sedley, *The Hellenistic Philosophers,* 2 vols. (Cambridge: Cambridge University Press, 1987); John M. Dillon, *The Middle Platonists: 80 B.C. to A.D. 220,* rev. ed. (Ithaca, NY: Cornell University Press, 1996).

64. Augustine, *retr.* prol. 3 (CCL 57: 6.51–7.53); trans. Mary Inez Bogan, *The Retractations* (Washington, DC: Catholic University of America Press, 1968). Compare Augustine's similar statement, made some fifteen years earlier, that he numbered himself among those "who, as they progress, write, and as they write, progress" (*qui proficiendo scribunt et scribendo proficiunt*) (*ep.* 143.2 [CSEL 44: 251.13–14]); trans. (altered) Roland J. Teske, *Letters,* WSA 2. 1–4.

65. Peter Brown, *Augustine of Hippo,* 139, 140, 150.

66. Robert A. Markus, *Conversion and Disenchantment in Augustine's Spiritual Career* (Philadelphia: Villanova University Press, 1989), 22. See also his *End of Ancient Christianity,* 27–83; Gerald Bonner, *St. Augustine: Life and Controversies,* 2d ed. (Norwich: Canterbury Press, 1986), 214; and Studer, *Grace of Christ,* 75.

67. Markus, *Conversion*, 34–35.

68. Reconsidering his own 1967 biography Peter Brown writes, "Central elements in Augustine's thought have been shown to be remarkably stable. They seem to bear little trace of discontinuity. Augustine's intellectual life as a bishop cannot be said to have been lived out entirely in the shadow of a 'Lost Future,' as I suggested in the chapter of my book which bears that title" (*Augustine of Hippo*, 490). See Carol Harrison, *Rethinking Augustine's Early Theology: An Argument for Continuity* (Oxford: Oxford University Press, 2006); eadem, "'The Most Intimate Feeling of Mind': The Permanence of Grace in Augustine's Early Theological Practice," *Augustinian Studies* 36 (2005): 51–58; Goulven Madec, *Introduction aux "Révisions" et à la lecture des œuvres de saint Augustin* (Paris: Études Augustiniennes, 1996), 127–46; idem, *La patrie et la voie*, 18–19. James Wetzel has argued for philosophical continuities even in Augustine's later reflections on grace and free will throughout his *Augustine and the Limits of Virtue* (Cambridge: Cambridge University Press, 1992). See also Paul R. Kolbet, "Formal Continuities between Augustine's Early Philosophical Teaching and Late Homiletical Practice," *Studia Patristica* 43 (2006): 149–54.

69. See, for example, Augustine's comment that while "public sermons, which the Greeks call homilies" have the advantage of including church congregations in the experience, his *Enarrationes in Psalmos* were composed "partly in sermons to the people and partly by dictation" (*en. Ps.* 118 prol. [CCL 40: 1664.3–4, 1665.24–25]; trans. Maria Boulding, *Expositions of the Psalms*, WSA, 3.15–3.20).

70. Observing that tractates 55–124 contain, among other things, "at least 30 sermons with examples of audience contact and direct address," Douglas Mileweski states that it may "be safely concluded that the later tractates do not constitute any profound rupture in Augustine's original intent and format" ("Augustine's 124 Tractates on the Gospel of John: The *Status Quaestionis* and the State of Neglect," *Augustinian Studies* 33 [2002]: 71, 75).

Notes to Chapter One

1. Suetonius, *Dom.* 21 (trans. J. C. Rolfe; LCL 38: 362); cf. Dio Cassius, *Hist. Rom.* 67.14 (trans. Earnest Cary; LCL 176: 350).

2. Suetonius, *Dom.* 7 (LCL 38: 334); Dio Cassius, *Hist. Rom.* 67.3 (LCL 176: 324).

3. Suetonius, *Dom.* 6 (LCL 38: 330–32); Dio Cassius, *Hist. Rom.* 67.6–7 (LCL 176: 328–34).

4. Suetonius notes that the soldiers were greatly grieved at the news and were prepared to avenge him. They eventually succeeded in demanding the execution of Domitian's murderers (*Dom.* 23 [LCL 38: 362–64]).

5. Philostratus, *Vit. Soph.* 1.7.488 (trans. Arthur Fairbanks; LCL 134: 20); Homer, *Od.* 22.1 (trans. A. T. Murray, rev. George E. Dimock; LCL 105: 344).

6. On the reason for his exile, Dio himself explains that he was exiled on account of his friendship with a man who was executed by Domitian (*Or.* 13.1). Dio Cassius records that under Domitian many perished under the "charge of philosophizing, and all the philosophers that were left in Rome were banished" (*Hist. Rom.* 67.13.3 [LCL 176: 346–48]). Philostratus states that Dio concealed himself in exile on account of the tyranny in the city [of Rome] which had driven out all philosophy (*Vit. Soph.* 1.7.488 [LCL 134: 18–20]). For a description of Dio's exile, see C. P. Jones, *The Roman World of Dio Chrysostom* (Cambridge, MA: Harvard University Press, 1978), 45–55.

7. Philostratus, *Vit. Soph.* 1.7.487 (LCL 134: 16). Philostratus describes Dio as carrying with him Plato's *Phaedo* and Demosthenes' *On the False Embassy* (*Vit. Soph.* 1.7.488 [LCL 134: 20]).

8. Philostratus, *Vit. Soph.* 1.7.488 (LCL 134: 20). As with all ancient historical sources, Philostratus' reliability can be questioned. Jones is skeptical of the account of Philostratus while acknowledging that others accept its historicity (*The Roman World*, 50–52). In the judgment of Graham Anderson, Philostratus remains "the most informative source on sophists . . . [although he] none the less fails all too often to tell us enough. . . . Yet he has left us a medium which is second to none for the evocation of sophists in action" (*The Second Sophistic*, 129). Note that while admonishing the city of Tarsus, Dio likens himself to Odysseus before the suitors (*Or.* 33.15), and elsewhere claims that while he was in exile, people would sometimes mistake him for a tramp or a beggar (*Or.* 13.10–11). Dio also recounts his open challenge to tyranny (*Or.* 45.1, 50.8). Even if Philostratus' account of Dio's conduct in the army camp is at points contrived, such embellishment effectively illustrates the ideal.

9. Philostratus, *Vit. Soph.* 1.7.488 (LCL 134: 20).

10. On the immense importance of rhetorical training from the fourth century BCE through the late Empire, see Henri I. Marrou, *A History of Education in Antiquity*, trans. George Lamb (Madison: University of Wisconsin Press, 1982); Robert A. Kaster, *Guardians of Language: The Grammarian and Society in Late Antiquity* (Berkeley: University of California Press, 1988); Catherine Steel, *Roman Oratory* (Cambridge: Cambridge University Press, 2006); Jeffrey Walker, *Rhetoric and Poetics in Antiquity* (Oxford: Oxford University Press, 2000), esp. 45–135.

11. Perhaps Gorgias was the earliest example of this (Philostratus, *Vit. Soph.* 1.9.493 [LCL 134: 30–32]), but see also Dio's *Or.* 12, Lucian's *Peregr.*, and Philostratus, *Vit. Soph.* 2.27.617.

12. The illustrations are drawn from Libanius' exemplary encomium of Antioch (Or. 11.35, 44, 57–58, and 229). An English translation is available by Glanville Downey, "Libanius' Oration in Praise of Antioch (Oration XI)," *Proceedings of the American Philosophic Society* 103.5 (1959): 652–86.

13. Plutarch, *Rect. rat. aud.* 13.44F (trans. Frank C. Babbitt; LCL 197: 240).

14. Synesius, *Caluitii encomium* (PG 66: 1167–1206). Philostratus also notes an *Encomium of a Parrot* that is no longer extant (*Vit. Soph.* 1.7.487 [LCL 134: 18]). See also Lucian's praise of the beauty, courage, and strength of a fly (*Musc. Enc.* [trans. A. M. Harmon; LCL 14: 82–94]).

15. Dio Chrysostom, *Or.* 11 (trans. J. W. Cohoon and H. Lamar Crosby; LCL 257: 446–564).

16. Philostratus, *Vit. Soph.* 1.21.518 (LCL 134: 80). See also Herodes, who is said to have studied at night and even while he drank wine (2.1.565 [LCL 134: 178]); and Aristeides (2.9.583 [LCL 134: 218]). From its first representative, Aeschines, extemporaneous speech was an important skill of the second sophistic (1.18.509–510 [LCL 134: 60])—although it was not unknown prior to him, see Alcidamas, *Soph.*, in John Victor Muir, *Alcidamas: The Works and Fragments* (London: Bristol Classical Press, 2001), 2–21.

17. Philostratus states that sophists tended to spend their days teaching boys. See, for example, where he asserts, "It is no great wonder that, while Scopelian [the sophist] taught at Smyrna, Ionians, Lydians, Carians, Maeonians, Aeolians also and Hellenes from Mysia and Phrygia flocked to his school. . . . But besides these he attracted Cappadocians and Assyrians, he attracted also Egyptians and Phoenicians, the more illustrious of the Achaeans, and all the youth of Athens" (*Vit. Soph.* 1.21.518 [LCL 134: 80]).

18. See Michael C. Leff's observations in his "The Material of the Art in the Latin Handbooks of the Fourth Century A.D.," in *Rhetoric Revalued: Papers from the International Society for the History of Rhetoric*, ed. Brian Vickers (Binghamton: State University of New York Press, 1982), 71–78.

19. There is a long-standing problem of explaining the relationship between Dio's sophistic exercises and his moralistic speeches. In Philostratus, they sit uneasily beside each other due to his desire to draw attention to his subject's rhetorical brilliance rather than to his philosophical sophistication. In the fifth century, Synesius attributes the differences in Dio's speeches to his development from an early sophist to a philosopher with different commitments (*De Dione* [LCL 385: 364–86]). Contemporary scholars have found Synesius' explanation not only unpersuasive, but unneeded (see Jones' treatment of the development thesis, *The Roman World*, 8–18). The diversity of Dio's works testifies to his rhetorical versatility—a much admired trait of the day. See, for example, how philosophical the introduction to his sophistic speech is on Troy's victory (*Or.* 11.1–3). The philosophical quality of Dio's speeches does not make him any less representative of the second sophistic. As Graham Anderson states, "If Dio cannot be classified as a sophist, then nobody can" ("The Second Sophistic: Some Problems of Perspective," in *Antonine Literature*, ed. D. A. Russell [Oxford: Clarendon Press, 1990], 104).

20. On the widely accepted ancient analogy between philosophy and medicine, see Julia E. Annas, "Philosophical Therapy: Ancient and Modern," in *Bioethics:*

Ancient Themes in Contemporary Issues, ed. Mark G. Kuczewski and Ronald Polansky (Cambridge, MA: MIT Press, 2000), 109–26; also André-Jean Voelke, *La philosophie comme thérapie de l'âme: Études de philosophie hellénistique* (Fribourg: Éditions universitaires, 1993); Martha Nussbaum, *Therapy of Desire.*

21. Dio Chrysostom, *Or.* 13.13–14.

22. Dio Chrysostom, *Or.* 34.4 (LCL 358: 340), also 32.11–12 (LCL 358: 182). Philostratus describes how Dio, on the one hand, "reproved unruly cities without seeming insulting or tactless, like a horse trainer guiding unruly horses with a bit rather than a whip," and, on the other hand, "praised well-behaved cities" while "warning them of the ruin change of their ways could bring" (*Vit. Soph.* 1.7.487 [LCL 134: 18]).

23. Dio Chrysostom, *Or.* 32.10 (LCL 358: 180) and *Or.* 33.6 (LCL 358: 278).

24. Dio Chrysostom, *Or.* 4.36–38 (LCL 257: 184). Dio's often-expressed criticism, however, was not a judgment against all other orators—"my [negative] remarks are not leveled at all sophists, for there are some who follow that calling honorably and for the good of others" (*Or.* 35.10 [LCL 358: 400]).

25. Dio Chrysostom, *Or.* 32.7 (LCL 358: 178).

26. See, for example Dio's references to the multitude present to hear him in Alexandria (*Or.* 32.20, 29).

27. Dio Chrysostom, *Or.* 32.25 (LCL 358: 196). See also *Or.* 34.24 (LCL 358: 358): "I came . . . that I might make plain (σαφὲς) to you how you stand with regard to one another."

28. Dio Chrysostom, *Or.* 33.16 (LCL 358: 288).

29. Dio Chrysostom, *Or.* 27.7 (LCL 339: 352).

30. Dio Chrysostom, *Or.* 11.1–3 (LCL 257: 446). For the Platonic and Stoic origins of the concepts and terms employed by Dio in his orations, see below.

31. Dio Chrysostom, *Or.* 33.13 (LCL 358: 284).

32. Dio Chrysostom, *Or.* 32.18 (LCL 358: 188): τῶν δυναμένων διὰ πειθοῦς καὶ λόγου ψυχὰς πραΰνειν καὶ μαλάττειν.

33. Dio Chrysostom, *Or.* 32.18 (LCL 358: 188).

34. Dio Chrysostom, *Or.* 33.7 (LCL 358: 280): εἰ μὴ πάνυ τις τῇ παρρησίᾳ χρῷτο. . . . Cf. *Or.* 32.34 (LCL 358: 204).

35. Dio Chrysostom, *Or.* 33.44 (LCL 358: 314).

36. Dio Chrysostom, *Or.* 33.32 (LCL 358: 302). See the story Dio uses to illustrate the ability to perceive the character of another's soul through outward signs (*Or.* 33.54). The anecdote also appears in Diogenes Laertius where it is used to describe Cleanthes (*Vit. phil.* 7.173), and in Maximus of Tyre (*Diss.* 25.3), and in Cicero (*Tusc. Disp.* 4.37.80) about Zopyrus.

37. Dio Chrysostom, *Or.* 33.33 (LCL 358: 302). He proceeds to chastise them for something far less severe, "snorting" or "snoring" (ῥέγκουσιν). His choice here is a clever way to help them perceive how a behavior that has social implications can exist apart from conscious awareness, without making them defensive.

38. Dio Chrysostom, *Or.* 33.17 (LCL 358: 288).

39. Dio Chrysostom, *Or.* 33.23 (LCL 358: 294).

40. Dio Chrysostom, *Or.* 32.37–38.

41. Dio Chrysostom, *Or.* 32.59 (LCL 358: 230). See Pierre Hadot's description of the practices implied by the verb προσέχειν, which he describes as "a technical term of ancient philosophy" ("Ancient Spiritual Exercises and 'Christian Philosophy,'" in *Philosophy as a Way of Life*, 130–34). Porphyry celebrates Plotinus' practice of continually "attending to himself" (πρὸς ἑαυτὸν προσοχὴν) (*Plot.* 8 [trans. A. H. Armstrong; LCL 440: 30.20–21]). See also Richard Sorabji's comments on the term in *Emotion and Peace of Mind: From Stoic Agitation to Christian Temptation* (Oxford: Oxford University Press, 2000), 13, 252.

42. Dio Chrysostom, *Or.* 34.51 (LCL 358: 384).

43. Dio Chrysostom, *Or.* 34.18–19 (LCL 358: 352–54).

44. Dio Chrysostom, *Or.* 32.16 (LCL 358: 186); cf. "it is self-control (σωφροσύνη) and mental perception (νοῦς) that save. These make blessed those who employ them" (*Or.* 33.28 [LCL 358: 300]).

45. Dio Chrysostom, *Or.* 32.16 (LCL 358: 186).

46. Glen W. Bowersock remarks, "Philosophers who performed in theaters, like Apuleius, and presented philosophy in an accessible way for large audiences were by no means uncommon" ("Philosophy in the Second Sophistic," in *Philosophy and Power in the Graeco-Roman World: Essays in Honour of Miriam Griffin*, ed. Gillian Clark and Tessa Rajak [Oxford: Oxford University Press, 2002], 166).

47. Philostratus, *Vit. Soph.* 1.481 (LCL 134: 6): "But the sophistic that followed it, which we must not call 'new,' for it is old, but rather 'second'. . ."; see also *Vit. Soph.* 1.484 (LCL 134: 12): "The ancients applied the term sophists not only to outstandingly eloquent and eminent rhetors, but to those philosophers who expressed their arguments with facility."

48. Dio, for example, remarks of his "recourse to an ancient appeal by a certain Socrates. . . . By no means, however, did I pretend that this appeal was mine, but gave credit where it was due" (*Or.* 13.14 [LCL 339: 100]).

49. Homer, *Od.* 1.105, 206–207, 215–216 (LCL 104: 20, 26–28); trans. Richmond Lattimore, *The Odyssey of Homer* (New York: Harper & Row, 1967).

50. On the theme of Telemachus' resemblance to his father, see Homer, *Od.* 3.122–125, 4.141–146 (LCL 104: 88, 128).

51. Homer, *Od.* 1.253–254 (LCL 104: 30). See the description of the plight of fatherless sons in *Il.* 22.482–507 (trans. A. T. Murray; LCL 171: 488).

52. Homer, *Od.* 1.269–270 (LCL 104: 32).

53. Homer, *Od.* 1.296–297, 307–308 (LCL 104: 34).

54. Homer, *Od.* 1.320–322 (LCL 104: 36).

55. Homer, *Od.* 2.225–227 (LCL 104: 62).

56. Homer, *Od.* 2.268 (LCL 104: 66), inter alia.

57. Homer, *Od.* 3.21–486, 4.609–620 (LCL 104: 80–116, 162).

58. Homer, *Od.* 4.668 (LCL 104: 166).

59. Homer, *Od.* 2.314–315 (LCL 104: 68): ἄλλων μῦθον ἀκούων πυνθάνομαι, καὶ δή μοι ἀέξεται ἔνδοθι θυμός.

60. Homer, *Od.* 24.506, 525–548 (LCL 105: 448, 450–52).

61. See also Homer's account of Phoenix, the instructor of Achilles (*Il.* 9.430–605 [LCL 170: 426–38]). In seeking to soothe Achilles' anger, Phoenix reminds him, "With you the old horseman Peleus sent me . . . a mere child, knowing nothing as yet of evil war. . . . For this reason he sent me to instruct you in all these things, to be both a speaker of words and a doer of deeds" (*Il.* 9.438–443 [LCL 170: 426]). Unlike Telemachus, who was successfully mentored, Achilles resists guidance and meets a tragic end.

62. Homer, *Il.* 4.219 (LCL 170: 180); Pindar, *Nem.* 3.53–55, 4.60, *Pyth.* 3.1, 3.63, 4.102–115, 9.38; Plato *Rep.* 391c, *Hipp. Min.* 371d; Xenophon, *Smp.* 8.23.

63. Maximus of Tyre, *Diss.* 28.1–2; Dio Chrysostom, *Or.* 6.24, 58.2; Lucian, *Dial. Mort.* 26.1.

64. On the early sophists and their diversity, cf. G. B. Kerferd, *The Sophistic Movement* (Cambridge: Cambridge University Press, 1981), or more generally, Marrou, *History of Education,* 46–60. The term "sophist" has been difficult to define especially since Plato's forceful criticism of the movement. As Marrou states, "Plato's treatment of the Sophists was always highly ambiguous and it has never been easy to grasp where invention and caricature and calumny begin and where they end" (*History of Education,* 48). After evaluating several proposed definitions, Graham Anderson concludes that "the word 'sophist' is as chameleon-like a term as Philostratus or any one of us may wish to make it" ("The Second Sophistic: Some Problems of Perspective," 109).

65. Werner Jaeger, *Paideia: The Ideals of Greek Culture,* trans. Gilbert Highet (New York: Oxford University Press, 1939–44), 1.288; Marrou, *History of Education,* 47.

66. Plato, *Prt.* 318a–b (LCL 165: 120); trans. (altered) John M. Cooper, ed., *Plato: Complete Works* (Indianapolis: Hackett, 1997).

67. Plato, *Prt.* 318e–319a (LCL 165: 124).

68. On the origins and use of such early sophistic models, see Thomas Cole's fine study, *The Origins of Rhetoric in Ancient Greece* (Baltimore, MD: Johns Hopkins University Press, 1991), 71–112.

69. Gorgias, *Hel.* 8 (*Die Fragmente der Vorsokratiker: griechisch und deutsch,* ed. Hermann Diels [Berlin: Weidmannsche Buchhandlung, 1935], 2.290.17–19): λόγος δυνάστης μέγας ἐστίν (trans. D. M. MacDowell, *Encomium of Helen* [Bristol: Bristol Classical Press, 1982]).

70. Gorgias, *Hel.* 10 (Diels, 2.291.1–2): συγγινομένη γὰρ τῆι δόξηι τῆς ψυχῆς ἡ δύναμις τῆς ἐπωιδῆς ἔθελξε καὶ ἔπεισε καὶ μετέστησεν αὐτὴν γοητείαι.

71. Gorgias, *Hel.* 13–14 (Diels, 2.292.4–293.3).

72. Gorgias, *Hel.* 13 (Diels, 2.292.8–10): τέχνηι γραφείς, οὐκ ἀληθείαι λεχθείς.

73. Plato, *Grg.* 456b–457c; see also 452e (LCL 166: 278, 290–94).

74. Plato, *Grg.* 459b–c (LCL 166: 300).

75. Plato, *Apol.* 31b (LCL 36: 112).

76. Plato, *Grg.* 465a (LCL 166: 318); cf. *Rep.* 493a–d (LCL 276: 38–40).

77. Plato, *Grg.* 481e (LCL 166: 378–80). A similar statement is found in the *Phaedrus* 272d–273b (LCL 36: 554–56): "For the fact is . . . the one who intends to be an able rhetorician has no need to know the truth about the things that are just and good or yet about the people who are such either by nature or upbringing. No one lawcourt, you see, cares at all about the truth of such matters. They only care about what is convincing. This is called 'the likely,' and that is what a man who intends to speak according to art should concentrate on. . . . Whatever you say, you should pursue what is likely and leave the truth aside. . . . No doubt you have churned through Tisias' book quite carefully. Then let Tisias tell us this also: By 'the likely' does he mean anything but what is accepted by the crowd?" Socrates' worry about the relativism implied by sophistic theory appears to be one he shared with his contemporaries and does seem to characterize the movement. See, for example, Gorgias' defense of Helen's adultery or his speech on nonbeing. Socrates' own philosophy, however, became subject to similar worries, since its difference from sophistic developments was apparently less than clear to his contemporaries, see the way in which he was charged with making the worse argument appear stronger (*Apol.* 18b, 23d [LCL 36: 74, 88]).

78. Plato, *Prt.* 356d–e (LCL 165: 238).

79. Kathryn Tanner, *The Politics of God* (Minneapolis, MN: Fortress Press, 1992), 67. Elsewhere she remarks with equal acuity: "Once social and ideal normative validity are uncoupled as distinct categories, the mores of a particular society are not validated simply by virtue of being established. . . . Socially valid norms as well as worldviews become subject to argumentative assessment" (55). The debate regarding the relative merits of natural (φύσις) and social norms (νόμος) preceded Plato and is part of his intellectual inheritance. See Aristotle, *En.* 5.7 and Felix Heinimann's classic study, *Nomos und Physis* (Basle: Reinhardt, 1945).

80. Plato, *Rep.* 514a–521c (LCL 27: 118–46).

81. Cf. Maximus of Tyre, *Diss.* 29.5, 36.4; Dio Chrysostom, *Or.* 11.1–3; Albinus/Alcinous, *Didascalicus* 27.3–4 (in the *Handbook of Platonism*, trans. John Dillon [New York: Oxford University Press, 1993], 12); Plotinus, *En.* 1.6.9, 3.8.8, 5.1.3–4, 6.9.11; Iamblichus, *Protrepticus* 15 (ed. H. Pistelli, *Iamblichi Protrepticus* [Leipzig: Teubner, 1888], 78–82). Martha Nussbaum writes of the "ascent" tradition that "it is such a pervasive feature of the history of Western philosophy and literature that one could write an illuminating history of moral thought from Plato to Nietzsche using that motif alone" (*Upheavals of Thought: The Intelligence of Emotions* [Cambridge: Cambridge University Press, 2001], 469). Later chapters will

show that Augustine often employs the imagery of the ascent tradition in both his homilies and writings.

82. Plato, *Rep.* 519a–b (LCL 276: 136–38).

83. Eric Pearl, "Sense Perception and Intellect in Plato," *Revue de Philosophie Ancienne* 15 (1997): 23–24. Compare Augustine's comment that "Plato did not err in saying that there is an intelligible world (*mundum intellegibilem*) if we are willing to consider not the word . . . but the thing itself. For he called the intelligible world that eternal and unchanging plan (*rationem*) according to which God made the world" (*retr.* 1.3.2 [CCSL 57: 12.24–13.29]).

84. Plato, *Sph.* 240d (LCL 123: 350).

85. For "doubled ignorance," see Plato's *Lg.* 863c, *Sph.* 229c. Diotima states in the *Symposium*, "For what is especially difficult about being ignorant is that you are satisfied with yourself. . . . If you do not think you need anything, of course you will not want what you do not think you need" (204a [LCL 166: 182]). This theme, however, appears to be Socratic (*Apol.* 21d, 22e, 29b).

86. Plato, *Rep.* 535d–e (LCL 276: 212): ἀνάπηρον ψυχήν.

87. Plato, *Rep.* 518c (LCL 276: 134).

88. Plato, *Smp.* 175d (LCL 166: 92).

89. Plato, *Rep.* 518c–d (LCL 276: 134).

90. See particularly Quintín Racionero, who describes how in the *Phaedrus* Plato "systematically develops" a "'positive strategy' in relation to rhetoric, the foundations of which were laid by the criticisms of the *Gorgias*" ("Logos, Myth and Probable Discourse in Plato's *Timaeus*" *Elenchos* 19 [1998]: 41). It should be kept in mind that while the term ῥήτωρ was commonly in use prior to Plato to refer to anyone who spoke in the law court or political assembly, Plato himself may well have coined the term ῥητωρική to introduce "a new level of specificity and conceptual clarity concerning different verbal arts" (Edward Schiappa, "Did Plato Coin Rhêtorikê?", *American Journal of Philology* 111 [1990]: 457–70, at 458).

91. Plato, *Phdr.* 261a (LCL 36: 516).

92. Plato, *Phdr.* 272b–c, 273e (LCL 36: 554, 558).

93. Plato, *Phdr.* 275b–c (LCL 36: 564).

94. Plato, *Phdr.* 261a, also 271c–d (LCL 36: 516–17, 552): ψυχαγωγία τις διὰ λόγων. Roos Meijering states that this text "might well be a quotation from Gorgias" and is "the oldest example of the term ψυχαγωγία in its technical sense of manipulation of (the soul of) another person" (*Literary and Rhetorical Theories*, 11). Plato employs the term in the *Timaeus* to refer to the appeal that irrational images have on that lower part of the soul which is not particularly responsive to reason (*Ti.* 71a [LCL 234: 184]). See the discussion of the term above in the introduction and by Elizabeth Asmis, "*Psychagogia*," 153–72; Anna Kélessidou, "La psychagogie du Phèdre et le long labeur philosophique," in *Understanding the Phaedrus: Proceedings of the II Symposium Platonicum*, ed. Livio Rossetti (Sankt Augustin: Academia Verlag, 1992), 265–68.

95. Plato, *Phdr.* 260a, 262c, 277b (LCL 36: 512, 522, 570). Plato commends the dialectical method of collection and division as the best way to pursue truth, *Phdr.* 263b–c, 265d–266c; *Plt.* 285a–c. See the discussion of the method by Charles L. Griswold, *Self-Knowledge in Plato's Phaedrus* (University Park: Pennsylvania State University Press, 1986), 173–86, 198–99.

96. Plato, *Phdr.* 270b (LCL 36: 546–48). This emphasis on the psychagogue's knowledge of the soul of the other is anticipated in the dialogue when Socrates remarks, "If I do not know Phaedrus, I must be forgetting who I am myself—and neither is the case" (228a [LCL 36: 416]), and echoed by Phaedrus (236c [LCL 36: 440]).

97. Plato, *Phdr.* 271b–272a (LCL 36: 550–52).

98. Plato, *Phdr.* 277c (LCL 36: 570).

99. Plato, *Phdr.* 271d–272b (LCL 36: 552–54). Plato's proposal has been criticized as being too ideal and otherworldly. Nowhere has this view been argued so elegantly and thoroughly as by Nussbaum, *Therapy of Desire,* and *The Fragility of Goodness: Luck and Ethics in Greek Tragedy and Philosophy* (Cambridge: Cambridge University Press, 1986). See also Roger Moss, "Plato's 'philosophical rhetor,' however, is a dubious entity . . . the gap between human need and Plato's idealism remains as great as ever" ("The Case for Sophistry," in *Rhetoric Revalued: Papers from the International Society for the History of Rhetoric,* ed. Brian Vickers [Binghamton: State University of New York Press, 1982], 217).

100. Plato, *Phdr.* 230c (LCL 36: 422).

101. Plato, *Phdr.* 228b, 230d (LCL 36: 416, 424).

102. Plato, *Phdr.* 229e–230a (LCL 36: 420–22).

103. As with all speech informed by psychagogic theory, Socrates' two speeches in the *Phaedrus* are temporary, occasional pieces adapted to the psychic state of the hearer. The contextual nature of the speech creates the problem of evaluating the degree to which the psychagogue intends the speech to be true in other contexts. For example, Socrates can refer back to his second speech and say, "We used a certain sort of image to describe love's passion; perhaps it had a measure of truth in it, though it may also have led us astray" (*Phdr.* 265b [LCL 36.532]).

104. Asmis, *"Psychagogia,"* 159.

105. Plato, *Phdr.* 262B (LCL 36: 522).

106. Plato, *Phdr.* 246a (LCL 36: 470).

107. Plato, *Phdr.* 246a–248b, 251b–c (LCL 36: 470–78, 486).

108. Plato, *Smp.* 203e–204a (LCL 166: 180–82).

109. Plato's Socrates states that "when someone's desires incline strongly for one thing, they are thereby weakened for others" (*Rep.* 485d [LCL 276: 8]).

110. Plato, *Phdr.* 249c–d (LCL 36: 480–82).

111. Plato, *Phdr.* 248b–c (LCL 36: 478).

112. Plato, *Phdr.* 241c (LCL 36: 456).

113. Plato, *Phdr.* 278b–c, 279b (LCL 36: 574, 576).

114. For varying accounts of the relationship between the positive appraisal of a certain kind of rhetoric in the *Phaedrus* and Plato's refutation of sophistry in other dialogues, see Rollin W. Quimby's argument for a maturation in Plato's rhetoric theory ("The Growth of Plato's Perception of Rhetoric," *Philosophy and Rhetoric* 7 [1974]: 71–79); Edwin Black's view that the *Phaedrus* is the positive compliment to Plato's earlier negative refutation ("Plato's View of Rhetoric," *Quarterly Journal of Speech* 44 [1958]: 361–74); and Marina McCoy, *Plato on the Rhetoric of Philosophers and Sophists* (New York: Cambridge University Press, 2007).

115. Cole, *Origins*, 140.

116. Cole, *Origins*, 90, 123. Jacques Derrida's provocative essay extends Plato's remarks to a more general theory ("Plato's Pharmacy," in *Dissemination*, trans. Barbara Johnson [Chicago: University of Chicago Press, 1981], 61–171).

117. Plato, *Phdr.* 275d, 276c (LCL 36: 564, 568).

118. Plato, *Phdr.* 275e–276a (LCL 36: 566).

119. Robert E. Cushman, *Therapeia: Plato's Conception of Philosophy* (Chapel Hill: University of North Carolina Press, 1958), 307.

120. Plato, *Rep.* 517a, 520a (LCL 276: 128, 140).

121. Plato, *Rep.* 520c (LCL 276: 142). Plato's philosopher would prefer to continue to press upward, but descends into the murkiness of human affairs out of duty (517c–d, 520e, 539e–540b).

122. Plato, *Rep.* 518c (LCL 276: 134); cf. 517a, 496c–e.

123. Plato, *Rep.* 518c–d (LCL 276: 134).

124. For example, in Plato's *Apology,* Socrates declares: "I shall not cease to practice philosophy, to exhort you and in my usual way to point out to any one of you whom I happen to meet: 'Good Sir, you are an Athenian, a citizen of the greatest city with the greatest reputation for both wisdom and power; are you not ashamed of your eagerness to possess as much wealth, reputation and honors as possible, while you do not care for nor give thought to wisdom or truth, or the best possible state of your soul?' Then if one of you disputes this and says he does care, I shall not let him go at once or leave him, but I shall question him, examine him and test him, and if I do not think he has attained the goodness that he says he has, I shall reproach him because he attaches little importance to the most important things" (29d–30a [LCL 36: 108]).

125. Plato, *La.* 187e–188a (LCL 165: 36).

126. Leonard Nelson, *Socratic Method and Critical Philosophy* (New Haven, CT: Yale University Press, 1949), 10.

127. Nelson, *Socratic Method,* 16.

128. Plato, *Sph.* 230b–d (LCL 123: 314).

129. Plato, *Sph.* 230c (LCL 123: 314); cf. *Tht.* 177b (LCL 123: 130).

130. Plato, *Sph.* 231b (LCL 123: 316).

131. Clearly such methods ascribed here to Plato are present in lesser degrees in some dialogues than in others. Although Plato's recommended strategies of

discussion are best studied through particular examples, scholars have sought to differentiate various methods. Henry Teloh quite rightly warns against attributing to Socrates "a single monolithic tactic," since *elenchus* and psychagogy "take on many different forms as we should expect since there are many different psychic conditions." Giving these qualifications, he offers his own "too crude" explanation of *elenchus* and psychagogy as "types of dialectical discussion" that "can be done separately, although *psychagogia* is usually done with *elenchus*," since "frequently Socrates starts with *elenchus* and moves to a mixture of both forms" (*Socratic Education in Plato's Early Dialogues* [Notre Dame, IN: University of Notre Dame Press, 1986], 22–23). According to Robert Cushman, "It is the province of *elenchos* to treat primarily of man's axiological experience and with judgments issuing from it, with a view toward ascertaining the implications for ultimate reality." Whereas, dialectic is a "*psuchagogia*, an art of leading souls by persuasion," which is the "reliable pedagogy of conversion" upon which "Plato rests his hope of the moral and intellectual betterment of men and politics" (*Therapeia*, 232, 234). Without employing the technical terminology, Martha Nussbaum similarly refers to two discrete movements in Platonic philosophy: "In less ideal circumstances, where we begin with adults who already have powerfully fettered souls, the educational and motivational process must be negative as much as positive: it must strike off the lead weights as well as inspiring the soul to look aloft. . . . *We* must be made conscious of *our* pain before we can be brought to a point at which we are ready to pursue a way of life that involves giving up, or radically revising, much that we now value" (*Fragility of Goodness*, 163). Richard Robinson asserts that the Socratic *elenchus* is "incorporated" by Plato "into the larger whole of dialectic, which somewhat changes its character. Though still negative and destructive in essence, it is harnessed to the car of construction" (*Plato's Earlier Dialectic*, 2d ed.[Oxford: Clarendon Press, 1953], 19).

132. Henry Teloh, *Socratic Education*, 20.

133. Plato, *Prt.* 358c (LCL 165: 244).

134. Plato, *Plt.* 278d–e (LCL 164: 80).

135. Plato, *Rep.* 534a (LCL 276: 204).

136. Plato, *Plt.* 277d (LCL 164: 76). See also Plato's discussion of the way that students of geometry first draw imperfect visible figures to help them think about perfect shapes that cannot be seen except in thought (*Rep.* 510d–e [LCL 276: 110–12]) and how astronomers should use the visible objects in the sky as a model in the study of other things grasped by reason and not by sight (*Rep.* 529c–d [LCL 276: 182–84]).

137. Plato, *Plt.* 278a–e (LCL 164: 78–80).

138. Plato, *Rep.* 477a–480a (LCL 237: 520–34).

139. Plato, *Men.* 97b (LCL 165: 358); the same is said of "right opinion" (ὀρθὴ δόξα) 97c (LCL 165: 360). See Cushman's thorough discussion of "true opinion," *Therapeia*, 101–34, and Johannes M. van Ophuijsen's essay on various belief states in Plato, "Making Room for Faith: Is Plato?" in *The Winged Chariot: Collected Es-*

says on Plato and Platonism in Honour of L. M. De Rijk, ed. Maria Kardaun and Joke Spruyt (Leiden: Brill, 2000), 119–34.

140. Plato, *Men.* 97a–b (LCL 165: 358).

141. Plato, *Plt.* 278c (LCL 164: 80): μίαν ἀληθῆ δόξαν.

142. Plato, *Phdr.* 275b (LCL 36: 564).

143. See Racionero, "Logos, Myth and Probable Discourse," esp. 44–46; Perceval Frutiger, *Les mythes de Platon: étude philosophique et littéraire* (New York: Arno Press, 1976); K. F. Moors, *Platonic Myth: An Introductory Study* (Washington, DC: University Press of America, 1982); Luc Brisson, *Plato the Myth Maker* (Chicago: University of Chicago Press, 1998), and for the use of myth specific to the *Phaedrus,* Griswold, *Self-Knowledge,* 138–56.

144. Plato, *Phdr.* 246a (LCL 36: 470); see also *Rep.* 488a (LCL 276: 16–18).

145. Plato, *Men.* 98a (LCL 165: 362): ἕως ἄν τις αὐτὰς δήσῃ αἰτίας λογισμῷ. Asmis states, "Myth is but a step toward understanding: it needs to be complemented by rational, dialectical examination if it is to be part of a genuine philosophical search" ("*Psychagogia,*" 165); Racionero describes a process of "sifting through the narrative elements of the myth by means of refutations" ("Logos, Myth, and Probable Discourse," 52).

146. See particularly the whole course of education elaborated in *Rep.* 522a–540b. Glenn Morrow concludes that the educational process in the *Republic* "is but an application of the art of psychagogy" as the various disciplines "enchant" the soul ("Plato's Conception of Persuasion," *Philosophical Review* 62 [1955]: 238).

147. Plato, *Rep.* 532c, 533d (LCL 276: 198, 202–4).

148. Pearl, "Sense Perception," 27. Note Plato's well-known description of the plight of someone who lacks these skills as being only familiar with beautiful instances but not with "beauty itself." These persons are portrayed as "living in a dream rather than in waking reality" (*Rep.* 476c [LCL 237: 518]). Cushman comments on the role of guidance in reshaping habits of perception: "Plato was aware of a 'habituation' of the mind which enforces ignorance and fixes it as an inverted outlook of the whole soul. Thus it was plain to Plato that *paideia* involved, not so much cogent argument and formal proof, as it did the art of waking men from sleep or turning them around and leading them out into the light of a brighter day. Only immediate acquaintance with reality, as it discloses itself to the rightly oriented mind, is able to convince men of its self-evidencing truth. Apparently, then, the valid political art is not one of conveying truth to a man in the form of propositions but rather one of conducting men, by an exacting scrutiny of opinions, into the presence of reality" (*Therapeia,* 45).

149. Plato, *Ep.* 7.341c–d (LCL 234: 530). The seventh letter is generally considered authentic. See also where the author refers to "pupil and teacher asking and answering questions in good will and without envy" (Plato, *Ep.* 7.344b [LCL 234: 540]).

150. Plato, *Rep.* 496a–b (LCL 276: 50); a point often reiterated, see 428e, 491a–b, 503b.

151. Plato, *Rep.* 494a (LCL 276: 42).

152. Listed in one passage, for example, as "by nature good at remembering, quick to learn, high-minded, graceful, and a friend and relative of truth, justice, courage, and moderation" (*Rep.* 487a [LCL 276: 12]).

153. See Plato's discussion of the manner in which enchantments are necessary to bring individuals into harmony with the law (*Lg.* 659d–e, 664b, 665c, 666c, 671a, 773d, 812c, 887d). Glenn Morrow writes, "Plato's legislation is, in short, one vast system of total persuasion, the climactic fulfillment of the art of psychagogy that he had outlined in the *Phaedrus*" ("Plato's Conception of Persuasion," 242).

Notes to Chapter Two

1. See George Kennedy, "Most sophists admired the dialogues of Plato for their literary art and their philosophical idealism" (*A New History of Classical Rhetoric*, 240); Graham Anderson, *Second Sophistic*, 75–78; cf. Gerald Sandy, *The Greek World of Apuleius: Apuleius and the Second Sophistic* (Leiden: Brill, 1997), 147.

2. Diogenes Laertius, *Vit. phil.* 3.45 (trans. R. D. Hicks; LCL 184: 316).

3. Michael B. Trapp, "Plato's *Phaedrus* in Second-Century Greek Literature," in *Antonine Literature*, ed. D. A. Russell (Oxford: Clarendon Press, 1990), 165, and note especially his useful appendix documenting manifold citations of the *Phaedrus* in the literature, 171–73. Glenn Morrow asserts, "Plato's conception is the germ of all later techniques of persuasion" ("Plato's Conception of Persuasion," 237).

4. See particularly Aristotle's discussion of states of soul (*Rh.* 2.2.1–11.7 [trans. J. H. Freese; LCL 193: 172–246]) and of adapting speech to specific types of character (*Rh.* 2.12.1–19.27 [LCL 193: 246–72]). Roger Moss describes the *Phaedrus* "being given a pivotal role in the process of rapprochement that takes place over three generations between what Socrates (presumably) said and what Aristotle is able to write in the *Rhetoric*" ("The Case for Sophistry," 217). When compared with Plato's influence on later rhetoric, Aristotle's was muted. As George Kennedy observes, "Although Greek and Roman writers on rhetoric not infrequently mention Aristotle at some point in their discussions and imply that they knew his treatise, its direct influence on the tradition was slight" (*A New History of Classical Rhetoric*, 62).

5. Henri Marrou, *A History of Education*, 212.

6. A. D. Nock, *Conversion*, 173.

7. A. D. Nock, *Conversion*, 185.

8. Ilsetraut Hadot, "Spiritual Guide," 451. Malherbe observes, "By the first century A.D., however, elements of the [psychagogic] system were widely used,

for example by the Stoics, Epictetus, Seneca and Dio Chrysostom, and by the Platonist Plutarch" ("Hellenistic Moralists," 301–2). Richard Sorabji writes, "Unlike the philosophical analysis of emotions, many of the therapeutic exercises are common to different philosophical schools (*Emotion and Peace of Mind*, 3).

9. Albinus/Alcinous, *Didascalicus* 6.8 (in *The Handbook of Platonism*, trans. John Dillon, 12).

10. Not to be confused with Zeno of Citium, Cyprus (c. 334–262 BCE), the founder of the Stoa. The papyrus of *De libertate dicendi* (Περὶ παρρησίας) is only partially preserved and the text has had to be reconstructed at many points. The edition used here is *Philodemus: On Frank Criticism: Introduction, Translation, and Notes*, trans. David Konstan, Diskin Clay, et al. (Atlanta: Scholars Press, 1998). Παρρησία was a common term in Hellenistic moral philosophy; see, for example, Plutarch's discussion of the role of frankness in friendship (*Adul. amic.* esp. 71d–74e [trans. Frank C. Babbitt; LCL 197: 376–78]).

11. Clarence Glad, "Introduction," in *Philodemus: On Frank Criticism*, trans. Konstan et al., 2. For further discussion, see also Glad, *Paul and Philodemus*, 101–60; idem, "Frank Speech, Flattery, and Friendship in Philodemus," in *Friendship, Flattery, and Frankness of Speech: Studies in Friendship in the New Testament World*, ed. John T. Fitzgerald (Leiden: E. J. Brill, 1996), 21–59; Elizabeth Asmis, "Philodemus' Epicureanism," ANRW 2.36.4 (1990), 2369–2406.

12. Epicurus, *Fr.* 54 (Usener 221, Porphyry, *Marc.* 31.479–481): κενὸς ἐκείνου φιλοσόφου λόγος, ὑφ᾽ οὗ μηδὲν πάθος ἀνθρώπου θεραπεύεται; see also *Fr.* 66 (Usener 457), *VS* 54 (Mühll 66), *VS* 64 (Mühll 67).

13. Philodemus, *Lib.* Col. XVIIa. For medical imagery, see especially *Fr.* 39, 63–69, 86.

14. Reading παρέδωκεν ἑαυτὸν θεραπεύειν (*Lib.* Fr. 40); cf. Fr. 36, 51, 88 (= 94N), Col. Xb, although others resist frank criticism, Fr. 31.

15. Philodemus, *Lib.* Fr. 57; cf. "For it is like when a doctor assumes because of reasonable signs (διὰ σημείων) that a certain man is in need of a purge . . ." (Fr. 63), and note as well the sage's knowledge of "common traits" (κοινότητας) of souls (Col. IVb).

16. Glad provides a detailed list, "Introduction," 12–13.

17. See also where the sage is said to speak in accord with the hearer's character (προσχαρακτηρικῶς [*Lib.* Fr. 8]).

18. Maximus of Tyre, *Diss.* 1.8 (*Maximus Tyrius: Dissertationes*, ed. Michael B. Trapp [Stuttgart and Leipzig: B. G. Teubner, 1994], 10.236–242); trans. (altered) Michael B. Trapp, *Maximus of Tyre: The Philosophical Orations* (Oxford: Clarendon Press, 1997).

19. Maximus of Tyre, *Diss.* 1.8 (Trapp, 11.249–260). For the technical meaning of ἦθος and πάθος, see Aristotle, *Rh.* 1.2.3–7, 2.1.1–2.11.7 (LCL 193: 16–18, 168–246).

20. Maximus of Tyre, *Diss.* 1.7 (Trapp, 9.214–219).

21. Maximus of Tyre, *Diss.* 1.2 (Trapp, 2.36–37).

22. Maximus of Tyre, *Diss.* 1.2 (Trapp, 2.27–28): ἀλλ᾽ ἐπεὶ ᾠδῆς μὲν καὶ τῆς ἐκ μελῶν ψυχαγωγίας ὀλίγη τοῖς ἀνθρώποις χρεία.

23. Maximus of Tyre, *Diss.* 30.2 (Trapp, 246.25–27).

24. Maximus of Tyre, *Diss.* 1.2 (Trapp, 3.57–60).

25. Maximus of Tyre, *Diss.* 1.7 (Trapp, 9.200–209).

26. Maximus of Tyre, *Diss.* 37.3 (Trapp, 297.41–42). Recall Philostratus' description of Dio's speech (λογοῦ) overcoming the disorder (ἀταξίαν) of the mutinous army.

27. Maximus of Tyre, *Diss.* 27.8 (Trapp, 232.159–168).

28. Maximus of Tyre, *Diss.* 25.6 (Trapp, 213.137–214.140).

29. Maximus of Tyre, *Diss.* 25.2 (Trapp, 209.32); cf. Seneca, "let speech harmonize with life" (*concordet sermo cum uita*) (*Ep.* 75.4 [LCL 76: 138], also 20.2–3, 34.4, 52.8, 108.35–36. Musonius Rufus asserts, "For only in this way will philosophy be of profit to anyone, if to sound teaching is added conduct in harmony with it" (Fr. 1 [ed. and trans. Cora E. Lutz, *Musonius Rufus: "The Roman Socrates"* (New Haven, CT: Yale University Press, 1947), 37]).

30. For example, Seneca states that "the best ideas are common property" (*Ep.* 12.11 [LCL 75: 72]); "I think we ought to do in philosophy as they are wont to do in the Senate: when someone has made a motion, of which I approve to a certain extent, I ask him to make his motion in two parts, and I vote for the part of which I approve" (*Ep.* 21.9 [LCL 75: 146]). He is particularly self-conscious of his use of Epicurus, *Ep.* 8.8, 11.9, 13.17, 33.2. For Plato, see *Ep.* 58.25–31, 65.7–17. Stephen Gersh finds that his "relatively sympathetic treatment" of Platonic doctrines "suggests that Seneca is well aware of the tradition of harmonizing Platonism and Stoicism which was established a century earlier by Antiochus and is prepared to view positively the contribution of thinkers outside his favorite school" (*Middle Platonism and Neoplatonism: The Latin Tradition*, 2 vols. [Notre Dame, IN: University of Notre Dame Press, 1986], 1:180–81).

31. Seneca, *Ep.* 8.3 (trans. Richard M. Gummere; LCL 75: 38).

32. Seneca, *Ep.* 38.1 (LCL 75: 256): "You are right when you urge that we increase our mutual traffic of letters. But the greatest benefit is to be derived from conversation (*sermo*), because it insinuates itself gradually into the soul"; cf. *Ep.* 40.1, 67.2, 75.1. For letter writing in antiquity, see Abraham J. Malherbe, *Ancient Epistolary Theorists* (Atlanta: Scholars Press, 1988).

33. Noting that Seneca's manipulation of his own identity for philosophic purposes has made his letters of little use for a purely historical reconstruction of Seneca's life, Catharine Edwards observes: "At times in the letters Seneca plays the role of Stoic sage, at times that of a lowly aspirant to philosophical improvement. Sometimes he mimics the voice of the traditional Roman moralist castigating the material luxuries of his fellows, sometimes that of the retired senator concerned

with his estates, sometimes that of the elderly invalid" ("Self-Scrutiny and Self-Transformation in Seneca's Letters," *Greece and Rome* 41 [1997]: 34).

34. Seneca, *Ep.* 8.2 (LCL 75: 36). I. Hadot studies Seneca's epistolary psychagogy in her *Seneca und die griechisch-römische Tradition der Seelenleitung* (Berlin: de Gruyter, 1969).

35. Seneca, *Ep.* 94.54 (LCL 77: 44–46). Elsewhere he states that "nothing but evil attends us from our early youth; for we have grown up amid the curses invoked by our own parents" (*Ep.* 60.1 [LCL 75: 422]). See also his opinion on the harmful effects of crowds on the soul—"none of us, no matter how much he cultivates his abilities, can withstand the shock of the faults that approach, as it were, with so great a retinue" (*Ep.* 7.6 [LCL 75: 32]); idem, "And just as it happens that in a great crush of humanity, when people push against each other, no one can fall down without drawing along another, and those that are in front cause destruction to those behind—this same thing you may see happening everywhere in life" (*Vit. beat.* 1.4 [trans. John W. Basore; LCL 254: 100]). Musonius Rufus likewise comments on the "longer and more thorough training" that philosophy requires since its students have been "born and reared in an environment filled with corruption and evil" (Fr. 6 [Lutz 52–54]).

36. Seneca, *Ep.* 53.7–8 (LCL 75: 356); cf. "The evil that afflicts us is not external, it is within us, situated in our very vitals; for that reason we attain health with all the more difficulty, because we do not know that we are diseased" (*Ep.* 50.4 [LCL 75: 332]).

37. Seneca, *Ep.* 94.26 (LCL 77: 28).

38. Seneca, *Ep.* 75.11 (LCL 76: 142).

39. Nussbaum, *Therapy of Desire,* 38.

40. Seneca, *Ira* 2.22.2 (trans. John W. Basore; LCL 214: 214).

41. Seneca, *Ira* esp. 2.26–34 (LCL 214: 220–44).

42. Seneca, *Ira* 3.5.8 (LCL 214: 266).

43. Indeed, Seneca warns that "unless the mind takes steps to intercede" one will "find occasion for anger everywhere" (*Ira* 3.28.1 [LCL 214: 324]). For the social context meriting the Hellenistic moralists' concern with anger, see Peter Brown, *Power and Persuasion,* 50–55; William V. Harris, *Restraining Rage: The Ideology of Anger Control in Classical Antiquity* (Cambridge, MA: Harvard University Press, 2004).

44. Seneca, *Ep.* 99.15–16 (LCL 77: 136–38).

45. Seneca, *Ep.* 13.4 (LCL 75: 74): *saepius opinione quam re laboramus;* cf. *Ep.* 78.13 (LCL 76: 188): "Everything depends on opinion: ambition, luxury, greed look back to opinion. It is according to opinion that we suffer. Each of us is as wretched as he believes"; Epictetus, "It is not things themselves that disturb people, but their judgments (δόγματα) about things" (*Ench.* 5 [trans. W. A. Oldfather; LCL 218: 486], see also 16, 20; *Diss.* 3.22.61). I proceed assuming with Phillip Mitsis

that Seneca's presentation "at least in its major outlines, is representative of an on-going consensus among orthodox Stoics about the nature of rules and their place in morality" ("Seneca on Reason, Rules, and Moral Development," in *Passions and Perceptions: Studies in Hellenistic Philosophy of Mind,* ed. J. Brunschwig and M. Nussbaum [Cambridge: Cambridge University Press, 1993], 293).

46. Seneca, *Ep.* 99.17 (LCL 77: 138).

47. Seneca, *Ep.* 99.7–13 (LCL 77: 132–34).

48. Seneca, *Ep.* 99.14 (LCL 77: 136).

49. Seneca, *Ep.* 99.18, 22 (LCL 77: 140, 143): *Omnia itaque ad rationem reuocanda sunt. . . . Aequo animo excipe necessaria.*

50. Seneca, *Ep.* 99.6 (LCL 77: 132).

51. See Nussbaum, *Therapy of Desire,* esp. 37–40, 104–39, 366–401; and also Long and Sedley, *Hellenistic Philosophers,* chapter 65.

52. See, for example, the Platonist Plutarch's treatise on anger (*Cohib. ira* 12.460d [trans. W. C. Helmbold; LCL 337: 136]) and James Hankinson's study of Galen's therapy of the passions articulated in the context of a Platonic anthropology ("Actions and Passions: Affection, Emotion, and Moral Self-Management in Galen's Philosophical Psychology," in *Passions and Perceptions,* ed. Brunschwig and Nussbaum, 184–222).

53. Seneca, *Ep.* 53.8 (LCL 75: 356): *Sola autem nos philosophia excitabit, sola somnum excutiet grauem.*

54. Seneca, *Ep.* 24.12–13 (LCL 75: 172).

55. Seneca, *Ep.* 94.54 (LCL 77: 44–46).

56. Seneca, *Otio* 4.1 (trans. John W. Basore; LCL 254: 186–88); cf. Seneca, *Ep.* 95.52 (LCL 77: 90), Cicero, *N.D.* 2.154 (trans. H. Rackham; LCL 268: 272).

57. Seneca, *Ep.* 7.7–8 (LCL 75: 32–34), Gretchen Reydams-Schils, "Roman and Stoic: The Self as a Mediator," *Dionysius* 16 (1998): 50; eadem, *The Roman Stoics: Self, Responsibility, and Affection* (Chicago: University of Chicago Press, 2005). Like Reydams-Schils, Nussbaum draws attention to Stoicism's critical capacity: "Stoicism conducts a radical critique of convention and ordinary belief, arguing that many deeply held ordinary beliefs will not pass appropriate tests of rationality" (*Therapy of Desire,* 322). There is a common opposing view that claims that Stoic political involvement tends to reduce their philosophy to conservative ideology. For example, James Francis states, "Stoicism turned the maintenance of the prevailing social and political order into a command of reason and nature hallowed by the dictates of philosophy" (*Subversive Virtue: Asceticism and Authority in the Second-Century Pagan World* [University Park: Pennsylvania State University Press, 1995], 19). Although the Stoics' commitment to political involvement did often lead to compromise, it is better understood as an attempt to mediate between norms (as outlined well by Reydams-Schils), even if from a later perspective we might assess some of those attempts as failures. For example, Augustine of Hippo admired Seneca's philosophical critique of Roman society so much as to devote a section of

his *City of God* to it, but laments the extent that Seneca continued to participate in customary practices that he no longer believed in (*ciu.* 6.10–11; trans. Henry Bettenson, *Concerning the City of God against the Pagans* [Harmondsworth, Middlesex: Penguin Books, 1984]). See also Augustine's description of the political compromises made by Cicero in his attempt to restore the liberty of the Roman Republic (*ciu.* 3.30).

58. Seneca, *Ep.* 18.4 (LCL 75: 116–18).

59. Seneca, *Ep.* 52.2–3 (LCL 75: 344). The need for guidance in the philosophic life is a common theme for Seneca, see esp. *Ep.* 11.9, 22.1–2, 25.5–6, 50.5.

60. Seneca, *Ep.* 94.55 (LCL 77: 46); see also Seneca's advice that if we wish to be happy, we "should not fail to find some expert guide who has explored the region toward which we are advancing" (*Vit. beat.* 1.2 [LCL 254: 100]).

61. Seneca, *Ep.* 94.59 (LCL 77: 48).

62. Seneca, *Ep.* 94.52–53 (LCL 77: 44).

63. Seneca, *Ep.* 94.72 (LCL 77: 56).

64. For further discussion of the issues raised in these letters, see Phillip Mitsis, "Seneca," 285–312; I. G. Kidd, "Moral Actions and Rules in Stoic Ethics," in *The Stoics*, ed. John M. Rist (Berkeley: University of California Press, 1978), 247–58; and Brad Inwood, "Seneca on Emotion and Action," in *Passions and Perception*, ed. Brunschwig and Nussbaum, 150–83.

65. Seneca, *Ep.* 95.10 (LCL 77: 64). The most prominent dogma found in Seneca's letters is his refrain, "live according to Nature" (*secundum naturam uiuere*) (*Ep.* 5.4 [LCL 75: 22]).

66. Seneca, *Ep.* 95.1 (LCL 77: 58), *Ep.* 94.39 (LCL 77: 36).

67. Seneca, *Ep.* 94.10–17, cf. 89.13. Diogenes Laertius reports that Aristo set aside both logic and physics in favor of ethics, and in ethical theory refused to recognize any ranking of goods he considered indifferent to virtue or vice (*Vit. phil.* 7.160–64 [LCL 185: 262–68]). See also Sextus Empiricus, *Math.* 7.12 (LCL 291: 6–8), 11.64–67 (LCL 311: 416–18).

68. Seneca, *Ep.* 94.5–6 (LCL 77: 12–14).

69. Seneca, *Ep.* 94.12 (LCL 77: 18).

70. Seneca, *Ep.* 94.8 (LCL 77: 16).

71. Seneca, *Ep.* 95.4–7 (LCL 77: 60–62).

72. Seneca, *Ep.* 94.1 (LCL 77: 10).

73. Seneca, *Ep.* 95.60 (LCL 77: 94–96): "Those who do away with doctrines do not understand that these doctrines are proved by the very arguments through which they seem to disprove them. . . . They are saying that precepts are sufficient to develop life, and that doctrines of wisdom, that is, dogmas, are superfluous. And yet this very utterance of theirs is a doctrine"; cf. *Ep.* 95.46 (LCL 77: 86): "as soon as a premise (*proposito*) is set out, doctrines (*decreta*) begin to be necessary"; *Ep.* 95.58 (LCL 95: 58): "One cannot attain the truth without doctrines (*sine decretis*); doctrines encompass life."

74. Seneca, *Ep.* 95.12 (LCL 77: 66).
75. Seneca, *Ep.* 95.64 (LCL 77: 98).
76. Seneca, *Ep.* 95.12 (LCL 77: 64).
77. Seneca, *Ep.* 95.37–39 (LCL 77: 80–82).
78. Seneca, *Ep.* 95.34 (LCL 77: 78).
79. Seneca, *Ep.* 47.10, 13–16 (LCL 75: 306–10).
80. Seneca, *Ep.* 45.9 (LCL 75: 294–96), *Ep.* 94.6–7 (LCL 77: 14).
81. Seneca, *Ep.* 95.45 (LCL 77: 86).
82. Seneca, *Ep.* 95.39–40 (LCL 77: 82–84).
83. Seneca, *Ep.* 95.59 (LCL 77: 94).
84. Seneca, *Ep.* 95.45 (LCL 77: 86).
85. Seneca, *Ep.* 95.12 (LCL 77: 64–66).
86. Seneca, *Ep.* 95.62 (LCL 77: 96).
87. Seneca, *Ep.* 95.61–64 (LCL 77: 96–98).
88. For theology, cf. *Ep.* 95.48 (LCL 77: 88): "No one will make sufficient progress without conceiving a right idea of God." Even as a Stoic skeptical of "Plato's ideas" (*ideae*), Seneca points out the practical value in this "doctrine" by drawing attention to its call to turn the soul toward those things that are eternal (*Ep.* 58.26–27 [LCL 75: 402–4]).
89. Seneca, *Ep.* 95.10 (LCL 77: 64).
90. Seneca, *Ep.* 94.36 (LCL 77: 34).
91. Seneca, *Ep.* 94.32 (LCL 77: 32).
92. Seneca, *Ep.* 71.30–32 (LCL 76: 164–66).
93. Seneca, *Ep.* 94.29 (LCL 77: 30).
94. Pierre Hadot has drawn attention to such exercises and states: "Every [Hellenistic] school practices exercises designed to ensure spiritual progress toward the ideal state of wisdom, exercises of reason that will be, for the soul, analogous to the athlete's training or the application of a medical cure" ("Forms of Life and Forms of Discourse," in *Philosophy as a Way of Life: Spiritual Exercises from Socrates to Foucault* [Cambridge: Blackwell, 1995], 59). See his other essays in *Philosophy as a Way of Life*, his *The Inner Citadel: The Meditations of Marcus Aurelius*, trans. Michael Chase (Cambridge, MA: Harvard University Press, 1998), esp. 35–53), as well as his attention to the subject throughout *What Is Ancient Philosophy?* See also Paul Rabbow, *Seelenführung*; Robert J. Newman, "*Cotidie Meditare*: Theory and Practice of the *meditatio* in Imperial Stoicism," *ANRW* 2.36.3 (1989), 1473–1517; Richard Sorabji, *Emotion and Peace of Mind*, 211–52; B.-L. Hijmans, *Askesis: Notes on Epictetus' Educational System* (Assen: Van Gorcum, 1959); and Michel Foucault's appropriation of this tradition in his advocacy of "technologies of the self" (*The Use of Pleasure*, vol. 2 of 3, *The History of Sexuality*, trans. Robert Hurley [New York: Random House, 1985], 10–11).
95. Musonius Rufus, *Fr.* 6 (Lutz 52).
96. P. Hadot, *Inner Citadel*, 51.

97. Seneca, *Ep.* 53.9 (LCL 75: 356–58).

98. Seneca, *Ep.* 72.1 (LCL 76: 96).

99. Seneca, *Ep.* 72.6 (LCL 76: 100).

100. Seneca, *Ep.* 15.5 (LCL 75: 98).

101. Seneca, *Ep.* 90.46 (LCL 76: 428): "Virtue is not attained by the soul unless that soul has been trained and taught, and by unremitting practice brought to perfection"; *Ep.* 4.5 (LCL 75: 16): "Rehearse this thought everyday (*cotidie meditare*)"; *Ep.* 2.4 (LCL 75: 8): "Each day acquire something that will fortify you"; *Ep.* 94.26 (LCL 77: 28): "Whatever is salutary should be often discussed and often brought before the mind, so that it may be not only familiar with us, but also ready to hand." In his *Letter to Herodotus,* Epicurus says that "mental tranquility means being released from all these troubles and retaining constantly in memory the general and most important principles (κυριωτάτων)" (Diogenes Laertius, 10.82 [LCL 185: 610]). Musonius Rufus refers to "habituating" (ἐθίζεσθαι) oneself to act according to the principles of a particular "teaching" (λόγου) (*Fr.* 5 [Lutz 50]). Epictetus observes, "It is not easy for a person to acquire a proper judgment (δόγμα), unless each day the same principles are said and heard, and at the same time applied to life" (Fr. 16 [LCL 218: 460]). Marcus Aurelius exhorts himself to always have his δόγματα ready, just as physicians have their instruments always "in hand" (πρόχειρα) (*De rebus suis* 3.13 [trans. C. R. Haines; LCL 58: 60]).

102. Seneca, *Ep.* 16.1 (LCL 75: 102).

103. Seneca, *Ep.* 16.3 (LCL 75: 104).

104. Seneca, *Ep.* 94.47–48 (LCL 77: 40–42). See also Seneca's comment about how "maxims" (*sententiae*) welcomed into the soul "mold" (*formant*) it (*Ep.* 94.47 [LCL 77: 40]).

105. Seneca, *Ep.* 22.1–3 (LCL 75: 148–50).

106. Seneca, *Ep.* 94.51 (LCL 77: 44).

107. Seneca, *Ep.* 94.25 (LCL 77: 28).

108. Seneca, *Ep.* 108.9–12; he cautions, nonetheless, against excessively ornate speech (*Ep.* 40.4–5).

109. Seneca, *Ep.* 94.29 (LCL 77: 30).

110. Seneca, *Ep.* 33.9 (LCL 75: 238).

111. Seneca, *Ep.* 33.7 (LCL 75: 236).

112. Seneca, *Ep.* 23.4 (LCL 75: 160).

113. Seneca, *Ep.* 33.9 (LCL 75: 238).

114. Seneca, *Ep.* 34.3 (LCL 75: 242); it is worth recalling Seneca's failed tutelage of Nero, despite the many instances in which Seneca tragically accommodated himself to the whims and desires of the young man (see Tacitus, *Ann.* 12.8, 13.2–6, 15.60–65).

115. Seneca, *Ep.* 31.5 (LCL 75: 224), *Ep.* 41.1 (LCL 75: 272). For a similarly negative evaluation of petitionary prayer, see Maximus of Tyre, *Diss.* 5.

116. Seneca, *Ep.* 20.3 (LCL 75: 134).

117. Seneca, *Ep.* 111.2–3 (LCL 77: 278); for an extended discussion of the Stoic sage's invulnerability to any sort of injury, see Seneca's *Const.* (LCL 214: 48–104).

118. Graham Anderson observes, "It is a familiarly accepted phenomenon that in the Early Empire the Greek world looked back with nostalgic self-awareness to the classical era, and that it did so as a reaction against the political impotence of the present" (*Second Sophistic*, 101); cf. E. L. Bowie, "Greeks and Their Past in the Second Sophistic," *Past and Present* 46 (1970): 3–41, revised in *Studies in Ancient Society*, ed. M. I. Finley (London: Routledge and K. Paul, 1974), 166–209; and Arthur Hilary Armstrong, "Pagan and Christian Traditionalism in the First Three Centuries A.D.," *Studia Patristica* 15 (1984): 414–30.

119. Anderson notes, "Among sophistic authors themselves the past could look still more immediate: the sensation of keeping in direct thought with remote antiquity, and in particular its literary canon, is obvious and real" (*Second Sophistic*, 102–3). As Anderson ably explains, the well-known resurgence of literary Attic even in spoken form is a function of this archaism (*Second Sophistic*, 86–100).

120. Maximus of Tyre, *Diss.* 11.1 (Trapp, 88.16–21).

121. Maximus of Tyre, *Diss.* 11.2 (Trapp, 88.30–89.43). See Plotinus' similar stance, "And [it follows] that these statements of ours are not new; they do not belong to our present time, but were made long ago, not explicitly, and what we have said in this discussion has been an interpretation of them, relying on Plato's own writings for evidence that these views are ancient" (*En.* 5.1.8 [trans. A. H. Armstrong; LCL 444: 40]).

122. P. Hadot, "Forms of Life and Forms of Discourse," in *Philosophy as a Way of Life*, 60. For a positive appraisal of this exegetical turn in philosophy, see P. Hadot, "Théologie, exégèse, révélation, écriture, dans la philosophie grecque," in *Les règles de l'interprétation*, ed. Michel Tardieu (Paris: Éditions du cerf, 1987), 13–34. The traditional quality of Hellenistic philosophy and its use of canonical authorities has often been viewed negatively as "a substitute for original thought" (see Gerald Sandy, *Greek World*, 148, and 30, 50, 59–60, 68, 88, 113, 130, 182–83). The visible limitations of the Hellenistic philosophers should not overshadow their hermeneutical and exegetical creativity in evolving methods of making the past usable for the present, see H. Gregory Snyder, *Teachers and Texts in the Ancient World: Philosophers, Jews, and Christians* (London and New York: Routledge, 2000), esp. 1–121.

123. Seneca, *Ep.* 64.7–9 (LCL 75: 440–42).

124. See especially Plato, *Rep.* 364b–365c, 383a–398b, 595a–608b; this famous argument, nonetheless, cannot be taken simply at face value due to the poetic qualities of Plato's own dialogues and his use of any number of genres (including epic poetry) in their composition (see Andrea Nightingale, *Genres in Dialogue: Plato and the Construct of Philosophy* [Cambridge: Cambridge University Press, 1995]).

125. The Epicureans rejected Homer as irretrievably introducing false fears and notions that disturb human tranquility, thus rejecting epic poetry's psychagogic value. For the Platonic tradition's later use of Homer, see Robert Lamberton's work,

"The Neoplatonists and the Spiritualization of Homer," in *Homer's Ancient Readers: The Hermeneutics of Greek Epic's Earliest Exegetes*, ed. Robert Lamberton and John J. Keaney (Princeton, NJ: Princeton University Press, 1992), 115–33; idem, *Homer the Theologian: Neoplatonist Allegorical Reading and the Growth of the Epic Tradition* (Berkeley: University of California Press, 1986); James A. Coulter, *The Literary Microcosm: Theories of Interpretation of the Later Neoplatonists* (Leiden: E. J. Brill, 1976). A. A. Long offers important observations on the distinctively Stoic interpretive traditions, "Stoic Reading of Homer," in *Homer's Ancient Readers*, 41–66; and his "Allegory in Philo and Etymology in Stoicism: A Plea for Drawing Distinctions," *Studia Philonica Annual* 9 (1997): 198–210.

126. Plutarch, *Adol. poet. aud.* 15f (trans. Frank C. Babbitt; LCL 197: 80). See Philip R. Hardie, "Plutarch and the Interpretation of Myth," ANRW 2.33.6 (1992), 4743–87, and, more generally, Robert Lamberton, *Plutarch* (Hermes Books; New Haven, CT: Yale University Press, 2001).

127. Plutarch, *Adol. poet. aud.* 16b–d (LCL 197: 82–84).

128. Plutarch, *Adol. poet. aud.* 16d, 28d, 31c.

129. Plutarch, *Adol. poet. aud.* 15b–c (LCL 197: 76–78).

130. Plutarch, *Adol. poet. aud.* 26a (LCL 197: 136).

131. Plutarch, *Adol. poet. aud.* 18b (LCL 197: 92). See Maximus of Tyre's similar statement of the utility of the mixed quality of myths: they "occupy the middle ground between rational knowledge and ignorance. Trusted because of the pleasure they give, yet mistrusted because of their paradoxical content, they guide (χειραγ-ωγοῦντας) the soul to search for the truth and to investigate more deeply" (*Diss.* 4.6 [Trapp, 33.102–106]). Maximus offers two further rationales — not in Plutarch's treatise, but similar to what Augustine will later state of Christian scripture — that attribute benefits to the very obscurity of myth. First, "given the boldness of its nature, the human soul tends to think little of what is close at hand, while it admires what is distant. Divining what it cannot actually see, it tries to hunt it out by the power of reason; failure simply intensifies its keenness in the chase, while success means that it loves what it has found as if it were its own handiwork" (*Diss.* 4.5 [Trapp, 33.94–99]). Second, myth is at times a more appropriate "vehicle for topics which our human frailty does not allow us to see clearly" (*Diss.* 4.5 [Trapp, 32.84–33.86]).

132. Plutarch, *Adol. poet. aud.* 37b (LCL 197: 196).

133. Plutarch, *Adol. poet. aud.* 36e (LCL 197: 194).

134. Plutarch, *Adol. poet. aud.* 15f–16a (LCL 197: 80).

135. Plutarch, *Adol. poet. aud.* 26b (LCL 197: 136).

136. Plutarch, *Adol. poet. aud.* 20d (LCL 197: 104).

137. Plutarch, *Adol. poet. aud.* 26a–b (LCL 197: 136).

138. Plutarch, *Adol. poet. aud.* 15d (LCL 197: 78).

139. Plutarch, *Adol. poet. aud.* 35f (LCL 197: 188).

140. Plutarch, *Adol. poet. aud.* 36d (LCL 197: 192).

141. Gerald L. Bruns, "The Problem of Figuration in Antiquity," in *Hermeneutics: Questions and Prospects*, ed. Gary Shapiro and Alan Sica (Amherst: University of Massachusetts Press, 1984), 147.

142. Plutarch, *Adol. poet. aud.* 20b–c (LCL 197: 102). Such common cause between philosophy and poetry was often asserted in the period. See how Dio Chrysostom contends, "Both Socrates and Homer . . . were devoted to the same ends and spoke about the same things, the one through the medium of his verse, the other in prose" (*Or.* 55.9 [LCL 376: 386]). Maximus of Tyre likewise states that "the philosophical doctrines of today are in essence no different from the myths of the past, except in their form (τῷ σχήματι) of composition. What descend to us via the whole philosophic tradition are doctrines about the gods that have their origin in a far more distant era" (*Diss.* 4.3 [Trapp, 31.60–62], also *Diss.* 18.5, 8).

143. Lucian, *Nigr.* pref. (trans. A. M. Harmon; LCL 14: 98).

144. Lucian, *Nigr.* 2–3 (LCL 14: 100–2).

145. Lucian, *Nigr.* 3 (LCL 14: 102).

146. Lucian, *Nigr.* 4 (LCL 14: 102–4).

147. Lucian, *Nigr.* 6 (LCL 14: 106).

148. Seneca, *Ep.* 108.13–16 (LCL 77: 238–40).

149. Epictetus, *Diss.* 3.23.29 (LCL 218: 180).

150. Epictetus, *Diss.* 3.23.30 (LCL 218: 180). Even in the classroom of a late first-century Stoic such as Epictetus, the influence of Platonic ideals is noteworthy. Robert Dobbin describes this influence on Epictetus as "of a more pervasive kind," and states that Epictetus cites Plato "more than sixty times," and refers to Socrates "more than fifty times" (*Epictetus: Discourses Book 1* [Oxford: Clarendon Press, 1998], xv–xvi).

151. Epictetus, *Diss.* 3.23.34 (LCL 218: 182).

152. An introductory comment in Epictetus, *Diss.* pref. 5 (LCL 131: 6).

153. For an example of pagan oratory from the fourth century, see Robert J. Penella, *The Private Orations of Themistius* (Berkeley: University of California Press, 2000) and *Politics, Philosophy, and Empire in the Fourth Century: Select Orations of Themistius*, trans. Peter J. Heather and David Moncur (Liverpool: Liverpool University Press, 2001).

154. For the influential school of Libanius and his impressive list of Christian and non-Christian students, see Raffaella Cribiore, *The School of Libanius in Late Antique Antioch* (Princeton, NJ: Princeton University Press, 2007).

Notes to Chapter Three

1. Symmachus' *relatio* (CSEL 82.3: 21–33) is translated by Boniface Ramsey, *Ambrose* (New York: Routledge, 1997), 179–84. See also Ambrose's letters to Emperor Valentinian regarding the matter (*ep.* 17 and 18).

2. For analysis of this relationship, see Neil B. McLynn, *Ambrose of Milan: Church and Court in the Christian Capital* (Berkeley: University of California Press, 1994), 263–75.

3. Augustine's own account of the appointment is found in *conf.* 5.12.22–23. For further details, see McLynn, *Ambrose*, 169–70; Serge Lancel, *Saint Augustine*, trans. Antonia Nevill (London: SCM Press, 2002), 61–66; Brown, *Augustine of Hippo*, 58–61; John J. O'Meara, *The Young Augustine: The Growth of St. Augustine's Mind up to His Conversion* (London: Longmans, Green, 1954), 92–93, 115; T. D. Barnes, "Augustine, Symmachus, and Ambrose," in *Augustine: From Rhetor to Theologian*, ed. Joanne McWilliam (Waterloo, Ontario: Wilfrid Laurier University Press, 1992), 7–13. For the role played by Augustine's Manichaean friends, see Samuel N. C. Lieu, *Manichaeism in the Later Roman Empire and Medieval China*, rev. ed. (Tübingen: J. C. B. Mohr [Siebeck], 1992), 173–74.

4. Augustine says of his parents, "Both of them . . . were very ambitious for me" (*conf.* 2.3.8 [CCL 27: 21.63]); and of his father in particular that he sacrificed for his son's education, but "did not care what character . . . I was developing, or how chaste I was so long as I possessed a cultured tongue" (*conf.* 2.3.5 [CCL 27: 20.16–17]). For similar pressures placed upon Augustine's friend Alypius, see *conf.* 6.8.13, 6.10.16.

5. See Symmachus' comment that "the road to civil office is frequently laid open by literature" (my translation; *ep.* 1.20, ed. Otto Seeck, *Q. Aurelii Symmachi quae supersunt*, Monumenta Germaniae Historica 6.1 [Berlin: Apud Weidmannos, 1883], 12.25). Carol Harrison observes how Augustine's social climb brought him "into the rank of the élite—an aristocracy, not of birth, but of educational formation" (*Augustine: Christian Truth and Fractured Humanity* [New York: Oxford University Press, 2000], 48).

6. Augustine, *conf.* 3.3.6.

7. Augustine, *conf.* 6.6.9 (CCL 27: 79.17–18).

8. Augustine, *conf.* 4.4.7, 5.7.13, 6.7.11; cf. Augustine's dedicatory preface to his patron Romanianus: "You alone were the one, when I returned to Carthage to get a more advantageous position, to whom I confided my plan and my hopes. . . . Though you hesitated for a little while out of love for your home town, since I was already teaching there, when you weren't able to overcome a young man's ambition for things that seemed better you turned your opposition into support" (*Acad.* 2.2.3 [CCL 29: 19.11–17]).

9. Augustine's lost *De pulchro et apto* (*conf.* 5.12.22, 5.8.14), whose title may have been drawn from Cicero, *Tusc. Disp.* 4.31 (trans. J. E. King; LCL 141: 358–60): *et ut corporis est quaedam apta figura membrorum cum coloris quadam suauitate eaque dicitur pulchritudo . . .* a text Augustine later rephrases in *ciu.* 22.19 (CCL 48: 838.41–43).

10. Augustine, *conf.* 6.11.19 (CCL 27: 87.37–38).

11. Augustine, *conf.* 6.6.9, 6.11.19 (CCL 27: 79.1, 87.39–42); see O'Donnell, *Confessions*, 2.374.

12. With his mother's encouragement (*conf.* 6.13.23–15.25).

13. See Augustine's mention of it in his *c. litt. Pet.* 3.30 (CSEL 52: 185.19–23).

14. For this skill, see the discussion above (chapter 1). Plotinus characterizes those giving panegyrics as being "incapable of making true speeches about their subjects" (*En.* 5.5.13 [LCL 444: 194]).

15. Augustine, *conf.* 1.20.31, 6.6.10 (CCL 27: 17.10–16, 80.46). Readers of the *Confessions* for biographical purposes should keep in mind that the account intentionally emphasizes philosophical and theological concepts that were important to Augustine the bishop (for example, his growing appreciation of the force of habit, his mature theology of grace, and sign theory). See, among others, the comments of O'Meara, *Young Augustine*, 6, 19; and O'Donnell, "Augustine: His Time and Lives," 23.

16. Augustine, *conf.* 9.2.2 (CCL 27: 133.2–3). Concern for the truthfulness of speech became one of Augustine's lifelong preoccupations, see Paul J. Griffiths, *Lying: An Augustinian Theology of Duplicity* (Grand Rapids, MI: Brazos Press, 2004).

17. Augustine, *conf.* 6.6.9 (CCL 27: 79.11–12).

18. Augustine, *conf.* 9.2.2 (CCL 27: 133.3–5).

19. Augustine, *conf.* 1.6.8–8.13.

20. Augustine, *conf.* 1.18.29–19.30 (CCL 27: 16.18–20, 1–3). See especially his comment on how "someone, who is educated in or is a teacher of the old conventional sounds, pronounces the word 'human' contrary to school teaching, without pronouncing the initial aspirate, he is socially censured more than if . . . he were to hate a human being" (1.18.29 [CCL 27: 16.21–24]).

21. Plutarch notes that "his fame for oratory abides to this day" (*Cic.* 2.4 [trans. B. Perrin; LCL 99: 86]).

22. Plutarch, *Cic.* 39.6–7 (LCL 99: 182); cf. Cicero's *Lig.* (trans. N. H. Watts; LCL 252: 454–93). Augustine was familiar with this speech (*ep.* 138.9).

23. Augustine, *conf.* 3.4.7 (CCL 27: 30.5–6): *exhortationem ad philosophiam.* Although Cicero's *Hortensius* remains lost, the fragmentary evidence provided by Augustine and others shows it to have been an instance of philosophical protreptic rhetorically summoning the reader to a philosophic life while addressing at least the following topics: the superiority of rigorous philosophical thinking to making judgments based on mere appearance; the manner in which bad habit becomes something of a second nature; philosophy as teaching how bad habits ruin nature; and how highmindedness and scorn of common opinion will strengthen one against any disaster. See *Marcus Tullius Cicero: Hortensius, Lucullus, Academici Libri,* ed. Laila Straume-Zimmermann, Ferdinand Broemser, and Olof Gigon (Munich: Artemis, 1990), 6–111; Hagendahl lists the fragments preserved by Augustine, *Augustine and the Latin Classics,* 81–94.

24. Augustine, *conf.* 3.4.7 (CCL 27: 30.13–14): *non ergo ad acuendam linguam referebam illum librum neque mihi locutionem, sed quod loquebatur persuaserat.*

25. Augustine, *conf.* 3.4.7–8 (CCL 27: 30.6–18); see also *conf.* 6.11.18, 8.7.17, *beata u.* 1.4, and *sol.* 1.10.17.

26. Plutarch, *Cic.* 3.1–4.5 (LCL 99: 86–90); Cicero states, "Philo, whom I often heard, made it his practice to teach rhetoric at one time, and philosophy at another. And since my friends have coaxed me to adopt this practice, I spent the time we had in my house at Tusculum this way" (*Tusc. Disp.* 2.9 [LCL 141: 154]). Malcolm Schofield has addressed Philo's influence on Cicero ("Academic Therapy: Philo of Larissa and Cicero's project in the *Tusculans*," in *Philosophy and Power in the Graeco-Roman World: Essays in Honour of Miriam Griffin*, ed. Gillian Clark and Tessa Rajak [Oxford and New York: Oxford University Press, 2002], 91–109).

27. As recorded by Arius Didymus, in Stobaeus, *Eclogae* 2.7.39.20–42.1. Greek text and translation adapted from Charles Brittain, *Philo of Larissa: The Last of the Academic Sceptics* (Oxford: Oxford University Press, 2001), 364–66.

28. Cicero was fully aware both of the force of Plato's critique of rhetoric as well as his compelling use of it. Concerning the *Gorgias,* Cicero remarks, "[W]hat impressed me most deeply about Plato in this book was, that it was in mocking orators that he himself seemed to me to be the most accomplished orator of all" (*De orat.* 1.47 [LCL 348: 34–36]). A. A. Long observes, "No other individual philosopher is cited by Cicero as fully and as frequently [as Plato]." In commenting on the particular significance of the *Phaedrus* for Cicero, Long contends that Cicero "wants his readers to compare his own work *Orator* with the *Phaedrus.* That dialogue, with its assimilation of authentic rhetoric to Platonic dialectic is, of course, the one that best suits Cicero's brief" ("Cicero's Plato and Aristotle," in *Cicero the Philosopher: Twelve Papers,* ed. J. G. F. Powell [Oxford: Oxford University Press, 1995], 44, 52). Cicero was not only widely read in Plato's dialogues, but engaged in translating some of them into Latin. For Cicero's translations, see J. G. F. Powell, "Cicero's Translations from Greek," in *Cicero the Philosopher,* ed. Powell, 273–300. For a list of Cicero's citations of Plato, see T. De Graff, "Plato in Cicero," *Classical Philology* 35 (1940): 143–53.

29. Cicero, *Tusc. Disp.* 5.4.10 (LCL 141: 434). See also Aristotle, *Metaph.* 987b.1–5, 1078b.17–19; Cicero, *Acad.* 1.4.15–16; Augustine, *ciu.* 6.2–10, 7.1–22, 8.3.

30. Cicero, *Orat.* 3.12 (LCL 342: 312–14).

31. Noted by Plutarch, *Cic.* 40.1–3. For Cicero's contributions to philosophy, see the essays in the volume, *Cicero the Philosopher,* ed. Powell.

32. Anderson, *Second Sophistic,* 123.

33. Wendy Olmsted observes of the *Confessions* that it "anatomizes the partial, distorted rhetorics that impeded Augustine's own search for God" ("Invention, Emotion, and Conversion in Augustine's *Confessions*," in *Rhetorical Invention and Religious Inquiry: New Perspectives,* ed. Walter Jost and Wendy Olmsted [New Haven, CT: Yale University Press, 2000], 65).

34. Cicero, *Tusc. Disp.* 3.1–2.2–3 (LCL 141: 224–28). On Augustine's thorough knowledge of the *Tusculans* and his continued use of them, see Hagendahl, *Augustine and the Latin Classics,* 138–56, 510–16; J.J. O'Donnell, "Augustine's Classical Readings," 156–57.

35. Cicero, *Tusc. Disp.* 3.5.10 (LCL 141: 234).

36. Cicero, *Tusc. Disp.* 3.1–2.2–3 (LCL 141: 224–28).

37. Cicero, *Tusc. Disp.* 5.27.78 (LCL 141: 504–6).

38. Cicero, *Tusc. Disp.* 3.6.13 (LCL 141: 240), 4.27.58 (LCL 141: 392). Describing the "effect of philosophy," Cicero remarks that "it is a physician of souls (*medetur animis*), takes away the load of empty troubles, sets us free from desires and banishes fears" (*Tusc. Disp.* 2.4.11 [LCL 141: 156]; also 2.18.43, and 3.34.84). For further elaboration, see, Stephen A. White, "Cicero and the Therapists," in *Cicero the Philosopher,* ed. Powell, 219–46.

39. Cicero, *Tusc. Disp.* 5.2.5 (LCL 141: 428); cf. *Tusc. Disp.* 2.4.12 (LCL 141: 158): "Now the cultivation of soul is philosophy; this pulls out vices by the roots and makes souls fit for the reception of seed."

40. Cicero, *Tusc. Disp.* 3.24.58 (LCL 141: 294), *Tusc. Disp.* 4.27.59 (LCL 141: 394): *aegritudine autem sublata propriis rationibus;* cf. *Tusc. Disp.* 4.38.83–84 (LCL 141: 422): "But there is one method of healing both distress (*aegritudinis*) and all other diseases of soul, namely to show that all are matters of belief (*omnes opinabiles*) and consent of the will and are submitted to simply because such submission is thought to be right. This deception, as being the root of all evil, philosophy promises to drag out utterly."

41. In *De orat.*, Cicero, on the one hand, repeatedly argues against the view that rhetoric can be an autonomous art in no need of philosophy and contends that the orator of necessity must possess broad philosophical learning. On the other hand, he claims that broad philosophical learning is of no value whatever unless the orator puts it into words that are persuasive (1.12.54 [LCL 348: 40]). Near the beginning of the *Tusc. Disp.* he states, "I have always judged that philosophy to be perfect which treats the greatest problems with adequate fullness and in an attractive style" (*copiose posset ornateque dicere*) (1.4.7 [LCL 141: 10]). See also his *Orat.* where he asserts that "no one can discuss great and varied subjects in a copious and eloquent style without philosophy—as, for example, in Plato's *Phaedrus* Socrates says that Pericles surpassed other orators because he was a pupil of Anaxagoras, the natural philosopher [269e]. From him Socrates thinks that Pericles learned much that was splendid and sublime, and acquired copiousness and fertility, and—most important to eloquence—knowledge of the kind of speech which arouses each part of the soul" (3.14–15 [LCL 342: 314]).

42. Cicero, *Part.* 23.79 (trans. H. Rackham; LCL 349: 368): *Nihil enim est aliud eloquentia nisi copiose loquens sapientia, quae ex eodem hausta genere quo illa quae in disputando est, uberior est atque latior et ad motus animorum uulgique sensus accommodatior.* See also *Orat.* 20.70 (LCL 342: 356).

43. Cicero, *Orat.* 33.117 (LCL 342: 392).

44. Augustine, *conf.* 3.5.9 (CCL 27: 31.5–7).

45. As Lieu states, "Manichaeism which, by the time of Augustine, had become actively anti-pagan and anti-Jewish, would not have been seen by Augustine as an exotic oriental cult like Mithraism but a higher and purer form of Christianity" (*Manichaeism*, 161).

46. See O'Meara's remark, "One might argue, however, that he fell under the spell of the Manichees because the *Hortensius* had already converted him to the pursuit of rational truth" (*Young Augustine*, 80–81).

47. Jason BeDuhn observes that Manichaeans presented "a regimen of life within the same discourse of concern as those imposed by other prophets, physicians and philosophers of the ancient world; these regimens were intended for the health of the individual—body and soul—and for the salvation of the individual from the condition of human suffering in all its manifestations" ("A Regimen for Salvation: Medical Models in Manichaean Asceticism," *Semeia* 58 [1992]: 121). Moreover, Lieu notes that "Manichaeans borrowed freely from Greek philosophical vocabulary in their translation of Manichaean writings" (*Manichaeism*, 159).

48. *The Cologne Mani Codex* 122, ed. A. Henrichs and L. Koenen (Opladen: Westdeutscher Verlag, 1988), 86. For Mani's teaching, see Lieu, *Manichaeism*, 7–32; and Manfred Heuser and Hans-Joachim Klimkeit, *Studies in Manichaean Literature and Art* (Leiden: Brill, 1998).

49. See BeDuhn's "Regimen," and *The Manichaean Body: In Discipline and Ritual* (Baltimore, MD: Johns Hopkins University Press, 2000).

50. BeDuhn notes the "absence of metaphoric or allegorical meaning in Manichaean statements" ("Regimen," 125). See also BeDuhn's citations of Augustine's testimony along with the similar testimony of the sixth-century Platonist, Simplicius, *In Epictetum Encheiridion* 27.71.44–72.16 (*Manichaean Body*, 71–72, 260–66). Also Lieu, *Manichaeism*, 31–32.

51. Augustine, *conf.* 5.3.6.

52. Augustine, *conf.* 5.3.3 (CCL 27: 58.8–10).

53. Augustine, *conf.* 5.6.11 (CCL 27: 62.28–31).

54. Augustine, *conf.* 5.6.11 (CCL 27: 62.35–42).

55. Augustine, *conf.* 5.7.12.

56. Augustine, *conf.* 5.6.10 (CCL 27: 61.10–62.15).

57. Augustine, *conf.* 5.7.13.

58. Augustine, *conf.* 5.13.23 (CCL 27: 70.14–19).

59. Augustine, *conf.* 5.14.24 (CCL 27: 71.4–7).

60. Augustine, *conf.* 5.13.23 (CCL 27: 70.8–9): *cuius tunc eloquia strenue ministrabant . . . sobriam uini ebrietatem.* Augustine's phrasing here evokes a well-known hymn composed by Ambrose, which itself has clear Philonic antecedents, see O'Donnell's discussion (*Confessions,* 2.322–23).

61. Paulinus of Milan, *Vit. Ambr.* 6 (PL 14: 29), also recounted by Theodoret, *Ecclesiastical History* 4.6. See also Ambrose's own remarks about the pressure put upon him to be ordained (*ep.* 63.65 [CSEL 82.3: 269]). For analysis of these events, see Daniel H. Williams, *Ambrose of Milan and the End of the Nicene-Arian Conflicts* (Oxford: Clarendon Press, 1995), 104–27.

62. Paulinus of Milan, *Vit. Ambr.* 5 (PL 14: 28); cf. Frederick Homes Dudden, *The Life and Times of St. Ambrose*, vol. 1 (Oxford: Clarendon Press, 1935), 1–21.

63. See Pierre Courcelle's study of Ambrose's use of Plotinus' *Enneads* in *Recherches sur les Confessions de saint Augustin*, new ed. (Paris: E. de Boccard, 1968), Appendix IV: "Aspects variés du platonisme ambrosien," and his "Anti-Christian Arguments and Christian Platonism: From Arnobius to St. Ambrose," in *The Conflict between Paganism and Christianity in the Fourth Century*, ed. Arnaldo Momigliano (Oxford: Clarendon Press, 1963), 151–92. See also Goulven Madec, *Saint Ambroise et la Philosophie* (Paris: Études Augustiniennes, 1974); Harald Hagendahl, *Latin Fathers and the Classics: A Study on the Apologists, Jerome and Other Christian Writers* (Gothenburg: University of Göteborg, 1958), 347–72; Mary D. Diederich, *Virgil in the Works of St. Ambrose* (Washington, DC: Catholic University of America Press, 1931). For Philo, see the summary of research provided by David T. Runia, *Philo in Early Christian Literature: A Survey* (Minneapolis, MN: Fortress Press, 1993), 291–311, and the studies of Hervé Savon, *Saint Ambroise devant l'exégèse de Philon le Juif,* 2 vols. (Paris: Études Augustiniennes, 1977), and "Saint Ambroise et saint Jérôme, lecteurs de Philon," ANRW 2.21.1 (1984), 731–59.

64. Ambrose's *De officiis ministrorum* in which he writes, "In the same way that Cicero wrote to instruct his son, I too am writing to mould you, my sons" (1.7.24 [CCL 15: 9.12–14]). Madec offers an assessment of Ambrose's "Cicéronianisme" (*Saint Ambroise,* 141–66). See also Davidson's *Ambrose,* 1.50–64.

65. Paulinus of Milan, *Vit. Ambr.* 7 (PL 14.29): *uerus philosophus Christi.*

66. Andrew Lenox-Conyngham, "Ambrose and Philosophy," in *Christian Faith and Greek Philosophy in Late Antiquity: Essays in Tribute to George Christopher Stead,* ed. Lionel R. Wickham and Caroline P. Bammel (Leiden: E. J. Brill, 1993), 114. Ambrose associated a consistent use of pagan philosophy with Christian heresy: "We must work towards a certain foolishness and evasion of worldly philosophy, in case through worldliness anyone might betray our faith and lead us from the truth, or through our effort the truth is pillaged through philosophy. For we know that the Arians rushed to their ruin by thinking that Christ's generation could be comprehended by the wisdom of this world. They have left the Apostle and follow Aristotle. They have left the wisdom which is close to God and opted for the snares of disputation and the nooses of dialectics" (*expos. Ps. cxviii* 22.10 [CSEL 62: 493.13–21]); trans. Íde Ní Riain, *Homilies of Saint Ambrose on Psalm 118 (119)* (Dublin: Halcyon Press, 1998). An association anticipated by Tertullian who states, "Indeed heresies are themselves instigated by philosophy" (*Praescr.* 7 [CCL 1: 192.6–7]).

67. Ambrose, *Luc.* prol. 1 (SC 45: 40); cf. *off.* 2.8.

68. As Ambrose does in *ex.* 1.2.7 (CSEL 32.1: 6.8–11); trans. (altered) John J. Savage, *Saint Ambrose: Hexameron, Paradise, and Cain and Abel* (Washington, DC: Catholic University of America Press, 1961), 3–283. Courcelle has argued that these sermons were heard by Augustine during his time in Milan (*Recherches*, 93–138), but see also Christine Mohrmann's review, *Vigiliae Christianae* 5 (1951): 249–54. Elsewhere Ambrose comments, "It was not by dialectic that it pleased God to save his people; for the kingdom of God consists in simplicity of faith, not in worldly contention" (*fid.* 1.5.42 [CSEL 78: 18.29–31]).

69. Ambrose, *ex.* 2.1.3 (CSEL 32.1: 42.14–18).

70. Ambrose, *expos. Ps. cxviii* 13.23–24 (CSEL 62: 294.22–295.24); Thomas Graumann describes how the "delight produced by the sweetness and grace of the biblical language and represented in the preacher's sermon" had "a kind of psychagogic influence on the audience" ("St. Ambrose on the Art of Preaching" in *Vescovi e pastori in epoca teodosiana: In occasione del XVI centenario della consacrazione episcopale di S. Agostino, 396–1996,* vol. 2 [Rome: Institutum patristicum Augustinianum, 1997], 587–600 at 598–99).

71. Ambrose, *sacr.* 5.3.17; *expos. Ps. cxviii* 15.28, 21.4.

72. Ambrose, *expos. Ps. cxviii* 14.11 (CSEL 62: 305.2–10): *multae foueae, multi scopuli in istius saeculi caligine non uidentur . . . contuere ubi pedem ponere mentis internae . . . bonus est caelestis ductus eloquii.*

73. Ambrose, *ep.* 55 (Maur. 8).6 (CSEL 82.2: 79.42–44).

74. In Ambrose's opinion, the best Greek philosophical developments were historically dependent on their leading philosophers' contact with ancient Jewish authorities. For example, he states, "Now I have used the writings of Esdras so that the pagans may know that the marvelous contents of their philosophical works have been taken from ours. And would they had not mixed them with superfluous and useless matter" (*bon. mort.* 10.45 [CSEL 32.1: 741.16–18]; trans. Michael P. McHugh, *Seven Exegetical Works* [Washington, DC: Catholic University of America Press, 1972], 70–113); cf. *Abr.* 2.2.6–7, 2.7.37, *bon. mort.* 5.19; *ep.* 6 (Maur. 28).1; *expos. Ps. cxviii* 2.5, 2.13; *off.* 1.31; *parad.* 3.14. On account of the legendary Eastern travels of Pythagoras and Plato, and because biblical figures like Moses and Jeremiah spent time in Egypt, this view was not utterly incredible at the time. For example, Philo of Alexandria could say that "some of the lawgivers among the Greeks did well when they copied from the most sacred tablets of Moses" (*De specialibus legibus* 4.10.61 [trans. F. H. Colson; LCL 341: 44–46]). See the discussion of Jewish and Christian contentions that the best elements of Graeco-Roman culture depended on biblical traditions in Peter Pilhofer, *Presbyteron kreitton: der Altersbeweis der jüdischen und christlichen Apologeten und seine Vorgeschichte* (Tübingen: J. C. B. Mohr [Paul Siebeck], 1990), esp. 144–220, and G. R. Boys-Stones, *Post-Hellenistic Philosophy: A Study of Its Development from the Stoics to Origen* (Oxford: Oxford University Press, 2001), 76–95, 176–202.

75. Ambrose, *Luc.* prol. 5 (SC 45: 42).

76. Ambrose, *Ios.* 1.1 (CSEL 32.2: 73.2–5); trans. McHugh, *Seven Exegetical Works*, 189–237: "Thus as we come to know Abraham, Isaac, and Jacob and the other just men by our reading, we may, as it were, follow in their shining footsteps along a kind of path of blamelessness opened up by their virtue." The influence of Philo and Origen upon Ambrose is particularly evident here. See Marcia L. Colish's lucid study, *Ambrose's Patriarchs: Ethics for the Common Man* (Notre Dame, IN: University of Notre Dame Press, 2005).

77. Ambrose, *fuga* 4.22 (CSEL 32.2: 182.7–8); trans. McHugh, *Seven Exegetical Works*, 281–323: *his ergo uirtutibus uelut gradibus quibusdam mens eius ascendit in caelum.*

78. Ambrose, *fuga* 5.28.

79. Ambrose, *fuga* 4.19 (CSEL 32.2: 180.1–2): *non corporis fuga, sed mentis ascensione.*

80. Following Madec, *Ambroise*, 279; and Lennox-Conyngham, "Ambrose," 121–28.

81. Ambrose, *ep.* 14 (Maur. 63).46–47 (CSEL 82.3: 259.465–470): *qui eligatur ex omnibus et qui medeatur omnibus. . . . Cuius se medicum etiam dominus. . . . Bonus medicus qui infirmitates nostras suscepit, sanauit aegritudines.*

82. Ambrose, *ep.* 36 (Maur. 2).7 (CSEL 82.2: 6.67–68); cf. *expos. Ps. cxviii* 4.23 (CSEL 62: 78.17–24): "The wound is great and longstanding. For a long, long time it has been spreading imperceptibly within us. . . . So with the virus of sin; once it has insinuated itself into the interior, it cannot be overcome with remedies applied exteriorly. Surgery is required, and fire or the knife. Unless the corrupt part is cut away, or the noxious virus burnt out, in vain are the doctor's hands applied to wounds."

83. Ambrose, *ep.* 36 (Maur. 2).5 (CSEL 82.2: 5.48–53); a practice Ambrose took seriously. He wrote to Emperor Theodosius urging him to repent of his massacre of the inhabitants of Thessalonica, "Should I keep silence? Then would my conscience be bound, my voice snatched from me — most wretched of conditions. And where would be the significance of the saying (Ez. 3:18) that if a bishop declare not to the wicked, the wicked shall die in iniquity, and the bishop shall be guilty of punishment because he has not warned the wicked?" (*ep.* 11 (Maur. 51).3 [CSEL 82.3: 213.25–29]). On the use of frank speech by late antique bishops, see Brown, *Power and Persuasion*, 61–70, 103–117. Anderson notes how in such situations "Christianity and sophistic *paideia* converge to face bureaucracy with a flourish" (*Second Sophistic*, 213).

84. Ambrose, *ep.* 36 (Maur. 2).6 (CSEL 82.2: 6.58–60), citing 1 Cor. 3:2.

85. Ambrose, *ep.* 36 (Maur. 2).28–29 (CSEL 82.2: 18.327–332, 19.340–342); cf. *ep.* 23 (Maur. 36).4 (CSEL 82.1: 169.31–35): "A good doctor knows what food is suitable for the state of illness, and at what stage in the course of recovery. Some-

times the taking of food brings back good health, but if one takes it at the wrong time or takes what is not suitable he is imperiled."

86. Ambrose, *ep.* 36 (Maur. 2).15 (CSEL 82.2: 11.173–176).

87. Ambrose, *ep.* 36 (Maur. 2).14 (CSEL 82.2: 10.165–166): *Alia piis mentibus consideranda statera, qua singulorum facta trutinantur.* For Ambrose's own efforts to shift his hearer's sense of value, see particularly his *Nab.* (CSEL 32.2: 469–516).

88. Ambrose, *ep.* 36 (Maur. 2).26 (CSEL 82.2: 17.312–313): *et tota mentis sedulitate erigere oculos ad caelestia, nihil ponere in lucro nisi quod vitae aeternae sit.*

89. Ambrose, *ep.* 36 (Maur. 2).25 (CSEL 82.2: 17.298–300); cf. *ep.* 14 (Maur. 63).64 (CSEL 82.3: 269.661–663): "The life of a priest ought to surpass others as its grace surpasses, and he who binds others by his precepts ought himself to keep the precepts of the law in himself."

90. Ambrose, *ep.* 36 (Maur. 2).2 (CSEL 82.2: 4.28–29): *Accipe ergo a Christo, ut et tuus sonus exeat.*

91. Ambrose, *ep.* 36 (Maur. 2).3 (CSEL 82.2: 4.30–5.36); cf. *expos. Ps. cxviii* 13.22–25.

92. Ambrose, *ep.* 36 (Maur. 2).4 (CSEL 82.2: 5.40–45).

93. Ambrose, *expos. Ps. cxviii.* 18.21 (CSEL 62: 407.23–25).

94. Ambrose, *expos. Ps. cxviii.* 18.20 (CSEL 62: 407.5–10).

95. Ambrose, *expos. Ps. cxviii.* 12.33 (CSEL 62: 271.23–24): *Sit nobis ergo cotidiana lectio pro exercitio, ut quae legimus meditemur imitari;* also *expos. Ps. cxviii.* 20.9 (CSEL 62: 449.13–15): "Consider, too, that divine scripture is anointing us with the oil of heavenly precepts and daily exercising (*exercet cotidie*) us"; and *Abr.* 2.5.22.

96. Ambrose, *Cain* 2.6.22 (CSEL 32.1: 397.22–398.4); trans. (altered) Savage, *Saint Ambrose: Hexameron, Paradise, and Cain and Abel,* 359–437.

97. Ambrose, *expos. Ps. cxviii.* 22.19 (CSEL 62: 497.14–15): "You, too, must eat the foods of the heavenly scriptures, so that they remain to eternal life, and eat them daily to avoid hunger"; *expos. Ps. cxviii.* 14.2 (CSEL 62: 299.14–19): "Christ himself feeds and refreshes us. His divine sacraments are good pastures. . . . The words of heavenly scripture are also good pastures, where we feed by our daily reading."

98. Ambrose, *ep.* 7 (Maur. 37).18 (CSEL 82.1: 52.175–176): *scriptum habens opus legis in tabulis cordi sui.*

99. Fully aware of the central place given to self-knowledge in Hellenistic moral philosophy (see the discussion of the verb πρόσεχω above), Ambrose continues in his usual fashion, "The pagans ascribe this maxim to the priestess of the Apollo at Delphi, as though Apollo were its author. We know, however, that it was taken from the book of Deuteronomy written by Moses long before it was engraved by the philosophers of Delphi" (*expos. Ps. cxviii.* 2.13 [CSEL 62: 27.15–24]). Ambrose may have known Basil's use of the Mosaic exhortation in this manner (PG 31: 197C–217B).

100. Ambrose, *expos. Ps. cxviii.* 2.13 (CSEL 62: 27.12–13).

101. Ambrose, *expos. Ps. cxviii.* 2.14 (CSEL 62: 27.25–28.17).

102. Augustine, *conf.* 6.3.3 (CCL 27: 75.11–12); cf. *conf.* 6.3.3 (CCL 27: 75.9–10): "He for his part did not know of my emotional crisis nor the abyss of danger threatening me"; *conf.* 6.11.18 (CCL 27: 86.14): "Ambrose is not available."

103. Assessing the exact parameters of this relationship has been difficult for scholars. As Peter Brown observes, "We are dealing, here, with a relationship between two people whose eddies may escape the historian. The influence of Ambrose on Augustine is far out of proportion to any direct contact which the two men may have had" (*Augustine of Hippo*, 77). O'Meara states judiciously, "Augustine frequently refers to Ambrose as one of the chief human instruments in his conversion, while at the same time conveying the impression that he had no intimate acquaintance with him. The problem is to discover how intimate or how distant were their relations and trace the influence of Ambrose upon Augustine" (*Young Augustine*, 116). See also Garry Wills, *Saint Augustine* (New York: Penguin, 1999), 42; and Philip Rousseau, "Augustine and Ambrose: The Loyalty and Single-Mindedness of a Disciple," *Augustiniana* 27 (1977): 151–65.

104. Augustine, *conf.* 5.13.23 (CCL 27: 71.24–25): "Gradually, though I did not realize it, I was drawing closer."

105. Augustine, *conf.* 5.13.23 (CCL 27: 70.21–71.23): *Ceterum rerum ipsarum nulla compatatio: nam ille per manichaeas fallacias aberrabat, ille autem saluberrime docebat salutem.*

106. Ambrose, *ep.* 36 (Maur. 2).22 (CSEL 82.2: 15.256–268).

107. Ambrose, *ep.* 7 (Maur. 37).36 (CSEL 82.1: 61.369–372); so also, "not philosophers but fishermen, not masters of dialectic but tax-gatherers, now find credence" (*fid.* 1.13.84 [CSEL 78: 37.49–50]).

108. For example, see Ambrose, *ex.* 1.8.30, 3.7.32.

109. Augustine, *conf.* 5.14.24.

110. Augustine, *conf.* 6.3.4 (CCL 27: 76.42–44).

111. Augustine, *conf.* 6.4.5 (CCL 27: 77.11): *confundebar et conuertebar.*

112. Augustine, *conf.* 6.1.1 (CCL 27: 73.21, 74.30–32).

113. Augustine, *conf.* 6.4.5 (CCL 27: 76.4–7).

114. Augustine, *conf.* 5.14.25 (CCL 27: 72.30–32); he states elsewhere that the Academics "somehow persuaded me of the plausibility . . . that man cannot find the truth. Accordingly, I had become lazy and utterly inactive, not daring to search for what the most intelligent and learned men were not permitted to find" (*Acad.* 2.9.23 [CCL 29: 30.32–36]); also "for a long time the Academics held the tiller of my ship" (*beata u.* 1.4 [CCL 29: 67.88–90]); trans. (altered) Mary T. Clark, *Augustine of Hippo: Selected Writings* (New York: Paulist Press, 1984), 163–93.

115. Cicero wrote that "our school maintains that nothing can be known for certain. . . . [Instead we] say that some things are probable, others improbable" (*Off.* 2.2.7 [trans. Walter Miller; LCL 30: 174]; a position elaborated fully in his *Acad.*

[trans. H. Rackham; LCL 268: 406–659]). Augustine preserves a fragment of the *Hortensius* that states, "If then nothing is certain . . . the wise man will never give his approval to anything" (*Acad.* 3.14.31 [CCL 29: 54.57–58]). See John Glucker, "Cicero's Philosophical Affiliations," in *The Question of "Eclecticism,"* ed. Dillon and Long, 34–69.

    116. See Nussbaum's discussion of "skeptic purgatives" (*Therapy of Desire,* 280–315).

    117. Augustine, *conf.* 5.14.25; also *conf.* 6.4.6 (CCL 27: 77.36–39): "Just as it commonly happens that a person who has experienced a bad physician (*malum medicum*) is afraid of entrusting himself to a good one, so it was with the health of my soul. While it could not be healed except by believing, it was refusing to be healed for fear of believing what is false."

    118. Augustine, *conf.* 5.14.25 (CCL 27: 72.33–37).

    119. See Courcelle's discussion of the situation in Milan at the time (*Late Latin Writers,* 131–48).

    120. Augustine, *beata u.* 1.4–5.

    121. See Claudian's panegyric on his eventual consulship, which takes note of his philosophical learning (trans. M. Platnauer; LCL 135: 336–93). He remarks particularly upon how Theodorus exchanged the "public responsibilities" (*curam populis*) of governance for the "leisure of the Muses" (*otio Musis*) (*Cons. Mall. Theod.* 61–66 [LCL 135: 342]); see also Augustine's comments in *ord.* 1.11.31.

    122. Augustine later states that "some books of the Platonists, translated from Greek into Latin" were brought to him "through a man puffed up with monstrous pride" (*conf.* 7.9.13 [CCL 27: 101.4–6]). Courcelle considers this to be a reference to Theodorus (*Late Latin Writers,* 138–40), but see O'Donnell's discussion of the issue (*Confessions,* 2.419–20). Determining exactly which Platonic sources Augustine knew and when he knew them has generated a great deal of scholarly debate. It is generally agreed that Augustine had firsthand knowledge at least of Plotinus *En.* 1.6, 1.8, 5.1 (*ciu.* 10.23), 3.2–3 (*ciu.* 10.14), but may have been aware of *En.* 4.3–5, 7–8, 5.8, and 6.4–5. He also appears to have known Cicero's translation of portions of Plato's *Timaeus,* Porphyry's now lost *De regressu animae* (*ciu.* 10.29.2; *retr.* 1.4.3), and Apuleius' *Soc.* (*ciu.* 8.14). Like his contemporaries, Augustine was not greatly interested in differentiating divergent strands of Platonism so it remains difficult to distinguish uniquely Porphyrian influences from Plotinian ones from concepts mediated by Ambrose for that matter. Augustine continued his reading of Platonic sources at varying times throughout his life and became more familiar with them over time. Even if the actual number of Platonic texts he had was quite minimal, Augustine would have been able to extend logically what he read to fill out the rest of the conceptual picture. A great deal of Platonism would have also come to him as mediated in Christian writings. For the debate, see John J. O'Meara, "The Neoplatonism of Saint Augustine," in *Neoplatonism and Christian Thought,* ed. Dominic J. O'Meara (Albany: State University of New York Press, 1982), 34–41;

O'Donnell, *Confessions*, 2.413–426; Pier Franco Beatrice, "*Quosdam Platonicorum Libros*: The Platonic Readings of Augustine in Milan," *Vigiliae Christianae* 43 (1989): 248–81; Robert Crouse, "*Paucis mutatis verbis*: St. Augustine's Platonism," in *Augustine and His Critics*, ed. Dodaro and Lawless, 37–50.

123. As Augustine says, "By the Platonic books I was admonished to return to myself" (*conf.* 7.10.16 [CCL 27: 103.1]), and elsewhere, "I was quickly returning to myself as a complete whole" (*Acad.* 2.2.5 [CCL 29: 21.59–60]). This feature of Plotinus' thought is well developed by Pierre Hadot, *Plotinus or the Simplicity of Vision*, trans. Michael Chase (Chicago: University of Chicago Press, 1993).

124. Plotinus, *En.* 1.6.9 (LCL 440: 258).

125. Plotinus, *En.* 4.4.31 (LCL 443: 230). This is not to say that Plotinus was unconcerned with pedagogy. Without resorting to sophisticated oratory he still strove to carry out in his teaching the critical and constructive tasks described in previous chapters. As he says, "One must therefore speak in two ways to men who are in this state of mind if one is going to turn them round to what lies in the opposite direction and is primary, and to lead them up to that which is highest, one, and first. What, then, are these two ways? One shows how contemptible are the things now honored by the soul . . . the other teaches and reminds the soul how high its birth and value are, and this is prior to the other one and when it is clarified will also make the other obvious" (*En.* 5.1.1 [LCL 444: 12]).

126. Porphyry, *Plot.* 14 and 18 (LCL 440: 38–40, 50).

127. Augustine, *conf.* 6.11.18.

128. Augustine, *conf.* 6.6.9–10.

129. Augustine, *conf.* 6.15.25.

130. Augustine, *conf.* 5.10.18

131. Augustine, *conf.* 7.3.4 (CCL 27: 94.5–6): "I had no clear and explicit grasp of the cause of evil."

132. Augustine, *conf.* 7.1.1 (CCL 27: 92.23–24): "I thought that anything from which space was abstracted was non-existent."

133. Augustine, *conf.* 7.5.7, cf. 7.1.1.

134. Augustine, *conf.* 7.3.5, a question connected with the one about the origin of evil since Augustine realized that if evil could be said to have its origin in the free exercise of the will it would exclude the Manichaean doctrine that evil is an unchangeable principle coeternal with God.

135. Augustine, *conf.* 7.1.2 (CCL 27: 92.28): *Ego itaque incrassatus corde.*

136. Augustine, *conf.* 7.1.2 (CCL 27: 92.31–93.32): *per quales enim formas ire solent oculi mei, per tales imagines ibat cor meum.*

137. Augustine, *conf.* 7.1.2 (CCL 27: 92.28–29).

138. Plotinus, *En.* 1.6.8 (LCL 440: 256–58).

139. Plotinus, *En.* 1.6.3 (LCL 440: 238–40).

140. Plotinus, *En.* 5.1.4–5 (LCL 444: 20–22).

141. At most, Plotinus ascribes to evil an existence "among non-existent things, as a sort of form of that which is not" (εἶδός τι τοῦ μὴ ὄντος) (*En.* 1.8.3 [LCL 440: 282]). As Denis O'Brien states concisely, matter is a "necessary" part of the soul's experience of evil, but it is not in itself a "sufficient cause" apart from the soul's internal inclinations ("Plotinus on Matter and Evil," in *The Cambridge Companion to Plotinus,* ed. Lloyd P. Gerson [Cambridge: Cambridge University Press, 1996], 186). For comparison with Augustine's mature view, see Gillian Rosemary Evans, *Augustine on Evil* (New York: Cambridge University Press, 1982); and Rowan D. Williams, "Insubstantial Evil," in *Augustine and His Critics,* ed. Dodaro and Lawless, 105–23.

142. Plotinus, *En.* 5.1.1 (LCL 444: 10): "The beginning of evil for them was audacity (τόλμα) and the first otherness and the wishing to belong to themselves." R. T. Wallis explains that "self-assertion is equivalent to self-isolation; the result is that a soul potentially containing the whole of Reality chooses instead to attach herself to, and so imprison herself in, a small part thereof" (*Neoplatonism,* 2d ed. [Indianapolis: Hackett, 1995], 78).

143. Plotinus, *En.* 1.8.14 (LCL 440: 314): "This is the fall of the soul, to come in this way to matter and to become weak, because all its powers do not come into action; matter hinders them from coming by occupying the place which soul holds and producing a kind of cramped condition, and making evil what it has got hold of by a sort of theft—until soul manages to escape back to its higher state."

144. Plotinus, *En.* 5.1.2 (LCL 444: 16–18): "All things live by the whole, and all soul is present everywhere, made like to the father who begat it in its unity and its universality. . . . [O]ur soul is of the same kind, and when you look at it without its accretions and take it in its purified state you will find that very same honorable thing which [we said] was soul, more honorable than everything which is body."

145. Plotinus, *En.* 5.1.12 (LCL 444: 50–52).

146. Plotinus, *En.* 1.6.6 (LCL 440: 250).

147. Plotinus, *En.* 5.1.1 (LCL 444: 12–14). As is most clearly seen in the (pseudo-) Platonic dialogue, *Alcibiades,* this is the common starting point for the Platonic tradition in its appropriation of the oracle at Delphi's injunction to know yourself. See Gerald J. P. O'Daly, *Plotinus' Philosophy of the Self* (Shannon: Irish University Press, 1972).

148. Plotinus, *En.* 5.1.2 (LCL 444: 14–18).

149. Plotinus, *En.* 2.9.15 (LCL 441: 284).

150. Plotinus, *En.* 1.6.7 (LCL 440: 252).

151. Plotinus, *En.* 1.6.5 (LCL 440: 248).

152. Plotinus, *En.* 1.8.4 (LCL 440: 288): "The perfect soul, then, which directs itself to intellect is always pure and turns away from matter and neither sees nor approaches anything undefined and unmeasured and evil. It remains, therefore, pure, completely defined by intellect." This is an ideal Plotinus himself appears to have reinforced by his own example (see Porphyry, *Plot.* 8–9, 23).

153. Courcelle states, "It was also Cicero who supplied St. Augustine with the most lucid information on ancient Greek philosophy. Furthermore, Augustine studied him very conscientiously" (*Late Latin Writers,* 167).

154. Augustine, *Acad.* 3.18.40 (CCL 29: 59.11–15): "Therefore, the Academicians knew the truth, and gave approval to falsehoods in which they recognized a commendable imitation of true things. Since it was neither right nor convenient to reveal this to the uninitiated, as it were, they left some indication of their view to posterity (and to any of their contemporaries they were able to)" (also *Acad.* 2.10.24, 3.17.38, 3.20.43). He explains the thesis in a letter to Hermogenianus saying, "For it seems to me that it well suited those times that, if any untainted stream were to flow from the Platonic spring, it be guided through shady and thorny thickets for the possession of a very few rather than allowed to wander through open spaces where cattle break through, and where it is impossible for it to be kept clear and pure. What is easier for the common herd than that the soul be thought to be a body? It was against men of this sort, I believe, that [the Academics] usefully devised that method or art of concealing the truth" (*occultandi ueri artem atque rationem*) (*ep.* 1.1 [CSEL 34.1: 1.8–15]); a thesis that also appears in *ep.* 118.3.20, 5.33). Cicero himself considered the "New" Academy to be the Old one (*Acad.* 1.12.46) and mentions the practice of concealing its doctrines (*Acad.* 2.18.60).

155. Basil Studer says of Augustine's debt to "the Ciceronian ideal of the 'wise speaker'" (*orator sapiens*) that "not only his sermons but his explanations of the Bible and even his treatises are profoundly permeated by this ideal" (*Grace of Christ,* 13).

156. Augustine, *conf.* 7.9.13 (CCL 27: 101.8–12).

157. Augustine, *conf.* 7.21.27 (CCL 27: 110.6–7).

158. Augustine, *conf.* 8.1.2.

159. Augustine, *conf.* 6.12.21.

160. Augustine, *conf.* 6.14.24 (CCL 27: 89.19–20).

161. Augustine, *conf.* 8.1.2 (CCL 27: 114.46–48): "And now I had discovered the good pearl. To buy it I had to sell all that I had; and I hesitated." Robert Dodaro aptly draws attention to the prominence of these issues in the *Confessions'* narrative: "Deception, career ambition and social reputation clearly overshadow sexual excess as the most serious moral issues at the heart of a conversion struggle that culminates in Augustine's rejection of a career as public orator for Milan and propagandist in the court of the Emperor Valentinian II" ("Augustine's Secular City," in *Augustine and His Critics,* ed. Dodaro and Lawless, 248); Claude Lepelley, "Un aspect de la conversion de saint Augustin: La rupture avec ses ambitions sociales et politiques," *Bulletin de Littérature Ecclésiastique* 88 (1987): 229–46.

162. Augustine, *conf.* 8.1.1 (CCL 27: 113.15–20). Ambrose himself testifies to Simplicianus' learning, see his *ep.* 65.1 (CSEL 82.1: 15).

163. Augustine, *conf.* 8.2.3 (CCL 27: 114.3–4).

164. Augustine, *conf.* 8.2.3–5 (CCL 27: 115.13–116.72).

165. Augustine, *conf.* 8.5.10 (CCL 27: 119.5–6): *loquacem scholam deserere maluit quam uerbum tuum, quo linguas infantium facis disertas.*

166. Augustine, *conf.* 8.5.10 (CCL 27: 119.2): "He had indeed told it to me with this object in view."

167. Augustine, *conf.* 8.12.28.

168. Augustine, *conf.* 8.12.29 (CCL 27: 131.33–36).

169. Many have observed the non-coincidental convergence between Augustine's own narration of his conversion and his theological convictions. See Stock, *Augustine the Reader,* 75–111.

Notes to Chapter Four

1. Augustine, *conf.* 9.2.2.

2. Augustine, *Acad.* 1.1.3 (CCL 29: 5.72–73); trans. Peter King, *Against the Academicians; The Teacher* (Indianapolis: Hackett, 1995), 1–93.

3. Augustine, *ord.* 1.2.4 (CCL 29: 91.31–32). See also his desire for *otium philosophandi* (*Acad.* 2.2.4 [CCL 29: 20.36–37]), and his wish that all his friends could join him in *liberali otio* (*sol.* 1.9.16 [CSEL 89: 25.15–21]). Augustine later reflects on the time at Cassiciacum as when "we rested in you from the agitation of the world" (*conf.* 9.3.5 [CCL 27: 135.16]), and as a period of *christianae uitae otium* (*retr.* 1.1.1 [CCL 57: 7.3–4]).

4. Augustine, *beata u.* 1.1 (CCL 29: 65.1): *philosophiae portum; Acad.* 2.1.1 (CCL 29: 18.22–23): *philosophiae tutissimus iucundissimusque portus;* a traditional image from Hellenistic philosophy which Augustine most likely knew from Cicero (*Tusc. Disp.* 5.2.5). See, for example, Lucian's reference to the peaceful harbor of philosophy (*Pisc.* 27–30).

5. Augustine, *Acad.* 2.2.4 (CCL 29: 20.30): *quaero intentissimus ueritatem;* "I am most intently searching for the truth."

6. Augustine, *Acad.* 1.6.16 (CCL 29: 12.14–15): Cicero, *Off.* 2.2.5; *Tusc. Disp.* 4.26.57.

7. Augustine, *ord.* 1.1 (CCL 29: 89.1–4).

8. Augustine ascribes the words to Trygetius, *Acad.* 1.5.15 (CCL 29: 12.49–52): *Sed nescio quo modo, cum mentis nostrae ueluti portum notio ipsa reliquerit et uerborum sibi quasi uela tetenderit, occurrent statim calumniarum mille naufragia.*

9. Augustine, *ord.* 2.7.20 (CCL 29: 118.8–9).

10. Dennis E. Trout, "Augustine at Cassiciacum: *Otium Honestum* and the Social Dimensions of Conversion," *Vigiliae Christianae* 42 (1988): 136. See also Seneca, *De otio* (LCL 254: 180–200). As Peter Brown observes, "This ideal was to

form the background of Augustine's life from that time until his ordination as a priest, in 391" (*Augustine of Hippo*, 108). R. J. Halliburton maintains that Augustine "did not, however, after the manner of Jerome, seek refuge in the deserts of Chalcis, nor after the manner of Rufinus.... The place of his retreat was rather the country residence in the regions of Cassiciacum, the architectural and geographical representation of the retreat of the Roman citizen from the storms of political life for centuries" ("The Inclination to Retirement—the Retreat of Cassiciacum and the "Monastery" of Tagaste," in *Studia Patristica* 5 [1962]: 338). See also Henri I. Marrou, *Saint Augustin et la fin de la culture antique*, 4th ed. (Paris: E. de Boccard, 1984), 169–79; Stock, *Augustine the Reader*, 113, 127; Carol Harrison, *Augustine's Early Theology*, 8–10.

11. Cicero had earlier written that after being "released from taking part in the government of the country, I seek from philosophy a cure (*medicinam*) from my grief and I deem this to be the most honorable delight of leisure" (*oti oblectationem hanc honestissimam*) (*Acad.* 1.3.11 [LCL 268: 420–22]).

12. Trout, "Augustine at Cassiciacum," 136–38; Conybeare writes, "While he certainly had a leave of absence from his teaching position in Milan, he may not yet have actually resigned his post" (*The Irrational Augustine* [Oxford: Oxford University Press, 2006], 6).

13. Augustine, *beata u.* 1.3 (CCL 29: 66.65–66): *superbum studium inanissimae gloriae.*

14. Augustine, *beata u.* 1.3 (CCL 29: 66.66–70); cf. Augustine's later description of his unhappiness at the apex of his secular career (*conf.* 6.6.9).

15. Augustine, *beata u.* 1.3 (CCL 29: 66.51–52). He lists those present as his mother Monnica, his brother Navigius, his son Adeodatus, Trygetius and Licentius, Lartidianus and Rusticus (*beata u.* 1.6). His friend Alypius was present as well aside from a trip to Milan (*ord.* 1.2.5, *Acad.* 1.2.5).

16. Augustine refers to "our school" (*scholam notram*) (*Acad.* 3.4.7 [CCL 29: 39.13], *ord.* 1.3.7 [CCL 29: 92.28]) and himself as "teacher" (*magistrum*) (*ord.* 1.10.29 [CCL 29: 104.56]).

17. Augustine, *beata u.* 1.5 (CCL 29: 68.120–21).

18. Augustine, *ord.* 1.3.6 (CCL 29: 91.11): *apud sese habitare consuefacerent animum.*

19. Augustine, *ord.* 1.10.29 (CCL 29: 103.39–104.44).

20. Augustine, *ord.* 1.10.30 (CCL 29: 104.60–71). Conybeare draws attention to this scene in her section, "Squabbling like Men" (*The Irrational Augustine*, 100–7).

21. Augustine, *ord.* 1.10.30 (CCL 29: 104.71–72): *quia uos ab ista uanitate morboque deterreo.*

22. Augustine, *ord.* 1.10.29 (CCL 29: 103.36–37).

23. Augustine, *ord.* 1.10.30 (CCL 29: 104.72–73); cf. *ord.* 1.3.9 (CCL 29: 93.67–68): "Because I had spoken in a tone of voice more severe than he [Licentius] was expecting, he kept quiet for some time."

24. Augustine consciously understood himself in continuity with this tradition, see *ord.* 1.11.31. For a detailed proposal of the relationship between the Cassiciacum writings and Cicero's dialogues, see Michael P. Foley, "Cicero, Augustine, and the Philosophical Roots of the Cassiciacum Dialogues," *Revue des Études Augustiniennes* 45 (1999): 51–77.

25. Augustine, *ep.* 1.1 (CSEL 34.1: 1.6–8).

26. Augustine, *ord.* 1.3.9 (CCL 29: 93.82).

27. Augustine, *Acad.* 1.1.3 (CCL 29: 5.77–80). Peter Brown cites this passage as "the heart of Augustine's message from Cassiciacum" (*Augustine of Hippo,* 115).

28. Augustine, *ord.* 2.5.16 (CCL 29: 116.47–50). On the prominence of the medical theme even in Augustine's earliest writings, see D. Doucet, "Le thème du médecin dans les premiers dialogues philosophique de saint Augustin," *Augustiniana* 39 (1989): 447–61.

29. Augustine, *ord.* 1.8.24 (CCL 29: 100.56–62).

30. Augustine, *Acad.* 3.19.42, *ord.* 2.11.32 (referring to Col. 2:8). For Augustine's understanding of Col. 2:8, see Djuth, "Philosophy in a Time of Exile."

31. Augustine, *Acad.* 3.17.37 (CCL 29: 57.15–21, informed by Cicero's narrative of the same, see his *Acad.* 1.4.17, 2.5.15).

32. Augustine, *Acad.* 3.18.41 (CCL 29: 60.43–46).

33. As Carol Harrison states, "What we find in the earliest works is, indeed, a 'Christian philosophy'—and they are none the worse for that. But they are, scholars would now generally agree, distinctively Christian" (*Christian Truth and Fractured Humanity,* 15); eadem, *Augustine's Early Theology,* 36–41. Augustine comments later that he and his friend Alypius disagreed at the time about "inserting the name of Christ in my books" since Alypius "wanted them to smell of the 'cedars' of the schools . . . rather than of the health giving herbs of the Church which are a remedy against serpents" (*conf.* 9.4.7 [CCL 27: 137.16–19]).

34. Augustine, *Acad.* 3.19.42 (CCL 29: 60.4–10).

35. Augustine, *Acad.* 3.20.43 (CCL 29: 61.18–19).

36. Augustine, *Acad.* 3.20.43 (CCL 29: 61.23–24).

37. Augustine, *ep.* 1.1 (CSEL 34.1: 2.3–8).

38. Augustine, *sol.* 2.7.14 (CSEL 89: 63.11–16).

39. Augustine, *beata u.* 2.9 (CCL 29: 70.74–77).

40. Augustine, *beata u.* 2.10 (CCL 29: 71.108–110): *Qua conditione hodie apud me ut epuleris, peto nec flagites, quod fortasse non est paratum.*

41. Augustine, *beata u.* 2.9 (CCL 29: 70.78–81).

42. Augustine, *beata u.* 3.17 (CCL 29: 74.4–8): *paucitatis ferculorum . . . exiguum repertum erat.*

43. Augustine, *beata u.* 2.13 (CCL 29: 72.174–175): *quasi scholastico melle confectum atque conditum.*

44. Augustine, *beata u.* 2.9 (CCL 29: 70.81–83).

45. Augustine, *beata u.* 2.13, 3.17.

46. Augustine, *beata u.* 2.14 (CCL 29: 73.197–202) (employing phrasing from Cicero's *Acad.* 2.24.75 and *Hortensius* [Straume-Zimmermann, Fr. 82.1]).

47. Augustine, *ord.* 1.9.27 (CCL 29: 102.5–7): *quasi in schola illa, unde me quoquo modo euasisse gaudeo, constitutus copiose atque ornate uobis ordinem laudem?*

48. Augustine, *ord.* 2.13.38 (CCL 29: 128.12–19).

49. Augustine, *sol.* 1.14.25 (CSEL 89: 37.20–38.8).

50. Augustine, *sol.* 1.13.23 (CSEL 89: 35.4–17).

51. Augustine, *sol.* 1.13.23 (CSEL 89: 36.1–15).

52. Augustine, *beata u.* 3.17 (CCL 29: 74.8–9): *Sed quid uobis praeparatum sit, ego quoque uobiscum nescio.*

53. Augustine, *Acad.* 2.7.17 (CCL 29: 27.27–29). The notion of "inquiry" occupies a central place in both Augustine's early writings and later ministerial works. See Charles T. Mathewes, "The Liberation of Questioning in Augustine's *Confessions*," *Journal of the American Academy of Religion* 70 (2002): 539–60.

54. Augustine, *Acad.* 2.9.22 (CCL 29: 30.15–16): *ubi libenter nobiscum philosophia quasi iocata est.*

55. Augustine, *ord.* 1.8.26 (CCL 29: 102.112–113): "It was my custom to go over half a book of Virgil with them before the evening meal"; cf. *Acad.* 1.5.15, 2.4.10, 3.1.1.

56. Augustine, *Acad.* 3.14.31. See also where Augustine comments how it was Cicero's *Hortensius* that had largely won his students over to philosophy (*Acad.* 1.1.4). He refers to Cicero as "one who began philosophy in the Latin language and brought it to perfection" (*Acad.* 1.3.8) and one who "above all, must carry authority with us" (*Acad.* 3.7.14).

57. Augustine, *beata u.* 4.25, 32; *ord.* 1.3.9.

58. Augustine, *Acad.* 3.1.1 (CCL 29: 35.24–27); see also *Acad.* 2.3.7. Phillip Cary traces Licentius' development in "What Licentius Learned: A Narrative Reading of the Cassiciacum Dialogues," *Augustinian Studies* 29 (1998): 141–63.

59. Augustine, *ord.* 1.3.8 (CCL 29: 93.61–65).

60. Augustine, *ord.* 1.8.21 (CCL 29: 99.5–7). Licentius, nonetheless, continued to struggle with this love long after his retreat at Cassiciacum. See Augustine's later letter in which he preserved a portion of Licentius' poetry (*ep.* 26).

61. Augustine, *ord.* 2.11.30 (CCL 29: 124.2–4).

62. Augustine, *Acad.* 3.17.38 (CCL 29: 57.35–58.37).

63. Augustine, *Acad.* 2.1.1 (CCL 29: 18.6–13).

64. Augustine, *beata u.* 1.1 (CCL 29: 65.5–6); cf. *ord.* 2.9.26 (CCL 29: 122.19): "To this knowledge, few are able to arrive in this life."

65. Augustine, *ord.* 2.5.17 (CCL 29: 116.64–67).

66. Augustine, *ord.* 2.2.5 (CCL 29: 109.29–31). A couple of years later, Augustine will describe "all sin" as a failure to find a higher criterion than uncertain sensation by which to order one's life (*lib. arb.* 1.16.34 [CCL 29: 234.13–235.22]). Soon after he is ordained, he, likewise, states flatly that sensation provides a "fatal

and utterly false standard" by which "to measure the ineffable inner sanctuary of truth" (*util. cred.* 1.1 [CSEL 25.1: 3.19–20]).

67. Augustine, *ord.* 2.9.27 (CCL 29: 123.45–46).

68. Augustine, *ord.* 1.1.3 (CCL 29: 90.51–53).

69. Augustine, *Acad.* 1.1.3 (CCL 29: 5.75–77).

70. Augustine, *ord.* 2.4.11 (subject in the Latin is singular rather than plural, CCL 29: 113.20–25).

71. Augustine, *ord.* 1.1.3 (CCL 29: 90.53–55).

72. Augustine, *Acad.* 3.3.5 (CCL 29: 36.2–4): *Sapientam ab studioso, ait, nulla re differe arbitror, nisi quod quarum rerum in sapiente quidam habitus inest.*

73. Augustine, *ord.* 2.5.14 (CCL 29: 115.10–14).

74. Augustine, *ord.* 2.5.14.

75. Augustine, *ord.* 2.19.50 (CCL 29: 134–35).

76. Augustine, *ord.* 1.2.4 (CCL 29: 91.34–35).

77. Augustine, *beata u.* 4.25 (CCL 29: 78.37–43).

78. Augustine, *beata u.* 4.25 (CCL 29: 79.56–60).

79. Augustine, *ord.* 2.19.51 (CCL 29: 135.61–70).

80. Augustine, *ord.* 1.2.3 (CCL 29: 90.11–12).

81. Augustine, *beata u.* 1.8; cf. *ep.* 2.1 (CSEL 34.1: 3.18–21): "while the body is engaged in its own activity, the mind should be carried away and entirely enamored of what alone remains unchanged, of what is not a passing attraction for us wayfarers."

82. Augustine, *ord.* 1.8.21–22. Young Licentius himself presumed that they had already arrived at the philosophic life: "We have been living in great mental tranquility . . . we have been taking pains, as far as humanly allowed, to cultivate reason, that is, to live according to the divine part of the spirit, and this we agreed yesterday was by definition the happy life" (*Acad.* 1.4.11 [CCL 29: 10.43–47]).

83. Augustine, *ord.* 1.3.6, 1.8.22; *sol.* 1.14.25.

84. Augustine, *ord.* 1.8.26.

85. Augustine, *conf.* 6.8.13 (CCL 27: 83.19–20).

86. Augustine, *ep.* 2 (CSEL 34.1: 4.9–10).

87. Augustine, *ep.* 3.5 (CSEL 34.1: 9.5–7).

88. Augustine, *sol.* 1.14.25 (CSEL 89: 38.8–17) referring back to *sol.* 1.10.17. Rowan Greer draws attention to this feature of this passage (*Broken Lights and Mended Lives: Theology and Common Life in the Early Church* [University Park: Pennsylvania State University Press, 1986], 74). So also Stephen A. Cooper, "Scripture at Cassiciacum: 1 Corinthians 13:13 in the Soliloquies," *Augustinian Studies* 27 (1996): 37–42.

89. Augustine, *sol.* 2.13.23 (CSEL 89: 78.2–5).

90. Augustine, *sol.* 2.14.26 (CSEL 89: 81.11–14).

91. Augustine, *ord.* 2.5.16 (CCL 29: 116.52–53).

92. Augustine, *ord.* 2.9.27 (CCL 29: 122.42–123.45).

93. Augustine, *ord.* 2.9.27 (CCL 29: 122.35–39).

94. Augustine, *beata u.* 2.10 (CCL 29: 70.89–71.104).

95. Augustine, *ord.* 1.11.32.

96. Augustine, *ord.* 1.11.32 (CCL 29: 106.55–57); compare how "philosophical" Monnica's instructions are regarding the problem of burying her body as she was about to die away from home (*conf.* 9.11.27). See also *beata u.* 2.10 (CCL 29: 71.92): "Mother, you have truly reached the very citadel of philosophy" (*arcem philosophiae*). Monnica's prominent presence in the dialogues has not gone unnoticed. She represents what becomes Augustine's typical valorization of the ordinary Christian life. See, especially, Conybeare, *The Irrational Augustine*, 64–138; and Ragnar Holte, "Monica, 'the Philosopher,'" *Augustinus* 39 (1994): 293–316.

97. Augustine, *ord.* 2.9.26 (CCL 29: 122.21–24).

98. Augustine, *beata u.* 2.8 (CCL 29: 69.50–70.55): *sterilitas et quasi fames animorum.*

99. Augustine, *sol.* 2.20.34 (CSEL 89: 94.3–6).

100. Only *De musica* and *De dialectica* are preserved from this ambitious project. See Augustine's own comments in *retr.* 1.6, *ep.* 101.3; Marrou, *Saint Augustin et la fin de la culture antique*, 277–327; Ilsetraut Hadot, *Arts libéraux et philosophie dans la pensée antique* (Paris: Études Augustiniennes, 1984), esp. 101–36; and O'Donnell, *Confessions,* 2:269–80.

101. Augustine, *ord.* 1.2.4 (CCL 29: 91.28): *qua purgatur et excolitur animus.*

102. Augustine, *retr.* 1.5.3 (CCL 57: 17.40–44).

103. Augustine, *mus.* 6.1.1 (PL 32: 1161); trans. (altered) Robert Catesby Taliaferro, in *Saint Augustine: The Immortality of the Soul; The Magnitude of the Soul; On Music; The Advantage of Believing; On Faith in Things Unseen,* ed. Ludwig Schopp (Washington, DC: Catholic University of America Press, 1947), 151–379.

104. Augustine, *ord.* 2.18.47 (CCL 29: 133.16–17).

105. For the state of Augustine's biblical knowledge to 385, see Anne-Marie La Bonnardière, "Augustine's Biblical Initiation," in *Augustine and the Bible,* ed. Pamela Bright (Notre Dame, IN: University of Notre Dame Press, 1997), 5–25. It is, however, a mistake to overlook the influence of scripture (especially the Pauline epistles) on Augustine at this point in his development, see Stephen Cooper, "Scripture at Cassiciacum," 21–47.

106. Augustine, *conf.* 9.6.14 (CCL 27: 140.1–2): "When the time came for me to give in my name for baptism, we left the country and returned to Milan."

107. Augustine, *conf.* 9.5.13.

108. Augustine, *conf.* 9.5.13 (CCL 27: 140.4–12).

109. For further details of the catechumenal process that Augustine and his friends would have experienced, see William Harmless, *Augustine and the Catechumenate,* 79–106.

110. Paulinus of Milan, *Vit. Ambr.* 38.

111. Ambrose, *myst.* 1.1 (SC 25bis: 156); trans. (altered) Ramsey, *Ambrose,* 145–65.

112. Ambrose, *expl. symb.* 2 (CSEL 73: 3.9–4.12); trans. (altered) R. H. Connolly, *The Explanatio symboli ad initiandos: A Work of Saint Ambrose* (Cambridge: Cambridge University Press, 1952): "The holy Apostles, having assembled together, made a brief summary of the faith, so that we might have the whole purport of our faith comprised in short. Brevity is necessary, that it may be always remembered and recalled to mind."

113. Ambrose, *expl. symb.* 9 (CSEL 73: 11–12). The manuscripts which preserve the homily omit the Creed itself and give "only catchwords, or the first and last words, of the clauses under comment which the preacher must have recited in full" (Connolly, *The Explanatio symboli,* 1).

114. Ambrose, *expl. symb.* 9 (CSEL 73: 12.7–12): *cottidiana meditatione. . . . Symbolum recense et scrutare intra te ipsum! Maxime recense intra te!*

115. Ambrose, *expl. symb.* 1 (CSEL 73: 3.5–7): *spiritale signaculum, quod symbolum cordis est nostri meditatio et quasi semper praesens custodia.*

116. Ambrose, *expl. symb.* 4 (CSEL 73: 6.12–26).

117. Ambrose, *myst.* 7.34 (SC 25bis: 174).

118. Ambrose, *sacr.* 1.2.4 (SC 25bis: 62); trans. Roy J. Deferrari, *Saint Ambrose: Theological and Dogmatic Works* (Washington, DC: Catholic University of America Press, 1963), 217–328.

119. Ambrose, *sacr.* 3.1.3 (SC 25bis: 92).

120. Ambrose, *myst.* 4.19 (SC 25bis: 164).

121. Ambrose, *sacr.* 1.3.10 (SC 25bis: 64–66): *Hoc est totum? Immo hoc est totum.*

122. Ambrose, *sacr.* 3.2.12 (SC 25bis: 98); cf. *sacr.* 1.3.10 (SC 25bis: 66): "You have seen what you were able to see with the eyes of your body, with human perception; you have not seen those things which are effected but those which are not seen. Those things which are not seen are much greater than those which are seen."

123. Ambrose, *sacr.* 3.2.15 (SC 25bis: 100).

124. Ambrose, *myst.* 3.15 (SC 25bis: 162).

125. Ambrose, *sacr.* 4.4.14 (SC 25bis: 108).

126. Ambrose, *sacr.* 4.2.6 (SC 25bis: 104).

127. Ambrose, *myst.* 9.58 (SC 25bis: 190).

128. Ambrose, *myst.* 9.54 (SC 25bis: 188): *Quod os loquitur, mens interna fateatur; quod sermo sonat, adfectus sentiat;* cf. *sacr.* 4.5.25 (SC 25bis: 116): *Quod confitetur lingua, teneat adfectus.*

129. Ambrose, *sacr.* 5.4.25 (SC 25bis: 132–34).

130. See Augustine, *conf.* 9.6.14 (CCL 27: 141.21–27): "During those days I found an insatiable and amazing delight in considering the profundity of your purpose for the salvation of the human race. . . . I was deeply moved by the music of the sweet chants of your Church. The sounds flowed into my ears and the truth

was distilled in my heart. This caused the feeling of devotion to overflow. Tears ran, and it was good for me to have the experience."

131. Van der Meer states, "It may be said that in all practical matters Augustine had a quite definite model before his eyes—his father in Christ, Ambrose" (*Augustine the Bishop: The Life and Work of a Father of the Church*, trans. Brian Battershaw and G. R. Lamb [London: Sheed and Ward, 1961], 570).

132. See *conf.* 9.8.17 (CCL 27: 143.4–6).

133. Brown, *Augustine of Hippo*, 120; cf. Lancel, *Augustine*, 128.

134. Augustine, *an. quant.* 14.24 (CSEL 89: 160.7–8); trans. John J. McMahon, in *Saint Augustine: The Immortality of the Soul*, ed. Schopp, 49–149. Augustine wrote *mor.* and the first book of *lib. arb.* as well.

135. Augustine, *an. quant.* 6.11 (CSEL 89: 143.27–144.1).

136. Augustine, *an. quant.* 33.76 (citing 1 Cor. 3:2) (CSEL 89: 224.11–15); cf. *an. quant.* 3.4, 34.77.

137. Augustine, *an. quant.* 7.12 (CSEL 89: 145.6–7, 10–12).

138. Augustine, *an. quant.* 15.25 (CSEL 89: 162.1–4).

139. Augustine, *an. quant.* 34.77 (CSEL 89: 226.18–20).

140. Augustine, *an. quant.* 29.57 (CSEL 89: 204.17–19).

141. Augustine, *an. quant.* 21.36 (CSEL 89: 175.7–10).

142. Augustine, *an. quant.* 21.36.

143. Augustine, *an. quant.* 19.33 (CSEL 89: 172.17–19); cf. *an. quant.* 16.28 (CSEL 89: 165.13–15): "You should not think that the soul makes progress in the same way as the body, by growing larger with age. For it advances by making progress in virtue."

144. Augustine, *an. quant.* 19.33 (CSEL 89: 172.5–6).

145. Augustine, *an. quant.* 33.70–76 (CSEL 89: 217.18–225.18).

146. Augustine, *an. quant.* 34.78 (CSEL 89: 228.1–8): "For, while these truths are scattered throughout many writings of the Church, and though we may seem to have made a convenient digest of them, yet they cannot be clearly understood, unless one strives mightily in the fourth of those seven degrees to preserve piety and to acquire health and strength to perceive them, and makes each of these degrees the object of the most diligent and perceptive inquiry. For, in each of those grades, which we would do better to call acts, there is a distinct and proper beauty."

147. Augustine, *an. quant.* 34.73 (CSEL 89: 220.22–221.12).

148. Augustine, *an. quant.* 34.76 (CSEL 89: 223.23–24).

149. Augustine, *an. quant.* 16.27 (CSEL 89: 164.23): *Fortis, et in se ipso totus, teres atque rotundus* (Horace, *Sat.* 2.7.86 [LCL 194: 230]).

150. Augustine, *lib. arb.* 1.9.19 (CCL 29: 224.33–35): *Eos enim sapientes uoco . . . qui regno mentis omni libidinis subiugatione pacati sunt.* He continues "human wisdom consists in the rule of the human mind" (*lib. arb.* 1.10.20 [CCL 29: 224.1–2]).

151. Augustine, *an. quant.* 28.55 (CSEL 89: 202.4–5). Thus, dependence on grace is a theme present in the earliest strata of Augustine's writings and emerges

well before the 390s. See Harrison, *Augustine's Early Theology,* esp. 238–87. While Augustine's convictions about the necessity of grace remain unchanged, it is his perception of the actual effects of grace on body and soul that deepens over time (see below).

152. However tempting it is to chart a path from Augustine's classical leisure at Cassiciacum to a Christian monasticism possibly already present at Thagaste, it is better (as George Lawless argues) to appreciate how genuinely innovative Augustine is in the structuring of Christian community and to observe him developing these notions at Cassiciacum and Thagaste and beyond (*Augustine of Hippo and His Monastic Rule* [Oxford: Clarendon Press, 1987], esp. 29–62). Compare Halliburton, "The Inclination to Retirement," 339.

153. Conybeare observes that the relation of the issues broached at Cassiciacum remained very much in play as Augustine arrived at Thagaste: "it is certainly not clear how he planned to marry the skills that had brought him worldly success with his Christian commitment" (*The Irrational Augustine,* 173).

154. Augustine, *Gn. adu. Man.* 2.4.5 (CSEL 91: 123.20–124.23); trans. (altered) Roland J. Teske, *On Genesis: Two Books on Genesis Against the Manichees; and, On the Literal Interpretation Of Genesis, an Unfinished Book* (Washington, DC: Catholic University of America Press, 1990).

155. Augustine, *Gn. adu. Man.* 2.15.22 (CSEL 91: 143.11–17).

156. Augustine, *Gn. adu. Man.* 2.16.24.

157. Augustine, *Gn. adu. Man.* 2.20.30.

158. Augustine states that he wrote *mag., Gn. adu. Man.,* and *mus.* at the same time in *retr.* 12 (CCL 57: 36.2). For a concise analysis of Augustine's somewhat diffuse argument, see M. F. Burnyeat, "Wittgenstein and Augustine *De magistro,*" in *The Augustinian Tradition,* ed. Gareth B. Matthews (Berkeley: University of California Press, 1999), 286–303.

159. Augustine, *mag.* 1.2 (CCL 29: 158.45–46); trans. (altered) King, *Against the Academicians; The Teacher,* 94–146.

160. Augustine, *mag.* 10.31 (CCL 29: 189.49): *nihil sine signis doceri.*

161. Augustine, *mag.* 10.33 (CCL 29: 192.115–117, 132–133): "When a sign (*signum*) is given to me, it can teach me nothing if it finds me ignorant of the thing (*rei*) of which it is a sign; but if I am not ignorant, what do I learn through the sign? . . . A sign is learned when the thing is known, rather than the thing being learned when the sign is given."

162. Augustine, *mag.* 11.36 (CCL 29: 194.5–6): *sonitum strepitumque uerborum.*

163. Augustine, *mag.* 5.14 (CCL 29: 171.94–172.97).

164. Augustine, *mag.* 10.34 (CCL 29: 193.153–155).

165. Augustine, *mag.* 10.30 (CCL 29: 189.43–45).

166. Augustine, *mag.* 4.8 (CCL 29: 165.35–36). See also Augustine's letter to Gaius (c. 390) accompanying some of his own early writings (*ep.* 19 [CSEL 34.1: 46.18–22]): "No one, after all, who reads believes that truth is in the bound book

or in the writer, but in himself, especially if his mind is illumined by the light of truth, that light which is farthest removed from any material torch or anything which is commonly called bright."

167. Augustine, *mag.* 1.2 (CCL 29: 159.63–68). Note that Augustine immediately declares to Adeodatus, *Recte intellegis* ("You understand correctly") (*mag.* 1.2 [CCL 29: 159.71]).

168. Augustine, *mag.* 14.46 (CCL 29: 202.21–23); a loose rephrasing of Matt. 23: 9–10. Augustine later identifies this theme as the central one in the dialogue. He described *mag.* as a book in which there is the discovery that "there is no teacher who teaches knowledge except God, according to what, in truth, is written in the Gospel: 'One is your Master, the Christ'" (*retr.* 12 [CCL 57: 36.3–5]).

169. Augustine, *Gn. adu. Man.* 2.5.6 (CSEL 91: 124.9–125.18); referring to John 4:14. Augustine suggestively states a similar view as early as Cassiciacum, see *Acad.* 3.19.42 (CCL 29: 60.11–16): "Yet the most subtle chain of reasoning would never call back to this intelligible world souls that have been blinded by the manifold shadows of error . . . had not God the highest, moved by a certain compassion for the multitude, humbled and submitted the authority of the Divine Intellect even to the human body itself."

170. Augustine, *mag.* 12.40. For the intricacies of what is commonly known as Augustine's doctrine of illumination, see Gerald J. P. O'Daly, *Augustine's Philosophy of Mind* (Berkeley: University of California Press, 1987). David Chidester brings out the role of the Word in this process ("The Symbolism of Learning in Augustine," *Harvard Theological Review* 76 [1983]: 73–90).

171. Augustine, *mag.* 14.46 (CCL 29: 202.23–25); cf. *en. Ps.* 84.1. For further elaboration of the—too often overlooked—christological argument in *De magistro*, see Louis H. Mackey, "The Mediator Mediated: Faith and Reason in Augustine's *De Magistro*," *Franciscan Studies* 42 (1982): esp. 143–48.

172. Augustine, *mag.* 1.2 (CCL 29: 159.56–60).

173. Augustine, *mag.* 12.40 (CCL 29: 198.40–48). Socrates' questioning in Plato's *Meno* is in the background here, but its success is explained without recourse to the myth of the soul's preexistence. Augustine needs no such hypothesis (although he never rules out the theoretical possibility of the soul's preexistence) due to his account of the inner teaching of the divine Word (see O'Daly, *Augustine's Philosophy of Mind*, 199–207).

174. Augustine, *mag.* 11.38 (CCL 29: 196.48–51).

175. Augustine, *mag.* 11.36 (CCL 29: 194.1–3).

176. Rist, *Augustine*, 32.

177. Augustine, *mag.* 11.38 (CCL 29: 195.45–196.46); cf. *uera rel.* 49.94 (CCL 32: 249.17–18), trans. John H. S. Burleigh, *Augustine: Earlier Writings* (Philadelphia: Westminster Press, 1953): "no one can reach truth who looks for it outside." The admonitionary function of signs is a central theme in Phillip Cary's forcibly

argued trilogy: *Augustine's Invention of the Inner Self: The Legacy of a Christian Platonist* (New York: Oxford University Press, 2000); *Inner Grace: Augustine in the Traditions of Plato and Paul* (New York: Oxford University Press, 2008); *Outward Signs: The Powerlessness of External Things in Augustine's Thought* (New York: Oxford University Press, 2008).

178. Augustine, *mag.* 8.21 (CCL 29: 180.19–22).

179. Augustine, *mag.* 8.21 (CCL 29: 180.14–17).

180. Augustine, *uera rel.* 7.13 (CCL 32: 196.20–23): *Huius religionis sectandae caput est historia et prophetia dispensationis temporalis diuinae prouidentiae pro salute generis humani in aeternam uitam reformandi atque reparandi.* Reiterated later in *uera rel.* 50.99 (CCL 32: 251.41–44): "Above all, we must ask how it profits the human race that divine providence has spoken to us by human rational and corporeal creatures."

181. Augustine, *uera rel.* 10.19 (CCL 32: 199.23–200.28).

182. Augustine, *uera rel.* 49.95 (CCL 32: 249.19–29). For the unusual prominence of this term in Augustine's writings and its range of meaning, see Jean-Luc Solère, "Les images psychiques selon S. Augustin," in *De la phantasia à l'imagination,* ed. Danielle Lories and Laura Rizzerio (Louvain: Peeters, 2003), 103–36.

183. Augustine, *uera rel.* 50.98 (CCL 32: 250.2–3), 51.100 (CCL 32: 252.5–6).

184. Augustine, *uera rel.* 50.98 (CCL 32: 250.3–11).

185. Augustine, *uera rel.* 16.30 (CCL 32: 205.8–206.13).

186. Augustine, *uera rel.* 54.106 (CCL 32: 255.33–36).

187. Augustine, *uera rel.* 24.45 (CCL 32: 215.10, 13–15).

188. Augustine, *uera rel.* 16.31 (CCL 32: 206.17): *Nihil egit ui, sed omnia suadendo et monendo.*

189. Augustine, *uera rel.* 28.51 (CCL 32: 221.25–28); cf. his later expression of the same sentiment (*Io. eu. tr.* 10.13).

190. Augustine, *uera rel.* 16.30 (CCL 32: 206.13–14): *Ipsa enim natura suscipienda erat quae liberanda.*

191. Augustine, *uera rel.* 16.30 (CCL 32: 205.1–3); cf. *uera rel.* 17.34 (CCL 32: 208.34–36): "The art of medicine remains the same and quite unchanged, but it changes its prescriptions for the sick, since the state of their health changes."

192. Augustine, *uera rel.* 1.1 (CCL 32: 187.15–17).

193. Augustine, *uera rel.* 4.6 (CCL 32: 192.17–19).

194. Augustine, *uera rel.* 5.8 (CCL 32: 193.12–16).

195. Augustine, *uera rel.* 3.5 (CCL 32: 191.86–89).

196. Quoting the eucharistic canon, "*Sursum cor habere ad dominum*" (*uera rel.* 3.5 [CCL 32: 191.86–192.97]). Note that Augustine's Latin is consistently the singular *cor* (heart) rather than plural *corda* (hearts). See the discussion below of Augustine's common use of the phrase in his sermons.

197. Augustine, *uera rel.* 4.6 (CCL 32: 192.10–12).

198. Augustine, *uera rel.* 16.32–17.33 (CCL 32: 207.51–55).

199. Augustine, *uera rel.* 28.51 (CCL 32: 220.12–16) following Paul's use of these psychagogic metaphors (1 Cor. 2.6).

200. Augustine, *uera rel.* 46.88 (CCL 32: 245.49–50).

201. Augustine, *uera rel.* 4.7 (CCL 32: 192.20–24).

202. Augustine, *uera rel.* 15.29 (CCL 32: 205.13–15).

203. Augustine, *uera rel.* 45.85 (CCL 32: 243.30–31).

204. Augustine, *uera rel.* 10.18 (CCL 32: 199.7–10).

205. Augustine, *uera rel.* 45.83 (CCL 32: 242.6–11).

206. Augustine, *uera rel.* 46.88 (CCL 32: 245.37–41); cf. *uera rel.* 46.88 (CCL 32: 245.41–42): "It is more inhuman not to love a man because he is human, but to love him because he is your son, that is, not to love that in him which belongs to God, but to love that which belongs to yourself."

207. Augustine, *uera rel.* 47.90 (CCL 32: 246.23–24).

208. Augustine, *uera rel.* 46.87 (CCL 32: 244.21–23). Also, *uera rel.* 46.86 (CCL 32: 244.3–4): "He who loves only what cannot be taken from him is indubitably unconquerable."

209. Augustine, *uera rel.* 47.90 (CCL 32: 246.25–31).

210. Augustine, *ep.* 10.2 (CSEL 34.1: 24.4–5): *deificari . . . in otio.* For this phrase, see Georges Folliet, "'Deificari in otio,' Augustin, *Epistula* 10, 2," *Recherches augustiniennes* 2 (1962): 225–36, with the corrections suggested by Roland J. Teske, "Augustine's *Epistula X*: Another Look at *Deificari in otio*," *Augustinianum* 32 (1992): 289–99.

211. Augustine, *ep.* 10.2 (CSEL 34.1: 23.23–26, 24.6–8).

212. Augustine, *conf.* 9.3.6, 9.6.14.

213. Augustine, *conf.* 9.12.30–31. A disposition which would have conformed entirely to the ideals he taught. Thus, "We have a thing without loving it when we can let it go without grieving" (*uera rel.* 47.92 [CCL 32: 248.68–69]). See Seneca's advice in *ep.* 99 (discussed above). Plotinus, who was never known to suffer such a lapse, states of the wise: "Even if the death of friends and relations causes grief, it does not grieve him but only that in him which has no intelligence, and he will not allow the distress of this to move him" (*En.* 1.4.4 [LCL 440: 184]).

214. Augustine, *conf.* 9.12.30–31, 33 (CCL 27: 150.22–24, 151.38–39, 152.70–72).

Notes to Chapter Five

1. Augustine, *mor.* 1.32.69 (CSEL 90: 74.9–12); trans. (altered) Donald A. Gallagher and Idella J. Gallagher, *The Catholic and Manichaean Ways of Life* (Washington, DC: Catholic University of America Press, 1966).

2. Augustine, *s.* 355.2 (PL 39: 1569); cf. "For you I am a bishop, with you I am a Christian. The former title is the name of an office undertaken, the latter a name of grace; the former means danger, the latter salvation" (*s.* 340.1 [PL 38: 1483]); trans. (altered) Edmund Hill, *Sermons,* WSA, part 3.1–3.11.

3. Possidius, *Vit. Aug.* 4 (PL 32: 37). Augustine, himself, attributes his tears at his ordination to his belief that priesthood was "a most dangerous duty" (*periculosissimum iudicarem hoc ministerium*) (*ep.* 21.2 [CSEL 34.1: 50.13–14]).

4. Augustine, *beata u.* 1.1–5.

5. Mary C. Preus remarks on the manner in which Augustine was "called back from his philosophic retreat to the affairs of the Christian community" to "find himself drawn into a kind of ψυχαγωγία" (*Eloquence and Ignorance in Augustine's On the Nature and Origin of the Soul* [Atlanta: Scholars Press, 1985], 20). For the daily duties of the bishop see Van der Meer, *Augustine the Bishop,* esp. 129–98; Bonner, *St. Augustine,* 121–56; Brown, *Augustine of Hippo,* 187–97; Lee Francis Bacchi, *The Theology of Ordained Ministry in the Letters of Augustine of Hippo* (San Francisco: International Scholars Publications, 1998), 8–52; Carol Harrison, *Christian Truth and Fractured Humanity,* 122–30; Michele Pellegrino, *The True Priest: The Priesthood as Preached and Practiced by Saint Augustine,* rev. ed. (Villanova, PA: Augustinian Press, 1988). For his involvement in political and legal affairs, see his own comments in *en. Ps.* 25(2).13 and Possidius, *Vit. Aug.* 19; Robert Dodaro, "Between the Two Cities: Political Action in Augustine of Hippo," in *Augustine and Politics,* ed. John Doody, Kevin L. Hughes, and Kim Paffenroth (Lanham, MD: Lexington Books, 2005), 99–115; Charles Munier, "*audientia episcopalis,*" *Augustinus-Lexikon,* ed. C. Mayer, vol. 1 (Basel: Schwabe, 1986–1994), 1.511–15; Kaufman, "Augustine"; Lancel, *Augustine,* 246–70; Raikas, "*Episcopalis audientia*"; Lenski, "Evidence for the *Audientia episcopalis.*"

6. Brown, *Augustine of Hippo,* 199. John Burnaby, and others, have rightly emphasized the manner in which Augustine's "ordination to the priesthood in 391 forced a re-orientation upon his thought" (*Amor Dei: A Study of the Religion of Saint Augustine* [London: Hodder and Stoughton, 1938], 63). The long-term effect of this crisis was "almost as profound as that of his conversion" (Henry Chadwick, *The Early Church* [Baltimore, MD: Penguin Books, 1967], 218–19); so also O'Donnell, *Augustine,* 26; and Carol Harrison, *Christian Truth and Fractured Humanity,* 122.

7. Augustine, *ep.* 21.1 (CSEL 34.1: 49.14–50.1).

8. Augustine, *ep.* 22.2–3 (CSEL 34.1: 50.22, 51.4).

9. Augustine, *ep.* 21.4 (CSEL 34.1: 52.5–6).

10. Augustine, *ep.* 21.3 (CSEL 34.1: 51.5): *Scripturarum eius medicamenta omnia; ep.* 21.6 (CSEL 34.1: 54.5–6): *saluberrimis consiliis de scriptures suis.*

11. Augustine, *util. cred.* 1.1 (CSEL 25.1: 3.12, 21–23); trans. (altered) Luanne Meagher, *Saint Augustine: The Immortality of the Soul,* ed. Schopp, 381–442. Since this chapter concerns only Augustine's theoretical reflections, it is sufficient

to let the term "Manichaean" stand for his perception of the movement rather than seeking to determine whether his description is an accurate representation of Manichaean psychagogic practices. Determining the degree to which "Manichaeism" in this treatise functions as a foil for the explication of his own views is therefore not pertinent to the present study. Mark Vessey has drawn attention to the prominence of the pedagogical concerns that are the subject of this study in *util. cred.* He states that "behind" all the concerns of the treatise "lies a single great unspoken question: what are the qualities that distinguish those ideal teachers . . . who embody the interpretive authority of the Catholic Church?" ("The Great Conference: Augustine and His Fellow Readers," in *Augustine and the Bible,* ed. Pamela Bright, 52).

12. Augustine, *util. cred.* 3.7 (CSEL 25.1: 9.10–13). Commentators often note the intellectual appeal of Manichaeism and its elite sophistication, see Peter Brown, *Augustine of Hippo,* 43; Gerald Bonner, *St. Augustine,* 161; O'Meara, *Young Augustine,* 63.

13. Augustine, *util. cred.* 1.2 (CSEL 25.1: 4.11–14, 18–19); see also Augustine's claim that with the Manichaeans he is "dealing with those who . . . insist that, first of all, a reason be given for everything" (*mor.* 1.2.3 [CSEL 90: 5.23–6.3]). Bonner posits that much of the appeal of Manichaeism had to do with its explanatory force: "the sheer massive structure of the system must have seemed very imposing, with each detail of the world provided for and suitably explained. The cosmic machine, established by the forces of Light for the liberation of the world and supposedly in harmony with astronomical theory, was calculated to impress the inquirer" (*St. Augustine,* 188).

14. Augustine, *util. cred.* 1.2, 9.21 (CSEL 25.1: 4.19, 26.10–11).

15. Augustine, *util. cred.* 6.13 (CSEL 25.1: 19.11–12); cf. *conf.* 6.5.7.

16. Augustine, *util. cred.* 2.4 (CSEL 25.1: 6.21–7.2). See also *mor.* 1.1.2; Roland J. Teske, "Augustine, the Manichees and the Bible," in *Augustine and the Bible,* ed. Pamela Bright, 208–21; and Hans-Joachim Klimkeit, "The Use of Scripture in Manichaeism," in *Studies in Manichaean Literature and Art,* ed. Heuser and Klimkeit, 111–22.

17. Augustine, *util. cred.* 9.21 (CSEL 25.1: 26.4–7).

18. Augustine, *util. cred.* 8.20 (CSEL 25.1: 24.18–25.2); referring to the Faustus of *conf.* 5.3.3 and *c. Faust.*

19. Augustine, *util. cred.* 8.20 (CSEL 25.1: 25.4–6): *Non putabam latere ueritatem, nisi quod in ea quaerendi modus lateret, eundemque ipsum modum ab aliqua diuina auctoritate esse sumendum.* On the sense of the term "authority," see Bonner's observation: "Authority—*auctoritas*—for the Roman is a non-coercive force, founded upon tradition and social position . . . an essentially moral influence, but not to be compared in everyday life with the *imperium,* the executive power of the consuls and, later, of the emperors" (*St. Augustine,* 231).

20. Augustine, *util. cred.* 8.20 (CSEL 25.1: 25.7–9): *inexplicabilis silua.*

21. Augustine, *util. cred.* 8.20 (CSEL 25.1: 25.12–14); similarly, see where Augustine says that as long as he was "buried under a mass of inane fables," he would not have been "able to get out from under them to breathe freely and begin to seek the truth," if his "love of finding the truth had not obtained divine help" (*opem diuinam*) (*lib. arb.*1.2.4 [CCL 29: 213.5–8]).

22. Augustine, *util. cred.* 8.20 (CSEL 25.1: 25.15–25): *sequere uiam catholicae disciplinae.* See also where Augustine states, "I anticipate that . . . you will hold fast with me to the way of wisdom" (*uiam sapientiae*) (*util. cred.* 2.4 [CSEL 25.1: 7.11–12]).

23. Augustine, *util. cred.* 2.4 (CSEL 25.1: 7.13–23). A similar posture is taken in his later invitation to Honoratus, "If you recognize in yourself what I say, then, I pray you, let us seek truth together" (*quaeramus uerum*) (*util. cred.* 7.14 [CSEL 25.1: 20.2–3]). Cf. "Let neither of us assert that he has found truth; let us seek it as if it were unknown to us both" (*c. ep. Man.* 3 [CSEL 25.1: 195.20–21]). Note how the later bishop continues to recount the temptations that still assail him throughout the tenth book of the *Confessions.*

24. Felix B. Asiedu writes, "Augustine . . . nowhere pretends to be urging his own ecclesiastical authority as the basis for his argument. . . . He comes not as a competent authority, but as a fellow inquirer" ("The Limits of Augustine's Personal Authority: The Hermeneutics of Trust in *De utilitate credendi*," in *Augustine and Liberal Education,* ed. Kim Paffenroth and Kevin L. Hughes [Aldershot and Burlington, VT: Ashgate, 2000], 131, 143).

25. Augustine, *util. cred.* 12.27 (CSEL 25.1: 35.19–21); also, "for the fool there is nothing closer for him to imitate beneficially than a wise person" (*util. cred.* 15.33 [CSEL 25.1: 41.24–25]).

26. Augustine, *util. cred.* 12.27 (CSEL 25.1: 34.24–26).

27. Augustine, *util. cred.* 13.28 (CSEL 25.1: 36.2–5): *neque enim quibuslibet signis cognoscere aliquid potest nisi illud ipsum, cuius ea signa sunt, nouerit.* The ultimate explanation for why some and not others find their way out of this closed system of foolishness remains difficult for Augustine. Just as he only found Ambrose after appealing to Divine providence, he states, "For this immense difficulty in our search for religion, then, only God can supply the remedy" (*deus solus mederi potest*) (*util. cred.* 13.29 [CSEL 25.1: 36.20–21]).

28. Augustine, *util. cred.* 7.17 (CSEL 25.1: 22.1–6); also "if any discipline, however, lowly and easy to understand, needs a teacher or a tutor, what is more indicative of rash pride, in all its fullness, than to refuse to learn the books of the divine mysteries from their own interpreters and then to dare to condemn them without understanding them?" (*util. cred.* 17.35 [CSEL 25.1: 46.2–4]).

29. Augustine, *util. cred.* 7.17 (CSEL 25.1: 21.25–28).

30. Augustine, *util. cred.* 6.13 (CSEL 25.1: 18.16–21). Brian Stock draws attention to this section of *util. cred.* (*Augustine the Reader,* 174–81).

31. Augustine, *util. cred.* 7.17 (CSEL 25.1: 22.6–14); see also *ep.* 95.6.

32. Augustine, *util. cred.* 1.1 (CSEL 25.1: 3.19–20). Augustine often asserts that many errors derive from habits of mind characterized by a naive acceptance of the data supplied by sense impressions, see *f. et symb.* 2.2, 9.20; *agon.* 15.17.

33. Augustine, *util. cred.* 6.13 (CSEL 25.1: 18.5); *util. cred.* 1.2 (CSEL 25.1: 4.23–25): *spernentum scilicet quasi aniles fabulas et ab eis promissum apertum et sincerum uerum tenere atque haurire cupientum.*

34. Augustine, *util. cred.* 14.31 (CSEL 25.1: 38.11–12): "Is it that your reason (*ratio tua*) will build a strong edifice on a foundation of rashness?" Stock refers to the "false rationalities of Manichaeism and skepticism" (*Augustine the Reader,* 176). See also Charles Cochrane's comments regarding *util. cred.* in *Christianity and Classical Culture: A Study of Thought and Action from Augustus to Augustine* (London and New York: Oxford University Press, 1944), 402.

35. Plato, *Smp.* 175d (LCL 166: 92); *util. cred.* 7.14 (CSEL 25.1: 19.28–20.1).

36. Augustine, *util. cred.* 11.25 (CSEL 25.1: 31.10); *util. cred.* 9.21 (CSEL 25.1: 26.11–13).

37. Plato, *Prt.* 318a–b (LCL 165: 120).

38. See *c. ep. Man.* 2–3 (CSEL 25.1: 194.13–195.12).

39. Augustine, *util. cred.* 13.29 (CSEL 25.1: 37.3–6).

40. Augustine, *util. cred.* 13.29 (CSEL 25.1: 37.7–10). The food metaphor is a topos of the psychagogic tradition and is present in the New Testament, compare Heb. 5:12–14, 1 Pet. 2:2, and especially 1 Cor. 3:2, which is discussed extensively by Clarence Glad, *Paul and Philodemus,* 185–336.

41. Augustine, *util. cred.* 14.32 (CSEL 25.1: 40.17–24, 41.4–5). Rowan Greer offers a discussion of Augustine's views on miracles in *The Fear of Freedom: A Study of Miracles in the Roman Imperial Church* (University Park: Pennsylvania State University Press, 1989), esp. 43–48, 150–51, 170–80.

42. Augustine, *util. cred.* 16.34 (CSEL 25.1: 43.16–19, 44.6–7).

43. Augustine, *util. cred.* 15.33 (CSEL 25.1: 41.25–42.9).

44. Augustine, *util. cred.* 15.33, 16.34 (CSEL 25.1: 42.3–4, 17–19). Augustine imagines this conversion to be by no means an easy process (*util. cred.* 17.35 [CSEL 25.1: 44.20–23]): "habits of any kind are so strong in their possession of people's minds that, even in the case of those that are perverse (and these usually come from the dominant passions), we can more easily condemn and detest them than we can abandon or change them."

45. Augustine, *util. cred.* 6.13 (CSEL 25.1: 18.9–12): *inest omnino ueritas et reficiendis instaurandisque animis adcomodatissima disciplina et plane ita modificata, ut nemo inde haurire non possit, quod sibi satis est, si modo ad hauriendum deuote ac pie, ut uera religio poscit, accedat;* cf. *mor.* 1.17.30 (CSEL 90: 34.18–35.2): "many things are expressed in humble language accommodated (*accommodatius*) to simple and uncultivated minds, so that they might rise through human things to the divine; and other things are expressed figuratively, so that the zealous mind, having exerted itself to discover their meaning, might rejoice more fully having found it."

On the interpretation of the Old Testament in *util. cred.*, see Christoph Schäublin, "Augustin, 'De utilitate credendi', über das Verhältnis des Interpreten zum Text," *Vigiliae Christianae* 43 (1989): 53–68.

46. Augustine, *util. cred.* 11.25 (CSEL 25.1: 33.18–20). Stock describes this process of belief and interpretation: "Conduct is reformed as individuals strive toward purity of mind using their agreed understanding of selected texts as an instrument of behavioural and intellectual change" (*Augustine the Reader*, 164).

47. Augustine, *util. cred.* 7.17 (CSEL 25.1: 22.18–22). Earlier Augustine had described how the skilled reader is aware of the danger of reading the scripture without attending to its full range of signification, for with "the profound inner figures, everything the interpretation elicits, forces an admission of their own misery from those who wish to condemn in advance rather than to learn" (*util. cred.* 3.9 [CSEL 25.1: 13.23–25]).

48. Augustine, *util. cred.* 7.17 (CSEL 25.1: 22.3–6.). See also Augustine's resulting assertion that a Manichee "is not subject to the authority of the scripture in faith, but subjects scripture to himself . . . so that he views something in scripture as correct, because he finds it congenial." In this way, "each mind becomes an authority unto itself" (*c. Faust.* 32.19 [CSEL 25.1: 780.19]); trans. (altered) Roland J. Teske, *Answer to Faustus, a Manichean*, WSA 1.20. The bishop queries, "Are you then the standard of truth?" (*tu es ergo regula ueritatis?*) (*c. Faust.* 11.2 [CSEL 25.1: 315.11]).

49. Augustine, *util. cred.* 10.24 (CSEL 25.1: 30.11–12).

50. Augustine, *util. cred.* 10.23 (CSEL 25.1: 29.3–4).

51. Augustine, *util. cred.* 10.24 (CSEL 25.1: 31.7–8): *quam et tibi esse auctorem periculi et ceteris temeritatis exemplum.*

52. Augustine, *util. cred.* 10.24 (CSEL 25.1: 29.22–30.5, 31.3–7). Augustine later clarified the skeptical implications of his argument by stating that it is "not that absolutely no truth can be found in this life which the mind can discern unless it be accepted on faith," but that the truths available to reason (such as mathematical equations) are too few to make us happy. "For whatever can be known in this life, however much it be, is not yet perfect happiness, since what remains unknown is by far an incomparably larger amount" (*retr.* 1.14.2 [CCL 57: 42.27–30, 43.49–51]).

53. Augustine, *conf.* 4.16.28.

54. Augustine, *conf.* 10.28.39 (CCL 27: 175.7–8): *Ecce uulnera mea non abscondo.*

55. Augustine, *conf.* 10.5.7 (CCL 27: 158.9–11): *ego uero quibus temptationibus resistere ualeam quibusque non ualeam, nescio.*

56. Augustine, *conf.* 10.3.4. Augustine confessed similar things in public: "I have plenty of trouble in my thoughts, fighting against my sinful impulses; I have a prolonged conflict, a conflict that never seems to stop, with the temptations of the enemy who strives to overpower me. I groan to God in my weakness" (*en. Ps.* 36.3.19 [CCL 38: 380.26–30]); cf. *ep.* 73.9.

57. Augustine, *conf.* 10.3.4 (CCL 27: 152.19–21): *euigilet in amore misericordiae tuae et dulcedine gratiae tuae, qua potens est omnis infirmus qui sibi per ipsam fit conscius infirmitatis suae.*

58. Augustine, *conf.* 9.12.33 (CCL 27: 152.73–74, 78–79). For a perceptive analysis of what William Werpehowski calls "sorrowing well" in the *Confessions,* see his "Weeping at the Death of Dido: Sorrow, Virtue, and Augustine's Confessions," *Journal of Religious Ethics* 19 (1991): 175–91.

59. Augustine, *conf.* 10.42.67 (CCL 27: 191.5–7).

60. Augustine, *retr.* 1.1.2 (CCL 57: 8.49–51): "To attain happiness, our mind ought not to be satisfied with itself but rather should subordinate itself to God."

61. Augustine, *conf.* 10.36.59 (CCL 27: 187.12–13): *Sed numquid, domine, qui solus sine typho dominaris, quia solus uerus dominus es.*

62. Augustine, *ciu.* 14.9 (CCL 48: 428.104–107): *quis hunc stuporem non omnibus uitiis iudicet esse peiorem.*

63. Augustine, *ciu.* 14.9 (CCL 48: 430.160–161): *humanitatem totam potius amittunt, quam ueram adsequuntur tranquillitatem.*

64. Augustine, *ciu.* 14.9 (CCL 48: 430.161–163): *Non enim quia durum aliquid, ideo rectum, aut quia stupidum est, ideo sanum.*

65. Augustine, *ciu.* 14.9 (CCL 48: 428.110–112).

66. Augustine, *ciu.* 14.13 (CCL 48: 434.5–8, 435.58–61).

67. Augustine, *ciu.* 14.9 (CCL 48: 426.4–8, 429.142–143): *omnes affectus istos uita recta rectos habet.* See also *ciu.* 14.6 and John Cavadini, "Feeling Right: Augustine on the Passions and Sexual Desire," *Augustinian Studies* 36 (2005): 195–217.

68. Augustine, *ciu.* 14.9 (CCL 48: 428.83): *cuius et infirmitas fuit ex potestate;* cf. *ciu.* 14.9 (CCL 48: 427.66–68): "For human emotion was not illusory in him who had a truly human body and truly human mind."

69. Cicero, *Tusc. Disp.* 5.23.68 (LCL 141: 494). The most notorious of these qualifications is perhaps Plato's myth of the god who fashions creatures with gold, silver, bronze, or iron natures (*Rep.* 415a–d [LCL 237: 304–6]).

70. As he had in *uera rel.* 1.1–5.8. Augustine was particularly disturbed by the disjunction between the Platonists' belief in one God and their continued attendance at customary polytheistic ceremonies (See *ciu.* 8.12, 10.9–11).

71. Augustine, *conf.* 9.4.7 (CCL 27: 136.5–6). See also *retr.* prol. 3.

72. Augustine, *retr.* 1.3.2 (CCL 57: 12.11–13). Brian Stock observes pointedly how Augustine "effectively domesticated the neoplatonic ascent by uniting its goals to those of Christian reading and meditation. The move permitted him to remain critical of philosophy while incorporating the key feature of meditative reflection in a programme accessible to all" (*Augustine the Reader,* 65).

73. Augustine, *trin.* 4.15.20 (CCL 50: 187.10–17); trans (altered) Edmund Hill, *The Trinity,* WSA 1.5.

74. Augustine, *lib. arb.* 3.18.52 (CCL 29: 305.41–45): "It is no wonder that because of our ignorance we lack the free choice of the will to choose rightly, or

that even when we do see what is right and will to do it, we cannot do it because of the resistance of carnal habit, which develops almost naturally because of the unruliness of our mortal inheritance."

75. Augustine, *ciu.* 14.11, 13 (CCL 48: 433.75–79, 95–96, 434.17–18).

76. Rist, *Ancient Thought Baptized,* 154, also 176; cf. Greer's comments, *Broken Lights,* 76. James Wetzel writes, "Augustine discovered that his philosophical inheritance, whether Stoic or Platonic, came up short when he turned to it to explicate the psychology of moral struggle. Pagan philosophers seemed to have little appreciation for the difficulties creatures of habit and passion would have in appropriating philosophical wisdom. Augustine made it his business to explore this uncharted terrain" (*Augustine and the Limits of Virtue,* 15).

77. Augustine would, thus, say as a slogan: "So think where you are, and from that infer what you are" (*en. Ps.* 36(3).19 [CCL 38: 381.54]).

78. Pelagius, *Dem.* 17.3 (PL 30: 31D); trans. B. R. Rees, *The Letters of Pelagius and His Followers* (Woodbridge: Boydell Press, 1991), 29–70. Augustine shows his firsthand knowledge of this letter in *ep.* 188, *gr. et pecc. or.* 1.37.40, 1.40.44.

79. Pelagius, *Dem.* 2.1 (PL 30: 16D–17A).

80. Pelagius, *Dem.* 3.3 (PL 30: 18C–D).

81. Pelagius, *Dem.* 24.1 (PL 30: 38A). He continues, "But to change one's moral life and to fashion in oneself special virtues of the mind and then to bring them to perfection is a matter which calls for intensive study and long practice (*Dem.* 24.1 [PL 30: 38B]).

82. Pelagius, *Dem.* 23.1 (PL 30: 37B).

83. Pelagius, *Dem.* 9.1.

84. Pelagius, *Dem.* 10.3 (PL 30: 26A).

85. Pelagius, *Dem.* 10.3, 4 (PL 30: 26B, C). As he notes "The greater value of a garment the greater precaution which must be taken to protect it from stain" (*Dem.* 19.1 [PL 30: 33B]).

86. Augustine, of course, rejected Pelagius' interpretation both of his works (*retr.* 1.8.1–6) and of those by Ambrose (*gr. et pecc. or.* 1.42.46–50.55). Carol Harrison observes, "Pelagius's thought was firmly rooted in the classical tradition of reflection upon man's moral and intellectual autonomy, and of his perfectibility in this life, which Augustine's understanding of the fall completely undermined and invalidated" (*Christian Truth and Fractured Humanity,* 100). Peter Brown writes, "Augustine, in a scrupulous examination of his abiding weakness, in his evocation of the life-long convalescence of the converted Christian, had tacitly denied that it was ever possible for a man to slough off his past: neither baptism nor the experience of conversion could break the monotonous continuity of life that was 'one long temptation.' In so doing, Augustine had abandoned a great tradition of Western Christianity. It is Pelagius who had seized the logical conclusions of this tradition: he is the last, the most radical, and the most paradoxical exponent of the ancient Christianity—the Christianity of discontinuity ("Pelagius and His Supporters: Aims

and Environment," *Journal of Theological Studies* n.s. 19 [1968]: 107). Augustine's contemporary, Jerome, also perceived an affinity between Pelagian teachings and Stoic ethics (see his *ep.* 133.1).

87. Carol Harrison states, "It is important to remember that Augustine's ethical thought, including his doctrine of the fall, original sin, grace, and free will, was well established long before his confrontation with Pelagianism, and that its defining characteristics were shaped not in the context of controversy, but in reflection upon the nature of human willing against the philosophical background of classical eudaemonism" (*Christian Truth and Fractured Humanity*, 114). Compare Markus, *End of Ancient Christianity*, 51.

88. Markus, *End of Ancient Christianity*, 43. Brown asserts that all the characteristic themes of Pelagius are "firmly based on a distinctive idea of the Church. For Pelagius and the Pelagian the aim remained not to produce only the perfect individual, but, above all, the perfect religious group" ("Pelagius," 102).

89. Pelagius, *Vit. chr.* 9.3 (PL 40: 1039); trans. Rees, *The Letters of Pelagius*, 106–26. This work can be attributed to Pelagius with slightly less certainty than *Dem.* For arguments for its authenticity, see Robert F. Evans, *Four Letters of Pelagius* (New York: Seabury Press, 1968) and Rees, *The Letters of Pelagius*, 105–6. Most importantly for our purposes, Augustine considered Pelagius its author (as noted by Rees, citing Augustine's, *gest. Pel.*, 6.16 ff [PL 44: 329f.], *The Letters of Pelagius*, 105).

90. Augustine, *Io. ep. tr.* 3.7, *ep.* 108.17. We have a letter of Augustine's written to his Donatist relative, Severinus, lamenting that they "do not live in the body of Christ in one society" though they are "brothers according to the flesh" (*ep.* 52.1). Kevin Coyle writes, "When Augustine arrived in Hippo Regius in 391, over half of that city's Christian population belonged to the Donatists who, until 411, outnumbered Catholics everywhere except in Africa Proconsularis" ("The Self-identity of North African Christians in Augustine's Time," in *Augustinus Afer: Saint Augustin, africanité et universalité: Actes du colloque international, Alger–Annaba, 1–7 avril 2001,* ed. Pierre-Yves Fux, Jean-Michel Roessli, and Otto Wermelinger, 2 vols. [Fribourg, Switzerland: Éditions Universitaires, 2003], 68). They, of course, claimed the title "Catholic" as their own and did not see themselves as "Donatists" but as the preservers of the authentic Christianity of North Africa. See Brent D. Shaw's admonitions against overlooking this fact ("African Christianity: Disputes, Definitions, and 'Donatists,'" in *Orthodoxy and Heresy in Religious Movements: Discipline and Dissent,* ed. Malcolm R. Greenshields and Thomas A. Robinson [Lewiston, NY: Edwin Mellen Press, 1992], 5–34).

91. Note the prominence of these themes in the revealing texts assembled and translated by Maureen A. Tilley (*Donatist Martyr Stories: The Church in Conflict in Roman North Africa* [Liverpool: Liverpool University Press, 1996]). Babcock states that the Donatists "could claim that they alone were continuing the tradition of the martyrs and had rejected the enticing prospect of an easy accommodation be-

tween church and world, a blurring of the boundary between the Christian and the non-Christian" ("Christian Culture and Christian Tradition," 41).

92. W. H. C. Frend, *The Donatist Church: A Movement of Protest in Roman North Africa* (Oxford: Clarendon Press, 1952), 327. Optatus contends that when Emperor Constans sent funds to assist in the relief of the North African poor, Donatus of Carthage rejected the gesture stating, "What has the Church to do with the Emperor?" (*Quid est imperatori cum ecclesia?*) (*De Schism. Donatist.* 3.3 [SC 413: 22]); trans. Mark Edwards, *Optatus: Against the Donatists* (Liverpool: Liverpool University Press, 1997). See Maureen Tilley's discussion of how the "Donatists used biblical texts to emphasize boundaries between Donatist orthopraxis and Catholic infidelity. They portrayed themselves as members of the *collecta*, tempted to apostasy in the midst of assimilationists" (*The Bible in Christian North Africa: The Donatist World* [Minneapolis: Fortress Press, 1997], 76), and her reminder that the Donatists were not monolithic ("From Separatist Sect to Majority Church: The Ecclesiologies of Parmenian and Tyconius," *Studia Patristica* 33 [1997]: 260–65). However much it was at odds with their theological convictions, the Donatists appealed to Roman authority against rivals when it was in their interest; see Jane E. Merdinger, *Rome and the African Church in the Time of Augustine* (New Haven, CT: Yale University Press, 1997), 88–110; Hermanowicz, *Possidius*, 83–220.

93. See Augustine's account of his own experience of a Donatist priest shouting *"traditores"* at him as he walked through an estate (*ep.* 35.4). Note Petilian's frequent invocation of the term in the portions of his letter preserved by Augustine in the second book of his *c. litt. Pet.* Tilley observes, "The basic reason behind the need for separation was to avoid ritual pollution resulting from associating with those who had committed the sin of apostasy. This sin inhered in the Catholics as descendants and supporters of the *traditores*" (*Bible in Christian North Africa*, 166). See also Bonner, *St. Augustine*, 237–39.

94. Optatus, *De Schism. Donatist.* 6.6 (SC 413: 182).

95. Augustine, *c. litt. Pet.* 1.8 (CSEL 52: 8.28–29): *non enim in ministrum per quem baptizor credo, sed in eum qui iustificat impium.* Augustine is preceded in this line of argumentation by Optatus (*De Schism. Donatist.* 5.1 [SC 413: 116]): *Has res unicuique credenti non eiusdem rei operarius, sed credentis fides et trinitas praestat.*

96. Augustine, *bapt.* 6.7 (CSEL 51: 302.12–14).

97. Augustine, *bapt.* 3.15 (CSEL 51: 205.24–28).

98. Augustine, *bapt.* 6.1 (CSEL 51: 298.12–15).

99. Augustine, *gest. Pel.* 12.27. See Brown's observation that Augustine approached "Pelagianism with the momentum of twenty years of controversy with the Donatists precisely on this issue — 'the state of the Church in this world'" ("Pelagius," 111).

100. Augustine, *c. litt. Pet.* 3.3 (CSEL 52: 163.10–13).

101. Augustine, *haer.* 41.19 (CCL 46: 319.191–197); cf. *en. Ps.* 140.8–12.

102. Augustine, *c. litt. Pet.* 3.3 (CSEL 52: 164.17–22). By contrast, Tilley explains that the Donatists "contended that parables of separation . . . dealt with division of sinners from the holy *just as soon as their identity was known,* not in the distant future" (*Bible in Christian North Africa,* 165). Augustine instructed the faithful that whenever "the scripture thunders at us that we must withdraw from the wicked, we are only being required to understand that we must withdraw in our hearts, or we may commit a greater evil in segregating the good, than the one we would flee from in being connected with the bad, which is what the Donatists have done" (*s.* 88.25 [PL 38: 553]).

103. Augustine, *ciu.* 1.35 (CCL 47: 34.15–16); cf. 18.51, 20.8.

104. Augustine, *s.* 105.9, 12. Augustine would later bring this message to a much broader audience: "The Roman Empire has been afflicted rather than changed. . . . There is no reason to despair of its recovery at the present time" (*ciu.* 4.7 [CCL 47: 104.39–42]). For a fuller account of Augustine's attitudes to Roman civic life, see Robert Markus, *Saeculum: History and Society in the Theology of St. Augustine,* 2d ed. (Cambridge: Cambridge University Press, 1988); John von Heyking, *Augustine and Politics as Longing in the World* (Columbia: University of Missouri Press, 2001).

105. Augustine, *s.* 105.9 (PL 38: 622).

106. Augustine, *s.* 105.10 (PL 38: 622–23), recalling Virgil, *Aeneid,* 1.278–279.

107. Augustine, *s.* 105.12 (PL 38: 624): "'But he should not say these things about Rome,' people have been saying about me. 'Oh, if only he would be quiet about Rome!'"

108. Augustine, *s.* 105.9 (PL 38: 622): *utinam et spiritualiter generetur, et nobiscum transeat ad aeternitatem.*

109. Augustine, *s.* 105.6 (PL 38: 620).

110. Augustine, *s.* 105.7 (PL 38: 621).

111. Augustine, *en Ps.* 61.7 (CCL 39: 777.4–6, 778.32–40).

112. Augustine, *ciu.* 19.17 (CCL 48: 685.62–63): *ordinatissima scilicet et concordissima societas fruendi Deo et inuicem in Deo.*

113. Augustine, *ciu.* 19.17 (CCL 48: 685.47–60).

114. Augustine, *en. Ps.* 61.8 (CCL 39: 779.37–40, 46–47).

115. Augustine, *en. Ps.* 61.8 (CCL 39: 778.4–6).

116. See Markus' description of Augustine as a defender of "Christian mediocrity" (*End of Ancient Christianity,* 43–62).

117. Augustine, *corrept.* 4.6 (PL 44: 919). Also, *corrept.* 2.4 (PL 44: 918): "Why are we preached to and given precepts in order to have us avoid evil and do good, if it is not we ourselves who do these things, but God who effects in us the will and the deed?"

118. Augustine, *corrept.* 2.4 (PL 44: 918): *orent, ut quod nondum habent accipiant.*

119. Augustine, *corrept.* 16.49 (PL 44: 946). See also Augustine's appeal to Paul's example saying, "he admonished, he taught, he exhorted, he chided. But he

knew that there was no value in all these things, which he did in a public way by
planting and watering, unless he who in secret makes things grow were to hear
and answer his prayers" (*corrept.* 2.3 [PL 44: 918]). Patout Burns concludes, "The
ministry of admonition through sensible signs remained a stable element in Augustine's theory of the process of salvation. Even when he had significantly modified his understanding of the interior divine assistance which makes external teaching effective, he insisted upon the essential role of this humanly mediated form of
grace" ("Providence as Divine Grace in St. Augustine," in *Augustinus Afer,* ed. Fux,
Roessli, and Wermelinger, 214).

120. Augustine, *corrept.* 5.7 (PL 44: 919).
121. Augustine, *corrept.* 16.49 (PL 44: 946).

Notes to Chapter Six

1. Augustine, *doctr. chr.* 1.1.1 (CCL 32: 6.1–3); he later identifies these tasks
with the subject matter of books 1–3 and book 4 respectively (4.1.1). On the writing of *doctr. chr.,* see Charles Kannengiesser, "The Interrupted *De doctrina christiana,*" in *De doctrina christiana: A Classic of Western Culture,* ed. Duane W. H.
Arnold and Pamela Bright (Notre Dame, IN: University of Notre Dame Press,
1994), 3–13. The meaning of Augustine's title for the work has not been entirely
clear to his readers (a problem thoroughly discussed by Gerald Press, "*Doctrina* in
Augustine's *De doctrina christiana,*" *Philosophy and Rhetoric* 17 [1984]: 98–120).
For the purpose of this analysis, when compared with his previous treatise, *De magistro,* the title, *De doctrina christiana* brings out more fully his mature view of psychagogic instruction. The title, in Mark Vessey's words, wards off any "confusion between the ultimate and proximate sources of true knowledge" and is "a phrase"
intended to "encompass the whole economy of saving instruction, without prejudg-
ing relations between the divine and human agencies involved" ("The Great Conference," 57). In this way, much as in his conversion Augustine lamented how his
classical education amounted to a "*doctrina* lacking heart" (*sine corde*) (*conf.* 8.8.19
[CCL 27: 125.5]), the bishop of Hippo promotes in this work a *doctrina christiana,* a *doctrina* with heart.

2. On the relation of book 4 to books 1–3, and particularly the manner in
which the rhetorical concerns of book 4 are integral to the exegetical ones in 1–3,
see John Cavadini's analysis: "In this way, book 4 of *De doctrina christiana,* precisely
because it is not a treatise on rhetoric *per se* but on (in effect) the dynamics of conversion, provides a kind of commentary on, or key to, the interpretation of the rest
of the work" ("The Sweetness of the Word: Salvation and Rhetoric in Augustine's
De doctrina christiana," in *De doctrina christiana: A Classic of Western Culture,* ed.
Arnold and Bright, 165). Other recent scholars have discerned a unified plan in
doctr. chr., cf. G. A. Press, "The Subject and Structure of Augustine's *De doctrina*

christiana," *Augustinian Studies* 11 (1980): 99–124; David Tracy, "Charity, Obscurity, Clarity: Augustine's Search for Rhetoric and Hermeneutics," in *Rhetoric and Hermeneutics in Our Time,* ed. Walter Jost and Michael J. Hyde (New Haven, CT: Yale University Press, 1997), 254–74. Augustine himself concludes the work by stating that in the course of four books there has been a unifying vision, "I have set out to the best of my poor ability, not what sort of person I am myself, lacking many of the necessary qualities as I do, but what sort of people those who apply themselves to sound teaching, that is to Christian doctrine, on behalf of themselves and others, ought to be" (*doctr. chr.* 4.31.64 [CCL 32: 167.5–9]).

3. Note the first line of the prologue where Augustine states, "There are certain rules for interpreting the scriptures, which I consider can be not inappropriately passed on to students, enabling them to make progress" (*doctr. chr.* prol. 1 [CCL 32: 1.1–4]).

4. Augustine, *doctr. chr.* prol. 9 (CCL 32: 6.144–146). Compare Plato and Seneca's appeal to the image discussed above.

5. Augustine, *doctr. chr.* prol. 5 (CCL 32: 3.60–61). The meaning of the prologue of *doctr. chr.* has been the subject of several studies, see among them: Peter Brunner, "Charismatische und methodische Schriftauslegung nach Augustins Prolog zu *De doctrina Christiana,"* *Kerygma und Dogma* 1 (1955): 59–69, 85–103; U. Duchrow, "Zum Prolog von Augustins *De doctrina christiana,"* *Vigilae Christianae* 17 (1963): 165–72; Eugene Kevane, "Paideia and Anti-Paideia: The *Prooemium* of St. Augustine's *De Doctrina Christiana,"* *Augustinian Studies* 1 (1970): 153–80.

6. Augustine, *doctr. chr.* prol. 4 (CCL 32: 2.44–3.53). See Athanasius, *Vita Antonii,* which was enormously popular and translated into several languages including Latin. In sections 1–3, Athanasius recounted how Antony's illiteracy was no obstacle to his understanding of scripture. Augustine had at least been told of the details of the work (*conf.* 8.6.15).

7. Augustine, *doctr. chr.* prol. 2 (CCL 32: 2.27).

8. Augustine, *doctr. chr.* prol. 6 (CCL 32: 4.83–91) (appealing to Acts 9–10).

9. Augustine, *doctr. chr.* prol. 7 (CCL 32: 4.102–108) (appealing to Acts 8:27–35).

10. Augustine, *doctr. chr.* prol. 6 (CCL 32: 4.91–97): *sed abiecta esset humana condicio, si per homines hominibus deus uerum suum ministrare nolle uideretur. . . .* See also his similar comment that "while nothing really worthy of God can be said about him, he has accepted the homage of human voices, and has wished us to rejoice in praising him with our words" (*doctr. chr.* 1.6.6 [CCL 32: 10.10–13]).

11. Augustine, *doctr. chr.* prol. 4 (CCL 32: 2.48–49); cf. "For from where does the sound of a word come to us except through the voice of the flesh? From where comes the pen, from where the writing?" (*Io. eu. tr.* 27.5.2 [CCL 36: 272.27–28]; trans. [altered] John W. Rettig, *St. Augustine: Tractates on the Gospel of John,* 5 vols. [Washington, DC: Catholic University of America Press, 1988–1995]).

12. Augustine, *doctr. chr.* prol. 5 (CCL 32: 3.62–66). See also what he later says about the necessity of the human traditions of instructing others that are the subject of book 4: "But anyone who says that people do not need to be given rules about what or how they are to teach, if the Holy Spirit is making them teachers, can also say that we do not need to pray either, because the Lord said, 'Your Father knows what you need before you ask it of him' (Matt. 6:8); or that the apostle Paul should not have instructed Timothy and Titus on how they are to instruct others—three letters of the apostle, by the way, which anyone charged with the role of teacher in the Church ought always to have before his eyes" (*doctr. chr.* 4.16.33 [CCL 32: 139.1–8]).

13. On the use of the term "culture," see Kathryn Tanner's useful analysis of the history of this term in the first half of her *Theories of Culture: A New Agenda for Theology* (Minneapolis, MN: Fortress Press, 1997). She notes that in contemporary usage, "culture cannot simply be identified with such high culture forms, or with articulate, formal expressions of belief and value. It encompasses as well the taken-for-granted, tacit background of beliefs, concepts, values, attitudes, and so forth, that are the constant accompaniment of everyday activities. Culture includes beliefs and values that, like language, are in unreflective use as well as those that are made the explicit focus of literature, song, or ritual activity" (31). As a term, then, culture refers to "the cumulative effect of past human interactions that have become habitual or routine over time. . . . Culture in this way becomes another name for traditional inheritance, for the customary behaviors that result from and are handed down by way of human historical processes" (28).

14. Augustine, *doctr. chr.* 1.24.25 (CCL 32: 20.32–33).

15. Augustine, *doctr. chr.* 1.4.4 (CCL 32: 8.4–18).

16. Augustine, *doctr. chr.* 1.3.3 (CCL 32: 8.10).

17. Augustine, *doctr. chr.* 1.9.9 (CCL 32: 11.5–12.11).

18. John Rist, *Augustine,* 175. See also Peter Brown's remark, "Like a single cloud that grows to darken the whole sky, this sense of the force of past habit deepens in Augustine" (*Augustine of Hippo,* 143), and John G. Prendiville's valuable study, "The Development of the Idea of Habit in the Thought of Saint Augustine," *Traditio* 28 (1972): 29–99.

19. Augustine, *doctr. chr.* 1.11.11 (CCL 32: 12.1–3).

20. *doctr. chr.* 1.17.16 (CCL 32: 15.1–7); cf. *en. Ps.* 84.2 (CCL 39: 1162.5–6): "he is the Truth (*ueritas*) to which we are hastening, and he is the Way (*uia*) by which we are running there." See also *trin.* 13.19.24 (CCL 50A: 417.52–54): "Through him we go straight to him . . . without ever turning aside from one and the same Christ."

21. Augustine, *doctr. chr.* 1.14.13 (CCL 32: 13.5–14.14).

22. Elsewhere Augustine presents the same argument in different terms: "the voice of the Word (*uocem uerbi*) by whom all things are made" is heard by means

of the "voice of the flesh (*uocem carnis*) that was made along with all things" so as to be "the voice of the medicine (*medicinae uocem*) by which you are healed" (*ep.* 140.18 [CSEL 44: 168.18–22]).

23. See John Rist's comment that in *doctr. chr.* "[a]ll value judgments are underpinned by God's actions as the sole non-conventional source of value" (*Augustine*, 165); also John Cavadini's observation about the manner in which "God's eloquence" in Christ "gives everything else a voice, invests the world of temporal things with significance" ("The Sweetness of the Word," 169). For salient studies of other christological features informing *doctr. chr.*, see Mark D. Jordan "Words and Word: Incarnation and Signification in Augustine's *De doctrina christiana*," *Augustinian Studies* 11 (1980): 177–96; and Robert W. Bernard, *In Figura: Terminology Pertaining to Figurative Exegesis in the Works of Augustine of Hippo*, Ph.D. dissertation, Princeton University, 1984, 259–313.

24. For other ascent passages, see, among many others, *ord.* 2.11.30–16.44, *sol.* 1.13.23, *an. quant.* 33.70–34.78, *doctr. chr.* 1.8.8, *conf.* 7.16, 7.23, 10.8–38, *en. Ps.* 119, 120, 121, 122, *ep.* 147.38–54, *Gn. adu. Man.* 1.25.43, *Io. eu. tract.* 18.11, *lib. arb.* 2.13.35–36, *s.* 263A, *s. dom. m.* 1.3.10–12, *trin.* 11.2.2–5, 12.1.1–4.4, *util. cred.* 2.4.

25. Augustine, *doctr. chr.* 2.7.9 (CCL 32: 36.1–6).

26. Augustine, *doctr. chr.* 2.7.9 (CCL 32: 37.10–12). The opposite posture is exemplified by those who "start finding more fault with scripture than with themselves. If this evil is allowed to spread, it leads to ruin. . . . Faith will start faltering if the authority of scripture is undermined; then with faith faltering, love itself languishes" (*doctr. chr.* 1.37.41 [CCL 32: 30.1–9]).

27. Augustine, *doctr. chr.* 2.7.10 (CCL 32: 37.13–14). The third stage holds a prominent place in *doctr. chr.* as a whole. This is indicated not only by the fact that the tasks elaborated in stage three are the preeminent concerns addressed throughout books 1–4, but also from Augustine's own statements. Only of the third stage does he say, "which I have undertaken to treat here and now," evidently referring to more than the passage at hand. Moreover, once he describes the culminating seventh stage, he remarks, "But let us turn our attention back to that third stage . . ." (*doctr. chr.* 2.8.12 [CCL 32: 38.1–2]). See Karla Pollmann's discussion of this passage, "Augustine's Hermeneutics as a Universal Discipline!?" in *Augustine and the Disciplines: From Cassiciacum to Confessions*, ed. K. Pollmann and M. Vessey (Oxford: Oxford University Press, 2005), 224–31. Perhaps Augustine assumes that it is the probable location of the implied reader, or that this stage is the most necessary for the Christian preacher to address. Indeed, as will be demonstrated later, Augustine's sermons rarely stray far from the tasks enumerated in this third stage.

28. Augustine, *doctr. chr.* 2.7.10 (CCL 32: 37.15–20); cf. *ep.* 55.21.38–39. On the role of *caritas* in *doctr. chr.*, see Karla Pollmann, *Doctrina Christiana: Untersuchungen zu den Anfängen der christlichen Hermeneutik unter besonderer Berücksichtigung von Augustinus, De doctrina christiana* (Fribourg, Switzerland: Universitätsverlag, 1996), 121–47.

29. Augustine, *doctr. chr.* 1.27.28 (CCL 32: 22.1–3).

30. Augustine, *doctr. chr.* 1.4.4 (CCL 32: 8.1–3): "Use consists in referring what has come your way to what your love aims at obtaining" while enjoyment "consists in clinging to something in love for its own sake." For discussion of these terms, see Oliver O'Donovan, "*Usus* and *fruitio* in Augustine, *De Doctrina Christiana* I," *Journal of Theological Studies* n.s. 33 (1982): 361–97.

31. Augustine, *doctr. chr.* 1.4.4 (CCL 32: 8.4–18).

32. Augustine, *doctr. chr.* 1.17.16 (echoing Plotinus *En.* 1.6.8 as he does in *conf.* 1.8.28, 8.8.19).

33. Augustine, *doctr. chr.* 2.9.14 (CCL 32: 40.2–41.3): *Cuius operis et laboris prima obseruatio est, ut diximus, nosse istos libros.*

34. Specifically, *doctr. chr.* 2.11.16–42.63. This feature of *doctr. chr.* was of immense interest to medieval readers, see the essays edited by Edward D. English, *Reading and Wisdom: The De doctrina christiana of Augustine in the Middle Ages* (Notre Dame, IN: University of Notre Dame Press, 1995).

35. Augustine, *doctr. chr.* 2.7.10 (CCL 32: 37.14–25). Thus, the liberal arts are not abandoned in Augustine's mature theory as much as they themselves have been transformed by their function in Augustine's ecclesial context. John Cavadini, consequently, describes *doctr. chr.* as "a revisioning of the projected encyclopedia, as that project which in effect replaced the encyclopedia" ("Sweetness of the Word," 171).

36. Augustine, *doctr. chr.* 2.7.10 (CCL 32: 37.32–35). Anticipating our later discussion of the sermons, the most common ending of Augustine's homilies begins with an exhortation: "*conuersi ad dominum.* . . . In the context of *doctr. chr.*, the homily frequently facilitates this ascent from stage three to stage four as sacred reading involves this specific type of conversion.

37. Augustine, *doctr. chr.* 2.7.11 (CCL 32: 38.56–61).

38. Musonius Rufus, *Fr.* 6 (Cora Lutz, 53); Augustine, *doctr. chr.* 4.14.30 (CCL 32: 137.1–5).

39. Augustine, *doctr. chr.* 4.5.7 (CCL 32: 120.7–9).

40. Augustine, *doctr. chr.* 4.12.28 (CCL 32: 136.29–30).

41. Augustine, *doctr. chr.* 4.5.7 (CCL 32: 120.10–12), citing Cicero, *Inu.* 1.1.1: "wisdom without eloquence is of little benefit to society; but eloquence without wisdom is often excessively destructive and profits no one" (trans. H. M. Hubbell; LCL 386: 2).

42. Augustine, *doctr. chr.* 4.11.26 (CCL 32: 135.11–14).

43. Augustine, *doctr. chr.* 4.25.55 (CCL 32: 160.9–10).

44. Augustine, *doctr. chr.* 4.26.55 (CCL 32: 161.26–30). See I. Sluiter's analysis of the function of *delectatio* in *doctr. chr.*, "Communication, Eloquence and Entertainment in Augustine's *De Doctrina Christiana*," in *The Impact of Scripture in Early Christianity*, ed. J. den Boeft, and M. L. van Poll–van de Lisdonk (Leiden: Brill, 1999), esp. 256–64.

45. Augustine, *doctr. chr.* 4.4.6 (CCL 32: 119.1–4).

46. Augustine, *doctr. chr.* 4.14.30 (CCL 32: 137.10–13). Apparently Augustine interprets God's command to Jeremiah to apply to his rhetoric. By means of it, he is "to uproot and to pull down, to destroy and to overthrow, and then to build and to plant" (Jer. 1:10), see *doctr. chr.* 11.17 and *en. Ps.* 50.11.

47. See John Cavadini's description of the function of the exposition of scripture in *doctr. chr.* as "the persuasive power of an eloquent speaking that will disentangle us from perverse sweetness and will delight us with that 'sweetness which actually would make us happy" (citing *doctr. chr.* 1.4.4, "Sweetness of the Word," 166); or, stated in different terms, "Charity," Augustine's principle of scriptural interpretation, "as it were, deconstructs those sweetnesses, dismantling them in the ultimate sign (*signum*), the sign of the cross" (171).

48. Augustine, *doctr. chr.* 2.6.7 (CCL 32: 35.1–7).

49. Augustine, *doctr. chr.* 3.6.10 (CCL 32: 83.4–5). Robert Markus is surely right that "Jews" in *doctr. chr.* are Augustine's "hermeneutical device to define a premature closure of biblical discourse, short of the new realm of meaning it would enter in the light of the incarnation," and "by no means the only people who enclosed themselves in a circumscribed, restricted world of meanings" ("World and Text in Ancient Christianity I: Augustine," in *Signs and Meanings: World and Text in Ancient Christianity* [Liverpool: Liverpool University Press, 1996], 24–25). For the ambivalent history of Augustine's "hermeneutical Jew," see Jeremy Cohen, *Living Letters of the Law: Ideas of the Jew in Medieval Christianity* (Berkeley: University of California Press, 1999), and Paula Fredriksen, *Augustine and the Jews: A Christian Defense of Jews and Judaism* (New York: Doubleday, 2008).

50. Augustine, *doctr. chr.* 3.5.9 (CCL 32: 83.9–12, 16–19).

51. Augustine, *doctr. chr.* 3.6.10 (CCL 32: 83.5–7).

52. Augustine, *doctr. chr.* 3.6.11 (CCL 32: 84.29–30). Augustine, therefore, disparages the philosophical exegesis of the poets as impotent even though it has formal similarities to what he advocates regarding Christian scripture. Although its method of referring signs to what they signify is admirable, it cannot succeed because it begins with "useless signs." As Augustine states, "What use is it to me that the image of Neptune is given symbolic meaning" to mean the sea "except perhaps to warn me off worshipping either of them?" (*doctr. chr.* 3.7.11 [CCL 32: 84.13–15]). For this long-standing Greek and Roman tradition, see the above first two chapters and the secondary literature cited there.

53. Augustine, *doctr. chr.* 3.8.12 (CCL 32: 85.1–11).

54. Augustine, *doctr. chr.* 2.7.10 (CCL 32: 37.21–25).

55. Augustine, *doctr. chr.* 4.20.39 (CCL 32: 146.32–43); see also Brian Stock's contention that "self-understanding and understanding of biblical texts are mutually supporting activities" (*Augustine the Reader,* 241).

56. Christoph Schäublin notes that Augustine's "fundamental distinction" between "branches of knowledge" concerned with "conventions" and those things that

are instituted by God as part of the natural order "derives ultimately from the ancient Greek antithesis between νόμος and φύσις." He proceeds, moreover, to observe that "Augustine applies an ancient concept more consistently than anyone before him: namely that language is not given by nature; its rules are laid down by men, as a social convention . . . which may change from one age to the next" (*"De doctrina christiana*: A Classic of Western Culture," in *De doctrina christiana: A Classic of Western Culture,* ed. Arnold and Bright, 56, 57).

57. Augustine's sign theory is received and transformed as well. See Robert A. Markus, "St. Augustine on Signs," *Phronesis* 2 (1957): 60–83; B. D. Jackson, "The Theory of Signs in St. Augustine's *De doctrina Christiana,*" *Revue des Études Augustiniennes* 15 (1969): 9–49; Marc Baratin, "Les origines stoïciennes de la théorie Augustinienne du signe," *Revue des Études Latines* 59 (1981): 260–68; Giovanni Manetti, *Theories of the Sign in Classical Antiquity,* trans. Christine Richardson (Bloomington: Indiana University Press, 1993); John Rist, *Augustine,* 23–40; Karla Pollmann, *Doctrina Christiana,* 159–96. On the relation of signs to affections highlighted here, see David Dawson, "Sign Theory, Allegorical Reading, and the Motions of the Soul," in *De doctrina christiana: A Classic of Western Culture,* ed. Arnold and Bright, 123–41. Robert Markus notes that although Augustine's initial "concern with signs" in *doctr. chr.* was "for the purpose of exploring the meaning of biblical signs," it "grew into something of far wider application," helping him "formulate his theology of the sacraments, and, gradually, into wider areas yet" ("World and Text," 24).

58. Robert Dodaro, thus, states, "Augustine never abandons the conviction, dear to classical rhetoricians, that human behavior is largely conditioned by the effects of language on the soul" (*Christ and the Just Society,* 66). See also Augustine's narrative in the first book of the *Confessions* on the inculcation of cultural signs in the educational process and its subsequent implications. Robert Markus contends that book two of *doctr. chr.* "explores the question of how communities are constituted by the way they understand and use the symbolic systems (i.e. all that Augustine includes under his category *signa data*) established within them" ("Augustine on Magic: A Neglected Semiotic Theory," in *Signs and Meanings,* 135).

59. *Doctr. chr.* draws quite a number of distinctions between various kinds of signs in scripture (and the world from which they are drawn). These range from certain sign systems, on the one hand, that can be seen to be instituted by God and only discovered by humans such as philosophy and rhetoric. Such disciplines are to be interpreted as good in themselves when they are put in service to God, but remain vulnerable to being systematically misused for other purposes. A sign system, on the other hand, such as astrology Augustine considers far from being a necessary feature of the social landscape; rather it is "given" such that it involves its participant in pacts with demons and likewise enlists their affections. For commentary on sign systems particularly of the latter kind, see Robert Markus, "Augustine on Magic" and his "World and Text," 30–31.

60. Augustine, *doctr. chr.* 4.12.28 (CCL 32: 136.40–43).

61. Augustine, *doctr. chr.* 2.1.1 (CCL 32: 32.5–7).

62. Augustine, *doctr. chr.* 2.5.6 (CCL 32: 35.1–8). See, for example, Augustine's description of the manner in which "the will" of the apostle Peter "is apparent" in his letter (*epistulam, in qua uoluntas apparet*) (*ep.* 29.10 [CSEL 34: 120.30–121.1]).

63. See Rowan Williams' perceptive analysis that "the incarnation manifests the essential quality of the world itself as 'sign' or trace of its maker. . . . Augustine has in effect defined Scripture as the paradigm of self-conscious symbolic awareness: it is a pattern of signs organized around—and by—the incarnate Word in such a way that all signs *remain* signs, all are kept open to the horizon of God, in virtue of their relation to their central acting out in cross and resurrection of God's otherness from the realm of representation" ("Language, Reality, and Desire in Augustine's *De doctrina*," *Literature and Theology* 3 [1989]: 141, 147).

64. Augustine, *doctr. chr.* 1.32.35 (CCL 32: 26.17–19): "This is the supreme reward—that we may thoroughly enjoy him and that all of us who enjoy him may enjoy one another in him."

65. Augustine, *doctr. chr.* 3.10.15 (CCL 32: 86.13–87.19).

66. Augustine, *doctr. chr.* 3.10.15, 3.18.26 (CCL 32: 87.19–25, 93.8–11). See William S. Babcock's apt summary: "Augustine fears, we will assume that Scripture's words are to be taken in their proper sense when they conform to our own standards of moral judgment and that they are to be construed in a figurative sense when they do not . . . [W]e will bring Scripture into conformity with our own culture either by investing the things signified by its verbal signs with a further signification that they do not really have or by stripping them of a further signification that they do. Plainly enough, here again, it is the social construction of meaning—in this instance of moral meaning—that lies at the heart of Augustine's concern" ("*Caritas* and Signification in *De doctrina christiana* 1–3," in *De doctrina christiana: A Classic of Western Culture,* ed. Arnold and Bright, 154).

67. Augustine, *doctr. chr.* 3.14.22 (CCL 32: 91.1–20).

68. Augustine, *doctr. chr.* 1.36.40 (CCL 32: 29.1–4). Thus Augustine can still hold with his earlier position in *mag.* that signs cannot be understood without preceding knowledge (10.33–13.41), but in *doctr. chr.* scripture itself, as an expression of divine grace, supplies such knowledge in the twofold commandment. Augustine had identified this twofold love as the core meaning of the law as early as *Gn. adu. Man.* 2.23.36. Compare Sluiter, "Communication, Eloquence, and Entertainment," 251.

69. Augustine, *doctr. chr.* 3.14.22 (CCL 32: 91.13–20); cf. *conf.* 3.7.13–8.15.

70. Augustine, nevertheless, does take into account the intentions of the human authors of scripture in their particular cultural context. He states that interpretation that conforms to the divine order but means something different from what the human author intended is not ultimately wrong but is indeed mistaken (*doctr. chr.* 1.36.41 [CCL 32: 30.21–28]). See Robert Markus' discussion of authorial

intention and his helpful distinction between "exegesis" and "interpretation" ("Word and Text," esp. 16–43).

71. Augustine, *doctr. chr.* 4.24.53 (CCL 32: 159.5–160.23); apparently, a form of ritual blood-letting. See Lancel, *Augustine,* 351; O'Donnell, *Augustine,* 258; Bonner, "Augustine's Visit to Caesarea in 418," in *Studies in Church History,* ed. C.W. Dugmore and C. Duggan (London: Nelson, 1964), 104–13. A useful parallel can be found in Augustine's own account in a letter to Alypius (c. 395) of his efforts to overcome the festal drunkenness of his congregation in Hippo (*ep.* 29). Recall the similar effects of Dio Chrysostom's oratory discussed in chapter 1.

72. As Robert Markus implies, "reading creatures as signs requires, as do the signs of the Old Testament, the right kind of reader, readers with the right semiotic intention" ("World and Text," 27).

73. Augustine, *ep.* 118.3.13 (CSEL 34.2: 677.14–17, 23–678.2).

74. Augustine, *s.* 133.4 (PL 38: 739).

75. Augustine, *s.* 68.7 (PLS 2: 506).

76. Augustine, *doctr. chr.* 4.15.32 (CCL 32: 138.4–7); see also the exhortation to prayer in *doctr. chr.* 4.30.63 (CCL 32: 167.1–15).

77. Augustine, *doctr. chr.* 4.16.33 (CCL 32: 140.29–141.42).

78. Thus, for Augustine's developing thought, the vision of God retains its importance as an eschatological hope for everyone rather than the immediate possession of a few. See the able analysis of Frederick van Fleteren, "Augustine and the Possibility of the Vision of God in this Life," *Studies in Medieval Culture* 11 (1977): 9–16.

79. As John Cavadini contends, "There is no question of a philosophical escape from temporal things into the eternal. As long as we live, we never leave the realm of sign and signification, of eloquence and word, to arrive at an inner world apart from them" ("Salvation and Rhetoric," 171).

80. Augustine, *doctr. chr.* 2.7.11 (CCL 32: 38.51–52). Stated more forcefully in Augustine's *cons. eu.* 4.10.20 (PL 34: 1227–28); trans. (altered) S. D. F. Salmond and M. B. Riddle, NPNF 1.6: 235: "But if anyone supposes that with man, living, as he still does, in this mortal life, it may be possible for a person to dispel and clear off every obscurity induced by corporeal and carnal images (*phantasiarum*), and to attain to the serenest light of changeless truth, and to cleave constantly and unswervingly to that with a mind thoroughly estranged from the custom of this present life, that man understands neither what he asks, nor who he is that put such a supposition." See also *ciu.* 22.29–30, *en. Ps.* 37.28, 43.5, *s.* 255.5, and the attention given to this theme by John Peter Kenney in his insightful *The Mysticism of Saint Augustine: Rereading the Confessions* (New York: Routledge, 2005).

81. Cf. Augustine, *en. Ps.* 38.14 (CCL 38: 416.27–33): "We learn, then, that in this life you can be perfect in no other way than by knowing that you cannot be perfect. Your perfection will consist in having leapt over certain things in order to hasten on toward certain others, but in having leapt over them in such a way that

there still remains something further, to which after all your efforts you must still leap. Faith like this is safe, for those who think they have already reached the goal are exalting themselves and are heading for a fall" (see also *s.* 306B.3). Of Augustine's mature reflections on the Trinity, Rowan Williams writes, "Growing into the image of God, then, is not a matter of perfecting our possession of certain qualities held in common with God. . . . It is for us to be at home with our created selves (our selves as produced, derived), and so to be at home with the action of a creator" ('*Sapientia* and the Trinity: Reflections on the *De trinitate*," in *Collectanea Augustiniana: Mélanges T. J. Van Bavel,* ed. B. Bruning, M. Lamberigts, and J. van Houtem, 2 vols. [Leuven: University Press, 1990], 1:321).

82. Cf. *conf.* 13.17.21 (CCL 27: 253.17–18): "We are moved to compassion by our own weakness."

83. As Karla Pollmann has noticed, "On the whole, *doctr. chr.* is almost always very concerned to avoid concrete historical ephemeral allusions that could diminish the generally valid, universal character of the work" ("African and Universal Elements in the Hermeneutics of Tyconius and Augustine," in *Augustinus Afer,* ed. Fux, Roessli, and Wermelinger, 357).

84. The following comments on *cat. rud.* address only those materials relevant to the traditions that are the subject of the present study. For more general treatments and bibliography, see Harmless, *Augustine and the Catechumenate,* esp. 107–55; Van der Meer, *Augustine the Bishop,* 453–67.

85. Augustine, *cat. rud.* 15.23 (CCL 46: 148.32–33); cf. *Simpl.* 53.4 (CCL 44: 90.127): "Souls are taught in accord with their degree of maturity."

86. Augustine, *cat. rud.* 15.23 (CCL 46: 148.33–36).

87. Augustine, *cat. rud.* 8.12 (CCL 46: 133.1–134.60).

88. Augustine, *cat. rud.* 9.13 (CCL 46: 135.1–136.36).

89. A population Augustine continually has in mind in the treatise. See, among other comments: "with slower minds we should use somewhat more words and illustrations, that they may not consider lightly what they see" (*cat. rud.* 9.13 [CCL 46: 136.37–38]); "if he is exceedingly slow-witted, and is unresponsive and averse to every such charm, we should bear with him in a compassionate spirit" (*cat. rud.* 13.18 [CCL 46: 142.21–23]); and his attention to the motives of uneducated townspeople (*cat. rud.* 16.24 [CCL 46: 148.1–8]).

90. Augustine, *cat. rud.* 1.1 (CCL 46: 121.6–8).

91. Augustine, *cat. rud.* 2.3 (CCL 46: 122.6–123.34).

92. Augustine, *cat. rud.* 2.4 (CCL 46: 123.48–55).

93. Augustine, *mag.* 10.34 (CCL 29: 193.153–155).

94. Augustine, *cat. rud.* 3.5 (CCL 46: 124.1–3). Note that the term *narratio* is a technical term of rhetoric with legal connotations of arguing the facts of a case, cf. Cicero, *Inu.* 1.19.27; *Part.* 1.4–5; and Christopher's philological commentary, *De Catechizandis Rudibus,* 128–29.

95. Augustine, *cat. rud.* 3.5 (CCL 46: 124.11–125.15). Note that in admonishing Deogratias to maintain the priority of scripture in the homily, the bishop further cautions him never to "abandon the course of the narration and permit our heart and tongue to stray into the more tangled mazes of disputation. But let the simple truth of the explanation that we employ be like the gold which holds together in harmonious arrangement the jewels of an ornament without becoming itself unduly conspicuous" (*cat. rud.* 6.10 [CCL 46: 131.26–31]).

96. Augustine, *cat. rud.* 3.5 (CCL 46: 124.10–11).

97. Cf. *ep.* 55.11.21 (CSEL 34.2: 192.8–13): "I believe that, as long as it is still involved in the things of earth, the feeling of the soul is set afire rather slowly, but if it is confronted with bodily likenesses and brought from there to spiritual realities that are symbolized by those likenesses, it is strengthened by this passage, and is set aflame like the fire in a coal when stirred up, and is carried with a more ardent love toward rest."

98. Augustine, *cat. rud.* 10.14 (CCL 46: 136.16–137.32).

99. Augustine, *cat. rud.* 10.15 (CCL 46: 138.66–78).

100. Augustine, *cat. rud.* 14.22 (CCL 46: 146.64–67).

101. Augustine, *cat. rud.* 6.10 (CCL 46: 130.4–131.14). See also along the same lines: "we must earnestly caution against placing hope in a human being" (7.11 [CCL 46: 132.33–34]); and the longer sample discourse begins, "one who desires true rest and true happiness must raise his hope from things that perish and pass away and place it in the Word of God" (16.24 [CCL 46: 149.29–31]).

102. Augustine, *cat. rud.* 3.5 (CCL 46: 125.14–15).

103. Augustine was, of course, all too familiar with this prejudice and its effects from his own experience (*conf.* 3.5.9; 5.13.23–14.24). His prominent place within the tradition of Christian "plain style" has been noted, see Erich Auerbach, "Sermo Humilis," in his *Literary Language and Its Public in Late Latin Antiquity and in the Middle Ages,* trans. Ralph Manheim (New York: Pantheon, 1965), 25–66; Kaster, *Guardians of Language,* 70–95; Peter Auksi, *Christian Plain Style: The Evolution of a Spiritual Ideal* (Montreal and Kingston: McGill-Queen's University Press, 1995), 110–73.

104. Augustine, *cat. rud.* 9.13 (CCL 46: 135.11–13).

105. Augustine, *cat. rud.* 9.13 (CCL 46: 135.17–19): *quid ualeant aenigmatum latebrae ad amorem ueritatis acuendum, discutiendumque fastidii torporem.*

106. Augustine, *cat. rud.* 9.13 (CCL 46: 135.19–25). See also the recommendation "to pick out some of those points that have been said mystically in the sacred scriptures, and particularly in the narration itself, the explanation and interpretation of which make our discourse more sweet" (*sermo dulcescat*) (*cat. rud.* 13.18 [CCL 46: 142.19–21]).

107. Augustine, *cat. rud.* 11.16 (CCL 46: 140.31–37).

108. Augustine, *cat. rud.* 26.50 (CCL 46: 173.10–174.18); cf. *doctr. chr.* 2.7.10.

109. Augustine, *cat. rud.* 3.6 (CCL 46: 125.20–24).

110. Augustine, *cat. rud.* 4.8 (CCL 46: 128.71–73).

111. Augustine, *cat. rud.* 4.8 (CCL 46: 128.73–129.79); cf. "the future humility of God, our King and Lord, Jesus Christ, that through faith in Him they might be cured of all pride and swelling arrogance" (*cat. rud.* 19.33 [CCL 46: 157.65–158.67]).

112. Augustine, *cat. rud.* 4.7 (CCL 46: 127.10–11): *Nulla est enim maior ad amorem inuitatio, quam praeuenire amando;* a conviction Augustine sees in Rom. 5:6–10.

113. Augustine, *cat. rud.* 4.8 (CCL 46: 128.57–59).

114. Augustine continues by noting that similar interpretive methods are, indeed, employed by respected pagan grammarians when teaching literature that Augustine considers far inferior: "For if, even as regards the fictitious tales of the poets, which were devised for the pleasure of minds that feed on trifles, the grammarians who are regarded and called good do nevertheless try to make them serve some useful purpose even though that very purpose be vain and greedy of worldly feasting, how much more careful ought we to be lest the truths, which we relate without a well-ordered statement of their causes, should be believed either on account of an artificial sweetness or even a harmful cupidity" (*cat. rud.* 6.10 [CCL 46: 131.18–25]).

115. Augustine, *cat. rud.* 14.22 (CCL 46: 146.67–70).

116. Augustine, *cat. rud.* 12.17 (CCL 46: 141.6–8). See Harmless' observation, "Augustine took this reciprocity between teacher and learner seriously and made it a routine theme in his catechesis" (*Augustine and the Catechumenate,* 136).

117. Augustine, *cat. rud.* 14.20 (CCL 46: 144.14–18, 145.22–23).

118. Augustine, *cat. rud.* 2.4 (CCL 46: 124.66–69); see also *cat. rud.* 12.17.

119. Augustine, *cat. rud.* 14.22 (CCL 46: 146.78–147.80), invoking one of Augustine's favorite biblical texts, Rom. 5:5.

120. Augustine, *cat. rud.* 11.16 (CCL 46: 140.48): *incertos exitus sermonis nostri.*

121. Augustine, *cat. rud.* 7.11 (CCL 46: 132.33–34, 38–43); cf. *cat. rud.* 11.16 (CCL 46: 140.58–59): "if we happily permit him to speak through us as best we are able."

122. Augustine, *doctr. chr.* 4.27.59 (CCL 32: 163.1–2).

123. See Peter Brown, *Augustine of Hippo,* 423–37; Lancel, *Augustine,* 470–75.

124. Possidius, *Vit. Aug.* 31.1–3 (PL 32: 63–64). Compare to Éric Rebillard's analysis which sees Augustine's manner of dying as emblematic of a broader societal shift from seeing death itself as a good to perceiving it as the unnatural destruction of a legitimate good. He states accordingly, "We find in the account of Possidius the key elements of Augustine's pastoral care" (my translation; *In hora mortis: Évolution de la pastorale chrétienne de la mort aux IVe et Ve siècles dans l'Occident latin* [Rome: École Française de Rome, 1994], 214).

125. Cf. *en. Ps.* 99.11 (CCL 39: 1400.20–21, 27–28): "We all want to have well-defended hearts. . . . Where then is our security? Nowhere here, certainly, nowhere in this life, but only in the hope of God's promises."

126. Compare Ambrose, *bon. mort.* 8.31 with Augustine, *s.* 172.1 (PG 38: 936): "About the dead, those who love them naturally feel a certain sadness. The horror of death is not a fact of opinion, but of nature." This juxtaposition is drawn by Rebillard, *In hora mortis,* 9, 45.

127. Augustine, *ep.* 21.3 (CSEL 34.1: 51.5).

128. In treating Augustine's theory before his practice, it should be kept in mind that his mature theory emerges out of his experience of Christian ministry rather than preceding it. Christine Mohrmann pointed out some time ago: "His theory is based upon this practice. His theoretical ideas are at the same time an elucidation and a defence of characteristic features of his own style" ("St. Augustine and the *Eloquentia,*" in *Études sur le latin des Chrétiens,* vol. 1 [Rome: Edizioni di storia e letteratura, 1961], 365).

Notes to Chapter Seven

1. Apuleius, *Flor.* 18.1 (Rudolf Helm, *Apulei Opera quae supersunt* [Stuttgart and Leipzig: B. G. Teubner, 1912], 2.2: 33.24–34.2); trans. (altered) H. E. Butler, *The Apologia and Florida of Apuleius of Madaura* (Westport, CT: Greenwood Press, 1970). *Flor.* 9, 15, 16, 17, 18, and 20 are excerpts from speeches given in Carthage. The other excerpts are less certain, but were likely given in Carthage as well. Apuleius mentions giving speeches there for some six years (*Flor.* 18.16 [Helm, 2.2: 35.16–18]). Stephen Harrison concludes, "It seems that . . . Apuleius spent much time in Carthage, which as a cosmopolitan provincial capital relatively close to Rome served as a good showcase for his talents" (*Apuleius: A Latin Sophist* [Oxford: Oxford University Press, 2000], 8).

2. Apuleius, *Flor.* 18.38 (Helm, 2.2: 38.16–17): "I will sing to you both in Greek and Latin a hymn to the God [Aesculapius]." See also his boast, "I write all these and much besides with equal fluency in Greek and Latin, with equal pleasure, like ardor and uniform skill" (*Flor.* 9.29 [Helm, 2.2: 13.21–23]); cf. *Apol.* 36.6–8 and the fifth excerpt from *Flor.* in *Soc.* 112–13 (C. Moreschini, *Apulei Opera quae supersunt* [Stuttgart and Leipzig: B. G. Teubner, 1991], 3: 6.2–10).

3. Apuleius, first excerpt from *Flor.* in *Soc.* 103–5 (Moreschini, 3: 1–2.12): "You have heard me speak prepared, now hear me unprepared. . . . In order for you to know me in all my infinite variety, make trial of me. . . . For the more I modify my style to suit your taste, the more I shall please you."

4. Apuleius, *Flor.* 16.1, 37–41. Stephen Harrison observes, "The award of a statue was a standard civic honor in the Roman empire, and was bestowed on

sophists and other intellectuals just as much as on others who had brought more tangible benefits to their city" (Harrison, *Apuleius*, 117). Philostratus mentions such monuments (*Vit. Soph.* 1: 8.490, 23.527, 25.543). A statue most likely of Apuleius was uncovered in Madaurus, a city where Augustine acquired some of his early training, with an inscription at the base of it which reads, "Platonic Philosopher." See Stéphane Gsell, *Inscriptions latines de l'Algérie* (Paris: E. Champion, 1922), 1.2115. Augustine himself was aware of a statue of Apuleius still standing in Oea (*ep.* 138.19).

5. Apuleius, *Flor.* 2.1 (Helm, 2.2: 1.14): *maior meum Socrates; Apol.* 10.6 (Helm, 2.1: 12.11): *Platonico philosopho;* see also *Flor.* 15.26, *Apol.* 13.1–2, 39.1, 41.7. For Apuleius' Platonism, especially that of his philosophical treatises, see Gersh, *Middle Platonism*, 1.215–328; Dillon, *The Middle Platonists*, 306–38; and B. L. Hijmans Jr., "Apuleius, *Philosophus Platonicus*," ANRW 2.36.1 (1987), 395–475.

6. Apuleius, *Flor.* 2.2–7 (Helm, 2.2: 1.16–2.13).

7. Apuleius, *Apol.* 4.1–5 (Helm, 2.1: 5.4–16).

8. Apuleius, *Flor.* 20.4–6 (Helm, 2.2: 41.2–9).

9. Apuleius, *Flor.* 13.1–3 (Helm, 2.2: 17.26–18.9).

10. Apuleius, *Flor.* 9.26 (Helm, 2.2: 13.13–14).

11. Apuleius, *Flor.* 11.1–2 (Helm, 2.2: 16.12–19).

12. Augustine, for example, comments about passing through Bulla Regia: "So it was God's will, my brothers and sisters, that I should pass this way. My brother detained me, ordered me, begged me, forced me to preach to you" (*s.* 301A.9 [MA 1: 89.17–18]). For Augustine's travels as a bishop, see Othmar Perler, *Les voyages de saint Augustin* (Paris: Études Augustiniennes, 1969), esp. 205–405.

13. On ascertaining its location, see Noël Duval, "Commentaire topographique et archéologique de sept dossiers des nouveaux sermons," in *Augustin Prédicateur*, ed. G. Madec, 172–75. The sermon is thought to have been preached in approximately 404 CE (see Dolbeau, *Vingt-six sermons*, 626, Hill, *Sermons* 3.11, 383–4 n.1).

14. Augustine, *s.* 360B.2 (Dolbeau, 25: 248.23–249.31).

15. Augustine, *s.* 360B.3 (Dolbeau, 25: 249.33–44); cf. *ep. Io. tr.* 7.10.

16. Augustine, *s.* 360B.3 (Dolbeau, 25: 249.48–49).

17. Augustine, *s.* 360B.4 (Dolbeau, 25: 249.56–250.63).

18. Augustine, *s.* 360B.8 (Dolbeau, 25: 252.146–147): *respuat ab animo suo . . . respuat et hanc cogitatione sua.*

19. Augustine, *s.* 360B.8 (Dolbeau, 25: 252.148–253.149): *Non est hoc, inquam, deus meus, opus est dei mei.*

20. Augustine, *s.* 360B.9 (Dolbeau, 25: 253.158–159): *Non enim corpus est anima, inuisibile quiddam est, et magnum quiddam est.*

21. Augustine, *s.* 360B.10 (Dolbeau, 25:254.190–193).

22. Augustine, *s.* 360B.12 (Dolbeau, 25: 255.235–237).

23. Augustine, *s.* 360B.10 (Dolbeau, 25: 254.189): *Transcende, si potes, et mentem tuam.*

24. Augustine, *s.* 360B.12 (Dolbeau, 25: 255.236–241).

25. Augustine, *s.* 360B.11 (Dolbeau, 25: 254.209–213); see also his assertion that the soul must "first learn to 'unfind' the one it wishes to find" (*s.* 360B.7 [Dolbeau, 25: 252.142–143]), or his more famous admonition "to find by 'unfinding' rather than by finding fail to find" (*conf.* 1.6.10 [CCL 27: 6.67–68]).

26. Augustine, *s.* 360B.16 (Dolbeau, 25: 258.319–320).

27. Augustine, *s.* 360B.12 (Dolbeau, 25: 255.224–228); cf. *ep. Io. tr.* 6.13.1 (SC 75: 306): "Let us go together with the heart and let us knock"; and *en. Ps.* 146.12 (CCL 40: 2130.8–2131.14): "When some text seems dark to you, be sure that the physician has made it so; he is inviting you to knock. He wanted it to puzzle you so that you may be exercised as you keep on knocking; he wants it to be so, that he may open to you when you knock. As you persevere in knocking you will be exercised; as you are exercised, your capacity will be enlarged; as your capacity grows, you will receive what comes to you as gift."

28. Augustine, *s.* 360B.11 (Dolbeau, 25: 255.220–222).

29. Augustine, *s.* 360B.14 (Dolbeau, 25: 256.265–257.296).

30. Augustine, *s.* 360B.15 (Dolbeau, 25: 257.297–298); cf. *s.* 278.1 (PL 38: 1269): "His is the medicine which cures the soul." On this theme, see the still valuable study by Rudolph Arbesmann, "The Concept of 'Christus Medicus' in St. Augustine," *Traditio* 10 (1954): 1–28.

31. Augustine, *s.* 360B.16 (Dolbeau, 25: 258.324–325).

32. Augustine, *s.* 360B.18 (Dolbeau, 25: 260.378–379); for this theme, see *s.* 49.9, 174.6, 175.3, 313B.4, *en. Ps.* 45.4, 109.3.

33. Augustine, *s.* 360B.18 (Dolbeau, 25: 260.368–373) quoting Acts 2:37; cf. *en. Ps.* 74.7, 138.8.

34. See the description of the ministry of the disciples (*s.* 360B.19 [Dolbeau, 25: 260.380–261.385]), and the more extended discussion in *en. Ps.* 87.10.

35. Augustine, *s.* 360B.17 (Dolbeau, 25: 258.326): *Humilitas Christi medicamentum superbiae tuae.*

36. Augustine, *s.* 360B.17 (Dolbeau, 25: 259.335): *accipe de scripturis ubi ars medici scripta est; s.* 360B.18 (Dolbeau, 25: 260.361–362): *Audi medicum pendentem in cruce: circumspecta turba saeuientium phreneticorum.*

37. Augustine, *s.* 360B.17 (Dolbeau, 25: 259.344): *Ideo humilis uenit deus, ne homini non esset imitandus.*

38. Augustine, *s.* 360B.16 (Dolbeau, 25: 258.321–324); a common theme, see *s.* 88.7, 142.6, *en. Ps.* 48(1).11, 98.3.

39. Augustine, *s.* 360B.17 (Dolbeau, 25: 259.348–52): *Humilitatem medici uides, tumorem superbiae tuae non uides. Inde tibi displicet humilis, superbiae tuae displicet, morbo tuo displicet medicamentum quod tibi dat medicus.*

40. Augustine, *s.* 360B.24 (Dolbeau, 25: 265.493–504).

41. Augustine, *s.* 360B.16 (Dolbeau, 25: 258.314–315): *nondum sani estis, sed adhuc curamini. Salus uestra in spe est, nondum in re;* also *s.* 360B.20 (Dolbeau, 25:

262.414): "so believe then, and walk in faith; your salvation lies in hope"; cf. *ep. Io. tr.* 4.2, 8.13, *Io. eu. tr.* 86.1.3.

42. Augustine, *s.* 360B.16 (Dolbeau, 25: 258.315–316).

43. Augustine, *s.* 360B.25 (Dolbeau, 25: 266.510–512).

44. Augustine, *s.* 360B.26 (Dolbeau, 25: 266.531–532).

45. Augustine, *s.* 360B.25 (Dolbeau, 25: 266.511–520).

46. Augustine, *s.* 360B.26 (Dolbeau, 25: 266.533–534).

47. Augustine, *s.* 360B.20 (Dolbeau, 25: 261.408).

48. Augustine, *s.* 360B.19 (Dolbeau, 25: 261.390–391, 396–397).

49. As noted in the text itself: *Et postquam pagani egressi sunt* (*s.* 360B.27 [Dolbeau, 25: 267.552]); cf. *s.* 49.8 (CCL 41: 620.201–202).

50. Augustine, *s.* 43.6 (CCL 41: 510.111–12): *et modo magnam laudem habet orator, si potuerit ab illo intellegi piscator.*

51. On the varying education levels of Augustine's audiences, see Pellegrino, "General Introduction," 85–88; Brown, *Augustine of Hippo*, 248; Pontet, *L'exégèse de saint Augustin*, 55–62; John C. Cavadini, "Simplifying Augustine," in *Educating People of Faith: Exploring the History of Jewish and Christian Communities*, ed. John H. Van Engen (Grand Rapids, MI: Eerdmans, 2004), 67–68 n.17; Rousseau, "'The Preacher's Audience,'" 391–400; and Ramsey MacMullen, "A Note on *sermo humilis*," *Journal of Theological Studies* n.s. 17 (1966): 108–112, who, in a later article, cautions that references to the poor in fourth-century sermons may require more interpretation than they have previously received ("The Preacher's Audience [AD 350–400]," *Journal of Theological Studies* n.s. 40 [1989]: 503–11). For Augustine adapting his preaching to the needs of his audience, see Éric Rebillard, "Interaction between the Preacher and His Audience: The Case-Study of Augustine's Preaching on Death," *Studia Patristica* 31 (1997): 86–96.

52. Peter Brown describes how "within two years" of his ordination the young priest "was patiently explaining the Creed to the assembled Catholic bishops of Africa! By allowing Augustine to preach, Valerius had infringed on a jealously-guarded privilege of the African hierarchy—that the bishop alone, seated on his raised throne, should expound the Catholic Scriptures" (*Augustine of Hippo*, 132–33; compare Bonner, *St. Augustine*, 115; Lancel, *Augustine*, 159–60). For further details about the council itself, see Jane Merdinger, *Rome and the African Church*, 63–87.

53. Augustine, *f. et symb.* 1.1 (CSEL 41: 3.6–7).

54. Augustine, *f. et symb.* 1.1 (CSEL 41: 3.13–4.5).

55. Augustine, *f. et symb.* 1.1 (CSEL 41: 4.7–10). When it was later his turn to hand over the Creed himself, Augustine similarly exhorted his hearers, "[W]rite it on your hearts" (*in corde scribite*), quoted Rom. 10:10, and proceeded to explain to them, "These words which you have heard are scattered throughout the divine scriptures, but they have been gathered from there and reduced to one short form,

so as not to overload the memories of slower minds, and so that all may be able to state, may be able to retain, what they believe" (*s.* 398 = *Sermo de symbolo ad Catechumenos* 1.1 [CCL 46: 185.10–13]). Compare also *s.* 212–215.

56. Augustine, *f. et symb.* 9.20 (CSEL 41: 26.24–27.3).

57. Augustine, *f. et symb.* 10.23 (CSEL 41: 29.1–2).

58. Augustine, *f. et symb.* 10.23 (CSEL 41: 28.20–22, 29.19–20).

59. Augustine, *f. et symb.* 10.23–24 (CSEL 41: 29.18–19).

60. Augustine, *f. et symb.* 10.24 (CSEL 41: 31.12): *gradibus ducendus est ad fidem.*

61. Van der Meer, *Augustine the Bishop,* 418–19.

62. Augustine, *s.* 16A.1 (CCL 41: 218.16–18). Note the familiar terminology of the Hellenistic schools that continually appealed to precepts, examples, and remedies. Precepts and examples, however, are now drawn from scripture and take on their particular healing capacity in the context of the sacraments. For the church as a school, see also *s.* 2.5, 32.2, 33A.4, 52.13, 74.1, 122.3, 177.2, 261.2; *en. Ps.* 90(2).1, 98.1.

63. Augustine, *s.* 16A.1 (CCL 41: 218.18–20): *Sunt ista medicamenta uulnerum nostrorum, et formenta studiorum nostrorum;* cf. *s.* 179A.7 (PLS 2: 715): "you are being cured in the church."

64. Augustine, *s.* 399.15 (CCL 46: 223.382–385).

65. Augustine, *s.* 179.7 (PL 38: 970); cf. *en. Ps.* 131.1 (CCL 40: 1911.7–8): "Within the one charity, we are all listeners to our one teacher in heaven."

66. Augustine, *s.* 153.1 (PL 38: 825).

67. Augustine, *s.* 270.3 (PL 38: 1240): *Scripturarum tractatores dicimur, non nostrarum opinionum affirmatores;* cf. *s.* 42.1 (CCL 41: 504.4–7): "My powers, brothers and sisters, are slight, but infinitely great are those of God's word. Give it free rein in your hearts. Then what I say rather feebly you can hear strongly, if you carry it out. The Lord has thundered at us through the prophet Isaiah as from his storm cloud"; or conversely his assertion that whenever bishops "speak not the words of God, not the words of Christ but our own, we shall be shepherds feeding ourselves, not the sheep" (*s.* 46.8 [CCL 41: 534.171–535.173]).

68. Augustine, *s.* 40.5 (PL 38: 245): *audi Scripturam sanctam praedicentem;* cf. *s.* 51.1 (PL 38: 332): "What I have to say to you is God's word and not mine"; *s.* 95.1 (PL 38: 581): "What I am dishing out to you is not mine. What you eat, I eat; what you live on, I live on"; *s.* 156.13 (PL 38: 857): "This is not what Augustine says; it is the Lord who says it"; *s.* 229E.4 (PLS 2: 561): "What we are setting before you is not being brought from our storeroom, but from his. We too live off it, for we are your fellow servants"; *Io. eu. tr.* 5.1 (CCL 36: 40.3–4): "For then, the things that we say, if they are useful for us and for you, are from him."

69. Augustine, *s.* 306B.2 (MA 1: 91.20–21). Due to this carefully crafted mutuality, any description of those hearing Augustine's sermons as "audience" is quite misleading.

70. Augustine, *s.* 270.1 (PL 38: 1237), *s.* 23.2, 261.2; *Io. eu. tr.* 16.3.1. See also his comment, "learn with me from the one who is teaching me" (*s.* 48.8 [CCL 41: 610.129).

71. Augustine, *s.* 179.1 (PL 38: 966).

72. Augustine, *s.* 244.2 (PL 38: 1149); cf. *s.* 23.1 (CCL 41: 309.12–14): "We bishops are called teachers, but in many matters we seek a teacher ourselves, and we certainly do not want to be regarded as masters."

73. Augustine, *s.* 179.1–2 (PL 38: 966–67).

74. Augustine, *ep. Io. tr.* 3.13.2 (SC 75: 210); cf. *s.* 52.18 (PL 38: 361): "I am not requiring you just to believe what I am about to say; do not accept anything I say unless you find it in yourself."

75. Augustine, *ep. Io. tr.* 3.13.2 (SC 75: 210): *Magisteria forinsecus, adjutoria quaedam sunt, et admonitiones;* a theme from his early *mag.* (see chapter 4) that informs his homilies.

76. Augustine, *ep. Io. tr.* 3.13.2 (SC 75: 210).

77. Augustine, *ep. Io. tr.* 3.13.3, 4.1.1 (SC 75: 212, 218). A theme Augustine takes from 1 Cor. 3:6–7; see also *Io. eu. tr.* 80.2.2, 97.1.3, *s.* 43.8, 102.2, 152.1, 153.1, 224.3, 260B.1, 376A.2.

78. Augustine, *s.* 399.1 (CCL 46: 208.28–31); cf. *s.* 126.8.

79. Augustine, *s.* 9.10 (CCL 41: 127.384–385).

80. Augustine, *ep. Io. tr.* 3.13.2, 4.1.1 (SC 75: 210, 218).

81. Augustine, *Io. eu. tr.* 98.5 (CCL 36: 579.5–10); cf. *en. Ps.* 38.6 (CCL 38: 408.46–49): "I know that . . . only those who have tasted the realities of which I speak understand me perfectly. Nonetheless, we speak to all of you, to those who have such a longing and to those who do not yet have it."

82. Augustine, *Io. eu. tr.* 97.5 (CCL 36: 575.40–576.7), citing 1 Cor. 3:1–2.

83. Augustine, *Io. eu. tr.* 98.4.1 (CCL 36: 578.2–7), reading Heb. 5:12–14.

84. Augustine, *en. Ps.* 38.3 (CCL 38: 405.69–70).

85. Augustine, *Io. eu. tr.* 97.1.3 (CCL 36: 573.45–49).

86. Augustine, *Io. eu. tr.* 98.1.2 (CCL 36: 576.14–19).

87. Augustine, *Io. eu. tr.* 98.3.1 (CCL 36: 577.1–2, 4–6). Thus, Augustine asserts that the one who advocates views beyond what is contained in "the rule of faith does not go forward in the way but goes back from the way" (*Io. eu. tr.* 98.7.4 [CCL 36: 581.45–46]). See Cavadini's study for the continuity between Augustine's "exoteric" sermons and that of his more formal "esoteric" treatises ("Simplifying Augustine," 63–84).

88. Augustine, *Io. eu. tr.* 98.2.1 (CCL 36: 576.1–2), 98.3.2 (CCL 36: 578.24–26) (citing 1 Cor. 1:30–31).

89. Augustine, *Io. eu. tr.* 98.6.2 (CCL 36: 580.22–23): *Christus autem crucifixus, et lac sugentibus, et cibus est proficientibus.*

90. Augustine, *Io. eu. tr.* 98.6.1 (CCL 36: 579.5–7).

91. Augustine, *Io. eu. tr.* 98.7.1 (CCL 36: 580.4–6): *magis magisque inhaerete Mediatori, per quem liberamini a malo, quod non est a uobis loco separandum, sed in uobis potius est sanandum.*

92. Augustine, *Io. eu. tr.* 97.1.1 (CCL 36: 573.18–20), explaining John 16:12–13.

93. Augustine, *Io. eu. tr.* 97.1.1 (CCL 36: 573.13–15).

94. Augustine, *Io. eu. tr.* 96.4.3 (CCL 36: 571.31–34): "I do not think that his words, "'He will teach you all truth,' or 'He will guide you in all truth' can be fulfilled in this life in anyone's mind"; cf. *Io. eu. tr.* 98.8.1 (CCL 36: 581.5–7): "If he wanted to open these to them in the same way as they are perceived in him by the angels, the human weakness in which they still were could not endure this."

95. Augustine, *Io. eu. tr.* 96.1.2 (CCL 36: 568.12–569.13).

96. Augustine, *Io. eu. tr.* 96.2.2–3.2. Augustine notes that even what the apostles did write down is beyond the capacity of many to bear (*Io. eu. tr.* 96.3.2).

97. Augustine, *Io. eu. tr.* 96.4.2 (CCL 36: 571.16–19).

98. Augustine, *Io. eu. tr.* 96.4.1 (CCL 36: 571.11–12); cf. *s.* 23.13.

99. Augustine, *Io. eu. tr.* 96.4.1 (CCL 36: 571.5–9).

100. Augustine, *Io. eu. tr.* 97.1.1 (CCL 36: 572.6–9).

101. Augustine, *Io. eu. tr.* 96.4.2 (CCL 36: 571.18–24), citing John 6:45.

102. Augustine, *Io. eu. tr.* 97.1.1 (CCL 36: 572.3–573.12), citing 2 Cor. 1:22 and 1 Cor. 2:9.

103. Neil McLynn, "Augustine's Roman Empire," *Augustinian Studies* 30 (1999): 36. McLynn continues, "Augustine lacked the social authority to bring his intellectual weight to bear upon even the gentry of Hippo, who could slip away from his sermons to belittle him at parties to which he was never invited" (42); cf. O'Donnell, "Augustine was a less important person in his world than in the intellectual history we have constructed since" (*Augustine*, 112).

104. Brown, *Augustine of Hippo*, 446. In reflecting on his own earlier works, Brown states, "I have found the Augustine of the Dolbeau sermons and of the Divjak letters to be considerably less the authoritarian, stern figure than my reading of the evidence available to me in the 1960s had led me to suspect" (445).

105. Brown, *Augustine of Hippo*, 457. See Michael C. McCarthy's description of how an anachronistic emphasis on the authority of Augustine's writings has caused subsequent generations to overlook the fact that Augustine's authority was most typically exercised in his preaching ("'We are Your Books': Augustine, the Bible, and the Practice of Authority," *Journal of the American Academy of Religion* 75 [2007]: 324–52).

106. Augustine, *s.* 51.2 (PL 38: 334); cf. *en. Ps.* 30(4).11, 32(2).1.

107. Augustine, *s.* 51.2 (PL 38: 333–34); cf. "Do not think, brothers and sisters, that the Lord, our God, has sent us away without spectacles; for if there are no spectacles, why have you come together today?" (*Io. eu. tr.* 7.6.4 [CCL 36: 70.24–26]).

For a discussion of Augustine's critique of Roman theater, see Donnalee Dox, *The Idea of the Theater in Latin Christian Thought: Augustine to the Fourteenth Century* (Ann Arbor: University of Michigan Press, 2004), 11–29. For the civic function of theater in Roman late antiquity and its competition with the evolving role of urban bishops, see Blake Leyerle, *Theatrical Shows and Ascetic Lives: John Chrysostom's Attack on Spiritual Marriage* (Berkeley: University of California Press, 2001).

108. Augustine, *s.* 51.1 (PL 38: 333): *et pro his qui nondum intenti sunt spectaculis ueritatis, sed dediti sunt spectaculis carnis;* cf. *en. Ps.* 39.16 (CCL 38: 438.41–43): "These are the Christian shows (*spectacula christiana*). God himself watches from on high, encourages us to participate, and gives us his help; he sets the prizes for the contests and awards them at the end."

109. Augustine, *s.* 51.2 (PL 38: 333–34): *quia et ipse spectatus est. . . . Illius corpus erigebatur in cruce: ille mentes cruci subdebat.*

110. Augustine, *s.* 51.2 (PL 38: 334); cf. *s.* 301A.7 (MA 1: 87.10–11): "Compare with this holy spectacle the pleasures and delights of the theaters. There the eyes are defiled, here the heart is purified." See also *s.* 49.11, 142.7, *en. Ps.* 39.8–9.

111. Augustine, *s.* 51.13 (PL 38: 340).

112. Augustine, *s.* 114B.1 (Dolbeau, 5: 435.3–5); *s.* 352.1, *en. Ps.* 138.1. For the premeditation that ordinarily preceded the homily, see *s.* 225.3 as well as the discussions by Roy J. Deferrari, "St. Augustine's Method of Composing and Delivering Sermons," *American Journal of Philology* 43 (1922): 97–123, 193–219 and G. W. Doyle, "Augustine's Sermonic Method," *Westminster Theological Journal* 39 (1977): 213–38.

113. *conuersi ad dominum.* For example, see Augustine, *s.* 15A, 16A, 16B, 18, 23A, 26, 30, 63, 67, 69, 76, 87, 100, 106, 111, 113, 113A, 113B, 122, 124, 127, 128, 129, 131, 136C, 138, 141, 145, 151, 153, 154, 155, 156, 162A, 163, 163B, 164, 165, 169, 173, 174, 175, 180, 182, 183, 234, 235, 254, 256, 272, 308A, 313D, 313F, 314, 320, 323, 324, 335A, 362, 399, etc. Van der Meer refers to this common ending as "the old fixed formula" (*Augustine the Bishop*, 397). See also Dolbeau's observations on the liturgical function of the formula "*conuersi ad dominum*" (*Vingt-six sermons*, 171–75 [translated without notes by Hill, *Sermons* 3.11, 128–30 n. 35]).

114. Augustine, *en. Ps.* 64.6 (CCL 39: 827.7–12); cf. *en. Ps.* 50.10 (CCL 38: 607.35–36): "Human beings are conceived in iniquity, and nourished on sins by their mothers while still in the womb."

115. Augustine, *s.* 4.2 (CCL 41: 20.21–24).

116. Augustine, *s.* 2.3 (CCL 41: 12.104–105).

117. Augustine, *s.* 399.10 (CCL 46: 218.259–260).

118. Augustine, *s.* 17.3 (CCL 41: 238.54–55).

119. Augustine, *s.* 142.3 (PLS 2: 727–728).

120. Augustine, *en. Ps.* 57.4 (CCL 39: 712.36–38).

121. Augustine, *s.* 52.17 (PL 38: 361). See also *s.* 13.7, 16A.7, 19.4, 34.7, 42.3, 47.23, 49.8, 52.22, 107.9, 142.3, *en. Ps.* 70(1).14, *ep. Io. tr.* 8.9.2, *passim.*

122. Augustine, *Io. eu. tr.* 18.10.1 (CCL 36: 186.6–7): *primo redi ad cor tuum, exsul a te uagaris foris; teipsum non nosti, et quaeris a quo factus es! Redi, redi ad cor.*

123. Augustine, *s.* 17.5 (CCL 41: 241.117–119).

124. Augustine, *s.* 17.5 (CCL 41: 241.120–121); cf. *s.* 399.6 (CCL 46: 213.167–168): "I was discussing what you really were; you have been found out, been shown up to yourself; you have seen yourself, taken a look at yourself"; *Io. eu. tr.* 18.5.1 (CCL 36: 182.5–6): "Now I agitate you by my inquiry, now I rouse you up against yourself, and I summon you to give witness against yourself."

125. Augustine, *s.* 142.3 (PLS 2: 728).

126. Augustine, *s.* 289.5 (PL 38: 1311): "How utterly feeble humanity is; we need a lamp to look for the daylight!" Elsewhere, he describes the light of Christ as being so intense that "bleary-eyed hearts could not take it." Instead "they were provided with the solace of a lamp, so that the lamp might bear witness to the daylight." He queried, "After all, could you endure him, if he was openly revealed?" (*s.* 379.5, 7 [Cyrille Lambot, "Sermons inédits de S. Augustin pour des fêtes de saints," *Revue Bénédictine* 59 (1949): 65.10, 68.17]).

127. Augustine, *en. Ps.* 54.24 (CCL 39: 674.5–8); cf. *en. Ps.* 38.3 (CCL 38: 405.69–72).

128. Augustine, *s.* 117.16 (PL 38: 670).

129. Augustine, *Io. eu. tr.* 35.9 (CCL 36: 322.21–323.24).

130. 2 Pet. 1:19; cf. *en. Ps.* 51.13, 76.4, 89.15, 118(23).1, *Io. eu. tr.* 23.3.1, 35.8, *s.* 49.3, 126.1, 210.6, 223D.3. For the resonance of this image within the traditions of Greek philosophy, it is worth recalling the celebrated image of Diogenes of Sinope walking the streets of Athens with a lamp saying that he was searching for a human being (recounted by Diogenes Laertius, *Vit. phil.* 6.41 [LCL 185: 42]).

131. Augustine, *s.* 126.1; cf. *s.* 189.1 (PL 38: 1005): "This night, you see, is passing, the night in which we are living now, in which the lamps of the scriptures are lit for us." For images and analysis of the actual ceramic lamps to which Augustine likens Christian scripture, see John J. Herrmann, Jr. and Annewies van den Hoek, *Light from the Age of Augustine: Late Antique Ceramics from North Africa,* 1st ed. (Cambridge, MA: Harvard Divinity School, 2002); 2d ed. (Austin: Institute for the Study of Antiquity and Christian Origins of the University of Texas at Austin, 2003).

132. Augustine, *s.* 289.6 (PL 38: 1311); cf. *s.* 317.4 (PL 38: 1436): "The house is the world, the lampstand is the cross of Christ, the lamp shining from the lampstand is Christ hanging on the cross." See also the manner in which he likens Christian preachers to lamps as they tend "the light of the word of truth in order to enlighten other people" (*s.* 46.5 [CCL 41: 532.100–102]), and *s.* 380.7, *Io. eu. tr.* 23.2.2.

133. Augustine, *s.* 4.10 (CCL 41: 27.219–221); cf. *s.* 47.9 (CCL 41: 580.254–255): "We all know, do we not, how quietly and gently scripture itself teaches us."

134. Augustine, *s.* 17.2 (CCL 41: 238.34–36). A common admonition in Augustine's preaching: "Use the holy scriptures like a mirror. This mirror has a reflective sheen that does not lie, a sheen that does not flatter, that does not respect the person of anyone. You are beautiful, you see yourself beautiful; you are ugly, you see yourself ugly. But when you come in front of it in your ugliness and see yourself ugly, do not blame the mirror. Go back to yourself, the mirror is not deceiving you, take care you do not deceive yourself. Pass judgment on yourself, be sorry about your ugliness, and so as you turn away and go off sorry and ugly, you may be able to correct yourself and come back beautiful" (*s.* 49.5 [CCL 41: 617.115–23]; see also *s.* 147A.3, 154A.2, 301A.1, 306B.4, *Io. eu. tr.* 10.7.2, *en. Ps.* 30(4).1, 103(1).4, 106.1, 118(4).3, 123.3). Augustine made similar statements about the function of sermons and creedal affirmations derived from scripture. Concerning the Creed, he instructed, "Call your faith to mind, look at yourself; treat your Creed as your own personal mirror. Observe yourself there, if you believe all the things you confess to believing, and rejoice every day in your faith. Let these be your riches, let them be in a kind of way the everyday clothes of the mind" (*s.* 58.13 [PL 38: 399]). Of his own preaching, moreover, he can say: "In all my sermons I am presenting you with a mirror. They are not my sermons, anyway; I only speak at the Lord's command" (*s.* 82.15 [PL 38: 513]).

135. See especially, chapters 4 and 6, and *doctr. chr.* 4.4.6, 4.13.29.

136. Hildegund Müller writes, "The structural qualities of Augustine's homiletic style are not mere literary values; they are obviously meant to have a direct impact on the recipients. Augustine forces his readers to join in, to permit themselves to be led along an emotional path of the preacher's making" ("Theory and Practice of Preaching: Augustine, *De doctrina christiana* and *Enarrationes in psalmos*," *Studia Patristica* 38 [2001]: 236).

137. Augustine, *s.* 32.1 (CCL 41: 398.1–9).

138. This conspicuous feature of the homilies has been previously noted. Willis states, "St. Augustine was a thoroughly liturgical preacher, whose addresses are very frequently based upon the readings of the day, and who makes constant references to lessons which have just been read" (*St. Augustine's Lectionary*, 12). Van der Meer remarks, "Augustine preached out of, with, and by means of, the Bible" (*Augustine the Bishop*, 405). Pontet writes poignantly that "la point de départ unique— ou presque— de la prédication de saint Augustin se trouve dans la Bible lue et chantée. L'orateur commente ce qui vient d'être entendu par tous" (*L'exégèse de saint Augustin*, 219); cf. Cavadini, "Simplifying Augustine," esp. 71–74.

139. Augustine, *s.* 36.1 (CCL 41: 434.7–9).

140. Augustine, *Io. eu. tr.* 4.15 (CCL 36: 39.16–17).

141. Augustine, *s.* 52.3, 8.17, 49.2, 261.2, 360B.12, *Io. eu. tr.* 18.6.2.

142. Augustine, *Io. eu. tr.* 4.16 (CCL 36: 39.8–9).

143. Augustine, *s.* 32.1–2 (CCL 41: 398.11–15, 31–35).

144. Augustine, *s.* 32.5 (CCL 41: 400.81–83).

145. Augustine, *s.* 32.26 (CCL 41: 410.444–446).

146. Augustine, *s.* 32.12 (CCL 41: 404.235–237).

147. Augustine, *s.* 32.26 (CCL 41: 410.446–450).

148. Augustine, *s.* 32.4–5 (CCL 41: 400.73–79, 91–95); cf. *en. Ps.* 45.13 (CCL 38: 527.41–528.43): "Throw away the weapons you relied on, and listen to the Lord telling you, 'My grace is sufficient for you.' You too must say, 'When I am weak, then I am strong'" (2 Cor. 12:9–10).

149. See also *en. Ps.* 33(1).4 (CCL 38: 276.13–27).

150. Augustine, *s.* 32.12 (CCL 41: 404.239–405.241).

151. Augustine, *s.* 32.9 (CCL 41: 403.180–186).

152. See where Augustine discusses how "anyone inexperienced listening to the divine scriptures" becomes confused and rendered mute by such an effort (*s.* 32.6 [CCL 41: 401.115–129]).

153. Recall how Augustine noted that some sayings in the scriptures appear to be covered in "a dense fog . . . in order to conquer pride with hard labor" (*doctr. chr.* 2.6.7 [CCL 32: 35.1–7]).

154. Augustine, *s.* 32.22 (CCL 41: 408.369–371); cf. *s.* 32.18 (CCL 41: 407.315–317): Augustine's similar statement that the Philistines "placed all their happiness in temporal things, all their enjoyment in shadows, not in the light itself, nor in the truth itself."

155. Augustine, *s.* 32.18 (CCL 41: 407.317–318).

156. Augustine, *s.* 9.3 (CCL 41: 109.78–79): *Sermo dei aduersarius tuus est.* A subject Augustine associates with Matt. 5:25; see also *s.* 40.5, 109.2–4, 251.7, 387.1.

157. Augustine, *s.* 109.3 (PL 38: 637): *Quamdiu tu tibi inimicus es, inimicum habes sermonem Dei.*

158. Augustine, *s.* 9.4 (CCL 41: 115.164–165): *Ita inuadens omnia consuetudo pro lege obseruatur;* cf. *s.* 392.4–5.

159. Augustine, *s.* 9.5; cf. *s.* 109.4, 387.3.

160. Augustine, *s.* 9.10; cf. *ep. Io. tr.* 6.8.

161. Augustine, *s.* 9.9 (CCL 41: 124.333–125.334): *corrigeris, et diriges in eam regulam cor tuum, a qua nunc alienus distortus es.*

162. See, for example, *Io. eu. tr.* 4.16 (CCL 36: 39.3–4): "But you should know that this question is of such a kind that it alone (*haec sola*) could destroy the sect of Donatus."

163. Augustine, *s.* 49.11 (CCL 41: 623.281–282); cf. *s.* 229J.2.

164. Augustine, *s.* 49.8 (CCL 41: 620.210): *Obserua te, attende te.*

165. Augustine, *s.* 49.7 (CCL 41: 619.176–620.188).

166. Augustine, *s.* 49.9 (CCL 41: 621.223–226).

167. Augustine, *s.* 49.8 (CCL 41: 620.211–621.212).

168. Augustine, *Io. eu. tr.* 19.7.3 (CCL 36: 191.15–192.18): "Therefore there is peace in the scripture, and all things have been set in order, not at all in conflict.

But you, cast aside the strife of the heart (*litem cordis*); understand the harmony of the scriptures."

169. Augustine, *s.* 16B.1 (CCL 41: 231.10–11); cf. *Io. eu. tr.* 8.10.2 (CCL 36: 89.22–24): "What is more, not only did Christ not have what you call fate, but neither do you, nor I, nor that man, nor any man at all."

170. Augustine, *s.* 16B.2 (CCL 41: 232.52–53): *Conuerte ergo te ab ista peruersitate. Esto correctus, et incipe contradicere tibi, et a contrario tibi loqui.* See the discussion of Augustine's "Stoic cognitivism" by Sarah C. Byers, "Augustine and the Cognitive Cause of Stoic 'Preliminary Passions' (*Propatheiai*)," *Journal of the History of Philosophy* 41 (2003): 433–48.

171. Augustine, *s.* 16B.2 (CCL 41: 232.48–52).

172. Augustine, *s.* 16B.4 (CCL 41: 234.123–124).

173. Augustine, *Io. eu. tr.* 18.7 (CCL 36: 184.8–10).

174. Augustine, *s.* 16A.2 (CCL 41: 219.68–69): *Quae, uidetis fratres, quae statera cordis facienda est.*

175. Augustine, *s.* 117.3 (PL 38: 663). See also where Augustine states, "The gospel of John exercises our minds, planes them smooth and defleshes (*excarnat*) them, to make sure we think about God in a spiritual, not a fleshly, material kind of way" (*s.* 140.6 [PL 38: 775]).

176. Augustine, *s.* 22.7 (CCL 41: 297.201–202): *Ergo pro facie dei, tibi pone interim scripturam dei. Liquesce ab illa.*

177. Augustine, *s.* 56.10 (PL 38: 381), cf. *s.* 37.11 (CCL 41: 457.261–263): "The one who speaks the word to us every day (*quotidie*), you see, is thereby as it were pouring in oil to save the lamps from going out"; *s.* 45.3 (CCL 41: 518.105–106): "scripture never stops warning us every day" (*cotidie*); *s.* 350A.1 (MA 1: 292.2–3): "I am certainly aware that the hearts of your graces are well and truly fed every day on the exhortations of the divine readings and the nourishment of the word of God." Of the eucharist as well he will say to the newly baptized, "You ought to know what you have received, what you are about to receive, what you ought to receive every day" (*quotidie*) (*s.* 227 [PL 38: 1099]).

178. Augustine, *s.* 5.1 (CCL 41: 50.1–2): *Haec maxime regula disciplinae necessaria est uiro christiano, ut uerbum dei audiat cum est in isto saeculo.*

179. Augustine, *en. Ps.* 32(3).1, 9 (CCL 38: 257.1–8, 261.4–5).

180. Augustine, *s.* 5.1 (CCL 41: 50.17–23); cf. *s.* 49.2 (CCL 41: 614.26–28): "You know what the work is, but I will remind you. Listen to what you know, and do what you hear"; *s.* 131.5 (PL 38: 731): "Listen then to what you know already; I am not teaching you, just reminding you by preaching it"; *en. Ps.* 61.7 (CCL 39: 777.6–7): "I am going to tell you something you know already, something to which you will give your assent. I am going to remind you of a truth already familiar to you; I am not teaching you anything you have not heard before"; *en. Ps.* 90(2).1 (CCL 39: 1265.13–14): "Dearly beloved, we have reminded you of these truths very often, but we are never tired of repeating them."

181. Augustine, *Io. eu. tr.* 100.4.1 (CCL 36: 590.2): *catholicis audite auribus, catholicis percipite mentibus.* Augustine commonly points out ways in which scripture uses linguistic expressions that depart from our customary usage. The scriptures have their own customary usage (*consuetudo scripturarum*) that readers are to learn (*Io. eu. tr.* 42.7, 10 [CCL 36: 368.3, 369.25–26]). Ultimately, scripture "has it own language" (*Io. eu. tr.* 10.2.2 [CCL 36: 101.10]).

182. Augustine, *Io. eu. tr.* 18.11 (CCL 36: 187.1–3): *Puto, fratres, quia cum loquimur ista, et cum meditamur, exercemus nos.*

183. Augustine, *s.* 88.5 (PL 38: 542).

184. Augustine, *en. Ps.* 57.7–11 (CCL 39: 714.1–718.21).

185. Augustine, *Io. eu. tr.* 18.11 (CCL 36: 187.3–17). Note that Augustine begins this sermon by observing that Christ's words were "written down that they might also be read by us afterwards. Therefore . . . let us consider more fully what happens in us when we hear these words" (*Io. eu. tr.* 18.1.1 [CCL 36: 180.22–25]).

186. Augustine, *en. Ps.* 121.2 (CCL 40: 1802.26–38).

187. Augustine, *en. Ps.* 122.2 (CCL 40: 1815.2); cf. *s.* 29A.4 (CCL 41: 380.81): "Listen to the psalm, and if you are wide awake notice your own voice in it."

188. Augustine, *en. Ps.* 121.11 (CCL 40: 1811.4): *Non enim pedibus imus, sed affectibus.* Although its context influences its meaning, note how this Plotinian phrase (*En.* 1.6.8) finds its way into Augustine's homilies as easily as it did into his theoretical writings. See also its homiletic use in *Io. eu. tr.* 32.1.

189. Augustine, *en. Ps.* 120.3 (CCL 40: 1787.1–3); cf. *s.* 142.1 (PL 38: 778): *Erigunt nos diuinae lectiones; s.* 350A.3 (PLS 2: 450): "See for yourselves whether the divine utterances have any other effect but that we should love; see whether they work toward anything else but to set us on fire, to inflame us, to kindle our desire, to get us sighing and groaning until we finally arrive."

190. Augustine, *en. Ps.* 103(1).11 (CCL 40: 1484.15–18).

191. Augustine, *en. Ps.* 121.1 (CCL 40: 1801.12–15).

192. Augustine, *en. Ps.* 121.8 (CCL 40: 1808.24–26): *Tunc est, quando uidet Deum. Tunc enim est, quando uidet eum qui est; et uidendo eum qui est, fit et ipse pro modo suo ut sit.*

193. Rom. 5:5. A favorite text of Augustine's throughout his life. Carol Harrison counts some 200 citations (*Christian Truth and Fractured Humanity,* 96 n.33). Even when he does not quote it explicitly, it echoes in the background. For example, see where he states, "Pay attention, therefore, and see how the Holy Spirit is going to come at Pentecost. . . . You see, he breathes into us the charity which should set us on fire for God, and have us think lightly of the world, and burn up our straw, and purge and refine our hearts like gold" (*s.* 227 [PL 38: 1100]). For a detailed discussion, see *trin.* 15.17.31–15.19.37.

194. Augustine, *s.* 350A.1 (MA 1: 292.15–16): *Caritas enim innouat hominem.*

195. Augustine, *s.* 350.3 (PL 39: 1535).

196. And many other practices including, among others—almsgiving (*s.* 9.17–21, 86.1–17, 164A), prayer and fasting (*s.* 9.17, 125.9, 207.1–3, 210.3–5), the kiss of peace (*s.* 227), the Lord's prayer (*s.* 49.8)—intended to engage and persuade not only the mind, but the whole human person.

197. Augustine, *Io. eu. tr.* 12.5.3 (CCL 36: 123.21–22): "A psalm sounds forth; it is the Spirit's voice. The gospel sounds forth; it is the Spirit's voice. God's word sounds forth; it is the Spirit's voice."

198. Augustine, *s.* 34.3 (CCL 41: 424.36–38).

199. Augustine, *Io. eu. tr.* 102.5 (CCL 36: 597.6–13); cf. *conf.* 13.31.46, and *en. Ps.* 127.8.

200. Augustine, *s.* 71.23 (PL 38: 457), *s.* 144.1 (PL 38: 788).

201. Augustine, *Io. eu. tr.* 18.6.3 (CCL 36: 184.41): "Put earthly things on Earth. Lift up your heart" (*sursum cor*); *s.* 52.15 (PL 38: 360): "The godhead is beyond material localization. . . . It is present everywhere, invisible and inseparable; not more in one part, less in another, but everywhere whole, nowhere divided. . . . Let the heart be stirred, the heart be lifted up to the mystery"; *s.* 56.16 (PL 38: 385): "Why always drag your heart along the ground? Listen; lift up your heart (*sursum cor*), stretch it; love your enemies"; *s.* 177.9 (PL 38: 959): "So lift your heart up (*sursum cor*), do not leave it down on the ground." See also *s.* 25.2, 7; 53.14–15; 68.6, 13; 86.1; 105.11; 165.4; 176.6; 177.5–9; 227; 229.3; 229A.3; 233.4; 237.3; 261.1; 296.7; 311.15; 330.2; 331.3; 345.5; 380.4; 395.1; 399.5; 114B.14 (Dolbeau, 5: 446.333); and *en. Ps.* 10.3; 31(2).21; 37.10; 39.28; 68(2).7; 85.6; 90(2).13; 93.2, 29; 96.10; 148.5.

202. Augustine, *Io. eu. tr.* 9.3.1–2 (CCL 36: 92.9–18).

203. Augustine, *Io. eu. tr.* 80.3.1 (CCL 36: 529.5–7): "The word is added to the elemental substance, and it becomes a sacrament, also itself, as it were, a visible word" (*uisibile uerbum*); cf. *c. Faust.* 19.16 (CSEL 25.1: 513.7–9): "After all, what else are certain material sacraments but certain visible words?"

204. Augustine, *Io. eu. tr.* 15.4.2 (CCL 36: 152.10–11).

205. Augustine, *en. Ps.* 68(2).7 (CCL 39: 923.5–10).

206. Augustine, *Io. eu. tr.* 17.5 (CCL 36: 172.6–7): *Significationibus pascimur, ut ad res ipsas praeuentae sunt;* cf. *en. Ps.* 146.8 (CCL 40: 2127.6–11): "These temporal sacred signs (*temporalia sacramenta*) that comfort us in this in-between time are the medicinal dressing suited to our condition. All the sermons we preach to you, the words that are heard and then fade away, all the temporal actions performed in the Church, are dressings applied to our wounds."

207. Augustine, *en. Ps.* 121.8 (CCL 40: 1808.43–45).

208. Augustine, *en. Ps.* 122.6 (CCL 40: 1819.28–29).

209. Augustine, *s.* 109.1 (PL 38: 636) since they were not only vulnerable to shattering accidents, but to decay as well.

210. Augustine, *en. Ps.* 122.2 (CCL 40: 1815.22–32); cf. *en. Ps.* 122.11 (CCL 40: 1823.18–19): "Even when we are healthy, let us realize that we are weak."

211. Augustine, *en. Ps.* 121.8 (CCL 40: 1809.65–66): *ad hoc adscendunt, ad confitendum nomini tuo, Domine* (Ps. 122.4); *en. Ps.* 38.18 (CCL 38: 419.43–44): "The first grace that God in his kindness confers on us is to bring us to confess our weakness"; cf. *s.* 76.6–7.

212. Cf. Augustine, *s.* 36.11; 58.6; 60A.4; 115.2–3; 136A.2–3; 136B.2; 169.9; 290.6; 29B.3 (Dolbeau, 8: 25.52–57); and *en. Ps.* 31(2).10–12: 58(1).7; 70(1).4; 74.10; 84.14; 90(1).6; 93.15; 105.2; 110.3; 128.9.

213. Augustine, *s.* 16B.4 (CCL 41: 233).

214. Augustine, *en. Ps.* 122.1 (CCL 40: 1814.5–8).

215. Augustine, *Io. eu. tr.* 123.4 (CCL 36: 677.27–28): "Now indeed by his gift let strength of heart (*firmitas cordis*), a true one, be taken up for undergoing death in the Lord's name. Let not a false strength be presumed by us in error"; *en. Ps.* 38.18 (CCL 38: 418.9–10): "There is a kind of strength that is really a vice"; *en. Ps.* 120.14 (CCL 40: 1800.31): "Let none of us rely on ourselves"; see also *s.* 145.4, 156.10.

216. Augustine, *s.* 150.5. As told by Augustine while commenting on Acts 17:18–34, these are the options presented by Epicureans and Stoics respectively; he told his audience, however, that such a choice was not merely about the merits of philosophical schools, but about ways of living.

217. Augustine, *s.* 150.9 (PL 38: 812).

218. Augustine, *s.* 348.3 (PL 39: 1528).

219. Augustine, *s.* 348.3 (PL 39: 1528). Augustine is particularly critical of the kind of autonomy he believes this strategy fosters: "What does 'calling themselves wise' (Rom. 1:24) mean, after all, but saying that they get it from themselves, they are self-sufficient" (*sibi sufficere*) (*s.* 150.9 [PL 38: 813]); "These too are being seduced by that proud enemy of souls . . . through the arrogance of human self-sufficiency, which stops them from seeking again in humility the one from whom they fell away in pride" (*s.* 198.36 [Dolbeau, 26: 394.857–859]).

220. Augustine, *en. Ps.* 122.6 (CCL 40: 1819.37–38).

221. Augustine, *s.* 348.3 (PL 39: 1528–29); cf. *Io. eu. tr.* 60.3.

222. Augustine, *en. Ps.* 122.6 (CCL 40: 1819.38–39).

223. Augustine, *s.* 150.8 (PL 38: 812). For further discussion, see John C. Cavadini, "The Darkest Enigma: Reconsidering the Self in Augustine's Thought," *Augustinian Studies* 38 (2007): 119–32.

224. Augustine, *ep. Io. tr.* 7.11.2 (SC 75: 334).

225. Augustine, *en. Ps.* 38.17 (CCL 38: 418.21–29).

226. Augustine, *ep. Io. tr.* 9.4.2 (SC 75: 386).

227. Augustine, *s.* 229A.3 (MA 1: 464.18): *Commemorate uos quod estis.*

228. Augustine, *en. Ps.* 66.4 (CCL 39: 861.27–29): "Do you not know that you have been made in the image of God, O precious soul of the Church redeemed by the blood of the stainless Lamb? Consider how valuable you are"; *en. Ps.* 32(2).4 (CCL 38: 249.3–8): "Do not be downcast and despair of yourselves. You are human

beings made in the image of God, and he who made you human became human himself for your sake. The blood of God's only Son was poured out for you so that you, all of you, might be adopted as a great family of God's children with rights of inheritance. If in your own estimation, you hold yourselves cheap because of your earthly frailty, esteem yourselves precious by reason of the ransom paid for you."

229. Augustine, *s.* 272 (PL 38: 1247); cf. *s.* 57.7 (PL 38: 389): "By being digested into his body and turned into his members we may be what we receive"; *s.* 227 (PL 38: 1099): "You are yourselves what you receive"; *s.* 228B.4 (MA 1: 20.12): "This sacrament, after all, does not present you with the body of Christ in such a way as to divide you from it. . . . So you are beginning to receive what you have also begun to be"; *ciu.* 10.6 (CCL 47: 279.52–55): "This is the sacrifice of Christians . . . which, as the faithful know, the Church continually celebrates in the sacrament of the altar, where it is shown to the Church that she herself is offered in the offering which she presents to God." The relationship between sign and sacrament is complex and resonates throughout Augustine's theology, see Pamela Jackson, "Eucharist," in *Augustine through the Ages: An Encyclopedia*, ed. A. Fitzgerald (Grand Rapids, MI: Eerdmans, 1999), with attendant bibliography, and Joanne McWilliam, "Weaving the Strands Together: A Decade in Augustine's Eucharistic Theology," *Augustiniana* 41 (1991): 497–506.

230. Augustine, *s.* 228B.2 (MA 1: 19.8–9).

231. Augustine, *s.* 272 (PL 38: 1247–48): *Estote quod uidetis, et accipe quod estis.*

Notes to Chapter Eight

1. So Peter Brown, "Augustine never faced the problem of replacing classical education throughout the Roman world. . . . Indeed, like many such 'withdrawals' on Augustine's part, it tacitly took for granted the resilience of the old ways. He hoped to gain some inner detachment from the traditional culture; but he assumed that it would continue" (*Augustine of Hippo,* 265).

2. Henri Marrou, *Saint Augustin et la fin de la culture antique,* esp. 352–55. Compare Press' assertion that Augustine's "polemic against the non-Christian ideal of *doctrina*" is "at the same time the exposition of a true, proper, sound vision of that ideal, a Christian vision of it, which retains the name and much of the form of the old ideal" ("*Doctrina* in Augustine's *De doctrina christiana,*" 113).

3. Margaret Atkins, "Old Philosophy and New Power: Cicero in Fifth-Century North Africa," in *Philosophy and Power in the Graeco-Roman World: Essays in Honour of Miriam Griffin,* ed. Gillian Clark and Tessa Rajak (Oxford and New York: Oxford University Press, 2002), 264.

4. Cicero, *Inu.* 1.2 (LCL 386: 4).

5. Cicero, *Inu.* 1.2 (LCL 386: 4), *N.D.* 2.148–149 (LCL 268: 266); cf. Aristotle, *Pol.* 1.1.10–11 (LCL 264: 10).

6. Cicero, *Inu.* 1.2 (LCL 386: 4): *deinde propter rationem atque orationem studiosius audientes ex feris et immanibus mites reddidit et mansuetos;* cf. *Inu.* 1.5 (LCL 386: 12): "I think that people, although lower and weaker than the animals in many respects, excel them most by having the power of speech."

7. Cicero, *Inu.* 1.5 (LCL 386: 12). Recall the ancient legends of Chiron the centaur whose human head governed his bestial body and was thereby able to guide others in doing the same.

8. Peter Brown, *The Body and Society: Men, Women, and Sexual Renunciation in Early Christianity* (New York: Columbia University Press, 1988), 6. Brown notes the studies of A. R. Burn, "Hic Breve Vivitur," *Past and Present* 4 (1953): 1–31; Keith Hopkins, "On the Probable Age Structure of the Roman Population," *Population Studies* 20 (1966): 245–64; and Bruce W. Frier, "Roman Life Expectancy: Ulpian's Evidence," *Harvard Studies in Classical Philology* 86 (1982): 213–51.

9. Peter Garnsey, "Responses to Food Crisis in the Ancient Mediterranean World," in *Hunger in History: Food Shortage, Poverty, and Deprivation,* ed. Lucille Newman (Cambridge, MA: Basil Blackwell, 1990), 126–46.

10. Cicero, *Inu.* 1.1 (LCL 386: 2).

11. Maximus of Tyre, *Diss.* 37.3 (Trapp, 297: 41–42).

12. Seneca, *Ep.* 31.5.

13. See, for example, the contentions of Plato's Socrates: "A good person is most self-sufficient (αὐτάρκης) when it comes to living well and is distinguished from other people by having the least need of anyone or anything else" (*Rep.* 387e [LCL 237: 206]) and *Mx.* 247e–248a (LCL 234: 374–76): "For that man is best prepared for life who makes all that concerns his welfare depend upon himself, or nearly so, instead of hanging his hopes on other men, whereby with their rise or fall his own fortunes also inevitably sway up or down. . . . Because he puts his trust in himself, he will neither be seen rejoicing nor yet grieving overmuch."

14. Seneca, *Ep.* 33.7 (LCL 75: 236).

15. Augustine, *s.* 360B.26 (Dolbeau, 25: 266.531–532).

16. Phrasing from Augustine's *cat. rud.* 9.13 (CCL 46: 135.12–16).

17. Recall Augustine's description of the "road of the affections" (*doctr. chr.* 1.17.16 [CCL 32: 15.1–7]).

18. Augustine, *s.* 5.4 (CCL 41: 53.130–131): *Et ideo Iacob ille, qui modo lectus est, populum significat christianum.*

19. Augustine, *s.* 5.8 (CCL 41: 59.295–296): *Tactus autem domini manus est domini corripiens et uiuificans.*

20. Augustine, *s.* 5.7–8 (CCL 41: 58.273–59.291).

21. See most recently, Martha Nussbaum, *Upheavals of Thought,* esp. 547–56; O'Donnell, "Augustine's view, elevated and devout, was deeply corrosive when it came to real secular societies" (*Augustine,* 249).

22. Arthur Hilary Armstrong, *St. Augustine and Christian Platonism* (Villanova, PA: Villanova University Press, 1967), 18. The disjunction between Plato's

idealism and the realm of this-worldly facts is too often over-played. Thus, when Machiavelli justifies the novelty of his own realistic approach to politics, he lampoons his predecessors who were content with constructing imaginary utopias (*The Prince* 15; trans. David Wootton, in *Selected Political Writings: Niccolò Machiavelli* [Indianapolis: Hackett, 1994], 48). Neither Plato nor Augustine were utopian in this sense, see Robert Calhoun's still insightful, "Plato as Religious Realist," in *Religious Realism*, ed. D. C. Macintosh (New York: Macmillan, 1931), 195–251. See also Dominic J. O'Meara, *Platonopolis: Platonic Political Philosophy in Late Antiquity* (New York: Oxford University Press, 2003), and Kai Trampedach, *Platon, die Akademie und die zeitgenössische Politik* (Stuttgart: F. Steiner, 1994).

23. Compare Conrad Leyser's statement: "The underlying pastoral purpose of Augustine's point of view was not to induce passivity, but to combat the divisive effects of spiritual elitism" (*Authority and Asceticism from Augustine to Gregory the Great* [Oxford: Clarendon Press, 2000], 7). For contemporary accounts that understand political engagement along Augustinian lines, see Eric Gregory, *Politics and the Order of Love: An Augustinian Ethic of Democratic Citizenship* (Chicago: University of Chicago Press, 2008) and Charles Mathewes, *A Theology of Public Life* (Cambridge: Cambridge University Press, 2007).

24. Robert Dodaro, "Augustine's Secular City," 247; see also his "Augustine's Revision of the Heroic Ideal," *Augustinian Studies* 36 (2005): 141–57; and George Lawless, "Augustine's Decentring of Asceticism," in *Augustine and His Critics*, ed. Dodaro and Lawless, 142–63.

25. Charles Taylor, *The Sources of the Self: The Making of the Modern Identity* (Cambridge, MA: Harvard University Press, 1989), 116. See also Burnaby, *Amor Dei*, 6.

26. Jaroslav Pelikan writes, "Augustine of Hippo occupies a place as the great line of demarcation in the intellectual history of the West. . . . Thus, although Alfred North Whitehead suggested in his Gifford Lectures that the history of Western thought could be read as a 'series of footnotes to Plato,' he could as well have said 'a series of footnotes to Augustine.' For during most of that history Plato has exerted his enormous influence not directly through his own writings, but through Neoplatonism, and this specifically in the form in which it was absorbed, recast, and transmitted by Augustine" (*The Mystery of Continuity: Time and History, Memory and Eternity in the Thought of Saint Augustine* [Charlottesville: University Press of Virginia, 1986], 3, 140).

27. Phrasing is borrowed from Rowan Williams, "Politics and the Soul: A Reading of the *City of God*," *Milltown Studies* 19–20 (1987): 62.

28. Van der Meer, *Augustine the Bishop*, 417.

29. Pierre Hadot, "Patristique Latine," 217 (in *Philosophy as a Way of Life*, 8).

30. Although Augustine's treatises are often shaped by psychagogic concerns; see for example, the gradual leading of the reader in *trin.*

31. See, for example, C. H. Dodd's assertion that "to the ordinary person of intelligence," Augustine's "mystification" of the parable of the Good Samaritan "must appear quite perverse" (*The Parables of the Kingdom,* rev. ed. [New York: Charles Scribner's Sons, 1961], 2).

32. Babcock concludes, "Augustine has preserved the North African tradition's vivid sense for the boundary between the Christian and the non-Christian, but he has transferred that boundary to a terrain in which it is no longer under human control or subject to human definition" ("Christian Culture and Christian Tradition," 46).

Bibliography

Allen, Pauline, and Wendy Mayer. "Through a Bishop's Eyes: Towards a Definition of Pastoral Care in Late Antiquity." *Augustinianum* 40 (2000): 345–97.

Anderson, Graham. *The Second Sophistic: A Cultural Phenomenon in the Roman Empire.* London: Routledge, 1993.

———. "The Second Sophistic: Some Problems of Perspective." In *Antonine Literature,* edited by D. A. Russell. Oxford: Clarendon Press, 1990.

Annas, Julia E. "Philosophical Therapy: Ancient and Modern." In *Bioethics: Ancient Themes in Contemporary Issues,* edited by Mark G. Kuczewski and Ronald Polansky. Basic Bioethics. Cambridge, MA: MIT Press, 2000.

Arbesmann, Rudolph. "The Concept of 'Christus Medicus' in St. Augustine." *Traditio* 10 (1954): 1–28.

Armstrong, Arthur Hilary. "Pagan and Christian Traditionalism in the First Three Centuries A.D." *Studia Patristica* 15 (1984): 414–30.

———. *St. Augustine and Christian Platonism.* The Saint Augustine Lecture Series. Villanova, PA: Villanova University Press, 1967.

Arnold, Duane W. H., and Pamela Bright, eds. *De doctrina christiana: A Classic of Western Culture.* Christianity and Judaism in Antiquity 9. Notre Dame, IN: University of Notre Dame Press, 1994.

Asiedu, Felix B. "The Limits of Augustine's Personal Authority: The Hermeneutics of Trust in *De utilitate credendi.*" In *Augustine and Liberal Education,* edited by Kim Paffenroth and Kevin L. Hughes. Burlington, VT: Ashgate, 2000.

Asmis, Elizabeth. "Philodemus' Epicureanism." ANRW 2.36.4 (1990), 2369–2406.

———. "*Psychagogia* in Plato's Phaedrus." *Illinois Classical Studies* 11 (1986): 153–72.

Atkins, Margaret. "Old Philosophy and New Power: Cicero in Fifth-Century North Africa." In *Philosophy and Power in the Graeco-Roman World: Essays in Honour of Miriam Griffin,* edited by Gillian Clark and Tessa Rajak. Oxford and New York: Oxford University Press, 2002.

Auerbach, Erich. "Sermo Humilis." In *Literary Language and Its Public in Late Latin Antiquity and in the Middle Ages.* Translated by Ralph Manheim. Bollingen Series 74. New York: Pantheon, 1965.

Auksi, Peter. *Christian Plain Style: The Evolution of a Spiritual Ideal.* Montreal and Kingston: McGill-Queen's University Press, 1995.

Ayres, Lewis. "Christology as Contemplative Practice: Understanding the Union of Natures in Augustine's Letter 137." In *In the Shadow of the Incarnation: Essays on Jesus Christ in the Early Church in Honor of Brian E. Daley, S.J.,* edited by Peter W. Martens. Notre Dame, IN: University of Notre Dame Press, 2008.

Babcock, William S. "*Caritas* and Signification in *De doctrina christiana* 1–3." In *De doctrina christiana: A Classic of Western Culture,* edited by Duane W. H. Arnold and Pamela Bright. Christianity and Judaism in Antiquity 9. Notre Dame, IN: University of Notre Dame Press, 1994.

———. "Christian Culture and Christian Tradition in Roman North Africa." In *Schools of Thought in the Christian Tradition,* edited by Patrick Henry. Philadelphia: Fortress Press, 1984.

Bacchi, Lee Francis. "A Ministry Characterized by and Exercised in Humility: The Theology of Ordained Ministry in the Letters of Augustine of Hippo." In *Augustine: Presbyter Factus Sum,* edited by Joseph T. Lienhard, Earl C. Muller, and Roland J. Teske. New York: Peter Lang, 1993.

———. *The Theology of Ordained Ministry in the Letters of Augustine of Hippo.* San Francisco: International Scholars Publications, 1998.

Baratin, Marc. "Les origines stoïciennes de la théorie Augustinienne du signe." *Revue des Études Latines* 59 (1981): 260–68.

Barnes, T. D. "Augustine, Symmachus, and Ambrose." In *Augustine: From Rhetor to Theologian,* edited by Joanne McWilliam. Waterloo, Ontario: Wilfrid Laurier University Press, 1992.

———. *Tertullian: A Historical and Literary Study.* Oxford: Clarendon Press, 1971.

Bastiaensen, A. "The Inaccuracies in the *Vita Augustini* of Possidius." *Studia Patristica* 16.2 (1985): 480–86.

Beatrice, Pier Franco. "*Quosdam Platonicorum Libros*: The Platonic Readings of Augustine in Milan." *Vigiliae Christianae* 43 (1989): 248–81.

BeDuhn, Jason. *The Manichaean Body: In Discipline and Ritual.* Baltimore, MD: Johns Hopkins University Press, 2000.

———. "A Regimen for Salvation: Medical Models in Manichaean Asceticism." *Semeia* 58 (1992): 109–34.

Berger, Peter. *The Sacred Canopy: Elements of a Sociological Theory of Religion.* Garden City, NY: Doubleday, 1967.

Berger, Peter, and Thomas Luckmann. *The Social Construction of Reality: A Treatise on the Sociology of Knowledge.* Garden City, NY: Doubleday, 1966.

Bernard, Robert W. *In Figura: Terminology Pertaining to Figurative Exegesis in the Works of Augustine of Hippo.* Ph.D. dissertation, Princeton University, 1984.

———. "The Rhetoric of God in the Figurative Exegesis of Augustine." In *Biblical Hermeneutics in Historical Perspective: Studies in Honor of Karlfried Froehlich on His Sixtieth Birthday,* edited by Mark S. Burrows and Paul Rorem. Grand Rapids, MI: Eerdmans, 1991.

Bettenson, Henry, trans. *Concerning the City of God against the Pagans.* Penguin Classics. Harmondsworth, Middlesex: Penguin Books, 1984.

Black, Edwin. "Plato's View of Rhetoric." *Quarterly Journal of Speech* 44 (1958): 361–74.

Bogan, Mary Inez, trans. *The Retractations.* Fathers of the Church. Washington, DC: Catholic University of America Press, 1968.

Bonner, Gerald. "Augustine's Visit to Caesarea in 418." In *Studies in Church History,* edited by C. W. Dugmore and C. Duggan. London: Nelson, 1964.

———. *St. Augustine of Hippo: Life and Controversies.* 2d ed. Norwich: Canterbury Press, 1986.

Borgomeo, Pasquale. *L'Église de ce temps dans la prédication de saint Augustin.* Paris: Études Augustiniennes, 1972.

Boulding, Maria, trans. *Expositions of the Psalms. The Works of St. Augustine: A Translation for the 21st Century,* edited by John E. Rotelle. Part 3.15–3.20. Hyde Park, NY: New City Press, 2000–2004.

Bowersock, Glen W. *Greek Sophists and the Roman Empire.* Oxford: Oxford University Press, 1969.

———. *Julian the Apostate.* Cambridge, MA: Harvard University Press, 1978.

———. "Philosophy in the Second Sophistic." In *Philosophy and Power in the Graeco-Roman World: Essays in Honour of Miriam Griffin,* edited by Gillian Clark and Tessa Rajak. Oxford: Oxford University Press, 2002.

———. "The Vanishing Paradigm of the Fall of Rome." *Bulletin of the American Academy of Arts and Sciences* 49.8 (1996): 29–43.

Bowie, E. L. "Greeks and Their Past in the Second Sophistic." *Past and Present* 46 (1970): 3–41. Revised in *Studies in Ancient Society,* edited by M. I. Finley, 166–209. London: Routledge and K. Paul, 1974.

Boys-Stones, G. R. *Post-Hellenistic Philosophy: A Study of Its Development from the Stoics to Origen.* Oxford: Oxford University Press, 2001.

Bright, Pamela, ed. *Augustine and the Bible.* The Bible through the Ages 2. Notre Dame, IN: University of Notre Dame Press, 1999.

Brisson, Luc. *Plato the Myth Maker.* Chicago: University of Chicago Press, 1998.

Brittain, Charles. *Philo of Larissa: The Last of the Academic Sceptics.* Oxford: Oxford University Press, 2001.

Brown, Peter. "Augustine and a Crisis of Wealth in Late Antiquity." *Augustinian Studies* 36 (2005): 5–30.

———. *Augustine of Hippo: A Biography.* 2d ed. Berkeley: University of California Press, 2000.

———. *The Body and Society: Men, Women, and Sexual Renunciation in Early Christianity.* Lectures on the History of Religions, new series 13. New York: Columbia University Press, 1988.

———. "Late Antiquity." In *A History of Private Life.* Vol. 1: *From Pagan Rome to Byzantium,* edited by Paul Veyne. Cambridge, MA: Harvard University Press, 1987.

———. "Pelagius and His Supporters: Aims and Environment." *Journal of Theological Studies* n.s. 19 (1968): 93–114.

———. *Poverty and Leadership in the Later Roman Empire.* Menahem Stern Jerusalem Lectures. Hanover, NH: Brandeis University Press, 2001.

———. *Power and Persuasion in Late Antiquity: Towards a Christian Empire.* The Curti Lectures. Madison: University of Wisconsin Press, 1992.

Browning, Robert. *The Emperor Julian.* Berkeley: University of California Press, 1976.

Brunner, Peter. "Charismatische und methodische Schriftauslegung nach Augustins Prolog zu *De doctrina Christiana.*" *Kerygma und Dogma* 1 (1955): 59–69, 85–103.

Bruns, Gerald L. "The Problem of Figuration in Antiquity." In *Hermeneutics: Questions and Prospects,* edited by Gary Shapiro and Alan Sica. Amherst: University of Massachusetts Press, 1984.

Brunschwig, J., and M. Nussbaum, eds. *Passions and Perceptions: Studies in Hellenistic Philosophy of Mind.* Cambridge: Cambridge University Press, 1993.

Burleigh, John H. S., trans. *Augustine: Earlier Writings.* Library of Christian Classics. Philadelphia: Westminster Press, 1953.

Burn, A. R. "Hic Breve Vivitur." *Past and Present* 4 (1953): 1–31.

Burnaby, John. *Amor Dei: A Study of the Religion of Saint Augustine.* London: Hodder and Stoughton, 1938.

Burns, J. Patout. "Delighting the Spirit: Augustine's Practice of Figurative Interpretation." In *De doctrina christiana: A Classic of Western Culture,* edited by Duane W. H. Arnold and Pamela Bright. Christianity and Judaism in Antiquity 9. Notre Dame, IN: University of Notre Dame Press, 1994.

———. "Providence as Divine Grace in St. Augustine." In *Augustinus Afer: Saint Augustin, africanité et universalité: Actes du colloque international, Alger-Annaba, 1–7 avril 2001,* edited by Pierre-Yves Fux, Jean-Michel Roessli, and Otto Wermelinger. 2 vols. Fribourg, Switzerland: Éditions Universitaires, 2003.

Burnyeat, M. F. "Wittgenstein and Augustine *De magistro.*" In *The Augustinian Tradition,* edited by Gareth B. Matthews. Philosophical Traditions 8. Berkeley: University of California Press, 1999.

Butler, H. E., trans. *The Apologia and Florida of Apuleius of Madaura.* Westport, CT: Greenwood Press, 1970.

Byers, Sarah C. "Augustine and the Cognitive Cause of Stoic 'Preliminary Passions' (*Propatheiai*)." *Journal of the History of Philosophy* 41 (2003): 433–48.

Calhoun, Robert Lowry. "Plato as Religious Realist." In *Religious Realism,* edited by D. C. Macintosh. New York: Macmillan, 1931.

Cameron, Averil. *Christianity and the Rhetoric of Empire: The Development of Christian Discourse.* Sather Classical Lectures 55. Berkeley: University of California Press, 1991.

———. *The Later Roman Empire: A.D. 284–430.* Cambridge, MA: Harvard University Press, 1993.

Cameron, Michael. "The Christological Substructure of Augustine's Figurative Exegesis." In *Augustine and the Bible,* edited by Pamela Bright. The Bible through the Ages 2. Notre Dame, IN: University of Notre Dame Press, 1999.

Cary, Phillip. *Augustine's Invention of the Inner Self: The Legacy of a Christian Platonist.* New York: Oxford University Press, 2000.

———. *Inner Grace: Augustine in the Traditions of Plato and Paul.* New York: Oxford University Press, 2008.

———. *Outward Signs: The Powerlessness of External Things in Augustine's Thought.* New York: Oxford University Press, 2008.

———. "What Licentius Learned: A Narrative Reading of the Cassiciacum Dialogues." *Augustinian Studies* 29 (1998): 141–63.

Cavadini, John C. "The Darkest Enigma: Reconsidering the Self in Augustine's Thought." *Augustinian Studies* 38 (2007): 119–32.

———. "Feeling Right: Augustine on the Passions and Sexual Desire." *Augustinian Studies* 36 (2005): 195–217.

———. "Simplifying Augustine." In *Educating People of Faith: Exploring the History of Jewish and Christian Communities,* edited by John H. Van Engen. Grand Rapids, MI: Eerdmans, 2004.

———. "The Sweetness of the Word: Salvation and Rhetoric in Augustine's *De doctrina christiana*." In *De doctrina christiana: A Classic of Western Culture,* edited by Duane W. H. Arnold and Pamela Bright. Christianity and Judaism in Antiquity 9. Notre Dame, IN: University of Notre Dame Press, 1994.

Chadwick, Henry. *The Early Church.* Penguin History of the Church 1. Baltimore, MD: Penguin Books, 1967.

———. "The Role of the Christian Bishop in Ancient Society." In *Protocol of the Thirty-Fifth Colloquy of the Center for Hermeneutical Studies in Hellenistic and Modern Culture,* edited by E. C. Hobbs and W. Wuellner. Berkeley, 1980.

———, trans. *Saint Augustine: Confessions.* Oxford: Oxford University Press, 1991.

Chidester, David. "The Symbolism of Learning in Augustine." *Harvard Theological Review* 76 (1983): 73–90.

Christopher, Joseph P. *S. Aureli Augustini: De Catechizandis Rudibus.* Washington, DC: Catholic University of America Press, 1926.

Chuvin, Pierre. *A Chronicle of the Last Pagans.* Translated by B. A. Archer. Revealing Antiquity 4. Cambridge, MA: Harvard University Press, 1990.

Clark, Mary T. *Augustine of Hippo: Selected Writings.* The Classics of Western Spirituality. New York: Paulist Press, 1984.

Cochrane, Charles Norris. *Christianity and Classical Culture: A Study of Thought and Action from Augustus to Augustine.* London and New York: Oxford University Press, 1944.

Cohen, Jeremy. *Living Letters of the Law: Ideas of the Jew in Medieval Christianity.* The S. Mark Taper Foundation Imprint in Jewish Studies. Berkeley: University of California Press, 1999.

Cole, Thomas. *The Origins of Rhetoric in Ancient Greece.* Ancient Society and History. Baltimore, MD: Johns Hopkins University Press, 1991.

Colish, Marcia L. *Ambrose's Patriarchs: Ethics for the Common Man.* Notre Dame, IN: University of Notre Dame Press, 2005.

———. *The Stoic Tradition from Antiquity to the Early Middle Ages.* Vol. 2: *Stoicism in Christian Latin Thought through the Sixth Century.* Studies in the History of Christian Thought 35. Leiden: E. J. Brill, 1985.

Comeau, Marie. *La rhétorique de Saint Augustin d'après les Tractatus in Ioannem.* Paris: Boivin, 1930.

———. *Saint Augustin exégète du quatrième Évangile.* 3rd ed. Paris: Gabriel Beauchesne, 1930.

Connolly, R. H. *The Explanatio symboli ad initiandos: A Work of Saint Ambrose.* Text and Studies 10. Cambridge: Cambridge University Press, 1952.

Conybeare, Catherine. "The Duty of a Teacher: Liminality and *disciplina* in Augustine's *De Ordine.*" In *Augustine and the Disciplines: From Cassiciacum to Confessions,* edited by K. Pollmann and M. Vessey. Oxford: Oxford University Press, 2005.

———. *The Irrational Augustine.* Oxford Early Christian Studies. Oxford: Oxford University Press, 2006.

Cooper, John M., ed. *Plato: Complete Works.* Indianapolis: Hackett, 1997.

Cooper, Stephen A. "Scripture at Cassiciacum: 1 Corinthians 13:13 in the Soliloquies." *Augustinian Studies* 27 (1996): 21–47.

Cottom, Daniel. *Text and Culture: The Politics of Interpretation.* Theory and History of Literature 62. Minneapolis: University of Minnesota Press, 1989.

Coulter, James A. *The Literary Microcosm: Theories of Interpretation of the Later Neoplatonists.* Columbia Studies in the Classical Tradition 2. Leiden: E. J. Brill, 1976.

Courcelle, Pierre. "Anti-Christian Arguments and Christian Platonism: From Arnobius to St. Ambrose." In *The Conflict between Paganism and Christianity in the Fourth Century*, edited by Arnaldo Momigliano. Oxford-Warburg Studies. Oxford: Clarendon Press, 1963.

———. *Late Latin Writers and Their Greek Sources.* Translated by Harry E. Wedeck. Cambridge, MA: Harvard University Press, 1969.

———. *Recherches sur les Confessions de saint Augustin.* New ed. Paris: E. de Boccard, 1968.

Coyle, J. Kevin. "The Self-identity of North African Christians in Augustine's Time." In *Augustinus Afer: Saint Augustin, africanité et universalité: Actes du colloque international, Alger-Annaba, 1–7 avril 2001,* edited by Pierre-Yves Fux, Jean-Michel Roessli, and Otto Wermelinger. 2 vols. Fribourg, Switzerland: Éditions Universitaires, 2003.

Cribiore, Raffaella. *The School of Libanius in Late Antique Antioch.* Princeton, NJ: Princeton University Press, 2007.

Crislip, Andrew T. *From Monastery to Hospital: Christian Monasticism and the Transformation of Health Care in Late Antiquity.* Ann Arbor: University of Michigan Press, 2005.

Crouse, Robert. *"Paucis mutatis verbis*: St. Augustine's Platonism." In *Augustine and His Critics: Essays in Honour of Gerald Bonner,* edited by Robert Dodaro and George Lawless. London and New York: Routledge, 2000.

Cushman, Robert E. *Therapeia: Plato's Conception of Philosophy.* Chapel Hill: University of North Carolina Press, 1958.

Daley, Brian E. "Building a New City: The Cappadocian Fathers and the Rhetoric of Philanthropy." *Journal of Early Christian Studies* 7 (1999): 431–61.

———. "A Humble Mediator: The Distinctive Elements in Saint Augustine's Christology." *Word and Spirit* 9 (1987): 100–17.

———. "Position and Patronage in the Early Church: The Original Meaning of 'Primacy of Honour.'" *Journal of Theological Studies* n.s. 44 (1993): 529–53.

Davidson, Ivor J. *Ambrose: De Officiis.* 2 vols. Oxford Early Christian Studies. Oxford and New York: Oxford University Press, 2002.

Dawson, David. *Allegorical Readers and Cultural Revision in Ancient Alexandria.* Berkeley: University of California Press, 1992.

———. "Sign Theory, Allegorical Reading, and the Motions of the Soul in *De doctrina christiana.*" In *De doctrina christiana: A Classic of Western Culture,* edited by Duane W. H. Arnold and Pamela Bright. Christianity and Judaism in Antiquity 9. Notre Dame, IN: University of Notre Dame Press, 1994.

Deferrari, Roy J., trans. *Saint Ambrose: Theological and Dogmatic Works.* Fathers of the Church. Washington, DC: Catholic University of America Press, 1963.

———. "St. Augustine's Method of Composing and Delivering Sermons." *American Journal of Philology* 43 (1922): 97–123, 193–219.

De Graff, T. "Plato in Cicero." *Classical Philology* 35 (1940): 143–53.

De Lacy, P. "Plato and the Intellectual Life of the Second Century AD." In *Approaches to the Second Sophistic: Papers presented at the 105th Annual Meeting of the*

American Philological Association, edited by G. W. Bowersock. University Park, PA: American Philological Association, 1974.

Derrida, Jacques. "Plato's Pharmacy." In *Dissemination.* Translated by Barbara Johnson. Chicago: University of Chicago Press, 1981.

Deuse, Werner. *Untersuchungen zur mittelplatonischen und neuplatonischen Seelenlehre.* Mainz: Akademie der Wissenschaften und der Literatur, 1983.

Diederich, Mary D. *Virgil in the Works of St. Ambrose.* Washington, DC: Catholic University of America Press, 1931.

Dihle, Albrecht. *The Theory of Will in Classical Antiquity.* Sather Classical Lectures 48. Berkeley: University of California Press, 1982.

Dillon, John M. *The Middle Platonists: 80 B.C. to A.D. 220.* Rev. ed. Ithaca, NY: Cornell University Press, 1996.

Dillon, John M., and A. A. Long, eds. *The Question of "Eclecticism": Studies in Later Greek Philosophy.* Berkeley: University of California Press, 1988.

DiLorenzo, Raymond D. "Ciceronianism and Augustine's Conception of Philosophy." *Augustinian Studies* 13 (1982): 171–76.

Djuth, Marianne. "Philosophy in a Time of Exile: *Vera Philosophia* and the Incarnation." *Augustinian Studies* 38 (2007): 281–300.

Dobbin, Robert. *Epictetus: Discourses Book 1.* Clarendon Later Ancient Philosophers. Oxford: Clarendon Press, 1998.

Dodaro, Robert. "Augustine's Revision of the Heroic Ideal." *Augustinian Studies* 36 (2005): 141–57.

———. "Augustine's Secular City." In *Augustine and His Critics: Essays in Honour of Gerald Bonner,* edited by Robert Dodaro and George Lawless. London and New York: Routledge, 2000.

———. "Between the Two Cities: Political Action in Augustine of Hippo." In *Augustine and Politics,* edited by John Doody, Kevin L. Hughes, and Kim Paffenroth. Augustine in Conversation. Lanham, MD: Lexington Books, 2005.

———. *Christ and the Just Society in the Thought of Augustine.* Cambridge: Cambridge University Press, 2004.

Dodaro, Robert, and George Lawless, eds. *Augustine and His Critics: Essays in Honour of Gerald Bonner.* London and New York: Routledge, 2000.

Dodd, C. H. *The Parables of the Kingdom.* Rev. ed. New York: Charles Scribner's Sons, 1961.

Dodds, E. R. *Pagan and Christian in an Age of Anxiety: Some Aspects of Religious Experience from Marcus Aurelius to Constantine.* The Wiles Lectures. Cambridge: Cambridge University Press, 1965.

Dolbeau, François. *Vingt-six sermons au peuple d'Afrique.* Collection des études augustiniennes, Série Antiquité 147. Paris: Institut d'Études Augustiniennes, 1996.

Doucet, D. "Le thème du médecin dans les premiers dialogues philosophique de saint Augustin." *Augustiniana* 39 (1989): 447–61.

Douglas, A. E. "Form and Content in the Tusculan Disputations." In *Cicero the Philosopher: Twelve Papers,* edited by J. G. F. Powell. Oxford: Oxford University Press, 1995.

Downey, Glanville. "Libanius' Oration in Praise of Antioch (Oration XI)." *Proceedings of the American Philosophic Society* 103.5 (1959): 652–86.

Dox, Donnalee. *The Idea of the Theater in Latin Christian Thought: Augustine to the Fourteenth Century.* Ann Arbor: University of Michigan Press, 2004.

Doyle, G. W. "Augustine's Sermonic Method." *Westminster Theological Journal* 39 (1977): 213–38.

———. *St. Augustine's "Tractates on the Gospel of John" Compared with the Rhetorical Theory of "De doctrina christiana."* Ph.D. dissertation, University of North Carolina, Chapel Hill, 1975.

Drobner, Hubertus R. *Augustinus von Hippo: Sermones ad populum.* Supplements to Vigiliae Christianae 49. Leiden: Brill, 2000.

———. "The Chronology of St. Augustine's *Sermones ad populum.*" *Augustinian Studies* 31 (2000): 211–18.

———. "Grammatical Exegesis and Christology in St. Augustine." *Studia Patristica* 18.4 (1990): 49–63.

———. *Person-Exegese und Christologie bei Augustinus: zur Herkunft der Formel Una Persona.* Philosophia patrum 8. Leiden: E. J. Brill, 1986.

Duchrow, U. "Zum Prolog von Augustins *De doctrina christiana.*" *Vigilae Christianae* 17 (1963): 165–72.

Dudden, Frederick Homes. *The Life and Times of St. Ambrose.* 2 vols. Oxford: Clarendon Press, 1935.

Duffy, Stephen J. *The Dynamics of Grace: Perspectives in Theological Anthropology.* New Theology Studies 3. Collegeville, MN: Liturgical Press, 1993.

Duval, Noël. "Commentaire topographique et archéologique de sept dossiers des nouveaux sermons." In *Augustin Prédicateur (395–411): Actes du Colloque International de Chantilly (5–7 Septembre 1996),* edited by G. Madec. Collection des Études Augustiniennes, Série Antiquité 159. Paris: Institut d'Études Augustiniennes, 1998.

Eden, K. "The Rhetorical Tradition and Augustine's Hermeneutics in *De doctrina christiana.*" *Rhetorica* 8 (1990): 45–63.

Edwards, Catharine. "Self-Scrutiny and Self-Transformation in Seneca's Letters." *Greece and Rome* 41 (1997): 23–37.

Edwards, Mark, trans. *Optatus: Against the Donatists.* Translated Texts for Historians 27. Liverpool: Liverpool University Press, 1997.

Engberg-Pedersen, Troels. "Plutarch to Prince Philopappus on How to Tell a Flatterer from a Friend." In *Friendship, Flattery, and Frankness of Speech: Studies on Friendship in the New Testament World,* edited by John T. Fitzgerald. Supplements to Novum Testamentum 82. Leiden: E. J. Brill, 1996.

English, Edward D., ed. *Reading and Wisdom: The De doctrina christiana of Augustine in the Middle Ages.* Notre Dame Conferences in Medieval Studies 6. Notre Dame, IN: University of Notre Dame Press, 1995.

Evans, Gillian Rosemary. *Augustine on Evil.* New York: Cambridge University Press, 1982.

Evans, Robert F. *Four Letters of Pelagius.* Studies in Pelagius. New York: Seabury Press, 1968.

Finan, Thomas. "St. Augustine and the '*mira profunditas*' of Scripture." In *Scriptural Interpretation in the Fathers: Letter and Spirit,* edited by Thomas Finan and Vincent Twomey. Dublin: Four Courts, 1995.

Finn, Richard D. *Almsgiving in the Later Roman Empire: Christian Promotion and Practice (313–450).* Oxford: Oxford University Press, 2006.

Foley, Michael P. "Cicero, Augustine, and the Philosophical Roots of the Cassiciacum Dialogues." *Revue des Études Augustiniennes* 45 (1999): 51–77.

Folliet, Georges. "'Deificari in otio,' Augustin, *Epistula* 10, 2." *Recherches augustiniennes* 2 (1962): 225–36.

Fontanier, Jean-Michel. *La beauté selon saint Augustin.* Rennes: Presses Universitaires de Rennes, 1998.

Fortin, E. L. "Augustine and the Problem of Christian Rhetoric." *Augustinian Studies* 5 (1974): 85–100.

Foucault, Michel. *The Use of Pleasure.* Vol. 2 of 3, *The History of Sexuality.* Translated by Robert Hurley. New York: Random House, 1985.

Francis, James A. *Subversive Virtue: Asceticism and Authority in the Second-Century Pagan World.* University Park: Pennsylvania State University Press, 1995.

Fredouille, Jean Claude. *Tertullian et la conversion de la culture antique.* Paris: Études Augustiniennes, 1972.

Fredrickson, David. "Parresia in the Pauline Epistles." In *Friendship, Flattery, and Frankness of Speech: Studies on Friendship in the New Testament World,* edited by John T. Fitzgerald. Supplements to Novum Testamentum 82. Leiden: E. J. Brill, 1996.

Fredriksen, Paula. *Augustine and the Jews: A Christian Defense of Jews and Judaism.* New York: Doubleday, 2008.

Frend, W. H. C. *The Donatist Church: A Movement of Protest in Roman North Africa.* Oxford: Clarendon Press, 1952.

Frier, Bruce W. "Roman Life Expectancy: Ulpian's Evidence." *Harvard Studies in Classical Philology* 86 (1982): 213–51.

Frutiger, Perceval. *Les mythes de Platon: Étude philosophique et littéraire.* New York: Arno Press, 1976.

Fux, Pierre-Yves, Jean-Michel Roessli, and Otto Wermelinger, eds. *Augustinus Afer: Saint Augustin, africanité et universalité: Actes du colloque international, Alger-Annaba, 1–7 avril 2001.* 2 vols. Fribourg, Switzerland: Éditions Universitaires, 2003.

Gallagher, Donald A., and Idella J. Gallagher, trans. *The Catholic and Manichaean Ways of Life.* Fathers of the Church. Washington, DC: Catholic University of America Press, 1966.

Garnsey, Peter. "Responses to Food Crisis in the Ancient Mediterranean World." In *Hunger in History: Food Shortage, Poverty, and Deprivation,* edited by Lucille Newman. Cambridge, MA: Basil Blackwell, 1990.

Gärtner, Hans Armin. "Cura." *Augustinus-Lexikon,* edited by C. Mayer. Vol. 2. Basel: Schwabe, 1986–1994.

Geffcken, Johannes. *Last Days of Greco-Roman Paganism.* Translated by Sabine MacCormack. Europe in the Middle Ages 8. Amsterdam and New York: North-Holland, 1978.

Gersh, Stephen. *Middle Platonism and Neoplatonism: The Latin Tradition.* 2 vols. Publications in Medieval Studies 23. Notre Dame, IN: University of Notre Dame Press, 1986.

Glad, Clarence. "Frank Speech, Flattery, and Friendship in Philodemus." In *Friendship, Flattery, and Frankness of Speech: Studies on Friendship in the New Testament World,* edited by John T. Fitzgerald. Supplements to Novum Testamentum 82. Leiden: E. J. Brill, 1996.

———. *Paul and Philodemus: Adaptability in Epicurean and Early Christian Psychagogy.* Supplements to Novum Testamentum 81. Leiden: E. J. Brill, 1995.

Glucker, John. "Cicero's Philosophical Affiliations." In *The Question of "Eclecticism": Studies in Later Greek Philosophy,* edited by John M. Dillon and A. A. Long. Berkeley: University of California Press, 1988.

Gowans, Coleen Hoffman. *The Identity of the True Believer in the Sermons of Augustine of Hippo: A Dimension of His Christian Anthropology.* Lewiston, NY: Edwin Mellen Press, 1998.

Graumann, Thomas. "St. Ambrose on the Art of Preaching." In *Vescovi e pastori in epoca teodosiana: In occasione del XVI centenario della consacrazione episcopale di S. Agostino, 396–1996.* 2 vols. Studia ephemeridis Augustinianum 58. Rome: Institutum patristicum Augustinianum, 1997.

Greer, Rowan A. *Broken Lights and Mended Lives: Theology and Common Life in the Early Church.* University Park: Pennsylvania State University Press, 1986.

———. *The Fear of Freedom: A Study of Miracles in the Roman Imperial Church.* University Park: Pennsylvania State University Press, 1989.

———. "Who Seeks for a Spring in the Mud: Reflections on the Ordained Ministry in the Fourth Century." In *Theological Education and Moral Formation,* edited by Richard John Neuhaus. Grand Rapids, MI: Eerdmans, 1991.

Gregory, Eric. *Politics and the Order of Love: An Augustinian Ethic of Democratic Citizenship.* Chicago: University of Chicago Press, 2008.

Griffiths, Paul J. *Lying: An Augustinian Theology of Duplicity.* Grand Rapids, MI: Brazos Press, 2004.

Griswold, Charles L. *Self-Knowledge in Plato's Phaedrus.* University Park: Pennsylvania State University Press, 1986.

Groh, D. E. "Tertullian's Polemic against Social Co-option." *Church History* 40 (1971): 7–14.

Gsell, Stéphane. *Inscriptions latines de l'Algérie.* 2 vols. Paris: E. Champion, 1922–1957.

Habinek, Thomas. *Ancient Rhetoric and Oratory.* Blackwell Introductions to the Classical World. Oxford: Blackwell, 2005.

Hadot, Ilsetraut. *Arts libéraux et philosophie dans la pensée antique.* Paris: Études Augustiniennes, 1984.

———. *Seneca und die griechisch-römische Tradition der Seelenleitung.* Quellen und Studien zur Geschichte der Philosophie 13. Berlin: de Gruyter, 1969.

———. "The Spiritual Guide." In *Classical Mediterranean Spirituality: Egyptian, Greek, and Roman,* edited by A. H. Armstrong. World Spirituality 15. New York: Crossroad, 1986.

Hadot, Pierre. *The Inner Citadel: The Meditations of Marcus Aurelius.* Translated by Michael Chase. Cambridge, MA: Harvard University Press, 1998.

———. *Philosophy as a Way of Life: Spiritual Exercises from Socrates to Foucault.* Translated by Michael Chase. Cambridge, MA: Blackwell. 1995.

———. *Plotinus or the Simplicity of Vision.* Translated by Michael Chase. Chicago: University of Chicago Press, 1993.

———. "Théologie, exégèse, révélation, écriture, dans la philosophie grecque." In *Les règles de l'interprétation,* edited by Michel Tardieu. Paris: Éditions du cerf, 1987.

———. *What Is Ancient Philosophy?* Translated by Michael Chase. Cambridge, MA: Harvard University Press, 2002.

Hagendahl, Harald. *Augustine and the Latin Classics.* 2 vols. Studia Graeca et Latina 20. Gothenburg: Acta Universitatis Gothoburgensis, 1967.

———. *Latin Fathers and the Classics: A Study on the Apologists, Jerome and Other Christian Writers.* Gothenburg, University of Göteborg, 1958.

Hala, J.-P. "Signum and Res: Wordplay and Christian Rhetoric." *Michigan Academy of Science, Arts, and Letters* 16 (1984): 315–28.

Halliburton, R. J. "The Inclination to Retirement—the Retreat of Cassiciacum and the 'Monastery' of Tagaste." *Studia Patristica* 5 (1962): 329–40.

Hamman, Adalbert G. "La transmission des sermons de Saint Augustin: Les authentiques et les apocryphes." *Augustinianum* 25 (1985): 311–27.

Hankinson, James. "Actions and Passions: Affection, Emotion, and Moral Self-Management in Galen's Philosophical Psychology." In *Passions and Perceptions: Studies in Hellenistic Philosophy of Mind,* edited by J. Brunschwig and M. Nussbaum. Cambridge: Cambridge University Press, 1993.

Hardie, Philip R. "Plutarch and the Interpretation of Myth." ANRW 2.33.6 (1992), 4743–4787.

Harmless, William. *Augustine and the Catechumenate.* Collegeville, MN: Liturgical Press, 1995.

Harris, William V. *Restraining Rage: The Ideology of Anger Control in Classical Antiquity.* Cambridge, MA: Harvard University Press, 2004.

Harrison, Carol. *Augustine: Christian Truth and Fractured Humanity.* Christian Theology in Context. New York: Oxford University Press, 2000.

———. *Beauty and Revelation in the Thought of Saint Augustine.* Oxford: Clarendon Press, 1992.

———. "'The Most Intimate Feeling of Mind': The Permanence of Grace in Augustine's Early Theological Practice." *Augustinian Studies* 36 (2005): 51–58.

———. *Rethinking Augustine's Early Theology: An Argument for Continuity.* Oxford: Oxford University Press, 2006.

———. "The Rhetoric of Scripture and Preaching: Classical Decadence or Christian Aesthetic?" In *Augustine and His Critics: Essays in Honour of Gerald Bonner,* edited by Robert Dodaro and George Lawless. London and New York: Routledge, 2000.

Harrison, Stephen J. *Apuleius: A Latin Sophist.* Oxford: Oxford University Press, 2000.

Heather, Peter J., and David Moncur, trans. *Politics, Philosophy, and Empire in the Fourth Century: Select Orations of Themistius.* Translated Texts for Historians 36. Liverpool: Liverpool University Press, 2001.

Heinimann, Felix. *Nomos und Physis.* Basle: Reinhardt, 1945.

Henrichs, A., and L. Koenen, eds. *The Cologne Mani Codex* 122. Papyrologia Coloniensia 14. Opladen: Westdeutscher Verlag, 1988.

Hermanowicz, Erika T. *Possidius of Calama: A Study of the North African Episcopate in the Age of Augustine.* Oxford Early Christian Studies. Oxford: Oxford University Press, 2008.

Herrmann, Jr., John J., and Annewies van den Hoek. *Light from the Age of Augustine: Late Antique Ceramics from North Africa.* 1st ed. Cambridge, MA: Harvard Divinity School, 2002; 2d ed. Austin: Institute for the Study of Antiquity and Christian Origins of the University of Texas at Austin, 2003.

Heuser, Manfred, and Hans-Joachim Klimkeit. *Studies in Manichaean Literature and Art.* Nag Hammadi and Manichaean Studies 46. Leiden: Brill, 1998.

Heyking, John von. *Augustine and Politics as Longing in the World.* Eric Voegelin Institute Series in Political Philosophy. Columbia: University of Missouri Press, 2001.

Hijmans, B. L. *Askesis: Notes on Epictetus' Educational System.* Wijsgerige teksten en studies 2. Assen: Van Gorcum, 1959.

Hijmans, Jr., B. L. "Apuleius, *Philosophus Platonicus.*" ANRW 2.36.1 (1987), 395–475.

Hill, Edmund. "St. Augustine's Theory and Practice of Preaching." *Clergy Review* 45 (1960): 589–97.

————, trans. *Sermons. The Works of St. Augustine: A Translation for the 21st Century*, edited by John E. Rotelle. Part 3.1–3.11. Hyde Park, NY: New City Press, 1990–1997.

————, trans. *Teaching Christianity. The Works of St. Augustine: A Translation for the 21st Century*, edited by John E. Rotelle. Part 1.11. Hyde Park, NY: New City Press, 1996.

————, trans. *The Trinity. The Works of St. Augustine: A Translation for the 21st Century*, edited by John E. Rotelle. Part 1.5. Hyde Park, NY: New City Press, 1991.

Hoare, Frederick R., trans. and ed. *The Western Fathers: Being the Lives of SS. Martin of Tours, Ambrose, Augustine of Hippo, Honoratus of Arles, and Germanus Auxerre*. The Makers of Christendom. New York: Sheed and Ward, 1954.

Holman, Susan R. *The Hungry Are Dying: Beggars and Bishops in Roman Cappadocia*. Oxford Studies in Historical Theology. New York and Oxford: Oxford University Press, 2001.

Holte, Ragnar. "Monica, 'the Philosopher.'" *Augustinus* 39 (1994): 293–316.

Hombert, Pierre-Marie. *Nouvelles recherches de chronologie augustinienne*. Collection des études augustiniennes, Série Antiquité 163. Paris: Institut d'Études Augustiniennes, 2000.

Hopkins, Keith. "On the Probable Age Structure of the Roman Population." *Population Studies* 20 (1966): 245–64.

Inwood, Brad. "Seneca on Emotion and Action." In *Passions and Perceptions: Studies in Hellenistic Philosophy of Mind*, edited by J. Brunschwig and M. Nussbaum. Cambridge: Cambridge University Press, 1993.

Jackson, B. Darrel. "The Theory of Signs in St. Augustine's *De doctrina christiana*." *Revue des Études Augustiniennes* 15 (1969): 9–49.

Jackson, Pamela. "Eucharist." In *Augustine through the Ages: An Encyclopedia*, edited by A. Fitzgerald. Grand Rapids, MI: Eerdmans, 1999.

Jaeger, Werner. *Paideia: The Ideals of Greek Culture*. Translated by Gilbert Highet. 3 vols. New York: Oxford University Press, 1939–44.

Johnson, W. R. "Isocrates Flowering: The Rhetoric of Augustine." *Philosophy and Rhetoric* 9 (1976): 217–31.

Jones, C. P. *The Roman World of Dio Chrysostom*. Loeb Classical Monographs. Cambridge, MA: Harvard University Press, 1978.

Jordan, Mark D. "Words and Word: Incarnation and Signification in Augustine's *De doctrina christiana*." *Augustinian Studies* 11 (1980): 177–96.

Kannengiesser, Charles. "The Interrupted *De doctrina christiana*." In *De doctrina christiana: A Classic of Western Culture*, edited by Duane W. H. Arnold and Pamela Bright. Christianity and Judaism in Antiquity 9. Notre Dame, IN: University of Notre Dame Press, 1994.

Kaster, Robert A. *Guardians of Language: The Grammarian and Society in Late Antiquity*. The Transformation of the Classical Heritage 11. Berkeley: University of California Press, 1988.

Kaufman, Peter Iver. "Augustine, Macedonius, and the Courts." *Augustinian Studies* 34 (2003): 67–82.

Kélessidou, Anna. "La psychagogie du Phèdre et le long labeur philosophique." In *Understanding the Phaedrus: Proceedings of the II Symposium Platonicum,* edited by Livio Rossetti. International Plato Studies 1. Sankt Augustin: Academia Verlag, 1992.

Kennedy, George. *A New History of Classical Rhetoric.* Princeton, NJ: Princeton University Press, 1994.

Kenney, John Peter. *The Mysticism of Saint Augustine: Rereading the Confessions.* New York: Routledge, 2005.

Kerferd, G. B. *The Sophistic Movement.* Cambridge: Cambridge University Press, 1981.

Kevane, Eugene. "Paideia and Anti-Paideia: The *Prooemium* of Augustine's *De Doctrina Christiana.*" *Augustinian Studies* 1 (1970): 153–80.

Kidd, I. G. "Moral Actions and Rules in Stoic Ethics." In *The Stoics,* edited by John M. Rist. Major Thinkers Series 1. Berkeley: University of California Press, 1978.

King, Peter, trans. *Against the Academicians; The Teacher.* Indianapolis: Hackett, 1995.

Klimkeit, Hans-Joachim. "The Use of Scripture in Manichaeism." In *Studies in Manichaean Literature and Art,* edited by Manfred Heuser and Hans-Joachim Klimkeit. Nag Hammadi and Manichaean Studies 46. Leiden: Brill, 1998.

Klingshirn, William. "Charity and Power: Caesarius of Arles and the Ransoming of Captives in Sub-Roman Gaul." *Journal of Roman Studies* 75 (1985): 183–203.

Kolbet, Paul R. "Formal Continuities between Augustine's Early Philosophical Teaching and Late Homiletical Practice." *Studia Patristica* 43 (2006): 149–54.

Konstan, David. "Friendship, Frankness, and Flattery." In *Friendship, Flattery, and Frankness of Speech: Studies on Friendship in the New Testament World,* edited by John T. Fitzgerald. Supplements to Novum Testamentum 82. Leiden: E. J. Brill, 1996.

Konstan, David, Diskin Clay, et al., trans. *Philodemus: On Frank Criticism: Introduction, Translation, and Notes.* Texts and Translations 43. Atlanta: Scholars Press, 1998.

Kovacs, Judith. "Divine Pedagogy and the Gnostic Teacher according to Clement of Alexandria." *Journal of Early Christian Studies* 9 (2001): 3–25.

La Bonnardière, Anne-Marie. "Augustine's Biblical Initiation." In *Augustine and the Bible,* edited by Pamela Bright. The Bible through the Ages 2. Notre Dame, IN: University of Notre Dame Press, 1997.

Laín Entrago, Pedro. *The Therapy of the Word in Classical Antiquity.* Translated by L. J. Rather and John M. Sharp. New Haven, CT: Yale University Press, 1970.

Lamberton, Robert. *Homer the Theologian: Neoplatonist Allegorical Reading and the Growth of the Epic Tradition.* The Transformation of the Classical Heritage 9. Berkeley: University of California Press, 1986.

———. "The Neoplatonists and the Spiritualization of Homer." In *Homer's Ancient Readers: The Hermeneutics of Greek Epic's Earliest Exegetes,* edited by Robert Lamberton and John J. Keaney. Magie Classical Publications. Princeton, NJ: Princeton University Press, 1992.

———. *Plutarch.* Hermes Books. New Haven, CT: Yale University Press, 2001.

Lambot, Cyrille. "Sermons inédits de S. Augustin pour des fêtes de saints." *Revue Bénédictine* 59 (1949): 55–81.

Lamoreaux, J. C. "Episcopal Courts in Late Antiquity." *Journal of Early Christian Studies* 3 (1995): 143–67.

Lancel, Serge. *Saint Augustine.* Translated by Antonia Nevill. London: SCM Press, 2002.

Lattimore, Richmond, trans. *The Odyssey of Homer.* New York: Harper & Row, 1967.

Lawless, George. *Augustine of Hippo and His Monastic Rule.* Oxford: Clarendon Press, 1987.

———. "Augustine of Hippo as Preacher." In *Augustine the Bishop: A Book of Essays,* edited by Fannie LeMoine and Christopher Kleinhenz. New York: Garland, 1994.

———. "Augustine's Decentring of Asceticism." In *Augustine and His Critics: Essays in Honour of Gerald Bonner,* edited by Robert Dodaro and George Lawless. London and New York: Routledge, 2000.

Leff, Michael C. "The Material of the Art in the Latin Handbooks of the Fourth Century A.D." In *Rhetoric Revalued: Papers from the International Society for the History of Rhetoric,* edited by Brian Vickers. Medieval and Renaissance Texts and Studies. Binghamton: State University of New York Press, 1982.

Lenox-Conyngham, Andrew. "Ambrose and Philosophy." In *Christian Faith and Greek Philosophy in Late Antiquity: Essays in Tribute to George Christopher Stead,* edited by Lionel R. Wickham and Caroline P. Bammel. Vigiliae Christianae, Supplements 19. Leiden: E. J. Brill, 1993.

Lenski, Noel E. "Evidence for the *Audientia episcopalis* in the New Letters of Augustine." In *Law, Society, and Authority in Late Antiquity,* edited by Ralph W. Mathisen. New York and Oxford: Oxford University Press, 2001.

Lepelley, Claude. "Un aspect de la conversion de saint Augustin: La rupture avec ses ambitions sociales et politiques." *Bulletin de Littérature Ecclésiastique* 88 (1987): 229–46.

———. "Facing Wealth and Poverty: Defining Augustine's Social Doctrine." *Augustinian Studies* 38 (2007): 1–17.

Leyerle, Blake. *Theatrical Shows and Ascetic Lives: John Chrysostom's Attack on Spiritual Marriage.* Berkeley: University of California Press, 2001.

Leyser, Conrad. *Authority and Asceticism from Augustine to Gregory the Great.* Oxford Historical Monographs. Oxford: Clarendon Press, 2000.

Lieu, Samuel N. C. *Manichaeism in the Later Roman Empire and Medieval China.* Rev. ed. Tübingen: J. C. B. Mohr (Siebeck), 1992.

Locke, John. *An Essay Concerning Human Understanding,* edited by Peter H. Nidditch. Oxford: Clarendon Press, 1975.

Long, A. A. "Allegory in Philo and Etymology in Stoicism: A Plea for Drawing Distinctions." *Studia Philonica Annual* 9 (1997): 198–210.

———. "Cicero's Plato and Aristotle." In *Cicero the Philosopher: Twelve Papers,* edited by J. G. F. Powell. Oxford: Oxford University Press, 1995.

———. "Epicureans and Stoics." In *Classical Mediterranean Spirituality: Egyptian, Greek, and Roman,* edited by A. H. Armstrong. World Spirituality 15. New York: Crossroad, 1986.

———. *Hellenistic Philosophy: Stoics, Epicureans, Sceptics.* 2d ed. Berkeley: University of California Press, 1986.

———. "Stoic Reading of Homer." In *Homer's Ancient Readers: The Hermeneutics of Greek Epic's Earliest Exegetes,* edited by Robert Lamberton and John J. Keaney. Magie Classical Publications. Princeton, NJ: Princeton University Press, 1992.

Long, A. A., and D. N. Sedley. *The Hellenistic Philosophers.* 2 vols. Cambridge: Cambridge University Press, 1987.

Loyd, A. C. "Emotion and Decision in Stoic Psychology." In *The Stoics,* edited by John M. Rist. Major Thinkers Series 1. Berkeley: University of California Press, 1978.

Lutz, Cora E., ed. and trans. *Musonius Rufus: "The Roman Socrates."* New Haven, CT: Yale University Press, 1947.

MacDowell, D. M., trans. *Encomium of Helen.* Bristol: Bristol Classical Press, 1982.

Mackey, Louis H. "The Mediator Mediated: Faith and Reason in Augustine's *De Magistro.*" *Franciscan Studies* 42 (1982): 135–55.

MacMullen, Ramsey. "A Note on *sermo humilis.*" *Journal of Theological Studies* n.s. 17 (1966): 108–12.

———. "The Preacher's Audience (AD 350–400)." *Journal of Theological Studies* n.s. 40 (1989): 503–11.

Madec, Goulven, ed. *Augustin Prédicateur (395–411): Actes du Colloque International de Chantilly (5–7 Septembre 1996).* Paris: Institut d'Études Augustiniennes, 1998.

———. *Introduction aux "Révisions" et à la lecture des œuvres de saint Augustin.* Collection des études augustiniennes, Série Antiquité 150. Paris: Études Augustiniennes, 1996.

———. *La patrie et la voie: Le Christ dans la vie et la pensée de Saint Augustin.* Paris: Desclée, 1989.

———. *Saint Ambroise et la Philosophie.* Paris: Études Augustiniennes, 1974.

Malherbe, Abraham J. *Ancient Epistolary Theorists.* Sources for Biblical Study 19. Atlanta: Scholars Press, 1988.

———. "Hellenistic Moralists and the New Testament." ANRW 2.26.1 (1992), 267–333.

———. *Paul and the Thessalonians: The Philosophic Tradition of Pastoral Care.* Philadelphia: Fortress Press, 1987.

Manetti, Giovanni. *Theories of the Sign in Classical Antiquity.* Translated by Christine Richardson. Advances in Semiotics. Bloomington: Indiana University Press, 1993.

Markus, Robert A. "Augustine on Magic: A Neglected Semiotic Theory." In *Signs and Meanings: World and Text in Ancient Christianity.* Liverpool: Liverpool University Press, 1996.

———. *Conversion and Disenchantment in Augustine's Spiritual Career.* The Saint Augustine Lecture. Philadelphia: Villanova University Press, 1989.

———. *The End of Ancient Christianity.* Cambridge: Cambridge University Press, 1990.

———. *Saeculum: History and Society in the Theology of St. Augustine.* 2d ed. Cambridge: Cambridge University Press, 1988.

———. "Signs, Communication, and Communities in Augustine's *De doctrina christiana.*" In *De doctrina christiana: A Classic of Western Culture,* edited by Duane W. H. Arnold and Pamela Bright. Christianity and Judaism in Antiquity 9. Notre Dame, IN: University of Notre Dame Press, 1994.

———. "St. Augustine on Signs." *Phronesis* 2 (1957): 60–83.

———. "World and Text in Ancient Christianity I: Augustine." In *Signs and Meanings: World and Text in Ancient Christianity.* Liverpool: Liverpool University Press, 1996.

Marrou, Henri I. *A History of Education in Antiquity.* Translated by George Lamb. Wisconsin Studies in Classics. Madison: University of Wisconsin Press, 1982.

———. *Saint Augustin et la fin de la culture antique.* 4th ed. Paris: E. de Boccard, 1949.

Mathewes, Charles T. "The Liberation of Questioning in Augustine's *Confessions.*" *Journal of the American Academy of Religion* 70 (2002): 539–60.

———. *A Theology of Public Life.* Cambridge Studies in Christian Doctrine. Cambridge: Cambridge University Press, 2007.

Maxwell, Jaclyn L. *Christianization and Communication in Late Antiquity: John Chrysostom and His Congregation in Antioch.* New York: Cambridge University Press, 2006.

McCarthy, Michael C. "'We Are Your Books': Augustine, the Bible, and the Practice of Authority." *Journal of the American Academy of Religion* 75 (2007): 324–52.

McCoy, Marina. *Plato on the Rhetoric of Philosophers and Sophists.* New York: Cambridge University Press, 2007.

McHugh, Michael P., trans. *Saint Ambrose: Seven Exegetical Works.* Fathers of the Church. Washington, DC: Catholic University of America Press, 1972.

McLynn, Neil B. *Ambrose of Milan: Church and Court in the Christian Capital.* The Transformation of the Classical Heritage 22. Berkeley: University of California Press, 1994.

———. "Augustine's Roman Empire." *Augustinian Studies* 30 (1999): 29–44.

McNeill, John T. *A History of the Cure of Souls.* New York and London: Harper and Row, 1951.

McNew, L. D. "The Relation of Cicero's Rhetoric to Augustine." *Research Studies of the State College of Washington* 25 (1957): 5–13.

McWilliam, Joanne. "The Study of Augustine's Christology in the Twentieth Century." In *Augustine: From Rhetor to Theologian,* edited by Joanne McWilliam. Waterloo, Ontario: Wilfrid Laurier University Press, 1992.

———. "Weaving the Strands Together: A Decade in Augustine's Eucharistic Theology." *Augustiniana* 41 (1991): 497–506.

Meeks, Wayne A. *The Origins of Christian Morality: The First Two Centuries.* New Haven, CT, and London: Yale University Press, 1993.

Meijering, Roos. *Literary and Rhetorical Theories in Greek Scholia.* Groningen: Egbert Forsten, 1987.

Merdinger, Jane E. *Rome and the African Church in the Time of Augustine.* New Haven, CT: Yale University Press, 1997.

Mileweski, Douglas. "Augustine's 124 Tractates on the Gospel of John: The *Status Quaestionis* and the State of Neglect." *Augustinian Studies* 33 (2002): 61–77.

Miller, Timothy S. *The Birth of the Hospital in the Byzantine Empire.* 2d ed. Baltimore, MD: Johns Hopkins University Press, 1997.

Mitsis, Phillip. "Seneca on Reason, Rules, and Moral Development." In *Passions and Perceptions: Studies in Hellenistic Philosophy of Mind,* edited by J. Brunschwig and M. Nussbaum. Cambridge: Cambridge University Press, 1993.

Mohrmann, Christine. *Die altchristliche Sondersprache in den sermones des hl. Augustinus.* Nijmegen: Dekker, 1932.

———. "Review of P. Courcelle, *'Recherches sur les Confessions de saint Augustin,'*" *Vigiliae Christianae* 5 (1951): 249–54.

———. "St. Augustine and the *Eloquentia.*" In *Études sur le latin des chrétiens.* Vol. 1. Rome: Edizioni di storia e letteratura, 1961.

Moors, K. F. *Platonic Myth: An Introductory Study.* Washington, DC: University Press of America, 1982.

Morgan, Michael L. *Platonic Piety: Philosophy and Ritual in Fourth-Century Athens.* New Haven, CT: Yale University Press, 1990.

Morrow, Glenn R. "Plato's Conception of Persuasion." *Philosophical Review* 62 (1953): 234–50.

Moss, Roger. "The Case for Sophistry." In *Rhetoric Revalued: Papers from the International Society for the History of Rhetoric,* edited by Brian Vickers. Medieval and Renaissance Texts and Studies. Binghamton: State University of New York Press, 1982.

Muir, John Victor. *Alcidamas: The Works and Fragments.* London: Bristol Classical Press, 2001.

Müller, Hildegund. "Theory and Practice of Preaching: Augustine, *De doctrina christiana* and *Enarrationes in psalmos.*" *Studia Patristica* 38 (2001): 233–37.

Munier, Charles. "*audientia episcopalis.*" *Augustinus-Lexikon,* edited by C. Mayer. Vol. 1. Basel: Schwabe, 1986–1994.

Nelson, Leonard. *Socratic Method and Critical Philosophy.* New Haven, CT: Yale University Press, 1949.

Neville, Graham, trans. *Saint John Chrysostom: Six Books on the Priesthood.* Crestwood, NY: St. Vladimir's Seminary Press, 1984.

Newman, Robert J. "*Cotidie Meditare:* Theory and Practice of the *meditatio* in Imperial Stoicism." ANRW 2.36.3 (1989), 1473–1517.

Nightingale, Andrea. *Genres in Dialogue: Plato and the Construct of Philosophy.* Cambridge: Cambridge University Press, 1995.

Nock, A. D. *Conversion: The Old and the New in Religion from Alexander the Great to Augustine of Hippo.* Oxford: Oxford University Press, 1933.

Norris, John. "Augustine and Sign in *Tractatus in Iohannis Euangelium.*" In *Augustine: Biblical Exegete,* edited by Frederick Van Fleteren and Joseph C. Schnaubelt. Augustinian Historical Institute. New York: Peter Lang, 2001.

Nussbaum, Martha C. *The Fragility of Goodness: Luck and Ethics in Greek Tragedy and Philosophy.* Cambridge: Cambridge University Press, 1986.

———. *The Therapy of Desire: Theory and Practice in Hellenistic Ethics.* Martin Classical Lectures, new series 2. Princeton, NJ: Princeton University Press, 1994.

———. *Upheavals of Thought: The Intelligence of Emotions.* Cambridge: Cambridge University Press, 2001.

Oberhelman, Steven M. *Rhetoric and Homiletics in Fourth-Century Christian Literature: Prose Rhythm, Oratorical Style, and Preaching in the Works of Ambrose, Jerome, and Augustine.* American Classical Studies 26. Atlanta: Scholars Press, 1991.

O'Brien, Denis. "Plotinus on Matter and Evil." In *The Cambridge Companion to Plotinus,* edited by Lloyd P. Gerson. Cambridge: Cambridge University Press, 1996.

O'Brien, M. "Apuleius and the Concept of a Philosophical Rhetoric." *Hermathena* 151 (1991): 39–50.

O'Connell, Robert J. *Soundings in St. Augustine's Imagination.* New York: Fordham University Press, 1994.

O'Daly, Gerald J. P. *Augustine's Philosophy of Mind.* Berkeley: University of California Press, 1987.

———. *Plotinus' Philosophy of the Self.* Shannon: Irish University Press, 1972.

O'Donnell, James J. *Augustine: A New Biography.* New York: Harper Collins, 2005.

———. "Augustine: His Time and Lives." In *The Cambridge Companion to Augustine,* edited by Eleonore Stump and Norman Kretzmann. Cambridge: Cambridge University Press, 2001.

————. "Augustine's Classical Readings." *Recherches augustiniennes* 15 (1980): 144–75.

————. *Confessions.* 3 vols. Oxford: Clarendon Press, 1992.

O'Donovan, Oliver. "*Usus* and *fruitio* in Augustine, *De Doctrina Christiana* I." *Journal of Theological Studies* n.s. 33 (1982): 361–97.

Olmsted, Wendy. "Invention, Emotion, and Conversion in Augustine's *Confessions.*" In *Rhetorical Invention and Religious Inquiry: New Perspectives,* edited by Walter Jost and Wendy Olmsted. New Haven, CT: Yale University Press, 2000.

O'Meara, Dominic J. *Platonopolis: Platonic Political Philosophy in Late Antiquity.* New York: Oxford University Press, 2003.

O'Meara, John J. "The Neoplatonism of Saint Augustine." In *Neoplatonism and Christian Thought,* edited by Dominic J. O'Meara. Studies in Neoplatonism 3. Albany: State University of New York Press, 1982.

————. *The Young Augustine: The Growth of St. Augustine's Mind up to His Conversion.* London: Longmans, Green, 1954.

Paffenroth, Kim, trans. *Soliloquies: Augustine's Interior Dialogue.* The Augustine Series 2. Hyde Park, NY: New City Press, 2000.

Pearl, Eric. "Sense Perception and Intellect in Plato." *Revue de Philosophie Ancienne* 15 (1997): 15–34.

Pelikan, Jaroslav. *Divine Rhetoric: The Sermon on the Mount as Message and as Model in Augustine, Chrysostom, and Luther.* Crestwood, NY: St. Vladimir's Seminary Press, 2001.

————. *The Mystery of Continuity: Time and History, Memory and Eternity in the Thought of Saint Augustine.* The Richard Lectures. Charlottesville; University Press of Virginia, 1986.

Pellegrino, Michele. "General Introduction." In *The Works of St. Augustine: A Translation for the 21st Century,* edited by John E. Rotelle. Part 3.1. Hyde Park, NY: New City Press, 1990.

————. *The True Priest: The Priesthood as Preached and Practiced by Saint Augustine.* Rev. ed. Villanova, PA: Augustinian Press, 1988.

Penella, Robert J. *The Private Orations of Themistius.* The Transformation of the Classical Heritage 29. Berkeley: University of California Press, 2000.

Pépin, Jean. *Mythe et allégorie: Les origines grecques et les contestations judéo-chrétiennes.* Rev. ed. Paris: Études Augustiniennes, 1976.

Perler, Othmar. *Les voyages de saint Augustin.* Paris: Études Augustiniennes, 1969.

Pilhofer, Peter. *Presbyteron kreitton: der Altersbeweis der jüdischen und christlichen Apologeten und seine Vorgeschichte.* Wissenschaftliche Untersuchungen zum Neuen Testament. Tübingen: J. C. B. Mohr (Paul Siebeck), 1990.

Pollmann, Karla. "African and Universal Elements in the Hermeneutics of Tyconius and Augustine." In *Augustinus Afer: Saint Augustin, africanité et universalité:*

Actes du colloque international, Alger-Annaba, 1–7 avril 2001, edited by Pierre-Yves Fux, Jean-Michel Roessli, and Otto Wermelinger. 2 vols. Fribourg, Switzerland: Éditions Universitaires, 2003.

———. "Augustine's Hermeneutics as a Universal Discipline!?" In *Augustine and the Disciplines: From Cassiciacum to Confessions,* edited by K. Pollmann and M. Vessey. Oxford: Oxford University Press, 2005.

———. *Doctrina Christiana: Untersuchungen zu den Anfängen der christlichen Hermeneutik unter besonderer Berücksichtigung von Augustinus, De doctrina christiana.* Fribourg, Switzerland: Universitätsverlag, 1996.

Pontet, M. *L'exégèse de saint Augustine prédicateur.* Paris: Aubier, 1946.

Poque, Suzanne. *Le langage symbolique dans la prédication d'Augustin d'Hippone: Images héroïques.* 2 vols. Dernières publications des Études Augustiniennes. Paris: Études Augustiniennes, 1984.

Powell, J. G. F. "Cicero's Translations from Greek." In *Cicero the Philosopher: Twelve Papers,* edited by J. G. F. Powell. Oxford: Oxford University Press, 1995.

Prendiville, John G. "The Development of the Idea of Habit in the Thought of Saint Augustine." *Traditio* 28 (1972): 29–99.

Press, Gerald A. "*Doctrina* in Augustine's *De doctrina christiana.*" *Philosophy and Rhetoric* 17 (1984): 98–120.

———. "The Subject and Structure of Augustine's *De doctrina christiana.*" *Augustinian Studies* 11 (1980): 99–124.

Preus, Mary C. *Eloquence and Ignorance in Augustine's On the Nature and Origin of the Soul.* American Academy of Religion Dissertation Series 51. Atlanta: Scholars Press, 1985.

Quimby, Rollin W. "The Growth of Plato's Perception of Rhetoric." *Philosophy and Rhetoric* 7 (1974): 71–79.

Rabbow, Paul. *Seelenführung: Methodik der Exerzitien in der Antike.* Munich: Kösel-Verlag, 1954.

Racionero, Quintín. "Logos, Myth and Probable Discourse in Plato's *Timaeus.*" *Elenchos* 19 (1998): 29–60.

Raikas, K. K. "*Episcopalis audientia*: Problematik zwischen Staat und Kirche bei Augustin." *Augustinianum* 37 (1997): 459–81.

Ramsey, Boniface. "Almsgiving in the Latin Church: The Late Fourth and Early Fifth Centuries." *Theological Studies* 43 (1982): 226–59.

———. *Ambrose.* The Early Church Fathers. New York: Routledge, 1997.

Rapp, Claudia. *Holy Bishops in Late Antiquity: The Nature of Christian Leadership in an Age of Transition.* The Transformation of the Classical Heritage 37. Berkeley: University of California Press, 2005.

Rebillard, Éric. *In hora mortis: Évolution de la pastorale chrétienne de la mort aux IVe et Ve siècles dans l'Occident latin.* Bibliothèque des écoles françaises d'Athènes et de Rome 283. Rome: École Française de Rome, 1994.

―――. "Interaction between the Preacher and His Audience: The Case-Study of Augustine's Preaching on Death." *Studia Patristica* 31 (1997): 86–96.

Rees, B. R. *The Letters of Pelagius and His Followers*. Woodbridge: Boydell Press, 1991.

Rettig, John W., trans. *St. Augustine: Tractates on the Gospel of John*. 5 vols. Fathers of the Church. Washington, DC: Catholic University of America Press, 1988–1995.

Reydams-Schils, Gretchen. "Roman and Stoic: The Self as a Mediator." *Dionysius* 16 (1998): 35–62.

―――. *The Roman Stoics: Self, Responsibility, and Affection*. Chicago: University of Chicago Press, 2005.

Riain, Íde Ní, trans. *Homilies of Saint Ambrose on Psalm 118 (119)*. Dublin: Halcyon Press, 1998.

Rist, John M. *Augustine: Ancient Thought Baptized*. Cambridge: Cambridge University Press, 1994.

―――. *Stoic Philosophy*. Cambridge: Cambridge University Press, 1969.

Robinson, Richard. *Plato's Earlier Dialectic*. 2d ed. Oxford: Clarendon Press, 1953.

Rollinson, Philip. *Classical Theories of Allegory and Christian Culture*. Duquesne Studies, Language and Literature Series 3. Pittsburgh: Duquesne University Press, 1981.

Rondet, H. "La Théologie de saint Augustin prédicateur." *Bulletin de littérature ecclésiastique* 62 (1971): 81–105, 241–57.

Rousseau, Philip. "Augustine and Ambrose: The Loyalty and Single-Mindedness of a Disciple." *Augustiniana* 27 (1977): 151–65.

―――. "'The Preacher's Audience': A More Optimistic View." In *Ancient History in a Modern University*, edited by T. W. Hillard et al. 2 vols. Grand Rapids, MI: Eerdmans, 1998.

Runia, David T. *Philo in Early Christian Literature: A Survey*. Compendia Rerum Iudaicarum ad Novum Testamentum: Section 3, Jewish Traditions in Early Christian Literature 3. Minneapolis, MN: Fortress Press, 1993.

Sandy, Gerald. *The Greek World of Apuleius: Apuleius and the Second Sophistic*. Mnemosyne, Bibliotheca Classica Batava Supplementum 174. Leiden: Brill, 1997.

Savage, John J., trans. *Saint Ambrose: Hexameron, Paradise, and Cain and Abel*. Fathers of the Church. Washington, DC: Catholic University of America Press, 1961.

Savon, Hervé. *Saint Ambroise devant l'exégèse de Philon le Juif*. 2 vols. Paris: Études Augustiniennes, 1977.

―――. "Saint Ambroise et saint Jérôme, lecteurs de Philon." ANRW 2.21.1 (1984), 731–59.

Schäublin, Christoph. "Augustin, 'De utilitate credendi', über das Verhältnis des Interpreten zum Text." *Vigiliae Christianae* 43 (1989): 53–68.

————. "*De doctrina christiana*: A Classic of Western Culture." In *De doctrina christiana: A Classic of Western Culture,* edited by Duane W. H. Arnold and Pamela Bright. Christianity and Judaism in Antiquity 9. Notre Dame, IN: University of Notre Dame Press, 1994.

Schenkeveld, Dirk M. "Philosophical Prose." In *Handbook of Classical Rhetoric in the Hellenistic Period 330 B.C.–A.D. 400,* edited by Stanley E. Porter. Leiden: Brill, 1997.

Schiappa, Edward. "Did Plato Coin Rhêtorikê?" *American Journal of Philology* 111 (1990): 457–70.

Schofield, Malcolm. "Academic Therapy: Philo of Larissa and Cicero's Project in the *Tusculans.*" In *Philosophy and Power in the Graeco-Roman World: Essays in Honour of Miriam Griffin,* edited by Gillian Clark and Tessa Rajak. Oxford and New York: Oxford University Press, 2002.

Schopp, Ludwig, ed. *Saint Augustine: Christian Instruction; Admonition and Grace; The Christian Combat; Faith, Hope, and Charity.* Fathers of the Church. Washington, DC: Catholic University of America Press, 1947.

————, ed. *Saint Augustine: The Immortality of the Soul; The Magnitude of the Soul; On Music; The Advantage of Believing; On Faith in Things Unseen.* Fathers of the Church. Washington, DC: Catholic University of America Press, 1947.

Seeck, Otto, ed. *Q. Aurelii Symmachi quae supersunt.* Monumenta Germaniae Historica. Vol. 6, pt. 1. Berlin: Apud Weidmannos, 1883.

Shaw, Brent D. "African Christianity: Disputes, Definitions, and 'Donatists.'" In *Orthodoxy and Heresy in Religious Movements: Discipline and Dissent,* edited by Malcolm R. Greenshields and Thomas A. Robinson. Lewiston, NY: Edwin Mellen Press, 1992.

Sider, Robert D. *Ancient Rhetoric and the Art of Tertullian.* Oxford Theological Monographs. Oxford: Oxford University Press, 1971.

Sieben, Hermann Joseph. "Die 'res' der Bibel: Eine Analyse von Augustinus, *De Doctrina Christiana* I–III." *Revue des Études Augustiniennes* 21 (1975): 72–90.

Siegert, Folker. "Homily and Panegyrical Sermon." In *Handbook of Classical Rhetoric in the Hellenistic Period 330 B.C.–A.D. 400,* edited by Stanley E. Porter. Leiden: Brill, 1997.

Sluiter, Ineke. "Communication, Eloquence, and Entertainment in Augustine's *De Doctrina Christiana.*" In *The Impact of Scripture in Early Christianity,* edited by J. den Boeft, and M. L. van Poll–van de Lisdonk. Supplements to Vigiliae Christianae 44. Leiden: Brill, 1999.

Smith, Philippa R. "'A Self-Indulgent Misuse of Leisure and Writing'? How Not to Write Philosophy: Did Cicero Get it Right?" In *Cicero the Philosopher: Twelve Papers,* edited by J. G. F. Powell. Oxford: Oxford University Press, 1995.

Smith, Rowland. *Julian's Gods: Religion and Philosophy in the Thought and Action of Julian the Apostate.* London and New York: Routledge, 1995.

Snyder, H. Gregory. *Teachers and Texts in the Ancient World: Philosophers, Jews, and Christians.* Religion in the First Christian Centuries. London and New York: Routledge, 2000.

Solère, Jean-Luc. "Les images psychiques selon S. Augustin." In *De la phantasia à l'imagination,* edited by Danielle Lories and Laura Rizzerio. Collection d'études classiques. Louvain: Peeters, 2003.

Sorabji, Richard. *Emotion and Peace of Mind: From Stoic Agitation to Christian Temptation.* Oxford: Oxford University Press, 2000.

Steel, Catherine. *Roman Oratory.* Greece and Rome, New Surveys in the Classics 36. Cambridge: Cambridge University Press, 2006.

Stock, Brian. *Augustine the Reader: Meditation, Self-Knowledge, and the Ethics of Interpretation.* Cambridge, MA: Harvard University Press, 1996.

Stowers, Stanley. "Paul on the Use and Abuse of Reason." In *Greeks, Romans, and Christians: Essays in Honor of Abraham J. Malherbe,* edited by David L. Balch, Everett Ferguson, and Wayne A. Meeks. Philadelphia: Fortress Press, 1990.

Straume-Zimmermann, Laila, Ferdinand Broemser, and Olof Gigon, eds. *Marcus Tullius Cicero: Hortensius, Lucullus, Academici libri.* Munich: Artemis, 1990.

Studer, Basil. *The Grace of Christ and the Grace of God in Augustine of Hippo: Christocentrism or Theocentrism.* Translated by Matthew J. O'Connell. Collegeville, MN: Liturgical Press, 1997.

———. *Trinity and Incarnation: The Faith of the Early Church.* Translated by Matthias Westerhoff. Collegeville, MN: Liturgical Press, 1993.

Tanner, Kathryn. *The Politics of God.* Minneapolis, MN: Fortress Press, 1992.

———. *Theories of Culture: A New Agenda for Theology.* Minneapolis, MN: Fortress Press, 1997.

Taylor, Charles. *The Sources of the Self: The Making of the Modern Identity.* Cambridge, MA: Harvard University Press, 1989.

Teloh, Henry. *Socratic Education in Plato's Early Dialogues.* Notre Dame, IN: University of Notre Dame Press, 1986.

TeSelle, Eugene. *Augustine the Theologian.* New York: Herder and Herder, 1970.

———. "Porphyry and Augustine." *Augustinian Studies* 5 (1974): 113–47.

Teske, Roland J., trans. *Answer to Faustus, a Manichean. The Works of St. Augustine: A Translation for the 21st Century,* edited by Boniface Ramsey. Part 1.20. Hyde Park, NY: New City Press, 2007.

———. "Augustine, the Manichees and the Bible." In *Augustine and the Bible,* edited by Pamela Bright. The Bible through the Ages 2. Notre Dame, IN: University of Notre Dame Press, 1999.

———. "Augustine's *Epistula X*: Another Look at *Deificari in otio.*" *Augustinianum* 32 (1992): 289–99.

———. "Criteria for Figurative Interpretation in St. Augustine." In *De doctrina christiana: A Classic of Western Culture,* edited by Duane W. H. Arnold and

Pamela Bright. Christianity and Judaism in Antiquity 9. Notre Dame, IN: University of Notre Dame Press, 1994.

———, trans. *Letters*. 4 vols. *The Works of St. Augustine: A Translation for the 21st Century*, edited by John E. Rotelle and Boniface Ramsey. Part 2.1–4. Hyde Park, NY: New City Press, 2001–2005.

———, trans. *On Genesis: Two Books on Genesis against the Manichees; and, On the Literal Interpretation of Genesis, an Unfinished Book*. Fathers of the Church. Washington, DC: Catholic University of America Press, 1990.

Tilley, Maureen A. *The Bible in Christian North Africa: The Donatist World*. Minneapolis, MN: Fortress Press, 1997.

———. *Donatist Martyr Stories: The Church in Conflict in Roman North Africa*. Translated Texts for Historians 24. Liverpool: Liverpool University Press, 1996.

———. "From Separatist Sect to Majority Church: The Ecclesiologies of Parmenian and Tyconius." *Studia Patristica* 33 (1997): 260–65.

Tracy, David. "Charity, Obscurity, Clarity: Augustine's Search for Rhetoric and Hermeneutics." In *Rhetoric and Hermeneutics in Our Time*, edited by Walter Jost and Michael J. Hyde. Yale University Studies in Hermeneutics. New Haven, CT: Yale University Press, 1997.

Trampedach, Kai. *Platon, die Akademie und die zeitgenössische Politik*. Stuttgart: F. Steiner, 1994.

Trapp, Michael B. *Maximus of Tyre: The Philosophical Orations*. Oxford: Clarendon Press, 1997.

———. "Plato in Dio." In *Dio Chrysostom: Politics, Letters, and Philosophy*, edited by Simon Swain. Oxford: Oxford University Press, 2000.

———. "Plato's *Phaedrus* in Second-Century Greek Literature." In *Antonine Literature*, edited by D. A. Russell. Oxford: Clarendon Press, 1990.

Troup, Calvin L. *Temporality, Eternity, and Wisdom: The Rhetoric of Augustine's Confessions*. Columbia: University of South Carolina Press, 1999.

Trout, Dennis E. "Augustine at Cassiciacum: *Otium Honestum* and the Social Dimensions of Conversion." *Vigiliae Christianae* 42 (1988): 132–46.

Van Bavel, Tarsicius J. *Recherches sur la christologie de saint Augustin*. Paradosis 10. Fribourg: Éditions Universitaires, 1954.

Van der Meer, Frederik. *Augustine the Bishop: The Life and Work of a Father of the Church*. Translated by Brian Battershaw and G. R. Lamb. London: Sheed and Ward, 1961.

Van Fleteren, Frederick. "Augustine and the Possibility of the Vision of God in This Life." *Studies in Medieval Culture* 11 (1977): 9–16.

———. "St. Augustine, Neoplatonism, and the Liberal Arts: The Background to *De doctrina christiana*." In *De doctrina christiana: A Classic of Western Culture*, edited by Duane W. H. Arnold and Pamela Bright. Christianity and Judaism in Antiquity 9. Notre Dame, IN: University of Notre Dame Press, 1994.

Van Ophuijsen, Johannes M. "Making Room for Faith: Is Plato?" In *The Winged Chariot: Collected Essays on Plato and Platonism in Honour of L. M. De Rijk*, edited by Maria Kardaun and Joke Spruyt. Brill's Studies in Intellectual History 100. Leiden: Brill, 2000.

Verbraken, Pierre-Patrick. *Études critiques sur les sermons authentiques de saint Augustin*. Instrumenta Patristica 12. Steenbrugis: Abbatia Sancti Petri, 1976.

————. "Saint Augustine's Sermons: Why and How to Read Them Today." *Augustinian Heritage* 33 (1987): 105–16.

Vessey, Mark. "The Great Conference: Augustine and His Fellow Readers." In *Augustine and the Bible*, edited by Pamela Bright. The Bible through the Ages 2. Notre Dame, IN: University of Notre Dame Press, 1999.

Voelke, André-Jean. *La philosophie comme thérapie de l'âme: Études de philosophie hellénistique*. Vestigia 12. Fribourg: Éditions universitaires, 1993.

Waldstein, W. "Zur Stellung der *episcopalis audientia* im spätrömischen Prozess." In *Festschrift für Max Kaser zum 70. Geburtstag*, edited by D. Medicus and H. H. Seiler. Munich: Beck, 1976.

Walker, Jeffrey. *Rhetoric and Poetics in Antiquity*. Oxford: Oxford University Press, 2000.

Wallis, R. T. *Neoplatonism*. 2d ed. Indianapolis: Hackett, 1995.

Werpehowski, William. "Weeping at the Death of Dido: Sorrow, Virtue, and Augustine's Confessions." *Journal of Religious Ethics* 19 (1991): 175–91.

Wetzel, James. *Augustine and the Limits of Virtue*. Cambridge: Cambridge University Press, 1992.

White, Stephen A. "Cicero and the Therapists." In *Cicero the Philosopher: Twelve Papers*, edited by J. G. F. Powell. Oxford: Oxford University Press, 1995.

Whitman, Jon. *Allegory: The Dynamics of Ancient and Medieval Technique*. Cambridge, MA: Harvard University Press, 1987.

Wilken, Robert L. "Alexandria: A School for Training in Virtue." In *Schools of Thought in the Christian Tradition*, edited by Patrick Henry. Philadelphia: Fortress Press, 1984.

Williams, Daniel H. *Ambrose of Milan and the End of the Nicene-Arian Conflicts*. Oxford Early Christian Studies. Oxford: Clarendon Press, 1995.

Williams, Rowan D. "Augustine's Christology: Its Spirituality and Rhetoric." In *In the Shadow of the Incarnation: Essays on Jesus Christ in the Early Church in Honor of Brian E. Daley, S.J.*, edited by Peter W. Martens. Notre Dame, IN: University of Notre Dame Press, 2008.

————. "Insubstantial Evil." In *Augustine and His Critics: Essays in Honour of Gerald Bonner*, edited by Robert Dodaro and George Lawless. London and New York: Routledge, 2000.

————. "Language, Reality, and Desire in Augustine's *De doctrina*." *Literature and Theology* 3 (1989): 138–50.

————. "Politics and the Soul: A Reading of the *City of God.*" *Milltown Studies* 19.20 (1987): 55–72.

————. "*Sapientia* and the Trinity: Reflections on the *De trinitate.*" In *Collectanea Augustiniana: Mélanges T. J. Van Bavel,* edited by B. Bruning, M. Lamberigts, and J. van Houtem. 2 vols. Bibliotheca Ephemeridum theologicarum Lovaniensium 92. Leuven: University Press, 1990.

Willis, Geoffrey G. *St. Augustine's Lectionary.* Alcuin Club Collections 44. London: SPCK, 1962.

Wills, Garry. *Saint Augustine.* Penguin Lives Series. New York: Penguin, 1999.

Wootton, David, ed. and trans. *Selected Political Writings: Niccolò Machiavelli.* Indianapolis: Hackett, 1994.

Xenakis, Jason. *Epictetus: Philosopher-Therapist.* Hague: Martinus Nijhoff, 1969.

Young, Frances M. "The Rhetorical Schools and Their Influence on Patristic Exegesis." In *The Making of Orthodoxy: Essays in Honour of Henry Chadwick,* edited by Rowan Williams. Cambridge: Cambridge University Press, 1989.

Index

338

PAUL R. KOLBET is assistant professor of theology at Boston College.